Richard Green Moulton

The Literary Study of the Bible

Richard Green Moulton

The Literary Study of the Bible

ISBN/EAN: 9783742810175

Manufactured in Europe, USA, Canada, Australia, Japa

Cover: Foto ©Lupo / pixelio.de

Manufactured and distributed by brebook publishing software (www.brebook.com)

Richard Green Moulton

The Literary Study of the Bible

THE
LITERARY STUDY OF THE BIBLE

AN ACCOUNT OF THE
LEADING FORMS OF LITERATURE REPRESENTED IN THE SACRED WRITINGS

INTENDED FOR ENGLISH READERS

BY

RICHARD G. MOULTON, M.A. (CAMBR.), PH.D. (PENNA.)

PROFESSOR OF LITERATURE IN ENGLISH IN THE UNIVERSITY OF CHICAGO
LATE UNIVERSITY EXTENSION LECTURER (CAMBRIDGE AND LONDON)

BOSTON, U.S.A.
D. C. HEATH & CO., PUBLISHERS
1895

COPYRIGHT, 1895,
BY RICHARD G. MOULTON.

Norwood Press
J. S. Cushing & Co.   Berwick & Smith
Boston, Mass., U.S.A.

PREFACE

An author falls naturally into an apologetic tone if he is proposing to add yet one more to the number of books on the Bible. Yet I believe the number is few of those to whom the Bible appeals as literature. In part, no doubt, this is due to the forbidding form in which we allow the Bible to be presented to us. Let the reader imagine the poems of Wordsworth, the plays of Shakespeare, the essays of Bacon, and the histories of Motley to be bound together in a single volume; let him suppose the titles of the poems and essays cut out and the names of speakers and divisions of speeches removed, the whole divided up into sentences of a convenient length for parsing, and again into lessons containing a larger or smaller number of these sentences. If the reader can carry his imagination through these processes he will have before him a fair parallel to the literary form in which the Bible has come to the modern reader; it is true that the purpose for which it has been split into chapters and verses is something higher than instruction in parsing, but the injury to literary form remains the same.

Of course earnest students of Scripture get below the surface of isolated verses. Yet even in the case of deep students the literary element is in danger of being overpowered by other interests. The devout reader, following the Bible as the divine authority for his spiritual life, feels it a distraction to notice literary questions. And thereby he often impedes his own purpose: poring over a passage of *Job* to discover the message it has for him, and forgetting all the while the dramatic form of the book, as a result of which the speaker of the very passage he is studying is in the end pronounced by God himself to have said the thing that is "not right." Another has been led by his studies to cast off the authority of the Bible, and he will not look for literary pleasure to that which has for him associations with a yoke from which he has been delivered. A third approaches Scripture with equal reverence and scholarship. Yet even for him there is a danger at the present moment, when the very bulk of the discussion tends to crowd out the thing discussed, and but one person is willing to read the Bible for every ten who are ready to read about it.

Now for all these types of readers the literary study of the Bible is a common meeting-ground. One who recognises that God has been pleased to put his revelation of himself in the form of literature, must surely go on to see that literary form is a thing worthy of study. The agnostic will not deny that, if every particle of authority and supernatural character be taken from the Bible, it will remain one of the world's great literatures, second to none. And the most polemic of all investigators must admit that appreciation is the end, and polemics only the means.

The term 'literary study of the Bible' describes a wide field of which the present work attempts to cover only a limited part. In particular, the term will include the most prominent of all types of Bible study, that which is now universally called the 'Higher Criticism.' There is no longer any need to speak of the splendid processes of modern Biblical Criticism, nor of the magnitude even of its undisputed results. I mention the Higher Criticism only to say that its province is distinct from that which I lay down for myself in this book. The Higher Criticism is mainly an historical analysis; I confine myself to literary investigation. By the literary treatment I understand the discussion of *what* we have in the books of Scripture; the historical analysis goes behind this to the further question *how* these books have reached their present form. I think the distinction of the two treatments is of considerable practical importance; since the historical analysis must, in the nature of things, divide students into hostile camps, while, as it appears to me, the literary appreciation of Scripture is a common ground upon which opposing schools may meet. The conservative thinker maintains that *Deuteronomy* is the personal composition of Moses; the opposite school regard the book as a pious fiction of the age of Josiah. But I do not see how either of these opinions, if true, or a third intermediate opinion, can possibly affect the question with which I desire to interest the reader, — namely, the structure of *Deuteronomy* as it stands, whoever may be responsible for that structure. And yet the structural analysis of our *Deuteronomy*, and the connection of its successive parts, are by no means clearly understood by the ordinary reader of the Bible.

The historical and the literary treatments are then distinct: yet sometimes they seem to clash. There are two points in particular as to which I find myself at variance with the accepted Higher Criticism. Historic analysis, investigating dates, sometimes finds itself obliged to discriminate between different parts of the same literary composition, and to assign to them different periods; having accomplished this upon sound evidence, it then often proceeds, no longer upon evidence, but by tacit assumption, by unconscious insinuations rather than by distinct statement, to treat the earlier parts of such a composition as 'genuine' or 'original,' while the portions of later date are made 'interpolations,' or 'accretions,' — in fact, are alluded to as something illegitimate. Thus, in the case of *Job*, few will hesitate to accept the theory that there is an earlier nucleus (to speak roughly) in the dialogue, while the speeches of Elihu and the Divine Intervention have come from another source. But nearly all commentators who hold this view seem to treat these later portions as if they were on a lower literary plane, and — so sensitive is taste to external considerations — they soon find them in a literary sense inferior. This whole attitude of mind seems to me unscientific: it is the intrusion of the modern conception of a fixed book and an individual author into a totally different literary age. The phenomena of floating poetry, with community of authorship and the perpetual revision that goes with oral tradition, are not only accepted but insisted upon by biblical scholars. But in such floating literature our modern idea of 'originality' has no place; the earliest presentation has no advantage of authenticity over the latest; nor have the later versions necessarily any superiority to the earlier. Processes of floating poetry produced the Homeric poems, and in this case it is the last form, not the first, that makes our supreme *Iliad*. My contention is that, whatever may be the truth as to dates, all the sections of such a poem as *Job* are equally 'genuine.' And as a matter of literary analysis, I find the Speeches of Elihu and the Divine Intervention, from whatever sources they may have come, carrying forward the previous movement of the poem to a natural dramatic climax, and in literary effect as striking as any part of the book.

My second objection to the characteristic methods of the Higher Criticism has to do with the divisions of the text. In analysing the contents of a book of Scripture many even of the best critics betray an almost exclusive preoccupation with subject matter, to the neglect of literary form; a powerful search-light is thrown upon minute historic allusions, while even broad indications of literary unity or diversity are passed by. I will take a typical example. In the latter part of our *Book of Micah* a group of verses (vii. 7-10) must strike even a casual reader by their buoyancy of tone, so sharply contrasting with what has gone before. Accordingly Wellhausen sees in this changed tone evidence of a new composition, product of an age long distant from the age of the prophet: "between *v*. 6 and *v*. 7 there yawns a century."[1] What really yawns between the verses is simply a change of speakers. The latter part of *Micah* is admittedly dramatic, and a reader attentive to literary form cannot fail to note a distinct dramatic composition introduced by the title-verse (vi. 9) : "The voice of the LORD crieth unto the city, and the man of wisdom will fear thy name." The latter part of the title—"and the man of wisdom will fear thy name"— prepares us to expect an addition in the 'Man of Wisdom' to the usual *dramatis personæ* of prophetic dramas, which are confined to God, the Prophet, and the ruined Nation. All

[1] Quoted in Driver's *Introduction, in loc.*

that follows the title-verse bears out the description. Verses 10-16 are the words of denunciation and threatening put into the mouth of God. Then the first six verses of chapter seven voice the woe of the guilty city. Then the Man of Wisdom speaks, and the disputed verses change the tone to convey the happy confidence of one on whose side the divine intervention is to take place:

> But as for me, I will look unto the LORD; I will wait for the God of my salvation: my God will hear me. Rejoice not against me, O mine enemy: when I fall, I shall arise, etc.

The sequence of verses follows quite naturally the dramatic form indicated by the title, and no break in the text is required. I have no objection in the abstract to the hypothesis of defects in textual transmission; but in judging of any alleged example it is reasonable to give to indications of literary form a weight not inferior to that of suggestions drawn from subject matter.

Besides this historic analysis other obvious lines of literary treatment are omitted from this book. I have scarcely touched such poetic criticism as was admirably illustrated by the digest of Hebrew imagery which Mr. Montefiore contributed some time since to the *Jewish Quarterly Review*. I have little or nothing to say about the style of biblical writers, although I welcome Professor Cook's introduction of the Bible as a model in the teaching of Rhetoric. I have even felt compelled to drop the survey of subject matter which was at first a part of my plan. The more I have studied the Bible from a literary standpoint, and considered also the conditions for making such a standpoint generally accessible, the more one single aspect of the subject has come into prominence — the treatment of literary morphology: how to distinguish one literary composition from another, to say exactly where each begins and ends; to recognise Epic, Lyric, and other forms as they appear in their biblical dress, as well as to distinguish literary forms special to the Sacred writers. Hence the book is "An account of the leading Forms of Literature represented in the Sacred Writings." The whole works up to what I

Hebrew thought? Whence then the neglect of the Bible in our higher schools and colleges? It is one of the curiosities of our civilisation that we are content to go for our liberal education to literatures which, morally, are at an opposite pole from ourselves: literatures in which the most exalted tone is often an apotheosis of the sensuous, which degrade divinity, not only to the human level, but to the lowest level of humanity. Our hardest social problem being temperance, we study in Greek the glorification of intoxication; while in mature life we are occupied in tracing law to the remotest corner of the universe, we go at school for literary impulse to the poetry that dramatises the burden of hopeless fate. Our highest politics aim at conserving the arts of peace, our first poetic lessons are in an *Iliad* that cannot be appreciated without a bloodthirsty joy in killing. We seek to form a character in which delicacy and reserve shall be supreme, and at the same time are training our taste in literatures which, if published as English books, would be seized by the police. I recall these paradoxes, not to make objection, but to suggest the reasonableness of the claim that the one side of our liberal education should have another side to balance it. Prudish fears may be unwise, but there is no need to put an embargo upon decency. It is surely good that our youth, during the formative period, should have displayed to them, in a literary dress as brilliant as that of Greek literature — in lyrics which Pindar cannot surpass, in rhetoric as forcible as that of Demosthenes, or contemplative prose not inferior to Plato's — a people dominated by an utter passion for righteousness, a people whom ideas of purity, of infinite good, of universal order, of faith in the irresistible downfall of all moral evil, moved to a poetic passion as fervid, and speech as musical, as when Sappho sang of love or Æschylus thundered his deep notes of destiny. When it is added that the familiarity of the English Bible renders all this possible without the demand upon the time-table that would be involved in the learning of another language, it seems clear that our school and college curricula will not have shaken off their mediæval narrowness and renaissance paganism until Classical and Biblical literatures stand side by side as sources of our highest culture.

My obligations will be obvious to the main representative works of Biblical Criticism, more especially to the works of Cheyne, Briggs, George Adam Smith, and the late Professor Milligan; to the lectures of President Harper; above all to Canon Driver's *Introduction to Old Testament Literature*, which has placed the best results of modern investigation within easy reach of the ordinary reader. I have made copious citations from the Revised Version of the Bible and Apocrypha, for the use of which I am under obligations to the University Presses of Oxford and Cambridge. I am indebted for assistance of various kinds to personal friends, amongst whom I ought to mention my brother, Dr. Moulton, of the Leys School, and — here as always — Mr. Joseph Jacobs, who has become to his large circle of friends a universal referee for all departments of study. I have other obligations in my memory, which it is not so easy to specify; obligations to public institutions and private individuals whose encouragement has assisted me at every step. For the last four years I have been lecturing on Biblical literature in churches of various denominations, in theological schools and universities, and in popular lecture rooms; my audiences in England and America have included clergy and laity, Christian and Jewish, not without a representation of that other public which never reads the Bible and hears with surprise its most notable passages. Though I have taken pains to inquire, I have never found examples of the difficulties which it was feared by some the handling of this topic on the lecture platform might create. On the contrary, my experience has uniformly confirmed what I have called above the foundation axiom of my work — that an increased apprehension of outer literary form is a sure way of deepening spiritual effect.

I think it right to state that the issue of this work — announced more than a year ago — has been delayed by circumstances for which neither author nor publishers are responsible.

RICHARD G. MOULTON.

August, 1895.

CONTENTS

INTRODUCTION

THE BOOK OF JOB: AND THE VARIOUS KINDS OF LITERARY INTEREST ILLUSTRATED BY IT 3

BOOK FIRST

LITERARY CLASSIFICATION APPLIED TO THE SACRED SCRIPTURES

CHAPTER		PAGE
I.	VERSIFICATION AND RHYTHMIC PARALLELISM . . .	45
II.	THE HIGHER PARALLELISM, OR PARALLELISM OF INTERPRETATION	68
III.	THE LOWER AND THE HIGHER UNITY IN LITERATURE	81
IV.	CLASSIFICATION OF LITERARY FORMS	105

BOOK SECOND

LYRIC POETRY OF THE BIBLE

V.	THE BIBLICAL ODE	127
VI.	OCCASIONAL POETRY, ELEGIES, AND LITURGICAL PSALMS	153
VII.	DRAMATIC LYRICS, AND LYRICS OF MEDITATION . . .	174
VIII.	LYRIC IDYL: 'SOLOMON'S SONG' . . .	194

BOOK THIRD

BIBLICAL HISTORY AND EPIC

IX.	EPIC POETRY OF THE BIBLE	221
X.	BIBLICAL HISTORY IN ITS RELATION WITH BIBLICAL EPIC .	244

BOOK FOURTH

THE PHILOSOPHY OF THE BIBLE, OR WISDOM LITERATURE

CHAPTER		PAGE
XI.	FORMS OF WISDOM LITERATURE	255
XII.	THE SACRED BOOKS OF WISDOM	284
XIII.	'THE WISDOM OF SOLOMON'	305

BOOK FIFTH

BIBLICAL LITERATURE OF PROPHECY

XIV.	FORMS OF PROPHETIC LITERATURE	327
XV.	FORMS OF PROPHETIC LITERATURE: THE DOOM SONG	353
XVI.	FORMS OF PROPHETIC LITERATURE: THE RHAPSODY	364
XVII.	THE RHAPSODY OF 'ZION REDEEMED' [*Isaiah* xl–lxvi]	395
XVIII.	THE WORKS OF THE PROPHETS	417

BOOK SIXTH

THE BIBLICAL LITERATURE OF RHETORIC

XIX.	THE EPISTLES: OR WRITTEN RHETORIC	439
XX.	SPOKEN RHETORIC: AND THE 'BOOK OF DEUTERONOMY'	444

APPENDICES

I.	LITERARY INDEX TO THE BIBLE	465
II.	TABLES OF LITERARY FORMS	499
III.	ON THE STRUCTURAL PRINTING OF SCRIPTURE	512
IV.	USE OF THE DIGRESSION IN 'WISDOM'	521

GENERAL INDEX . . 527

INTRODUCTION

THE BOOK OF JOB: AND THE VARIOUS KINDS OF LITERARY INTEREST ILLUSTRATED BY IT

INTRODUCTION

I

THE story in the *Book of Job* opens by telling how there was a man in the land of Uz whose name was Job; how he was perfect and upright, a man that feared God and eschewed evil. It tells of his great substance in sheep and camels and oxen, and how he was the greatest of all the children of the east. Then it speaks of his seven sons and three daughters, and describes their joyous family life. And so scrupulous was the piety of Job that, when his sons and daughters had concluded a round of feastings at one another's houses, Job rose early and sanctified them, lest *perchance* in their gaiety they had offended God. Book of Job: The Story Opens i, ii

Then the story passes to a Council in Heaven, at which the sons of God came, each from his several province, to present themselves before the Lord; and amongst them came the Adversary from his sphere of inspection, the Earth. He in his turn was questioned as to his charge, and Job was instanced by the Lord as a type of human perfection. But the Adversary, as his office was, began to raise doubts as to this perfection. God had made a hedge of prosperity about the man: if he were to put forth his hand, and destroy all at a stroke, Job might yet renounce his worship.

The Lord gave consent for this experiment to be made. So it came about that in the midst of Job's prosperity there came a messenger to him and said:

> The oxen were plowing,
> and the asses feeding beside them;
> and the Sabeans fell upon them
> and took them away;
> yea, they have slain the servants
> with the edge of the sword;
> and I only am escaped alone to tell thee!

While he was yet speaking there came also another, and said :

> The fire of God is fallen from heaven,
> and hath burned up the sheep, and the servants,
> and consumed them;
> and I only am escaped alone to tell thee!

While he was yet speaking there came also another, and said :

> The Chaldeans made three bands,
> and fell upon the camels,
> and have taken them away,
> yea, and slain the servants with the edge of the sword;
> and I only am escaped alone to tell thee!

While he was yet speaking there came also another, and said :

> Thy sons and thy daughters
> were eating and drinking wine in their eldest brother's house;
> and behold,
> there came a great wind from the wilderness,
> and smote the four corners of the house,
> and it fell upon the young men,
> and they are dead;
> and I only am escaped alone to tell thee!

Then Job arose, and rent his mantle, and shaved his head, and fell down upon the ground, and worshipped ; and he said :

> Naked came I out of my mother's womb,
> and naked shall I return thither!
> The Lord gave,
> and the Lord hath taken away:
> Blessed be the Name of the Lord!

So the experiment of the Adversary was over, and Job had not fallen into sin.

A second Council in Heaven followed, and a second time came the sons of God, and the Adversary among them, and made their reports. When the Lord triumphed in the matter of Job, that he still retained his integrity notwithstanding the destruction done to him, the Adversary did honour to the goodness of the man by suggesting a yet severer test:

> Skin for skin, yea, all that a man hath will he give for his life. But put forth thine hand now, and touch his bone and his flesh, and he will renounce thee to thy face.

Even in this case the Almighty had no fear for his servant. So the Adversary went forth, and smote Job with sore boils from the sole of his foot unto his crown. And Job silently passed out, as one unclean, and crept up the ash-mound, and there he sat and suffered; until his good wife — who had uttered no word of complaint when all the substance was swallowed up and her children perished — broke down in the presence of this helpless pain:

> Dost thou still hold fast thine integrity? renounce God, and die!

But Job rebuked this momentary lapse from her wisdom:

> What? shall we receive good at the hand of God, and shall we not receive evil?

So the second experiment was over, and still Job sinned not with his lips.

But a third trial awaited Job, which needed no Council in Heaven to decree it, — the trial of time. Day followed day, but no relief came; and Job sat patiently on the ash-mound, an outcast and unclean. And gradually a reverence grew about the silent sufferer: the children no longer jostled him as they sported to and fro, and groups of sympathising spectators would gather about the mound to gaze for a while on the fallen child of the east. And the travellers as they passed by the way smote on their breasts at the sight; and they made a token of it, and carried the news into distant countries, until it reached the ears of Job's three Friends, all of them great chieftains like himself: the stately Eliphaz the Temanite, and Bildad the sturdy Shuhite, and Zophar the Naamathite, with his venerable grey hairs. These three made an appointment together to visit Job; and, when they came in sight of him, with one accord they lifted up their voices and wept. And the crowd of spectators made way for the great men to ascend the mound; and they sat down upon the ground opposite Job. Day after day they took their station there, yet they could only weep with their friend; for, though they longed to speak, their utter courtesy forbade them to disturb the majesty of that silent suffering.

At last it was Job himself who broke the long silence, in order to curse, not God, but his own life. And at this point the introductory story in which the poem is framed begins to give place to dialogue; but not before the introduction has made its contribution to the general argument. The topic of the whole book is the *Mystery of Human Suffering:* the introduction has suggested a *First Solution of the Mystery: Suffering presented as Heaven's test of goodness;* the test being made the severer where the goodness is strong enough to stand it.

(Problem of the poem and First Solution)

Job opened his mouth, and cursed the day of his birth. Would that it might be blotted from among the days of the year, that the cloud, and the thick darkness, and the shadow of death, and all the degrees of blackness might seize it for their own! If the best of all gifts — never to have existed — must be denied him, why might not that day of his birth have also brought to him the Grave, and the long quiet sleep with the stately dead, and with the wicked and the weary, the prisoner and his task-master, the small and the great, all at their ease together? Why should life be forced upon the bitter in soul?

Job's Curse
iii

In these later thoughts Job seems to reflect upon the order of God's providence: he must be checked, and yet gently; and Eliphaz takes this task upon himself. He dreads to give pain to his friend, yet how can he refrain from speaking, and laying down to Job the foundations of hope and fear with which Job himself has so often comforted the afflicted? *The Dramatic Dialogue First Cycle iv-xiv*

> Now a thing was secretly brought to me,
> And mine ear received a whisper thereof:
>   In thoughts from the visions of the night,
>   When deep sleep falleth on men,
>   Fear came upon me, and trembling,
>   Which made all my bones to shake.
>   Then a spirit passed before my face;
>   The hair of my flesh stood up.
>   It stood still, but I could not discern the appearance thereof;
>   A form was before mine eyes:
>   There was silence, and I heard a voice, saying,
> "Shall mortal man be more just than God?
> Shall a man be more pure than his Maker?"

With the awful solemnity of this vision Eliphaz enforces the view which the three Friends maintain throughout the discussion, and which is put forward as a *Second Solution of the Problem: The very righteousness of God* (they think) *is involved in the doctrine that all Suffering is a judgment upon Sin.* Affliction, says Eliphaz, does not spring up of itself like the grass, but it is they who have sown trouble that reap the same. But he puts the doctrine gently, as constituting so much hope for Job: when the sinner has once sought unto God he will find what great and unsearchable wonders God doeth. Then happy will have been the chastening of the Almighty, for if he maketh sore he bindeth up.

> He shall deliver thee in six troubles;
> Yea, in seven there shall no evil touch thee.
>   In famine he shall redeem thee from death;
>   And in war from the power of the sword.
>   Thou shalt be hid from the scourge of the tongue;

> Neither shalt thou be afraid of destruction when it cometh.
> At destruction and dearth thou shalt laugh:
> Neither shalt thou be afraid of the beasts of the earth.
> For thou shalt be in league with the stones of the field;
> And the beasts of the field shall be at peace with thee.
> And thou shalt know that thy tent is in peace;
> And thou shalt visit thy fold and shalt miss nothing.
> Thou shalt know also that thy seed shall be great,
> And thine offspring as the grass of the earth.
> Thou shalt come to thy grave in a full age,
> Like as a shock of corn cometh in in its season.
> Lo this, we have searched it, so it is;
> Hear it, and know thou it for thy good.

Job is bitterly disappointed at thus meeting reproof where he had looked for consolation.

> My brethren have dealt deceitfully as a brook,
> As the channel of brooks that pass away;
> Which are black by reason of the ice,
> And wherein the snow hideth itself:
> What time they wax warm, they vanish:
> When it is hot, they are consumed out of their place.
> The paths of their way are turned aside,
> They go up into the waste and perish.
> The caravans of Tema looked,
> The companies of Sheba waited for them.
> They were ashamed because they had hoped;
> They came thither and were confounded.

The comfort Job longs for is the crushing pain that would cut him off altogether. And has he not a right to look for it? Is not man's life a warfare for a limited time?

> As a servant that earnestly desireth the shadow,
> And as an hireling that looketh for his wages,

so Job passes his wearisome nights and months of vanity.

> If I have sinned, what can I do unto thee,
> O thou watcher of men?
> Why hast thou set me as a mark for thee,
> So that I am a burden to myself?

> And why dost thou not pardon my transgression,
> And take away mine iniquity?
> For now shall I lie down in the dust;
> And thou shalt seek me diligently,
> But I shall not be!

Job never claims to be sinless, but he knows that no sin of his can be proportionate to the total ruin that has fallen upon him. But this does not satisfy the second speaker.

> Doth God pervert judgement?
> Or doth the Almighty pervert justice?

Will not Job disentangle himself from the transgression which has already found victims in his children? For so surely as the flag cannot grow without water: though it be green and spreading above, with roots wrapped round and round its solid bed, yet it perishes as if it had never been seen: so surely God will not uphold the evil-doer. But neither will God cast away a perfect man.

> He will yet fill thy mouth with laughter,
> And thy lips with shouting.
> They that hate thee shall be clothed with shame,
> And the tent of the wicked shall be no more.

Job knows of a truth that it is so. Yet how can a man be just with God:

> Which removeth the mountains, and they know it not,
> When he overturneth them in his anger.
> Which shaketh the earth out of her place,
> And the pillars thereof tremble.
> Which commandeth the sun, and it riseth not;
> And sealeth up the stars.

What answer but supplication is possible before that overpowering Strength? a Strength that can destroy both the perfect and the wicked alike: for if it be not God who does this, who is it? Certain it is that the earth is given into the hand of the wicked. However innocent the accused may be, before that Strength his own mouth would condemn him.

> If I wash myself with snow water,
> And make my hands never so clean:
> > Yet wilt thou plunge me in the ditch,
> > And mine own clothes shall abhor me.
> For he is not a man, as I am, that I should answer him,
> That we should come together in judgement;
> There is no daysman betwixt us,
> That might lay his hand upon us both.

And Job appeals to God himself against this oppression of his own handiwork.

> Thine hands have framed me
> And fashioned me together round about;
> > Yet thou dost destroy me.
> Remember, I beseech thee, that thou hast fashioned me as clay;
> > And wilt thou bring me into dust again?
> Hast thou not poured me out as milk,
> And curdled me like cheese?
> Thou hast clothed me with skin and flesh,
> And knit me together with bones and sinews.

It is but a small boon that the creature asks of his Creator: that he may be let alone for a brief space —

> Before I go whence I shall not return:
> Even to the land of darkness
> > And of the shadow of death;
> A land of thick darkness,
> As darkness itself;
> > A land of the shadow of death,
> > Without any order,
> And where the light is as darkness.

Zophar is deeply shocked at a spectacle he has never beheld in all his long life, — a good man questioning a visible judgment of God.

> Canst thou by searching find out God?
> Canst thou find out the Almighty unto perfection?
> > It is high as heaven; what canst thou do?
> > Deeper than Sheol; what canst thou know?
> > The measure thereof is longer than the earth,
> > And broader than the sea.

There is no course for Job but to set his heart aright, and put iniquity far away; then shall he again lift up a spotless countenance before God.

> For thou shalt forget thy misery;
> Thou shalt remember it as waters that are passed away:
> And thy life shall be clearer than the noonday;
> Though there be darkness, it shall be as the morning.

Before the persistent dogmatism of the three Friends Job loses more and more the patience which had stood the shocks of the Adversary.

> No doubt but ye are the people,
> And wisdom shall die with you.
> But I have understanding as well as you;
> I am not inferior to you:
> Yea, who knoweth not such things as these?

The just man is made a laughing-stock, and the tents of robbers prosper: and yet the very beasts of the field can tell the inquirer that the hand of the Lord is responsible for every breath of every living thing. What, do the Friends stand forth as representatives of Wisdom? Nay,

> With HIM is wisdom and might;
> He hath counsel and understanding.

Priests and counsellors spoiled, kings bound and unbound, the mighty overthrown, speech reft from the trusty, and understanding from the elders, contempt poured upon princes, and the belt of the strong loosed: these declare the Wisdom to which alone Job will appeal. Will the Friends lie on God's behalf? Will they be partial advocates in his cause?

> Though he slay me, yet will I wait for him:
> Nevertheless I will maintain my ways before him.

Job appeals to God against God's own dealings, and never doubts the issue of his appeal. And yet he is so feeble to plead his cause: a driven leaf, a fettered prisoner, a moth-eaten rag! And the time left for his vindication is so short!

> Man that is born of a woman
> > Is of few days, and full of trouble;
> > He cometh forth like a flower, and is cut down,
> > He fleeth also as a shadow and continueth not.
>
> For there is hope of a tree, if it be cut down,
> > That it will sprout again,
> > And that the tender branch thereof will not cease;
> Though the root thereof wax old in the earth
> And the stock thereof die in the ground,
> > Yet through the scent of water it will bud,
> > And put forth boughs like a plant.
> But man dieth, and wasteth away:
> Yea, man giveth up the ghost, and where is he?
> > As the waters fail from the sea,
> > And the river decayeth and drieth up,
> So man lieth down and riseth not;
> > Till the heavens be no more,
> They shall not awake,
> Nor be roused out of their sleep.

A strange fancy plays for a moment with the emotions of the sufferer, — the fancy that the Grave itself might be sweet, if only there might come the vindication beyond it.

> Oh that thou wouldest hide me in Sheol,
> That thou wouldest keep me secret, until thy wrath be past,
> That thou wouldest appoint me a set time, and remember me!
> > — If a man die, shall he live again? —
> All the days of my warfare would I wait,
> > Till my release should come;
> > Thou shouldest call,
> > And I would answer thee:
> Thou wouldest have a desire to the work of thine hands.

But Job dismisses the thought as vain.

> > Surely the mountain falling cometh to nought,
> > And the rock is removed out of its place,
> > The waters wear the stones,
> > The overflowings thereof wash away the dust of the earth:
> > > And thou destroyest the hope of man:

> Thou prevailest for ever against him, and he passeth;
> Thou changest his countenance, and sendest him away;
> His sons come to honour,
> And he knoweth it not;
> And they are brought low,
> But he perceiveth it not of them;
> Only for himself his flesh hath pain
> And for himself his soul mourneth.

It has come to the turn of Eliphaz again to speak: he is shocked that Job should resist the united appeals of his Friends. Second Cycle
xv-xxi

> Art thou the first man that was born?
> Or wast thou brought forth before the hills?
> Hast thou heard the secret counsel of God?
> And dost thou restrain wisdom to thyself?

On his side, Eliphaz says, and perhaps as he speaks he lays his hand upon the shoulder of Zophar, are the aged and greyheaded, men much older than Job's father. Then he proceeds to formulate again the doctrine of the unfailing judgment upon sin, a judgment never so certain as when it appears for the time to be delayed.

> The wicked man travaileth with pain all his days,
> Even the number of years that are laid up for the oppressor.
> A sound of terrors is in his ears;
> In prosperity the spoiler shall come upon him:
> He believeth not that he shall return out of darkness,
> And he is waited for of the sword.

Job cries out against such miserable consolation as this: for his comfort he will go to a very different source.

> O earth, cover not thou my blood,
> And let my cry have no resting-place.
> Even now, behold, my Witness is in heaven,
> And He that voucheth for me is on high.

But once more the certainty of an ultimate vindication is overshadowed by the thought of the rapidly flitting life.

> If I look for Sheol as mine house;
> If I have spread my couch in the darkness;
> If I have said to corruption, Thou art my father;
> To the worm, Thou art my mother, and my sister;
> Where then is my hope?

Bildad rebukes Job's discomposure of manner.

> Thou that tearest thyself in thine anger,
> Shall the earth be forsaken for thee?
> Or shall the rock be removed out of its place?

He sternly reiterates the doctrine of judgment, and images of doom flow freely. Nets and toils are under the feet of the sinner, gins and snares are all about him; his strength is hungerbitten and the firstborn of death devours his members; brimstone is scattered upon his habitation; he is driven from light into darkness and chased out of the world.

Such reiteration simply drives Job to stronger and stronger self-assertion: in set terms he declares that God subverteth him in his cause, and denies him the judgment for which he calls. And God has removed all other succour from him: his kinsfolk have failed him, his acquaintance are estranged, his very household look upon him as an alien.

> Have pity upon me, have pity upon me,
> O ye my friends,
> For the hand of God hath touched me!

But the weakness of a moment is transformed into a burst of strength, as he proceeds to lay his hopes upon a help from above.

> Oh that my words were now written!
> Oh that they were inscribed in a book!
> That with an iron pen and lead
> They were graven in the rock for ever!
> For I know that MY VINDICATOR LIVETH,
> And that he shall stand up at the last upon the earth;
> And after my skin hath been thus destroyed,
> Yet without my flesh shall I see God!
> Whom I shall see on my side,
> And mine eyes shall behold, and not another!

With the overpowering emotions called up by this thought Job almost faints :

— My reins are consumed within me —

but after a pause he recovers himself, and is able to bring his speech to a conclusion.

Zophar can scarcely wait his opportunity for speaking; his thoughts anticipate his words on the favourite topic.

> Knowest thou not this of old time,
> Since man was placed upon earth,
> That the triumphing of the wicked is short,
> And the joy of the godless but for a moment?

And many wise saws are poured forth by Zophar, testifying to this mockery of the sinner.

> His children shall seek the favour of the poor,
> And his hands shall give back his wealth.
> His bones are full of his youth,
> But it shall lie down with him in the dust. . . .
> The heavens shall reveal his iniquity
> And the earth shall rise up against him.

The doctrine thus thrust upon him again and again Job at last begins to look fairly in the face; and the more he considers it the more he trembles at the doubts that come crowding into his mind.

> How oft is it that the lamp of the wicked is put out?
> That their calamity cometh upon them?
> That God distributeth sorrows in his anger?
> That they are as stubble before the wind,
> And as chaff that the storm carrieth away? . . .
> One dieth in his full strength,
> Being wholly at ease and quiet:
> His breasts are full of milk,
> And the marrow of his bones is moistened.
> And another dieth in bitterness of soul,
> And never tasteth of good.
> They lie down alike in the dust,
> And the worm covereth them.

Eliphaz will not notice these doubts of Job; his righteous indignation with his friend has reached a climax, and casting restraint aside he openly accuses Job of sin.

Third Cycle xxii-xxx

> Thou hast taken pledges of thy brother for nought,
> And stripped the naked of their clothing.
> Thou hast not given water to the weary to drink,
> And thou hast withholden bread from the hungry.

Therefore has trouble come upon him: but there is yet a place for repentance. If Job will acquaint himself with God and put unrighteousness away, he may still delight himself again in the Almighty.

Job makes no reply as yet to the cruel accusations: his thoughts are upon the heavenly Vindicator.

> Oh that I knew where I might find him:
> That I might come even to his seat!

There he would have a judge that would not use his greatness to confound him.

> Behold I go forward,
> But he is not there;
> And backward,
> But I cannot perceive him:
> On the left hand, when he doth work,
> But I cannot behold him;
> He hideth himself on the right hand,
> That I cannot see him.
> But he knoweth the way that I take;
> When he hath tried me,
> I shall come forth as gold.

His spirit purified by this meditation, Job is able with calm deliberateness to lay before his Friends the new thoughts which are troubling him: the doubt whether his own is after all an exceptional case, whether it be not rather the truth that in life taken as a whole the times of the Almighty are not plainly to be seen. He speaks of the violence in the world, and the poverty that violence brings in its train: how men remove the ancient landmarks and drive the needy out of the way, until they have to seek precarious subsistence from the inclement wilderness, or labour in the fields of which they may never eat. He tells of violence in the city, and cries rising to a regardless God; of the thief, the adulterer, the murderer,—men who rebel altogether against the light, and the dawn comes upon them like a shadow of death. Yet all these fare just like the rest of mankind.

> They are exalted; yet a little while, and they are gone;
> Yea, they are brought low, they are gathered in, as all other!

Bildad cannot meet these questionings of Job: his thoughts are filled with the overpowering greatness of God. He rises on the wave of a great theme, as he pictures the Ruler of the Universe engaged in matters of high celestial policy, or discovering blemishes in the brightness of the stars; before him the Shades beneath the sea tremble;[1] Destruction and the Abyss reveal their secrets; his work is to hang the earth upon nothing, to support the mighty waters in the flimsy clouds, to divide light and darkness by a boundary circle. xxv. 1-6
xxvi. 5-14

> Lo, these are but the outskirts of his ways;
> And how small a whisper do we hear of him!
> But the thunder of his power who can understand?

The Friends have persisted in ignoring the arguments that Job has offered, and Job can only fall back into self-assertion. xxvi. 1-4 and xxvii. 1-6

> As God liveth, who hath taken away my right;
> And the Almighty, who hath vexed my soul;
>   All the while my breath is in me,
>   And the spirit of God is in my nostrils:
> Surely my lips shall not speak unrighteousness,
> Neither shall my tongue utter deceit.

---

[1] In reference to the rearrangement of the speeches at this point see *Job* in Literary Index (Appendix I).

Once more, and for the last time, the doctrine of unfailing judgment on sin is to be asserted, and Zophar commences:

xxvii. 7-
xxviii. 28

> Let mine enemy be as the wicked —

His long experience has filled him with instances of the godless frustrated in their hopes: their children multiplied for the sword, their heaped-up silver divided amongst the innocent, and themselves swept by the tempest out of their place. To Zophar this confidence in the unerring stroke of doom seems the very foundation of Wisdom. There are mines out of which may be dug gold and silver and precious stones, but where is the place of Wisdom?

> The deep saith, It is not in me:
> And the sea saith, It is not with me:
> It cannot be gotten for gold,
> Neither shall silver be weighed for the price thereof.

God only is the source of it, and when he laid the foundations of the universe he inwrought this into the structure of his world: that the fear of the Lord and his judgments on evil — this should be Wisdom and Understanding.

Job is gathering himself together for his final vindication. But first, softly to himself, he meditates upon the contrast between then and now.

> Oh that I were as in the months of old,
> As in the days when God watched over me;
> When his lamp shined upon my head,
> And by his light I walked through darkness.

In the rich imagery of the East he paints a prosperity that washed his steps in butter; he describes the hush that fell upon the assembly of the great when he advanced to join them; how among the people every ear that heard him blessed him, and every eye that saw him was a witness to the deeds of kindness by which he spread happiness around him. But now! He is derided by those whose fathers were not to be ranked with the dogs of his

flock; the very rabble thrust him aside as he walks. And — worse than all —
> Thou art turned to be cruel to me:
> With the might of thy hand thou persecutest me.

But before friend and foe, and in the presence of God himself, Job stands forth to make solemn vindication. Towering above the seated accusers, he waves his arm in the full ritual of the Oath of Clearing. Article by article he repudiates the lust of the eye, oppression of the weak, failure in charity to the poor or hospitality to the stranger, secret trust in gold or secret worship of the heavenly host; if there be any other transgression — and Job passionately longs to see the indictment of an adversary — he makes the very concealment of it a fresh sin. Once more he breaks out: *(Job's Vindication xxxi)*

> If my land cry out against me,
> And the furrows thereof weep together;
> If I have eaten the fruits thereof without money,
> Or have caused the owners thereof to lose their life:
> Let thistles grow instead of wheat,
> And cockle instead of barley!

Then, with a wave of dismissal — "The words of Job are ended" — he seats himself and covers his face with his robe; and the Friends understand that the discussion is closed.

Religious tradition, embodied in the speeches of the three Friends, has spent its energies and failed. But there is youthful enthusiasm represented among the crowd of spectators round the ash-mound, in the person of Elihu, of the great family of Ram. He has stood listening with indignation in his heart; indignation against Job because he justified himself and not God, and indignation against the Friends because they had been unable to silence such presumption. Elihu now breaks through the circle and ascends the ash-mound, standing respectful but *(Interposition of Elihu xxxii)* *(xxxii. 6–xxxiii)* passionate before the seated elders. He had said that days must speak and multitude of years show wisdom : but he has an understanding as well as they ; yea, his spirit feels like wine that can find no vent but by bursting its bottle. Thus, with juvenile profuseness, he pours forth some fifty lines in saying that he is about to speak, before he confronts Job — who had longed to meet God face to face — with the words :

> Behold, I am according to thy wish, in God's stead.

He thus reaches the point which makes his contribution to the discussion, — a facet of the truth which his generation was seeing a little more clearly than the generation before him. It may be made a *Third Solution of the Mystery: Suffering is one of the voices by which God warns and restores men.* He describes a man chastened with pain upon his bed until his life abhorreth bread, and his soul the daintiest meat :

(Third Solution)

> If there be with him an angel,
> An interpreter, one among a thousand,
> To shew unto man what is right for him;
> Then he is gracious unto him, and saith,
> " Deliver him from going down to the pit,
> I have found a ransom."

An idyllic picture follows of restored purity and happy penitence ; and Elihu urges this view upon Job, and pauses for Job's reply.

But Job vouchsafes no reply ; and receives the new light with contemptuous indifference.

Disappointed at this reception, Elihu turns to the three Friends — as wise men with an ear to try words — and hopes to take them with him, and all men of understanding, in his protest against this Job, who drinketh up scorning like water, who addeth rebellion unto sin, and clappeth his hands against God. He enlarges upon the presumption of mankind and the judgments with which it is overwhelmed, and looks to the three Friends for assent.

xxxiv

But the three Friends make no sign; they meet their youthful champion with chilling silence.

Slighted on both sides, Elihu, like Job, is driven to look upwards: as his glance sweeps the sky, another flood of inspiration comes upon him. _{xxxv-xxxvii}

Look unto the Heavens, and see:

he cries, alike to Job and to his companions. Is the God of those heavens, he asks, a God to be harmed by a man's sin, or benefited by his righteousness? Thus, "fetching his knowledge from afar," he makes the heavens a starting-point for a fresh vindication of the providence that brings low and builds up again mighty kings, or cuts off whole peoples in a night. A rumble of distant thunder recalls him to his text; and, when he looks up a second time, the brilliant sky of the land of Uz has begun to show signs of change. *Rise of the Whirlwind xxxvi. 22-xxxvii. 24*
Now his whole discussion of providential might is bound up with the manifestations of power that are being exhibited at the moment in the changing heavens. His words bring before us the small drops of water and the spreading clouds, the play of lightning and the noise that tells of God, down to the very cattle standing expectant of the coming storm. When a nearer burst of thunder makes his heart tremble and move out of its place, Elihu still keeps his eyes fastened upon the sky: he finds fresh texts in the roaring voice of the heavens, and the lightning that lightens to the ends of the earth, in the snow intermingled with mighty rain as the icy breath of the north encounters the storm out of the chambers of the south, in the thick clouds wearied with waterings, and their delicate balancings as they descend, and descend, until they have wrapped in their folds speaker and hearers, and they cannot order their speech by reason of the darkness, and the impetuous eloquence of Elihu has died down into dread:

If a man speak, surely he shall be swallowed up!

Now the whirlwind is upon them: in marvellous wise its blasts seem to cleanse the mirky darkness into order; flashes of unearthly bright out of the dark make them cast their eyes downward; until the flashes at last grow together into one terrible majesty of golden splendour in the northern heart of the storm, and the whirlwind has become the

VOICE OF GOD

Divine Intervention
xxxviii-xlii. 6

> Who is this that darkeneth counsel
> By words without knowledge?
> Gird up now thy loins like a man;
> For I will demand of thee, and declare thou unto me.

As the Voice comes out of the storm a new aspect of the discussion unfolds itself. The perplexities of Job and his Friends rested upon a one-sided view that confined its survey to Evil, as if it alone were exceptional and unintelligible; the speech attributed to the Divine Being comes to restore the balance by taking a more comprehensive survey. It may be reckoned as a *Fourth* *Solution of the Problem: That the whole universe* (Fourth Solution) *is an unfathomed Mystery, in which the Evil is not more mysterious than the Good and the Great.* The idea of the whirlwind is maintained throughout: the tone of overmastering might — so often mistaken for the meaning of this Theophany — is no more than the outward form in which the words of God are embodied; the traditional association of thunder with the voice of God leading our poet to convey the speech of Deity in the form of short sharp interrogatories, like explosions of thunder, each outburst putting some startling mystery of nature.

> Who shut up the sea with doors,
>   When it brake forth and issued out of the womb;
>   When I made the cloud the garment thereof,
>   And thick darkness a swaddling band for it,
>   And prescribed for it my decree,
>   And set bars and doors,
>   And said, "Hitherto shalt thou come, but no further;
>   And here shall thy proud waves be stayed"?

INTRODUCTION

> Have the gates of death been revealed unto thee,
> Or hast thou seen the gates of the shadow of Death?
>
> Where is the way to the dwelling of light,
> And as for darkness, where is the place thereof?
>
> Hath the rain a father?
> Or who hath begotten the drops of dew?
> Out of whose womb came the ice?
> And the hoary frost of heaven, who hath gendered it?

There is no pause in the succession of wonders: the wonder of the lioness hunting her prey; of the young ravens crying to God for their food; the wonder of the wild goats bringing forth their young; the wonder of the wild ass ranging loose in the wilderness, and the ox abiding patiently by his crib; the wonder of the ostrich, foolish over her young because God has deprived her of wisdom, glorious in flight, putting to scorn the horse and his rider; the wonder of the war-horse pawing in the valley and rejoicing in his strength, swallowing the ground in fierceness and rage amid the thunder of the captains and the shouting. There is a momentary lull in the storm, when Job's voice is heard in awe-struck humility:

> Once have I spoken, and I will not answer:
> Yea twice, but I will proceed no further.

Then again the swirl of mystery rages around: the Voice tells of Behemoth, with bones of brass and limbs of iron, his larder a mountain and a jungle his bower, watching unconcernedly the swelling of the boisterous waterfloods; or of Leviathan himself, panoplied against the hook of the fisher or snare of the fowler, and scorning even the hunter's spear and the arrows of the warrior, flashing light and breathing smoke as he goes, terror dancing before him, and ocean turning hoary in his wake.

At last the storm begins to abate, and Job is able to make his submission. He knows that God is all-powerful, and that no purpose of his can be restrained.

— " Who is this that hideth counsel without knowledge ? " —

comes like an echoing rumble of the retiring storm. Job admits the charge: he has uttered that which he understood not, and meddled in things too high for him.

— " I will demand of thee, and declare thou unto me " —

again sounds forth, like a more distant echo of the tempest. Job comprehends his whole submission in one utterance.

> I had heard of thee by the hearing of the ear;
> But now mine eye seeth thee,
> Wherefore I abhor myself, and repent
> In dust and ashes.

Then the storm has entirely cleared away. And with it the dramatic poem has given place to the frame of story: which resumes to relate how, when Job had thus spoken, the anger of the Lord was kindled against the three Friends, because they had not said of Him the thing that was right as His servant Job had. Thus the Epilogue furnishes a *Fifth Solution: the proper attitude of mind towards the Mystery of Human Suffering: that the strong faith of Job, which could even reproach God as a friend reproaches a friend, was more acceptable to Him than the servile adoration which sought to twist the truth in order to magnify God.* It only remains to tell how the Lord turned the captivity of Job, and his wealth and prosperity returned in greater measure than before; and he begat sons and daughters, and saw his sons' sons to the fourth generation. So Job died, being old and full of years.

The Story Closes xlii. 7-17

(Fifth Solution)

II

Such is the *Book of Job* presented as a piece of literature. The questions of Theology or historic criticism that it suggests are outside the scope of the present work. Our immediate concern is with the various kinds of literary interest which have touched us as we have traversed this monument of ancient literature. *[sidenote: Literary Interest in the Book of Job]*

The dominant impression is that of a magnificent drama. No element of dramatic effect is wanting; and that which we might least have expected, the scenic effect, is especially impressive. The great ash-mound outside an ancient village or town makes a stage just suited for the single scene — and that an open-air scene — to which a Greek tragedy would be confined. And resemblance to a Greek drama is further maintained by the crowd of spectators who stand round this ash-mound like a silent Chorus; — unless, indeed, we are to consider that their sentiments are conveyed by Elihu as Chorus-Leader. When we reach the crisis of the poem we are able to see what advantage a drama addressed purely to the imagination may have over plays intended for the theatre. No stage machinery could possibly realise the changes of sky and atmosphere which in *Job* make a dramatic background for the approach of Deity. It is true that the original poem does not describe these changes, as I have done, in straightforward narrative. But every scholar is aware that the 'stage directions' of modern plays are wanting in the dramas of antiquity: whatever variations of movement and surroundings these involve have to be collected from the words of the personages who take part in the dialogue. And in the transformation traced above, from a day of brilliant sunshine to a thunderstorm, and yet further to a supernatural apparition, every detail of change is implied in the words of Elihu. We watch the changing scene through the eyes of those who are in the midst of it. *[sidenote: Dramatic Interest of Background]*

Interest of character abounds in the poem. I must confess I cannot follow the subtle differences which some commentators see

of Character

between the characters of the three Friends. It is easy to recognise in Eliphaz a stately personage with a wider range of thought than his colleagues. But Bildad and Zophar leave different impressions on different readers. To me Bildad seems a touch more blunt in his manner than the rest. Of Zophar I would only say that the speeches assigned him fit well with the suggestion of his being a generation older than the

xv. 10

other personages of the poem; though of course the words of Eliphaz which claim such a personage as on his side need not necessarily refer to anyone present. But whatever may be thought about the individualities of the Friends, no one can miss the contrast between the whole group and Job; between the interest of static character in various modifications of conformity to current ideals, and the interest of a dynamic personality like that of Job, which can look back to a realisation of the perfection his friends describe, and can yet at the call of circumstances fling his former beliefs to the winds, and probe passionately among the mysteries of providence for new conceptions of divine rule. And the welcome addition to the poem of Elihu adds the ever fresh interest of youth in contrast with age. In the impetuous self-confidence of this personage, his flowing yet jejune eloquence, and in the chilling reception it meets alike from Job and Job's adversaries, we have youth presented from the one side. But, on the other hand, youth has dramatic justice done to it when we find Elihu's heart beating responsive to every change of the changing heavens, and eagerly drinking in the accumulating terrors of the storm, until his wild speech stops only before the voice of God.

But scenery and character might almost be called secondary elements of drama: its essence lies in action. The whole world

and of Movement

of literature hardly contains a more remarkable piece of dramatic movement than the changes of position taken up by Job in the course of his dialogue with the

Friends. Before it commenced Job had met his ruin with that ideal patience which has forever been associated with his name. At last we find just a shadow of resistance in his plaintive enquiry, why life should be forced upon the miserable. His friends fasten upon this, and make it a starting-point for the discussion in which they urge that the sufferer is a sinner. Almost in an instant the patient Job is transformed into an angry rebel, tearing to shreds optimist views of righteous providence, and, with the passion of a Titan, painting God as an Irresponsible Omnipotence that delights to put righteousness and wickedness on an equality of helplessness to resist Him. The Friends continue their pressure, and Job is driven to appeal to God against their misconstruction; more and more as the action advances Job is led to rest his hopes of vindication on the Being he began by maligning. At last he is found to have traversed a circle: and the same God whom, in the ninth chapter, he had accused of exercising judgment only to show his omnipotence, he contrasts with the Friends in the twenty-third chapter as a judge who would not contend with him in the greatness of his power. When the climax of the Theophany comes, this movement of the drama is carried forward into a double surprise. Job had felt that if only he could find his way into the presence of God his cause would be secure. His prayer is strangely granted, and with what result?

> I had heard of thee by the hearing of the ear;
> But now mine eye seeth thee,
> Wherefore I abhor myself, and repent
> In dust and ashes.

Yet was Job's first thought a mistake? The answer is a second surprise. While the tempest lasts the Theophany appears wholly directed against Job. But when the storm has cleared it is found to be the adversaries who have incurred the wrath of God, and his servant Job has said of him the thing that is right. The deep moral significance of these various presentations of Deity need not make us overlook the dramatic beauty in the transition from one to another.

The dialogue in *Job* is introduced and concluded by a narrative story, and to dramatic effect must be added epic: I use this word without meaning to convey any judgment on the question whether the incidents of the book are to be regarded as imaginary or as historically true. The narrative is one of grand simplicity, like the epics of antiquity. A few touches create for us a whole picture of life and scheme of society. The first note struck is that of perfection; and the life of which Job is declared the perfect type is that of a simple pastoral age. His substance of cattle is given in ideal figures; and he is called the greatest of all the children of the east. It is an age in which the 'state' is not yet born, but family life is pictured on the highest scale. The great seasons which break the monotony of such patriarchal existence are rounds of festal gatherings among the seven sons of Job, each receiving on his day with a regularity never broken; the sons moreover invite their sisters, and so women's society raises a revel into a dignified ceremonial. Such interchange of festivity would represent the highest ordinary ideals of the age. But behind this, Job, who lives in a wider world, has his high day of religious devotion, rising early in the morning to sanctify his children against possible sin.

In an instant, without any connecting link or wordy preparation, after the fashion of the old epics which have the doings of gods and men alike in their grasp, we are transported to the heavenly counterpart of such earthly festivities. Heaven too has its high day on which the sons of God gather together from their several provinces; in the description of two such assemblies the recurrence of identical phrases conveys the notion of ritual and ceremonial observance. We reach a point in the story at which the utmost care is needed to guard against a misconception of the whole incident. Among the sons of God, it is said, comes 'The Satan.' It is best to use the article and speak of '*The* Satan,' or as the margin gives it, 'The Adversary': that is, the Adversary *of the Saints*. Elsewhere in Scripture the title of this office has become the name of

Epic Interest

(The Satan of Job)

a personage — the Adversary *of God*, or 'Satan.'[1] But here (as in a similar passage of *Zechariah*) the Satan is an official of the Court of Heaven. There is nothing in his reception to distinguish him from the other sons of God; as they may come from sun or moon or other parts of the Universe, so the Satan is the Inspector of Earth, and describes his occupation as "going to and fro in the earth, and walking up and down in it." When once the associations with the other 'Satan' are laid aside, it is easy to see that in the dealings of this personage with Job there is no malignity; he simply questions where others accept, and in an inspector such distrust is a virtue. The Roman Church has exactly caught this conception in its 'Advocatus Diaboli': such an advocate may be in fact a pious and kindly ecclesiastic, but he has the function assigned him of searching out all possible evil that can be alleged against a candidate for canonisation, lest the honours of the Church might be given without due enquiry. In the present case the Satan merely points out possible weaknesses in Job, and a means of testing them. The Court of Heaven sanctions the 'experiment': — the word 'experiment' has only to be changed into its equivalent 'probation' for the whole proceeding to be brought within accepted notions of divine government.

Zechariah iii. 1

Epic power is again exhibited in the description of the mode in which this experiment is carried out. Slow history brings about results by what means are in its power, with much of makeshift, and accidents which mar the symmetry of events. But epic poetry can make its action harmonious; and it seems to be a conspiracy of heaven and earth that compasses Job's destruction. The Sabeans take his oxen, the sky rains fire upon the sheep, the

---

[1] Bishop Bickersteth in his epic poem *Yesterday, To-day, and Forever* ingeniously harmonises these two conceptions of Satan. He makes his Lucifer Guardian Spirit of Earth and Man; as part of his office he tempts Adam; then flies to Heaven to be fallen Man's accuser: gradually the spirit in which he has executed his office intensifies and makes more and more pronounced his own fall, until he at last sinks into an open Adversary of God. See the poem, books iv-vi, and the bishop's defence of this view in the *St. James's Sermons*.

Chaldeans carry away the camels, and the winds of the wilderness overwhelm Job's children: while the separate destructions are worked into a concerto of ruin by the recurrence of the messenger's wail —

> I only am escaped alone to tell thee.

It is an ideally grand shock. But at this stage Job's character is epic, and the shock is met by an ideal grandeur of acceptance. One by one the customary gestures of distress are exhibited, and then slowly succeed the words which have become the world's formulary for the emotion of bereavement. They are sublime words, that first proclaim simply the essential manhood to which the whole of life is but an accessory, and then throw over pious submission a grace of oriental courtesy that would make the resumption of a gift an occasion for remembering the giver.

> Naked came I out of my mother's womb,
> And naked shall I return thither!
> The Lord gave,
> And the Lord hath taken away:
> Blessed be the Name of the Lord!

Our epic plot intensifies, and when the second assembly in heaven is held, God and the Satan concur in honouring Job's constancy by severer tests. In what follows there is no realistic description; epic poetry can act by reticence, and a word or two are sufficient to convey the picture of Job shrinking away silent and unclean from among his fellows, with a patience terrible to look upon; until the silence is broken by a second of those utterances of his which are so colossal in their simplicity. The oriental nomad life has two ideals specially its own. One is the solemn giving and receiving of gifts. The other is an instinct of authority that knows no bounds to its submission: an oriental seems to feel a pride in self-prostration before his natural lord. Both ideals are united in Job's answer to his wife's murmur:

> What? shall we receive good at the hands of God and shall we not receive evil?

INTRODUCTION 31

The simple power of epic poetry has raised us to a high plane of thought and feeling: upon that plane the action of the poem is to move with a passionateness that is proper to drama. But there is a transition stage between the one and the other in that portion of the book entitled 'Job's Curse.' This is not narrative, and so cannot be epic; it is clearly distinct from the dramatic poetry to which it is a starting-point. Examination of it shows at once the musical elaboration and accumulation of musings on a situation or thought which we associate with lyric poetry. The Curse is a counterpart to such English lyrics as Wordsworth's *Intimations of Immortality* or Gray's *Bard*. I subjoin the whole here, that it may be read in this connection as a separate lyric: — an Elegy of a Broken Heart.

The Curse a Lyric Poem

I

Let the day perish wherein I was born;
And the night which said, There is a man child conceived!

    Let that day be darkness;
    Let not God regard it from above,
    Neither let the light shine upon it!
    Let darkness and the shadow of death claim it for their own;
    Let a cloud dwell upon it;
    Let all that maketh black the day terrify it!

    As for that night, let thick darkness seize upon it;
    Let it not rejoice among the days of the year;
    Let it not come into the number of the months!
    Lo, let that night be barren;
    Let no joyful voice come therein!
    Let them curse it that curse the day,
    Who are ready to rouse up leviathan!
    Let the stars of the twilight thereof be dark!
    Let it look for light, but have none;
    Neither let it behold the eyelids of the morning:

    Because it shut not up the doors of my mother's womb,
    Nor hid trouble from mine eyes!

2

Why died I not from the womb?
 Why did I not give up the ghost when I came out of the belly?
Why did the knees receive me?
 Or why the breasts, that I should suck?
For now should I have lien down and been quiet;
I should have slept; then had I been at rest,
 With kings and counsellors of the earth,
 Which built solitary piles for themselves;
 Or with princes that had gold,
 Who filled their houses with silver;
Or as an hidden untimely birth I had not been;
As infants which never saw light.
 There the wicked cease from troubling;
 And there the weary be at rest.
 There the prisoners are at ease together;
 They hear not the voice of the taskmaster.
 The small and great are there;
 And the servant is free from his master.

Wherefore is light given to him that is in misery,
And life unto the bitter in soul?
 Which long for death, but it cometh not;
 And dig for it more than for hid treasures;
 Which rejoice exceedingly,
 And are glad when they can find the grave.
Why is light given to a man whose way is hid,
And whom God hath hedged in?
 For my sighing cometh before I eat,
 And my roarings are poured out like water.
 For the thing which I fear cometh upon me,
 And that which I am afraid of cometh unto me.
 I am not at ease,
 Neither am I quiet,
 Neither have I rest;
 But trouble cometh.

Our result then so far is that the *Book of Job* contains specimens of epic, lyric, and dramatic composition; all the three main elements of poetry find a representation in it, and a representation of the most impressive kind. I pass now to those departments of literature which are usually considered to be furthest removed from poetry,—philosophy and science: philosophy that seeks to find a meaning underlying life as a whole, and science that observes in detail and arranges its observations. Interest of Philosophy

The whole work is a philosophical discussion dramatised. The subject discussed is the mystery of human suffering, and its bearing upon the righteous government of the world: this is one of the stock questions of philosophy. Each section of the book is the representation of a different philosophical attitude to this question. Various Attitudes to the problem discussed

The three Friends present a cut and dried theory of suffering — that it is always penal. They are brought before us as behaving in the usual fashion of persons finally committed to a theory: they pour out stores of facts that make for their view, they ignore and refuse to examine facts that tell against it, and they hint moral obliquity as the real explanation of refusal to concur in their doctrine. Elihu introduces the same theory modified and corrected to date; with him suffering is punishment for sin, but that special kind of punishment which is corrective in character. He accordingly stands for a philosophic school of the second generation; and we are not surprised to find him maintaining his position with as much inflexibility as the Friends have shown, and at the same time magnifying his slight difference from them, and appearing no less an adversary to the Friends than to Job himself. The Friends: A Theory Elihu: Theory modified

> Beware lest ye say, "We have found wisdom;
> God may vanquish him, not man":
> For he hath not directed his words against me;
> Neither will I answer him with your speeches.

At the furthest remove from these is found Job, who takes a negative attitude, shattering other theories but providing none of his own. Of course no one will understand Job really to accept what some of his words imply, as where he sees in God an omnipotence that judges only to display power. But these wild words are not out of place as a poetically strong representation of the perplexities that encounter one who would explain providential action. Job simply cannot solve these perplexities; he trusts in a divine vindication at some time, but meanwhile can only pronounce the problem of life insoluble. This is distinctly a philosophic attitude: it is nothing but the famous *epoché*, or suspension of mind, which from the time of Socrates has been recognised as a natural tone of mind for an enquirer. Of course there is a vast difference between the cold brightness of Plato's dialogues and the heated debate in *Job;* the Hebrew poem is not the discussion in the Porch or Garden, but represents philosophy as it is talked in the school of affliction. Job represents the *epoché* in a passion.

Job's Negative Attitude

Yet another philosophical position is embodied in the Divine Intervention. As I have suggested above, this portion of the poem has been often misunderstood. It has been assumed, not unnaturally, that the Divine Intervention — like the *Deus ex machinâ* of the Greek drama — must be a final settlement of the questions in dispute. When the speeches attributed to God are examined in this light they are found to be no settlement at all, or, what were worse than any settlement, an indignant denial of man's right to question. But such interpretations overlook one important consideration: that in the epilogue Job is pronounced by the Lord to have said of him the thing that is right, while Job's Friends, who maintained the wickedness of questioning, are declared to have incurred the Divine anger. The interpretation involves a double mistake. On the one hand the Divine Intervention is not a settlement of the matter in dispute; at the end of the poem the problem of human suffering remains a mystery. But this section of the work, like others, is a distinct contribution towards a solution. In estimating what that contribution is a second mistake must be avoided.

Divine Intervention: Reference to a wider category

by which form and substance have been confused. The tone of scorn which rings through the sentences of the Divine utterance must, as I have said above, be considered part of the dramatic form thrown over the discussion; the poet has conceived the thunder tone to be the proper embodiment for the Divine voice, and the explosive interrogatories of which the speeches are composed are just as much a portion of this dramatic setting as the signs of a rising tempest which are put into the mouth of Elihu. The whole is introduced with the explanation: "The Lord answered Job out of the whirlwind." But when we go below this outer form, and enquire what is the general drift of the Divine utterance as a whole, we find, as I have said before, that its effect is to widen the field of discussion. Job has fastened his attention simply upon Evil, and successfully maintained its inexplicableness against his friends. The Divine Intervention brings out that the Good and the Great, all that men instinctively admire in the universe, is just as inexplicable as Evil. Now this is distinctly a contribution towards the solution of the problem; in philosophic terms, it has included the matter under discussion in a wider category, and this represents a stage of philosophic advance. Moreover, it implies consolation to the human sufferer as well as progress to the discussion. Job had met loss and pain without a murmur; he broke down when long musing made him realise the isolation his ruin had brought him, and how he was an outcast from intelligible law. He recovers his self-control when he is led to feel that his burden is only part of the world-mystery of Good and Evil, for the solution of which all time is too short.

Two sections of the work have yet to be considered in the present connection, the prologue and the epilogue. From the side of philosophy no part of *Job* is more important than the brief epilogue. Other sections suggest distinct solutions of the problem under discussion. But when a question is so wide as to admit of no final settlement, but only of tentative treatment, philosophy can have no more important task than to discover a practical attitude

<small>Epilogue : Practical bearings of the question</small>

which we may assume towards it while advancing slowly towards theoretic knowledge. This is what the epilogue does in its pronouncement that Job has been right and his friends wrong. As suggested above, this can have no other meaning than to imply that the bold faith of a Job, which could reproach his God as friend reproaches friend where the Divine dealings seemed unjust, was, though founded on ignorance, more acceptable to that God than the servile adoration which sought to twist facts in order to magnify His name. The deep significance of such a pronouncement must be welcomed by every school of thought; it for ever stamps the God of the Bible as a God on the side of enquiry.

But before this principle has been laid down in the epilogue, before Job and his friends have commenced to discuss the mystery of suffering, another explanation of that mystery has been suggested to our thoughts in the prologue. When we are made to see the Powers of Heaven discussing the character of Job as if it were an item in which the welfare of the universe was concerned, and contriving visitations of suffering as means of testing whether the character be really all that it seems to be, it is impossible for our minds not to generalise, and wonder whether large part of the visible suffering in the actual world be not a probationary visitation of this nature. Here then there is another solution presented: how is the treatment to be classified from our immediate point of view? The thinker has other weapons besides philosophic discussion. Philosophy deals with that which can be known by its own methods; but the thinker may recognise a region outside this, which therefore from the philosophic point of view is the unknowable, which may nevertheless have influences operating upon the region of what is known. In reference to such a region he will not employ the method of discussion, but rather the form of philosophic suggestion that has come to be called 'speculation.' The prologue to *Job* may be regarded as giving the authority of Holy Writ to reverent speculation upon the higher mysteries. No doubt here difference of interpretation comes in. Those who

Prologue: Speculation upon a Transcendental Explanation

consider that the first two chapters of *Job* represent an historic fact — incidents which actually happened — will not use the word 'speculation': to them this prologue will be the final settlement of the whole question. But the great majority of readers will take these chapters to be part of the parable into which the history of Job has been worked up; the incidents in heaven, like the incidents of the Prodigal Son, they will understand to be spiritually imagined, not historically narrated. And these will recognise that the prologue gives completeness to the *Book of Job* viewed from the standpoint of philosophy; the problem of human suffering, which has in other parts of the book been treated by theory and theory modified, by negative positions and reference to a wider category, and even by pronouncement upon its practical bearings, has a further illumination cast upon it by a speculation which refers the origin of suffering to the mysteries of the supernatural world.

I have spoken of science as well as philosophy. Science observes nature and life; observation of nature is the special work of modern science, antiquity turned its reflection chiefly on human life. It is hardly necessary to point out that proverb-like reflections on society and life form large part of the material out of which the dialogue in *Job* is constructed. I will be content with a single one of the more extended illustrations. It is remarkable that the whole course of what the most modern thought calls 'the land question' is sketched in a single chapter of *Job*. The patriarch is describing what seems to him the misgovernment of the world. He commences with the encroachments of private ownership upon the common land:

<small>Interest of Science: The Land Question</small>

<small>xxiv</small>

> There are that remove the landmarks. . . .
> They turn the needy out of the way.
> <small>2, 4</small>

There is consequently the formation of a class of the poor, who are either driven to the barren regions, or become a mere labouring class without rights in the land of the community.

4, 5	The poor of the earth hide themselves together:
	Behold, as wild asses in the desert
	They go forth to their work, seeking diligently for meat;
	The wilderness yieldeth them food for their children. . . .
7, 8	They lie all night naked without clothing,
	And have no covering in the cold.
	They are wet with the showers of the mountains,
	And embrace the rock for want of a shelter.

Poverty, Job sees, necessitates borrowing, and the fresh distress that is its natural sequel.

2, 3	They violently take away flocks and feed them,
	They drive away the ass of the fatherless,
	They take the widow's ox for a pledge.

Poverty is seen side by side with wealth, forced into close relationship with it that increases the distress of want.

6	They cut his provender in the field;
	And they glean the vintage of the wicked. . . .
10, 11	And being an-hungered they carry the sheaves;
	They make oil within the walls of these men;
	They tread their winepresses, and suffer thirst.

As a next stage we get the crowding of population in cities, with hints of fresh distress and turbulence.

12	From out of the populous city men groan,
	And the soul of the wounded crieth out,
	Yet God imputeth it not for folly.

The climax comes in the formation of a purely criminal class.

13-17	These are of them that rebel against the light;
	They know not the ways thereof,
	Nor abide in the paths thereof.
	The murderer riseth with the light,
	He killeth the poor and needy;
	And in the night he is as a thief.
	The eye also of the adulterer waiteth for the twilight;
	Saying, No eye shall see me;
	And he putteth a covering on his face.

> In the dark they dig through houses:
> They shut themselves up in the daytime.
> They know not the light.
> For the morning is to all of them
> As the shadow of death;
> For they know the terrors of the shadow of death.

It is noteworthy that when Job makes his general vindication he finds a climax in disowning sins against the rights and duties of land. xxxi. 38

It appears then that both philosophy and science have their representation in this ancient book of the Bible. Yet every reader will feel that these words are an imperfect description of the matter which makes up the poem of *Job*. Philosophy is based upon reason; but in the present case there is a section of the poem which represents God himself as entering into the discussion, and holding up a view of the truth from which no one appeals. It is clear that in the *Book of Job* yet another element of Revelation mingles side by side with Philosophy; and the new element implies a new division of literature. The student who comes to the Bible from other literatures must be prepared to recognise a special literary type, that of Prophecy: a department which is distinguished from others not by form — for Prophecy may take any form — but by spirit, its *differentia* being that it presents itself as an authoritative Divine message. The literary study of the Bible has no more important task than that of describing Prophecy from the literary point of view. Interest of Prophecy

The varieties of literary form illustrated in the work we are considering are not yet exhausted. We have called the *Book of Job* a drama and a philosophic discussion; yet neither of these descriptions will account for the strange character of the individual speeches which strikes every reader. Their length, if nothing else, would distinguish them from the speeches of other dramas; and their tone is equally far removed from the tone of philosophic disquisition. Interest of Rhetoric

They have in them plenty of dramatic force, and also clear and effective strokes of argument. But they do not stop with these; the dramatic thrust gives place to ornate moralising which, from the dramatic point of view, seems so much waste; and the point of the argument is again and again lost in an accumulation of beautiful irrelevancy. He would be a very perverse reader who should cry out against these characteristics of *Job* as literary faults: on the contrary, they are evidence that the character of the work is insufficiently described by the terms drama and discussion. A further element comes in of Rhetoric: not in the debased sense which the word is coming to bear to modern ears, but the Rhetoric of antiquity which was the delight in speech for its own sake. Each delivery of a speaker in the poem of *Job* is to be looked upon as a work of art in itself. If Job in the course of the discussion interjects the parenthetic thought, "What is the good of arguing?" this parenthesis is found to be a finished meditation of twenty-eight lines. The speech in which it occurs is answered by Bildad, and he meets Job's eloquence by a *tour-de-force* of imagery painting the whole universe watching to destroy the sinner, and this piece of word-beauty runs to thirty-four lines. Zophar in the same round of discussion varies the beauty by a string of wise saws on the same topic, and these extend to sixty lines. All this is over and above the portions of the speeches which are strictly argumentative. It is clear then that the personages of the poem answer one another, not only with argument and dramatic passion, but also with counterpoises of rhetoric weight. The whole becomes like a controversy carried on in sonnets, a discussion waged in perorations. Once more the many-sidedness of the Bible is apparent; and the student who would fully appreciate it must train himself in the literary interest of Rhetoric.

One word more has yet to be said. The literary varieties mentioned so far are such as appeal chiefly to the mind. But there is one main distinction in literature that appeals to the eye and the ear also; the distinction between the 'straight-forward' speech

xvi. 6-17

xviii. 5-21

xx. 4-29

called 'prose,' and that kind of speech which 'measures' itself into metres and verses. A glance at the *Book of Job* in any properly printed version shows that this work, like the plays of Shakespeare or the later stories of William Morris, presents an interchange between the two fundamental forms of language, being a dialogue in verse enclosed in a frame of prose story. When however the English reader calls in his ear to supplement his eye, he finds that the verse passages of *Job* differ essentially from what he is accustomed to find in English verse. There is no rhyme, nor do the lines correspond in meters or syllables. The *Book of Job*, then, in addition to its other literary suggestiveness, raises the elementary questions of Biblical versification. *[Interest of Versification]*

The purpose of this Introduction is now accomplished. I have engaged the reader's attention with a single book of the Bible; we have seen that, over and above what it yields to the theological faculty or the religious sense, the *Book of Job* is a piece of literature, the analysis of which brings us into contact with all the leading varieties of literary form. What the Introduction has done in reference to a single book, the work as a whole is to do in reference to the whole Bible, proceeding however by a method more regular than has been necessary so far. The work will be divided into six books. The first book will start with the point last reached — Biblical Versification — and widening from this will search out other distinctions which may serve as a basis for the Classification of Literature under such heads as Lyric, Epic, Philosophic, Prophetic, Rhetoric. The subsequent books will take up these departments one by one, illustrating each, with the subdivisions of each, from the most notable examples in the Sacred Writings. The reader who has thus given his attention to the general literary aspects of the Bible will then find, in an Appendix, Tabular arrangements into which the whole of the Bible enters, intended to assist him when he desires to read the Sacred Writings from the literary point of view. *[Plan of the whole work]*

Book First

LITERARY CLASSIFICATION APPLIED TO THE SACRED SCRIPTURES

Chapter	Page
I. Versification and Rhythmic Parallelism	45
II. The Higher Parallelism, or Parallelism of Interpretation	68
III. The Lower and the Higher Unity in Literature	81
IV. Classification of Literary Forms	105

CHAPTER I

VERSIFICATION AND RHYTHMIC PARALLELISM

THE Bible is the worst-printed book in the world. No other monument of ancient or modern literature suffers the fate of being put before us in a form that makes it impossible, without strong effort and considerable training, to take in elements of literary structure which in all other books are conveyed directly to the eye in a manner impossible to mistake. *Literary form of Scripture obscured by ordinary modes of printing*

By universal consent the authors of the Sacred Scriptures included men who, over and above qualifications of a more sacred nature, possessed literary power of the highest order. But between their time and ours the Bible has passed through what may be called an Age of Commentary, extending over fifteen centuries and more. During this long period form, which should be the handmaid of matter, was more and more overlooked; reverent, keen, minute analysis and exegesis, with interminable verbal discussion, gradually swallowed up the sense of literary beauty. When the Bible emerged from this Age of Commentary, its artistic form was lost; rabbinical commentators had divided it into 'chapters,' and mediæval translators into 'verses,' which not only did not agree with, but often ran counter to, the original structure. The force of this unliterary tradition proved too strong even for the literary instincts of King James's translators. Accordingly, one who reads only the 'Authorized Version' incurs a double danger: if he reads his Bible by chapters he will, without knowing it, be often commencing in the middle of one composition and leaving off in the middle of another; while, in whatever way he may read it, he will know no distinction between prose and verse. It is only in our own day that a better state of things has arisen. The Church of England led the way by issuing its 'New Lectionary'; the new lessons will be found to differ from the old chiefly in the fact that the passages marked out for public reading are no longer limited by the beginnings and endings of chapters. Later still the 'Revised Version' of the Bible, whatever it may have left undone, has at all events made an attempt to rescue Biblical poetry from the reproach of being printed as prose.

<small>in particular: verse printed as prose</small>

It is to the latter of these two points — the distinction between verse and prose — that I address myself in the present chapter.

No doubt the confusion of the two would have been impossible, were it not that the versification of the Bible is of a kind totally unlike that which prevails in English literature. Biblical verse is made neither by rhyme nor by numbering of syllables; its long-lost secret was discovered by Bishop Lowth more than a century after King James's time. Its underlying principle is found to be the symmetry of clauses in a verse, which has come to be called 'Parallelism.'

<small>Biblical Versification based on parallelism of clauses</small>

> Hast thou given the horse his might?
> Hast thou clothed his neck with the quivering mane?
> Hast thou made him to leap as a locust?
>   The glory of his snorting is terrible.
>   He paweth in the valley, and rejoiceth in his strength:
>   He goeth out to meet the armed men.
>   He mocketh at fear, and is not dismayed;
>   Neither turneth he back from the sword.
>   The quiver rattleth against him,
>   The flashing spear and the javelin.
>   He swalloweth the ground with fierceness and rage;
>   Neither standeth he still at the voice of the trumpet.
>   As oft as the trumpet soundeth he saith, Aha!
>   And he smelleth the battle afar off,
>   The thunder of the captains, and the shouting.

It is abundantly clear, first, that this is a passage of the highest rhythmic beauty; secondly, that the effect depends neither on rhyme nor metre. Like the swing of a pendulum to and fro, like the tramp of an army marching in step, the versification of the Bible moves with a rhythm of parallel lines.

How closely the effect of this versification is bound up with the parallelism of the clauses, the reader may satisfy himself by a simple experiment. Let him take such a psalm as the one hundred and fifth; and, commencing (say) with the eighth verse, let him read on, omitting the second line of each couplet: what he reads will then make excellent historic prose.

> He hath remembered his covenant for ever: the covenant which he made with Abraham, and confirmed the same unto Jacob for a statute, saying, "Unto thee will I give the land of Canaan," when they were but a few men in number, and they went about from nation to nation. He suffered no man to do them wrong, saying, "Touch not mine anointed ones."

Let him now read again, putting in the lines omitted: the prose becomes transformed into verse full of the rhythm and lilt of a march.

> He hath remembered his covenant for ever,
>   The word which he commanded to a thousand generations;
> The covenant which he made with Abraham,
>   And his oath unto Isaac;
> And confirmed the same unto Jacob for a statute,
>   To Israel for an everlasting covenant:
> Saying, "Unto thee will I give the land of Canaan,
>   The lot of your inheritance":
> When they were but a few men in number;
>   Yea, very few, and sojourners in it;
> And they went about from nation to nation,
>   From one kingdom to another people
> He suffered no man to do them wrong;
>   Yea, he reproved kings for their sakes;
> Saying, "Touch not mine anointed ones,
>   And do my prophets no harm."

48 *LITERARY CLASSIFICATION OF SCRIPTURE*

The alphabet, then, of Scriptural versification will be the figures
The Couplet and of Parallelism. Of these figures the simplest and
Triplet most fundamental are the Couplet and Triplet. A
Couplet consists of two parallel clauses, a Triplet of three.

> The LORD of Hosts is with us;
> The God of Jacob is our refuge.

> He maketh wars to cease unto the end of the earth;
> He breaketh the bow, and cutteth the spear in sunder;
> He burneth the chariots in the fire.

It is remarkable that the musical rendering of the psalms by
chants, which in some points is carried to such a degree of nicety,
entirely ignores this foundation difference of Couplet and Triplet,
the same chant being sung to both. To take a typical case.

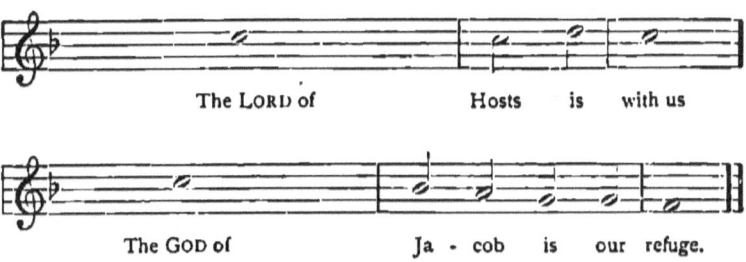

This is correct, because a piece of music which is two-fold in
its structure is sung to a couplet verse. But presently the same
music will be sung to the triplet verse.

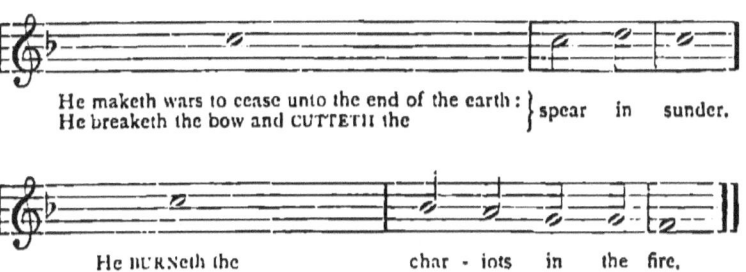

Every ear must detect that this is a clumsy makeshift: it runs counter to a rhythmic distinction as fundamental as the distinction of common time and triple time in music. The remedy is very simple. Chants of this nature are made up of two parts.

As such they are only fitted to couplet verses. For the triplet verse a *variant* is needed to the first part, sufficiently like it to be recognised, yet differing in a note or two. For

a simple variant would be

The couplet verse would be sung as before; for the triplet the variant would be inserted between the first and second parts.

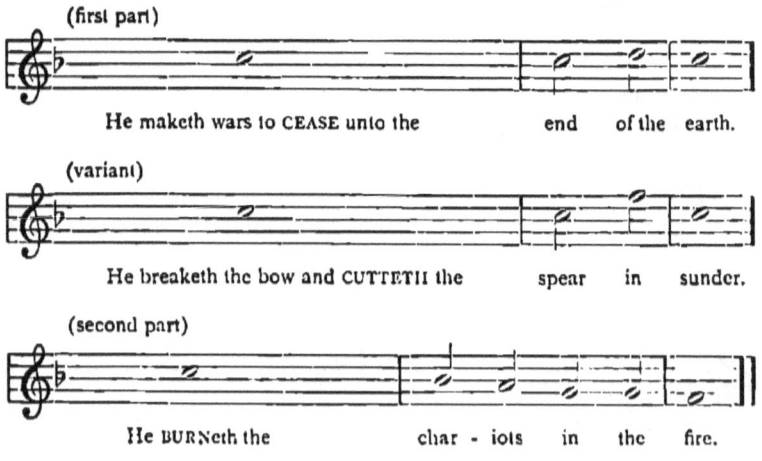

I am loth to delay the reader with what may seem to be merely technical matters. But attention to just a few of the elementary forms of Hebrew verse will richly repay itself in increased susceptibility to the rhythmic cadence of Biblical poetry. Passing then to other figures, it is natural to mention first the Quatrain, which has four lines. The four lines may be related to one another in various ways, of which the commonest is <u>Alternation</u>, the first line being parallel with the third, and the second with the fourth.

Quatrains and Double Triplets

> With the merciful
>   Thou wilt show thyself merciful:
> With the perfect man
>   Thou wilt show thyself perfect.[1]

In the Quatrain Reversed, or Introverted, the first line corresponds with the fourth, and the two middle lines with one another.

> Have mercy upon me, O God,
>   According to thy loving kindness:
>   According to the multitude of Thy tender mercies
> Blot out my transgressions.[2]

Usually such introversion is merely a matter of form; but sometimes it is found to be closely bound up with the sense.

> Give not that which is holy unto the dogs,
>   Neither cast your pearls before the swine:
>   Lest haply they [*the swine*] trample them under their feet,
> And [*the dogs*] turn and rend you.[3]

---

[1] *Psalm* xviii. 25. The following verse is another example, and this figure is very common.

[2] *Psalm* li. 1. Compare the metre of *In Memoriam*. Other examples are *Psalm* ciii. 1; ix. 15.

[3] *Matthew* vii. 6. It will be observed that Hebrew parallelism strongly influences the language of the New Testament, and of Apocryphal books originally Greek. It is therefore technically correct to treat 'Biblical' literature as a department by itself.

Very rarely the couplets of a Quatrain are not only parallel but interwoven, so that the sense of the first line is carried on by the third, and the sense of the second by the fourth.

> I will make mine arrows drunk with blood,
> And my sword shall devour flesh:
> With the blood of the slain and the captives,
> [*Flesh*] From the head of the leaders of the enemy.[1]

As we have Quatrain and Quatrain Reversed, so we have the Double Triplet and the Triplet Reversed.

> Ask, and it shall be given you;
> Seek, and ye shall find;
> Knock, and it shall be opened unto you.
> For every one that asketh receiveth,
> And he that seeketh findeth,
> And to him that knocketh it shall be opened.[2]

The eye catches what the ear confirms in this arrangement: how the first line of the second triplet balances the first line of the first triplet, the second the second, and the third the third. But in what follows the order of the second triplet is reversed, so that the beginning of the whole corresponds with the end, and the middle lines with one another:

> No servant can serve two masters:
> For either he will hate the one,
> And love the other;
> Or else he will hold to one,
> And despise the other.
> Ye cannot serve God and mammon.[3]

It is to be observed that such figures occur either pure or intermixed with a sequence of words that   *Recitative additions to Figures*

---
[1] *Deut.* xxxii. 42.
[2] *Matthew* vii. 7, 8. Other examples are *Matthew* xii. 35; *Isaiah* xxxv. 5.
[3] *Luke* xvi. 13. Other examples are *Proverbs* xxx. 8, 9; *Ezekiel* i. 27.

remains outside the rhythm, like the 'recitative' of a chant. Such a recitative may occur at the beginning:

And in that day thou shalt say

> I will give thanks unto thee, O Lord,
> For though thou wast angry with me,
> Thine anger is turned away,
> And thou comfortest me.

or at the end:

> Make the heart of this people fat,
> And make their ears heavy,
> And shut their eyes:
> Lest they see with their eyes,
> And hear with their ears,
> And understand with their heart:
> *and turn again and be healed.*

Or the recitative may even occur by interruption in the middle of the figure: a passage in *St. Matthew* has two Reversed Quatrains in succession thus interrupted.

> Whosoever shall swear by the Temple, it is nothing,
> But whosoever shall swear by the Gold of the Temple, he is a debtor:
>   (*Ye fools and blind*)
> For whether is greater, the Gold?
> Or the Temple that hath sanctified the Gold?
>
> And, Whosoever shall swear by the Altar, it is nothing,
> But whosoever shall swear by the Gift that is upon it, he is a debtor:
>   (*Ye fools and blind*)
> For whether is greater, the Gift?
> Or the Altar that sanctifieth the Gift?

The Chain Figure

There is no limit to the length or variety of such figures in Biblical versification. Of the more elaborate it will be enough to instance two. The Chain Figure is made up of a succession of clauses so linked that the goal of one clause becomes the starting-point of the next.

> That which the palmerworm hath left
>   hath the locust eaten;
> and that which the locust hath left
>   hath the cankerworm eaten;
> and that which the cankerworm hath left
>   hath the caterpillar eaten.[1]

The figure is all the more impressive when an additional line comes to complete the chain of ideas by connecting the end with the beginning.

> For her true beginning is
>   desire of discipline;
> And the care for discipline is
>   love of her;
> And love of her is
>   observance of her laws;
> And to give heed to her laws
>   confirmeth incorruption;
> And incorruption bringeth near unto God;
> So then desire of wisdom promoteth to a kingdom.

But perhaps the most important figure, and the one most attractive to the genius of Hebrew poetry, is the Envelope Figure, by which a series of parallel lines running to any length are enclosed between an identical (or equivalent) opening and close. *The Envelope Figure*

> By their fruits ye shall know them.
>   Do men gather grapes of thorns?
>   Or figs of thistles?
>   Even so every good tree bringeth forth good fruit,
>   But the corrupt tree bringeth forth evil fruit:
>   A good tree cannot bring forth evil fruit,
>   Neither can a corrupt tree bring forth good fruit.
>   Every tree that bringeth not forth good fruit
>   Is hewn down, and cast into the fire.
> Therefore by their fruits ye shall know them.[2]

---

[1] *Joel* i. 4. Other examples are in *Hosea* ii. 21, 22; *Romans* x. 14, 15; *II Peter* i. 5-7. The passage next cited is from *Wisdom* vi. 17-20.

[2] Compare *Psalm* viii: or, in English poetry, the opening stanza of Southey's *Thalaba*.

The same artistic effect of envelopment is produced when in such a figure the close is not a repetition of the opening, but completes it, so that the opening and the close make a unity which the parallel clauses develop.

> Consider the ravens:
>   that they sow not,
>   neither reap:
>   which have no store-chamber nor barn;
>   and God feedeth them:
> Of how much more value are ye than the birds![1]

The general subject of versification includes not only these Figures of Parallelism, the ultimate form by which Biblical verse separates itself from prose, but also those larger aggregations of lines and verses making integral parts of a poem, which may be called 'Stanzas.' Four points may be noted in regard to the position of the stanzas in the structure of Hebrew verse.

Stanzas

First, a poem may be composed of similar figures throughout: this is the treatment most familiar to the reader of English literature. The hundred and twenty-first psalm is made up of four similar quatrains.

1. Stanzas of Similar Figures

Psalm cxxi

> I will lift up mine eyes unto the mountains:
>   From whence shall my help come?
>   My help cometh from the LORD,
>   Which made heaven and earth.
>
> He will not suffer thy foot to be moved:
>   He that keepeth thee will not slumber;
>   Behold, he that keepeth Israel
>   Shall neither slumber nor sleep.
>
> The LORD is thy keeper:
>   The LORD is thy shade upon thy right hand;
>   The sun shall not smite thee by day,
>   Nor the moon by night.

[1] *Luke* xii. 24.—The figure made by a Question and its Answer comes under this head; e.g. *Psalm* xv, or *Psalm* xxiv. 3-6.

> The LORD shall keep thee from all evil:
> He shall keep thy soul;
> The LORD shall keep thy going out and thy coming in,
> From this time forth and for evermore.

Here may be mentioned a device of versification which applies to this as to all varieties of structure. It is the Refrain: the recurrence of a verse (or part of a verse) the repetition of which, besides being an artistic effect in itself, assists also in marking off such divisions as stanzas. *{The Refrain as a structural device}* A refrain in stanzas of this first kind will be given by the familiar hundred and thirty-sixth psalm; the poem is wholly composed of couplets, and the second line of each couplet is the refrain,

> For his mercy endureth for ever.

A second treatment of stanzas is seen where a psalm is found to be composed of different figures. The analysis of the first psalm yields a result of this nature. First we have a triple triplet preceded by a recitative. *{2. Stanzas of Varying Figures}*

> *Blessed is the man*   Psalm i
> > that walketh not
> > > in the counsel
> > > > of the wicked,
> >
> > Nor standeth
> > > in the way
> > > > of sinners,
> >
> > Nor sitteth
> > > in the seat
> > > > of the scornful.

This is followed by a quatrain reversed.

> > But his delight
> > > is in the law of the LORD:
> > > And in his law
> >
> > Doth he meditate day and night.

The next verse is a good example of the closeness with which form reflects matter. Its form is found to be a double quatrain with an introduction. On examination this recitative introduction will be seen to put forward the general thought — the comparison of the devout life to a tree; while the figure works this thought out into particulars, on the plan of the left-hand members of the figure suggesting elements of vegetable life — the planting, the fruitage, the foliage — and the right-hand members predicating perfection of each.

> *And he shall be like a Tree*
> Planted
> by the streams of water,
> That bringeth forth its fruit
> in its season;
> Whose leaf also
> doth not wither,
> And whatsoever he doeth
> shall prosper.

Next, we have a single couplet, sharply contrasting with what has gone before the mere worldly life.

> The wicked are not so,
> But are like the Chaff which the wind driveth away.

A simple quatrain and a quatrain reversed bring the poem to a conclusion.

> Therefore the wicked shall not stand
> in the judgement,
> Nor sinners
> in the congregation of the righteous.
>
> For the LORD knoweth
> the way of the righteous,
> But the way of the wicked
> shall perish.

As much lyric beauty is here produced by the avoidance of similar figures in successive verses as in the former case by the repetition of them.

Where lyrics are constructed on this second plan the refrain may still come to emphasise the divisions. The forty-sixth psalm is arranged in the Revised Version in two stanzas of six lines and one of seven: the refrain — a shout of triumph — brings each to a climax. It has, however, dropped out by accident from the first stanza in the received text, and must be restored.[1]

    God is our refuge and strength,   Psalm xlvi
    A very present help in trouble.
        Therefore will we not fear, though the earth do change,
        And though the mountains be moved in the heart of the seas;
        Though the waters thereof roar and be troubled,
        Though the mountains shake with the swelling thereof.
    THE LORD OF HOSTS IS WITH US;
    THE GOD OF JACOB IS OUR REFUGE!

    There is a river, the streams whereof make glad the city of God,
    The holy place of the tabernacles of the Most High.
        God is in the midst of her; she shall not be moved:
        God shall help her, and that right early.
        The nations raged, the kingdoms were moved:
        He uttered his voice, the earth melted.
    THE LORD OF HOSTS IS WITH US;
    THE GOD OF JACOB IS OUR REFUGE!

    Come, behold the works of the LORD,
    What desolations he hath made in the earth.
        He maketh wars to cease unto the end of the earth;
        He breaketh the bow, and cutteth the spear in sunder;
        He burneth the chariots in the fire.
        "Be still, and know that I am God:
        I will be exalted among the nations, I will be exalted in the earth."
    THE LORD OF HOSTS IS WITH US;
    THE GOD OF JACOB IS OUR REFUGE!

---

[1] On the general subject of textual emendation, I would lay down the principle that, where the sense is affected by a proposed change, it is prudent to be conservative and chary of admitting it. But where (as with a repetition) it is only a question of form, the long period of tradition mentioned above, during which the literary form of Scripture was overlooked, justifies us in expecting many omissions and misplacements.

We have a more elaborate symmetry of parallelism when we come to *Antistrophic* stanzas. The word is Greek, and the spirit of this beautiful form of structure is best caught from the complete realisation of it in Greek lyrics. A Greek ode was performed by a body of singers whose evolutions as they sang a stanza carried them from the altar towards the right: then turning round they performed an answering stanza, repeating their movements, until its close brought them to the altar from which they had started. Then a stanza would take them to the left of the altar, and its answering stanza would bring them back to the starting-point: and of such pairs of stanzas an ode was normally made up. From a Greek word meaning 'a turning' the first stanza of a pair was called a *strophé*, its answering stanza an *antistrophé*: and the metrical rhythms of the antistrophe reproduced those of the corresponding strophe line by line, though the rhythm might be wholly changed between one pair of stanzas and another. Hebrew lyrics contain examples of this disposition of stanzas in pairs; and the two stanzas of a pair agree, not of course in metre, but in number of parallel lines. Though somewhat rare in the Bible, this structure is worthy of close study wherever it occurs. The simplest case is where each antistrophe immediately follows its strophe, and of this the thirtieth psalm is an example.

<small>3. Antistrophic structure of stanzas</small>

Strophe 1

Psalm xxx I will extol thee, O LORD; for thou hast raised me up,
And hast not made my foes to rejoice over me.
O LORD my God,
I cried unto thee, and thou hast healed me.
O LORD, thou hast brought up my soul from Sheol:
Thou has kept me alive, that I should not go down to the pit.

Antistrophe

Sing praise unto the LORD, O ye saints of his,
And give thanks to his holy name.
For his anger is but for a moment,
In his favour is life:
Weeping may tarry for the night,
But joy cometh in the morning.

Strophe 2

As for me, I said in my prosperity,
I shall never be moved.
Thou, LORD, of thy favour hadst made my mountain to stand strong:

Antistrophe

Thou didst hide thy face; I was troubled.
I cried to thee, O LORD;
And unto the LORD I made supplication:

Strophe 3

"What profit is there in my blood when I go down to the pit?
Shall the dust praise thee? Shall it declare thy truth?
Hear, O LORD, and have mercy upon me:
LORD, be thou my helper."

Antistrophe

Thou hast turned for me my mourning into dancing;
Thou hast loosed my sackcloth, and girded me with gladness:
To the end that my glory may sing praise to thee, and not be silent.
O LORD my God, I will give thanks unto thee for ever.

But in the parallelism of stanzas, as well as the parallelism of lines in a figure, the device of introversion is found, by which, it will be recollected, beginning corresponds with end, and middle part with middle part. An example of such antistrophic introversion is found in the hundred and fourteenth psalm, which thought and form combine to make one of the most striking of Hebrew lyrics. It is a song inspired, not only by the deliverance from Egypt, but also by the new conception of Deity which that deliverance exhibited to the world. In the age of the exodus the prevailing conception of a god was that of a being sacred to a particular territory, out of the bounds of which territory the god's power did not extend. But the Israelites in the wilderness presented to the world the spectacle of a nation moving from country to country and carrying the presence of their God with them; it was no

_{Antistrophic Introversion}

_{Psalm cxiv}

longer the land of Goshen, but the nation of Israel itself that constituted the sanctuary and dominion of Jehovah. The wonder of this conception the psalm expresses by the favourite Hebrew image of nature in convulsion; and the effect of introversion in giving shape (so to speak) to the whole thought of the poem may be conveyed to the eye by the following scheme:

> A new conception of Deity!
> Nature convulsed!
> Why Nature convulsed?
> At the new conception of Deity.

Those phrases sum up the thought of the successive stanzas, which are so related to one another that the first strophe is followed by a second, and the antistrophe to the second strophe precedes the antistrophe to the first.

Strophe 1

> When Israel went forth out of Egypt,
>   The house of Jacob from a people of strange language;
> Judah became his sanctuary,
>   Israel his dominion.

Strophe 2

> The sea saw it and fled;
> Jordan was driven back.
> The mountains skipped like rams,
> The little hills like young sheep.

Antistrophe 2

> What aileth thee, O sea, that thou fleest?
> Thou Jordan, that thou turnest back?
> Ye mountains, that ye skip like rams?
> Ye little hills, like young sheep?

Antistrophe 1

> Tremble, thou earth, at THE PRESENCE OF THE LORD,
>   At the presence of the God of Jacob;
> Which turned the rock into a pool of water,
>   The flint into a fountain of waters!

Again, we find as a rare effect in Hebrew poetry what is common in Greek, an interweaving of stanzas similar to the interweaving of couplets in a quatrain noted above; the first strophe is followed by a second of different length, then succeed the antistrophe to the first and the antistrophe to the second. The ninety-ninth psalm has this structure; and the effect is assisted by a double refrain: the longer strophe of five lines has a short refrain, while the shorter strophe of three lines has a longer refrain.[1]

Antistrophic Interweaving

Strophe 1

The LORD reigneth: let the peoples tremble: Psalm xcix
He sitteth upon the cherubim; let the earth be moved.
The LORD is great in Zion;
And he is high above all the peoples.
Let them praise thy great and terrible name.
Holy is He!

Strophe 2

The king's strength also loveth judgement;
Thou dost establish equity,
Thou executest judgement and righteousness in Jacob.
EXALT YE THE LORD OUR GOD
AND WORSHIP AT HIS FOOTSTOOL.
HOLY IS HE!

Antistrophe 1

Moses and Aaron among his priests,
And Samuel among them that call upon his name;
They called upon the LORD, and he answered them.
He spake unto them in the pillar of cloud:
They kept his testimonies and the statute that he gave them.
Holy is He!

Antistrophe 2

Thou answeredst them, O LORD our God,
Thou wast a God that forgavest them,
Though thou tookest vengeance of their doings.
EXALT YE THE LORD OUR GOD,
AND WORSHIP AT HIS HOLY HILL;
FOR THE LORD OUR GOD IS HOLY!

---

[1] The short refrain has dropped out of Antistrophe 1, and must be restored (at the end of verse 7).

But the commonest treatment of stanzas in Biblical poetry is that which is also the freest: where a poem is allowed to fall into well-marked divisions, which have, however, no distinct relations with one another as regards length or parallelism. By an awkwardness of nomenclature, such irregular divisions have come to be called 'strophes': it is too late to change the usage, but the reader must be on the watch to distinguish the 'strophic structure,' where the stanzas may be unequal, from the 'antistrophic structure,' in which the two stanzas of a pair are exact counterparts. A simple example of such division by natural cleavage only will be afforded by the twentieth psalm.

4. Strophic structure of stanzas

Strophe 1 — The People

Psalm xx
The LORD answer thee in the day of trouble;
The name of the God of Jacob set thee up on high;
Send thee help from the sanctuary,
And strengthen thee out of Zion;
Remember all thy offerings,
And accept thy burnt sacrifice;
Grant thee thy heart's desire,
And fulfil all thy counsel.
We will triumph in thy salvation,
And in the name of our God we will set up our banners:
The LORD fulfil all thy petitions.

Strophe 2 — The King

Now know I that the LORD saveth his anointed;
He will answer him from his holy heaven
With the saving strength of his right hand.

Strophe 3 — The People

Some trust in chariots, and some in horses:
But we will make mention of the name of the LORD our God.
They are bowed down and fallen:
But we are risen, and stand upright.
O LORD, save the king;
And answer us when we call.

In this strophic structure the refrain has a special value for marking out the stanzas which have no other rhythmic distinction. A splendid example of such treatment is given by the poem which opens the second book of Psalms. _{Psalms xlii-xliii} The allusion of one of its verses seems to associate it with some high ground — mountains of Hermon, or hill Mizar — which was the last point from which the Holy Land could be seen by an exile carried eastwards; in any case, it is appropriately named 'The Exile's Lament.' The spirit of the whole lyric is summed up in its refrain, which is a struggle between despair and hope.

> *Why art thou cast down, O my soul?*
> *And why art thou disquieted within me?*
> *Hope thou in God:*
> *For I shall yet praise him,*
> *Who is the health of my countenance*
> *And my God!*

This refrain is found to unify into a single poem the psalms numbered forty-two and forty-three; and the whole falls into three strophes. Though the refrain does not change, yet its repetition is made to suggest advance. The first strophe has nothing but longing memories: how the poet was wont to mingle with the throng, or perhaps lead them in procession to the house of God, with the voice of joy and praise, a multitude keeping holyday. Its struggle towards hopefulness is so unsuccessful that, after the refrain, the second strophe opens with the deepest note of despondency. A single ray of light, however, is cast into the future, and there is just a mention of loving-kindness by day and songs in the night, after which thoughts of mourning and oppression resume their sway. But the third stanza begins with a more resolute appeal to God as the judge, or righter of the oppressed; the turn has been taken, and we advance through ideas of light and truth to joy and praise of harp, until the third repetition of the refrain makes us feel that its summons to hope has proved successful.

Strophe 1

As the hart panteth after the water brooks,
So panteth my soul after thee, O God.
My soul thirsteth for God, for the living God:
When shall I come and appear before God?
My tears have been my meat day and night,
While they continually say unto me, Where is thy God?
These things I remember, and pour out my soul within me,
How I went with the throng, and led them to the house of God,
With the voice of joy and praise, a multitude keeping holyday.

> *Why art thou cast down, O my soul?*
> *And why art thou disquieted within me?*
> *Hope thou in God:*
> *For I shall yet praise him,*
> *Who is the health of my countenance*
> *And my God!*

Strophe 2

My soul is cast down within me!
Therefore do I remember thee from the land of Jordan,
And the Hermons, from the hill Mizar.
Deep calleth unto deep at the noise of thy waterspouts:
All thy waves and thy billows are gone over me!
Yet the LORD will command his loving-kindness in the day-time,
And in the night his song shall be with me,
Even a prayer unto the God of my life.
I will say unto God my rock, " Why hast thou forgotten me?
Why go I mourning because of the oppression of the enemy?
As with a sword in my bones, mine adversaries reproach me;
While they continually say unto me, Where is thy God?"

> *Why art thou cast down, O my soul?*
> *And why art thou disquieted within me?*
> *Hope thou in God:*
> *For I shall yet praise him,*
> *Who is the health of my countenance*
> *And my God!*

Strophe 3

Judge me, O God, and plead my cause against an ungodly nation:
O deliver me from the deceitful and unjust man.
For thou art the God of my strength; why hast thou cast me off?

Why go I mourning because of the oppression of the enemy?
O send out thy light and thy truth; let them lead me:
Let them bring me unto thy holy hill, and to thy tabernacles.
Then will I go unto the altar of God,
Unto God my exceeding joy:
And upon the harp will I praise thee, O God, my God.
    WHY ART THOU CAST DOWN, O MY SOUL?
    AND WHY ART THOU DISQUIETED WITHIN ME?
      HOPE THOU IN GOD:
      FOR I SHALL YET PRAISE HIM,
      WHO IS THE HEALTH OF MY COUNTENANCE
      AND MY GOD!

But the maximum of lyric effect drawn from this combination of the strophic structure and the refrain is found in a portion of the hundred and seventh psalm. Here there is a double refrain: one puts in each stanza a cry for help, the other the outburst of praise after the help has come; each refrain has a sequel verse which appropriately changes with the subject of each stanza. Thus the form of the strophes is that which the eye catches in the subjoined mode of printing it; the body of each stanza consists of short lines putting various forms of distress; then the stanza lengthens its lines into the first refrain with its sequel verse, and enlarges again into the second refrain with its sequel. *Psalm cvii. 4-32*

Strophe 1

    They wandered in the wilderness
    In a desert way;
    They found no city of habitation.
    Hungry and thirsty,
    Their soul fainted in them.
    Then they cried unto the Lord in their trouble,
    And he delivered them out of their distresses.
    He led them also by a straight way,
    That they might go to a city of habitation.
OH THAT MEN WOULD PRAISE THE LORD FOR HIS GOODNESS,
AND FOR HIS WONDERFUL WORKS TO THE CHILDREN OF MEN!
For he satisfieth the longing soul,
And the hungry soul he filleth with good.

Strophe 2

Such as sat in darkness
And in the shadow of death,
Being bound in affliction and iron;
Because they rebelled against the words of God,
And contemned the counsel of the Most High:
Therefore he brought down their heart with labour,
They fell down, and there was none to help.
Then they cried unto the Lord in their trouble,
And he saved them out of their distresses.
He brought them out of darkness and the shadow of death,
And brake their bands in sunder.
OH THAT MEN WOULD PRAISE THE LORD FOR HIS GOODNESS,
AND FOR HIS WONDERFUL WORKS TO THE CHILDREN OF MEN!
For he hath broken the gates of brass,
And cut the bars of iron in sunder.

Strophe 3

Fools because of their transgression,
And because of their iniquities, are afflicted.
Their soul abhorreth all manner of meat;
And they draw near unto the gates of death.
Then they cry unto the Lord in their trouble,
And he saveth them out of their distresses.
He sendeth his word, and healeth them,
And delivereth them from their destructions.
OH THAT MEN WOULD PRAISE THE LORD FOR HIS GOODNESS,
AND FOR HIS WONDERFUL WORKS TO THE CHILDREN OF MEN!
And let them offer the sacrifices of thanksgiving,
And declare his works with singing.

Strophe 4

They that go down to the sea in ships,
That do business in great waters,
These see the works of the LORD,
And his wonders in the deep.
For he commandeth,
And raiseth the stormy wind,
Which lifteth up the waves thereof:
They mount up to the heaven,

They go down again to the depths;
Their soul melteth away because of trouble :
They reel to and fro,
And stagger like a drunken man;
And are at their wits' end.
*Then they cry unto the Lord in their trouble,
And he bringeth them out of their distresses.*
He maketh the storm a calm,
So that the waves thereof are still.
Then are they glad because they be quiet :
So he bringeth them unto the haven where they would be.
OH THAT MEN WOULD PRAISE THE LORD FOR HIS GOODNESS,
AND FOR HIS WONDERFUL WORKS TO THE CHILDREN OF MEN!
Let them exalt him also in the assembly of the people,
And praise him in the seat of the elders.

It is just such structural variations as these that it is the special mission of a musical rendering to express.[1] In the psalm just cited the melancholy monotony of men's voices in unison might be used to bring out the various phases of distress which make the subjects of successive strophes. **Musical expression of structure** Children's voices in harmony and unaccompanied would fitly express the cry for help (refrain and sequel verse), while full choir and organ would give out the thanksgiving. In the more extended final stanza a monotone of men's voices in unison would leave more scope for organ accompaniment to bring out the changes of the sea. Then as before the whole would resolve into the silvery harmony of children's voices heard alone ; while all that full choir and instrument could do would be needed for the final climax.

[1] Bishop Westcott's *Paragraph Psalter* (Macmillan) is a step in the direction of such structural chanting. A musical setting of *Psalms* lxxviii and civ in illustration of it has been published by Dr. Naylor, Organist of York Minster (Novello).

CHAPTER II

THE HIGHER PARALLELISM, OR PARALLELISM OF INTERPRETATION

Parallelism in general

THE preceding chapter has sufficiently exhibited Biblical Versification in its leading forms and devices of structure. In the present chapter I consider further the general spirit of parallelism which underlies it. I wish to show that the study of such parallelism is not a mere matter of technicalities, but that it connects itself directly with the higher interests of literature.

Parallelism a factor in interpretation

In interpreting the meaning of Scripture parallelism plays no unimportant part. I will commence with a very simple example. The Song of the Sword,[1] which gives expression to the excitement attending the first invention of deadly weapons, contains the following couplet:

> I have slain a man to my wounding,
> And a young man to my hurt.

Does this passage imply the slaying of one person or two persons? This question cannot be called a mere matter of technicalities. Commentators of the period when the secret of parallelism was lost understood the words to mean that two men were slain; and connecting the passage with the succeeding couplet—

> If Cain shall be avenged sevenfold,
> Truly Lamech seventy and sevenfold —

they found an interpretation for the whole by supposing that when

[1] Otherwise called Song of Lamech (*Gen.* iv. 23-24).

Lamech became advanced in years he carried with him a youth to show him where to point his arrows; that this youth directing him to shoot into a certain bush Lamech thereby slew Cain, and made himself liable to the curse invoked on the slayer of that outcast. In his rage Lamech shot a second arrow at his youthful attendant; and thus two slayings are accounted for. But to an ear accustomed to parallelism it is clear enough that no such violence of interpretation is required. The second line of a couplet need not be a separate statement from that of the first line, but may be, in the spirit of parallelism, a saying over again of what has been said. Thus the couplet need only imply the death of a single person, or better, slaying as a general idea. And the second couplet merely gives expression to the enlarged possibilities of destruction that come with the invention of the sword: even the vengeance for Cain — a thing that had perhaps passed into a proverbial expression — becomes a small matter in comparison with the power of vengeance the armed warrior will possess. Thus the whole meaning of the passage has been changed by attention to a detail of versification.

The intrinsic importance of this first example is not great. But no one will consider the 'Lord's Prayer' unimportant: and yet it would seem that the great majority of those who repeat the Lord's Prayer in public fail to bring out the full thought that underlies it. This prayer is almost always rendered as a succession of isolated clauses which may be represented thus: *The Lord's Prayer*

> Our Father which art in heaven, Hallowed be thy name. Thy kingdom come. Thy will be done in earth as it is in heaven.

But the true significance of these words is only seen when they are arranged so as to make an envelope figure.

> Our Father which art in heaven:
> Hallowed be thy Name,
> Thy Kingdom come,
> Thy Will be done,
> In earth as it is in heaven.

In the former version the words, "In earth as it is in heaven" are attached only to the petition, "Thy will be done." But it belongs to the envelope structure that all the parallel clauses are to be connected with the common opening and close. The meaning thus becomes: "Hallowed be thy name in earth as it is in heaven, Thy kingdom come in earth as it is in heaven, Thy will be done in earth as it is in heaven." It is something more than literary beauty that is gained by the change.

One more illustration of the close connection between parallelism of structure and interpretation will be afforded by the eighth psalm. The whole of this poem makes a single envelope figure.

Psalm viii

> O LORD, our Lord,
> How excellent is thy name in all the earth!
>> Who hast set thy glory upon the heavens,
>>> Out of the mouth of babes and sucklings hast thou established strength,
>>> Because of thine adversaries,
>>> That thou mightest still the enemy and the avenger.
>>> When I consider the heavens, the work of thy fingers,
>>> The moon and the stars which thou hast ordained;
>>> What is man, that thou art mindful of him?
>>> And the son of man, that thou visitest him?
>>> For thou hast made him but little lower than God,
>>> And crownest him with glory and honour.
>>> Thou madest him to have dominion over the works of thy hands;
>>> Thou hast put all things under his feet:
>>> All sheep and oxen,
>>> Yea, and the beasts of the field;
>>> The fowl of the air, and the fish of the sea,
>>> Whatsoever passeth through the paths of the seas.
> O LORD, our Lord,
> How excellent is thy name in all the earth!

By neglect of the true structure, three lines instead of two have been taken into the opening verse:

> 1. O LORD, our Lord,
>   How excellent is thy name in all the earth!
>   Who hast set thy glory upon the heavens.

Accordingly, the verse which follows this, and presumably opens the regular thought of the poem, is made to read:

> 2. Out of the mouth of babes and sucklings hast thou established strength, etc.

So arranged this verse becomes obscure, and the ingenuity of commentators has been much exercised to determine what is the allusion its words contain. But the envelope structure conveys at once to the eye that the first two lines must be isolated as the enveloping refrain, and then the opening verse becomes this:

> Who hast set thy glory upon the heavens,
> Out of the mouth of babes and sucklings hast thou established strength, etc.

That the Artificer of the mighty heavens should have chosen man — a mere babe and suckling in comparison — to be the representative of his might to the rest of the universe: this is the wonder with which the poem really opens, and the thought of feeble man as God's Viceroy over the creation is precisely the idea which is found to bind the whole psalm into a unity.

These are particular examples: it is possible to generalise. In Biblical interpretation the question will repeatedly arise, whether a particular passage is to be understood as a simple narrative of facts or an idealised description: in such a case parallelism of clauses will undoubtedly be one factor in the interpretation. I have already suggested that the extreme symmetry of the clauses which describe Job's misfortunes descending upon him tells in favour of the view that the narrative is not a history so much as an incident worked up into a parable. In a more important matter the same principle has been applied to the opening chapter of *Genesis*. The account of the Creation which this passage contains is found, upon examination, to be arranged with the most minute parallelism of matter and form. Not only are the six days furnished with opening and closing formulæ which correspond, but

[margin: Parallelism a criterion for idealisation]
[margin: Genesis i]

the whole divides into two symmetrical halves of three days and three days, and each day of the first three is exactly parallel with the corresponding day of the second half. A table will illustrate the structure.

And God said—
    [Creation of Light]
 And there was evening and there was morning, one day.
	And God said—
	    [Creation of Lights]
	 And there was evening and there was morning, a fourth day.

And God said—
    [Creation of the Firmament dividing waters from waters]
 And there was evening and there was morning, a second day.
	And God said—
	    [Creation of Life in the Firmament and in the Waters]
	 And there was evening and there was morning, a fifth day.

{ *And God said*—
    [Creation of Land]
   And God said—
    [Creation of Vegetation, climax of inanimate nature]
 And there was evening and there was morning, a third day.
	{ *And God said*—
	    [Creation of Life on Land]
	   And God said—
	    [Creation of Man, climax of animate nature]
	 And there was evening and there was morning, the sixth day.

When this structure and the fulness of its parallelism is grasped, it will appear reasonable that it should be urged as one argument in favour of understanding the chapter to be, not a narration of incidents in their order of succession, but a logical classification of the elements of the universe, with the emphatic assertion of Divine creation in reference to each.

The reader will understand that it is not essential to my argument that such interpretations as I have been advancing should seem to him correct. Parallelism is only one factor amongst many in exegesis. I am merely concerned to show that those who address themselves to determining the matter and meaning of Scripture nevertheless appeal to its form and structure. Indeed, the reader unaccustomed to this subject will be greatly astonished at the extent and minuteness

<small>Recognition of Parallelism in exegesis</small>

to which symmetry of form in Scripture is made to obtain in the exegesis of competent theologians; when, for example, not a paragraph but a long poem, or the whole of an epistolary treatise, is represented as being constructed on a single intricate system. Such elaborations of parallelism must be considered each on its own merits; but there is in them nothing inherently improbable. When the genius of a language rests the whole system of its versification upon symmetry of clauses, it becomes a safe presumption that parallelism will penetrate very deeply into its logical processes of thought.[1]

We have been led to see then that there are two points of view from which parallelism may be considered: that of Rhythm and that of Interpretation. The musical element of Biblical language rests on parallels and recurrences, and an ear for rhythm is as essential for the appreciation of Scriptural style as an ear for time is essential for the appreciation of music. But thought may be rhythmic as well as language, and the full meaning and force of Scripture is not grasped by one who does not feel how thoughts can be emphasised by being differently re-stated, as in the simplest couplet; or how a general thought may reiterate itself to enclose its particulars, as in the envelope figure, or, in such cases as the Lord's Prayer, hold its conclusion in suspense until all to which it applies has been set forth; or again, as in the opening of *Genesis*, how a passage can suggest logical symmetries while in form it is only narrating. Accordingly the structural analysis of Biblical language must distinguish a Lower Parallelism of Rhythm and a Higher Parallelism of Interpretation. The two can never clash, since in Hebrew rhythm largely depends on recurrence of clauses corresponding in thought; but one or other parallelism will preponderate in accordance with the nature of a particular passage or the purpose of a citation. Sometimes the musical form will be felt to preponderate, and in this case the

The Lower Parallelism of Rhythm and the Higher Parallelism of Interpretation

---

[1] Dr. Forbes's *Symmetrical Structure of Scripture* (Clark, Edinburgh) may be regarded as a text-book of the general subject.

structural arrangement of the passage will be such as will make prominent the recurrence of fixed figures. In other cases the arrangement will bring out how distant sequences of words from all over a lengthy passage co-ordinate together, and this effect will throw into the background the parallelisms of couplets and triplets, which nevertheless are to be found when looked for.[1]

The matter is best treated by illustrations; and I proceed to give two arrangements of the same passage, based respectively on the Lower and the Higher Parallelism.

Job x. 3-13 arranged for Lower Parallelism

Is it good unto thee that thou shouldest oppress,
That thou shouldest despise the work of thine hands,
And shine upon the counsel of the wicked?

    Hast thou eyes of flesh,
    Or seest thou as man seeth?

    Are thy days as the days of man,
    Or thy years as man's days,

    That thou inquirest after mine iniquity,
    And searchest after my sin,

    Although thou knowest that I am not wicked;
    And there is none that can deliver out of thine hand?

    Thine hands have framed me and fashioned me
    Together round about; yet thou dost destroy me.

    Remember, I beseech thee, that thou hast fashioned me as clay;
    And wilt thou bring me into dust again?

    Hast thou not poured me out as milk,
    And curdled me like cheese?

    Thou hast clothed me with skin and flesh,
    And knit me together with bones and sinews.

---

[1] On the whole subject compare Appendix III: On the Structural Printing of Scripture.

Thou hast granted me life and favour,
And thy visitation hath preserved my spirit.

Yet these things thou didst hide in thine heart;
I know that this is with thee.

In the above citation I have followed the Revised Version of the Bible in conveying nothing to the eye beyond the elementary rhythm of couplets and triplets. Such an arrangement involves the minimum of interpretation, and therefore the minimum difference of opinion. Where the higher symmetry is expressed individual interpretations will of course differ. In my second arrangement of the passage figures of mere rhythm are suppressed in order that parallelisms of thought may stand out.

Arranged for Higher Parallelism

Is it good unto thee that thou shouldest oppress,
That thou shouldest despise the work of thine hands,
   And shine upon the counsel of the wicked?
Hast thou eyes of flesh,
   Or seest thou as man seeth?
Are thy days as the days of man,
   Or thy years as man's days,
That thou inquirest after mine iniquity,
   And searchest after my sin,
Although thou knowest that I am not wicked;
   And there is none that can deliver out of thine hand?
Thine hands have framed me,
And fashioned me together round about;
   Yet thou dost destroy me.
Remember, I beseech thee, that thou hast fashioned me as clay;
   And wilt thou bring me into dust again?
Hast thou not poured me out as milk,
And curdled me like cheese?
Thou hast clothed me with skin and flesh,
And knit me together with bones and sinews;
Thou hast granted me life and favour,
And thy visitation hath preserved my spirit:
   Yet these things thou didst hide in thine heart;
   I know that this is with thee.

Two distinct trains of thought are interwoven in this passage: in one Job makes appeal to God as being God's own handiwork; in the other he protests against the righteous Lord following the oppressive ways of unjust judges. In this second arrangement the two elements of the thought are separated: lines belonging to the first are indented to the left, lines belonging to the second are indented to the right. Thus the whole play of thought in the passage is reflected to the eye, or, in other words, the structural arrangement has brought out the Parallelism of Interpretation.[1]

One more observation must be made on Biblical parallelism considered as an element in literary style. It is that such symmetry of clauses is closely bound up with a literary effect of an opposite kind — that of surprise. It is just when the ear is being led by the general form of a passage to expect what is coming that the disappointment of this expectation, and the substitution of something new, strikes with most telling force. Here, again, illustrations will make the best exposition.

Parallelism implies its opposite effect of surprise

There is no passage in the Bible in which parallelism is carried further than in the peroration (if the word may be allowed) of the Sermon on the Mount, with its comparison of the two kinds of hearers to the builders on the rock and on the sand. The passage is antistrophic, and for every clause in the one picture there is a corresponding clause in the other. Yet here the effect of surprise is produced by a subtle and delicate variation which has been recovered for us by the Revised Version. The word which describes the action of the wind differs in the two strophes; for the blasts labouring in vain to destroy the one house a word is used which is translated by the English 'beat'; for the wind in the other case the Greek word is changed to something which the Revisers render 'smote'— the very sound of which, as well as the sense, pictures a single blow sufficing to bring the structure down.

Matthew vii. 24-27

---

[1] In my edition of the *Book of Job* this mode of printing that reflects the Higher Parallelism is followed throughout. [Macmillan & Co.]

Strophe

Every one therefore which heareth these words of mine,
    and doeth them,
shall be likened unto a Wise Man,
which built his house upon the Rock:
    And the rain descended,
    and the floods came,
    and the winds blew
    and *beat* upon that house;
and it fell not:
for it was founded upon the Rock.

Antistrophe

And every one that heareth these words of mine,
    and doeth them not,
shall be likened unto a Foolish Man,
which built his house upon the Sand:
    And the rain descended,
    and the floods came,
    and the winds blew,
    and SMOTE upon that house;
and it fell:
and great was the fall thereof!

In this example the effect of surprise is produced by a verbal alteration. It is more pertinent to the subject of the present chapter to consider cases in which the variation extends to a whole clause. An admirable illustration is afforded by the hundred and thirty-ninth psalm. This exquisite lyric is in structure a very extended form of the envelope figure. But the opening verse, when it appears at the close, has undergone an important change: for the indicative mood of the opening —

Psalm cxxxix

    O LORD, thou hast searched me —

we have at the end the imperative mood —

    Search me, O God —

and the whole movement of the poem is to lead from the one state of mind to the other. At the outset the thought of Divine omniscience and omnipresence lies like a weight upon the poet's mind.

> O Lord, thou hast searched me, and known me!
> Thou knowest my downsitting and mine uprising,
> Thou understandest my thought afar off.
> Thou searchest out my path and my lying down,
> And art acquainted with all my ways.
> For there is not a word in my tongue,
> But, lo, O Lord, thou knowest it altogether.
> Thou hast beset me behind and before,
> And laid thine hand upon me.

The burden becomes intolerable, and the poet would fain throw it off.

> Such knowledge is too wonderful for me;
> It is high, I cannot attain unto it.
> Whither shall I go from thy spirit?
> Or whither shall I flee from thy presence?
> If I ascend up into heaven, thou art there:
> If I make my bed in Sheol, behold, thou art there.
> If I take the wings of the morning,
> And dwell in the uttermost parts of the sea;
> Even there shall thy hand lead me,
> And thy right hand shall hold me.
> If I say, Surely the darkness shall overwhelm me,
> And the light about me shall be night;
> Even the darkness hideth not from thee,
> But the night shineth as the day:
> The darkness and the light are both alike to thee.

The sense of oppression can intensify yet further, and the next verse extends it backwards in time, as previous verses had made it stretch through all space.

> For thou hast possessed my reins:
> Thou hast covered me in my mother's womb.

It is just here, where the effect is at its height, that the turn comes. The mysteries of the womb suggest to the poet that this Divine watchfulness from which he cannot escape is the same watchfulness which, in his helplessness, built him up into the being he is. The current of thought begins to flow back — for the structure of the psalm is antistrophic as well as enveloped.

> I will give thanks unto thee; for I am fearfully and wonderfully made:
> Wonderful are thy works,
> And that my soul knoweth right well.
> My frame was not hidden from thee,
> When I was made in secret,
> And curiously wrought in the lowest parts of the earth.
> Thine eyes did see mine unperfect substance,
> And in thy book were all my members written,
> Which day by day were fashioned,
> When as yet there was none of them.

The besetting watchfulness now becomes a precious thought to the psalmist; most precious of all, the incalculableness of its extent.

> How precious also are thy thoughts[1] unto me, O God!
> How great is the sum of them!
> If I should count them, they are more in number than the sand:
> When I awake, I am still with thee.

The new thought has gained force, and takes fire in a burst of purity.

> Surely thou wilt slay the wicked, O God:
> Depart from me therefore, ye bloodthirsty men.
> For they speak against thee wickedly,
> And thine enemies take thy name in vain.
> Do not I hate them, O LORD, that hate thee?
> And am not I grieved with those that rise up against thee?
> I hate them with perfect hatred:
> I count them mine enemies.

The new train of thought has reached its goal, and, as the envelope figure completes itself, the refrain reappears changed and enlarged, so that the burden has become an aspiration.

[1] That is, the thoughts which God bestows on the psalmist,

> Search me, O God, and know my heart:
> Try me, and know my thoughts:
> And see if there be any way of wickedness in me,
> And lead me in the way everlasting.

The analysis of this psalm is an excellent illustration, both of the general principle that the most deeply spiritual trains of thought are reflected in beauty of external literary structure, and also of the special observation immediately under discussion, that parallelism carries with it the literary effect of climax or surprise when the exactness of the parallelism is artistically violated.

CHAPTER III

THE LOWER AND THE HIGHER UNITY IN LITERATURE

LITERARY classification has so far been applied only to the external structure of Sacred Scripture, and its distinction of prose and verse; though it has appeared that here, as always, structure reacts on spirit, and the parallelism of rhythm generates a parallelism of thought. Before we can proceed to that higher literary classification which recognises structure and spirit alike, another preliminary consideration needs attention. The bond uniting clauses into a verse and verses into a stanza may be considered as the Lower Unity in comparison with a Higher Unity which is the subject of the present chapter. This Higher Unity is the Unity of Poem: the bond which unites successive verses and stanzas into a poem complete in itself.[1] *The Lower Unity and the Higher Unity*

Here again are difficulties special to the literary study of the Bible, arising from the arrangement of our printed bibles and of the manuscripts on which they are founded, and still more from the habits of reading which these by long tradition have fostered. In dealing with any other literature the student would naturally, and as a matter of course, look for the higher unity in what he reads. He would not study Virgil merely to get quotable hexameters, nor Shakespeare to find pithy sentences: he would wish to comprehend the drift of a scene, or the plot of a whole play; he would

The Higher Unity obscured by reading the Bible in verses

---

[1] For convenience of illustration I speak throughout the chapter of poems: but the argument applies, *mutatis mutandis*, to prose compositions.

read a whole eclogue at once, or even sustain his attention through the twelve books of the *Æneid*. But the vast majority of those who read the Bible have never shaken off the mediæval tendency to look upon it as a collection of isolated sentences, isolated texts, isolated verses. Their intention is nothing but reverent; but the effect of their imperfect reading is to degrade a sacred literature into a pious scrap-book.

I have called this tendency mediæval: it is a relic of the Middle Ages under the influence of which arose our earliest translations of the Bible into modern tongues. The thought of the Middle Ages is distinguished by disconnectedness. The Schoolmen were not remarkable for successful investigation or wide reflectiveness, but they surpassed all men in subtlety of discussion; indeed, it would almost seem that with them the process of discussing was more important than the conclusion attained. Accordingly their age gave special prominence to the isolated proposition. Its thinkers were not confined to books as a medium for expressing thought; it was equally open to them to issue a series of propositions, and, setting these up on some church door or elsewhere, offer discussion with all comers. To formulate truth into these brief independent sentences, adapted for attack and defence, made the characteristic literary activity of the period. In modern thought detail truths are so many bricks to be built into an edifice, each valued according as it contributes to the common stability; the independent propositions of the mediæval thinker were rather footballs to be driven to and fro in an exercise of dialectic strength. Translations of the Bible made amid such surroundings took shape from the minds of the translators. Hebrew and Greek literature — poem, dialogue, discourse — all assumed a monotonous uniformity of numbered sentences, each to be treated as a good saying in itself, rather than a component part of a literary whole.

The influence of these earliest translations is still felt. There are three versions of the Bible in familiar use amongst us: one is the recent 'Revised Version'; a second is the 'Authorised

[sidenote: This tendency a relic of mediæval influence]

Version,' executed under King James I; while for a third the earlier translation of Coverdale is represented in the Psalter of the Prayer Book. These three versions stand at three different points of the line separating us from the Middle Ages: Coverdale's translation was executed wholly amid mediæval surroundings;[1] the Authorised Version belongs to the borderland between mediæval and modern, while the Revised Version is entirely modern. When these three translations are compared what is the result? If the comparison be made in respect of phraseology and single verses there will be little to choose between the three: the earliest will strike our sense of beauty quite as much as the latest. But when attention is given to the connection between verse and verse, to the drift of an argument and the general unity of a whole poem, only the Revised Version will be found reliable; the reader of the Authorised Version, when he wishes to catch the teaching of a whole epistle, or the sequence of thought in a minor prophet, must go to the Hebrew and Greek to find out what his English version means.

Three popular versions of the Bible

Similar in what concerns the Lower Unity

The 'Revised Version' stands alone as regards the Higher Unity

It is most important for the English student of the Bible to remember that these versions are different in kind, and must therefore not be discussed as if they represented different degrees of success in attaining a common object. It will be well to emphasise this matter by examples.

Let our first example be taken from the translation of Coverdale. The eighteenth psalm will be specially suitable for our purpose, because in the case of this poem the Authorised and Revised versions substantially agree; moreover the impression they give of the psalm — that of a thanksgiving for recent deliverance — is one not open to dispute, inasmuch as the

Prayer Book Version compared with the other two Psalm xviii

---

[1] Coverdale's version is in actual date (1535) earlier than A. V. by three-quarters of a century; in spirit it is earlier still, being avowedly not original, but founded upon previous 'interpretations.' See Dr. W. F. Moulton's *History of the English Bible* (Cassell), chapters vii and viii.

poem is cited at full length in the book of *Samuel*, and is there expressly connected with the escape of David from the persecution of Saul. As we read in the Authorised or Revised versions, every line of the poem carries out this idea. At the commencement epithets of adoration succeed one another with an exuberance of diction that is like a flourish of trumpets opening some set piece of music. With the fourth verse the psalm settles down to its regular movement, and in subdued tones describes the perilous extremity out of which the singer has found deliverance.

> The sorrows of death compassed me, and the floods of ungodly men made me afraid.
> The sorrows of hell compassed me about; the snares of death prevented me.
> In my distress I called upon the LORD, and cried unto my God: he heard my voice out of his temple, and my cry came before him, even into his ears.

Then a burst of imagery rushes upon us, sustained through nine verses, presenting all nature agitated to its centre as the Almighty descends to the help of the sufferer who has called upon him. A strain of tenderness comes in with the deliverance itself.

> He sent from above, he took me, he drew me out of many waters.
> He delivered me from my strong enemy, and from them which hated me: for they were too strong for me.
> They prevented me in the day of my calamity: but the LORD was my stay.
> He brought me forth also into a large place; he delivered me, because he delighted in me.

With the last clause the conception has widened. The poet considers that with his personal deliverance the cause of righteousness has triumphed, and so he is led to the generalisation:

> With the merciful thou wilt shew thyself merciful; with an upright man thou wilt shew thyself upright.
> With the pure thou wilt shew thyself pure: and with the froward thou wilt shew thyself froward.

The latter half of the psalm no less clearly carries on the conception of the earlier half; review of past deliverances carries with it confidence for the future, when whole nations will run in submission to the conqueror marked out by Divine favour. Towards the close the rapture of the opening verses reappears:

> The LORD liveth: and blessed be my rock; and let the God of my salvation be exalted.

Then in the very last line, like the signature to a document, comes the name of 'David,' at once the singer and the hero of the song.

Let the reader now study this psalm in the Psalter of the Prayer Book. Let him remember what is the exact point of the present argument. If he takes any particular verse, he will find it just as striking in the translation of Coverdale as in the later versions; it will be when he proceeds to note the linking of verse to verse that the difference will appear. At the third verse (in the numbering of the Prayer Book) the psalm appears, as in the other version, to start upon the description of a perilous extremity.

> The sorrows of death compassed me: and the overflowings of ungodliness made me afraid.
> The pains of hell came about me: the snares of death overtook me.

But when we pass to the next verse, instead of a continuation of the description, we find a general statement.

> In my trouble I will call upon the Lord: and complain unto my God.

Of course, if a reader has come to his Bible simply as a storehouse of good words, he may find as great a spiritual stimulus in the declaration, "I will call upon the Lord," as in the statement, "I did call upon the Lord." But to the reader of a sacred literature this substitution in the Prayer Book Version of future tense for past has destroyed the connection of the verses, and the unity is gone. Again, at the seventh verse Coverdale's translation returns to the tense of description; but at verse 16 — just where in the other case we found the actual deliverance come in — we are thrown back upon general expressions:

> He shall send down from on high to fetch me, etc.

In verse 18 we read, "They *prevented* me," but in verse 20, "The Lord *shall* reward me": and so throughout the poem past, present, future tenses are indiscriminately mingled. What does this mean? That the translator was a bungler? Certainly not: every verse, with its felicity of diction and beauty of rhythm, belies such a suggestion. The meaning is that Coverdale formed a different conception of the literature he was translating from that which both ourselves and the later versions assume. It did not belong to Coverdale's age to look upon a psalm as a poem with a unity running through it; he understood it simply as a collection of pious thoughts, and he used all his skill to make each thought as beautiful as the English language would permit. He has succeeded in his attempt, and given us in the eighteenth psalm a chaplet of very pearls; but it is a chaplet with the string broken.

It is even more important to compare the Authorised and the Revised versions as regards this matter of the connection between verse and verse. Let the reader study in the older translation the twenty-eighth chapter of *Job*, and set himself, without the aid of commentators who have had the original before them, to think out from the English alone the unity linking successive verses.

<small>A. V. compared with R. V.
Job xxviii</small>

> 1. Surely there is a vein for the silver, and a place for gold where they fine it.
> 2. Iron is taken out of the earth, and brass is molten out of the stone.

[Already the clauses fall sweetly upon the ear, though the point of what is being said is hardly yet apparent.]

> 3. He setteth an end to darkness, and searcheth out all perfection: the stones of darkness, and the shadow of death.

[This seems like some very general glorification of God: but the drift of the whole is still vague.]

4. The flood breaketh out from the inhabitant; even the waters forgotten of the foot: they are dried up, they are gone away from men.

[Can any clear sense be attached to these words? The only certainty seems to be that they have no connection with the preceding verse, as that had none with what went before. Yet the words which immediately follow seem to announce a new topic.]

5. As for the earth, out of it cometh bread: and under it is turned up as it were fire.
6. The stones of it are the place of sapphires: and it hath dust of gold.

[Various as are the topics presented so far, yet the next words announce one more.]

7. There is a path which no fowl knoweth, and which the vulture's eye hath not seen:
8. The lion's whelps have not trodden it, nor the fierce lion passed by it.
9. He putteth forth his hand —

[Apparently we have here returned to the general glorification of God in nature upon which the third verse touched.]

9. He putteth forth his hand upon the rock; he overturneth the mountains by the roots.
10. He cutteth out rivers among the rocks; and his eye seeth every precious thing.
11. He bindeth the floods from overflowing; and the thing that is hid bringeth he forth to light.

At this point, in place of a string of distinct topics, we suddenly come upon a train of connected reasoning. Where, asks the speaker, shall wisdom be found? and, after searching all possible sources, and weighing wisdom against every form of wealth, he comes to the conclusion that only God knows the origin of wisdom, and that he who created the universe interwove righteousness into its structure. Is it not strange that within the limits of the same chapter should be found, first the wandering from topic to topic, and then the coherent working from question to answer? Yet more strange that the discordant halves of the chapter should be linked by the conjunction *But?*

Now let the same passage be read in the Revised Version.

> Surely there is a mine —

[At the very outset has come the key word to the whole.]

> Surely there is a mine for silver,
> And a place for gold which they refine.
> Iron is taken out of the earth,
> And brass is molten out of the stone.
> Man setteth an end to darkness,

[What we are reading is not a description of God, but of the miner.]

> And searcheth out to the furthest bound
> The stones of thick darkness and of the shadow of death,
> He breaketh open a shaft away from where men sojourn;
> They are forgotten of the foot that passeth by;
> They hang afar from men, they swing to and fro.

[We can almost see the miner descending in his cage into the depths of the earth, far beneath the heedless passers-by on the surface. And now a relevancy appears for the next verse.]

> As for the earth, out of it cometh bread:
> And underneath it is turned up as it were by fire.
> The stones thereof are the place of sapphires,
> And it hath dust of gold.
> That path —

[Of course, the path of the miner in the bowels of the earth.]

> That path no bird of prey knoweth,
> Neither hath the falcon's eye seen it:
> The proud beasts have not trodden it,
> Nor hath the fierce lion passed thereby.
> He putteth forth his hand upon the flinty rock;

[It is still the miner that is spoken of.]

He overturneth the mountains by the roots;
He cutteth out channels among the rocks;
And his eye seeth every precious thing.
He bindeth the streams that they trickle not;
And the thing that is hid bringeth he forth to light.

Read in a version which brings the idea of connected literature to bear upon the Bible, the passage which before seemed a series of disconnected sayings is seen to resolve itself into a simple unity, — a brilliant picture of mining operations. Nay, the whole chapter now becomes a unity, for we catch the connection of its two halves: there are mines out of which men dig gold and silver and precious stones, but where is the mine out of which we may bring wisdom?

It is impossible to insist too strongly upon this difference between the Revised Version of the Bible and its predecessors, a difference of kind and not of degree, and one which is as wide as the distinction between the words 'text' and 'context.' The English reader need not feel any difficulty on the ground of the disfavour with which the Revised Version has in many quarters been received. Such reception has been the regular fate of revisions from St. Jerome's day downwards. The Authorised Version had itself to encounter the same opposition. It is said to have been a full half century before this work of King James's translators came into general use; and in the interval we have on record the opinion of a scholar and divine, who, asked by the king, declared he would be torn by wild horses rather than urge so badly executed a version upon the churches. The whole discussion of the subject seems to me to have been conducted on a wrong footing. The critics will take single verses or expressions, and, as it were, test them with their mental palate to see whether the literary flavour of the old or the new be superior. But comparisons of this kind are a sheer impossibility. No one, least of all a cultured critic, can separate in his mind between the sense of beauty which comes from association, and the beauty which is intrinsic; the softening

Thus R. V. essential for literary study

effect of time and familiarity is needed before any translation can in word and phrase assume the even harmony of a classic. Meanwhile the consideration here contended for — the unique excellence of the Revised Version in the matter of connectedness and the Higher Unity — is beyond dispute. The true issue between the Authorised and the Revised versions is the question whether the Bible is to be treated as a collection of sayings, each verse an independent whole, or whether the first duty of an interpreter is to associate a text with its context. What answer the theologian will return to this question it is not the province of this book to determine. But speaking from the literary point of view, I make bold to say that the reader who confines himself to the Authorised Version excludes himself from half the beauty of the Bible.

To vindicate the importance of the Higher Unity in application to Biblical literature is our first duty. Our second is to guard ourselves from forming too limited a conception of it. When we try to think out the connectedness of some sacred poem or discourse, we must be prepared to find its unity assuming forms other than those with which we are familiar in the literature of the present day.

The Higher Unity assumes variety of form

The simplest type of unity is where a whole poem is no more than the working out of a single idea. I have had occasion in a former chapter to cite the hundred and fourteenth psalm, and have shown how it connects the deliverance from Egypt with the new conception of a Deity accompanying with his presence a journeying nation. Every line of the psalm is filled with this idea; there is no other thought in the poem. A unity so clear presents no difficulty.

Simple Unity Psalm cxiv

Again, I have in the chapter immediately preceding this analysed the hundred and thirty-ninth psalm. This is a lyric of fifty-two lines; its opening and closing thoughts are antagonistic to one another, the Divine Omnipresence being dreaded in the one case and in the other case desired. Yet the poem presents no difficulty in regard

Unity of Transition Psalm cxxxix

to the connection of its thought, for we were able to see the exact point where the one train of feeling began to change into the other. The psalm is made one by the Unity of Transition.

A more difficult case arises where a portion of literature is seen to commence with one topic, to end with a topic entirely different, while no part of it can be indicated as conveying a transition from the one set of ideas to the other. A notable instance is the much discussed nineteenth psalm. The first six verses of this psalm are entirely occupied with the heavens above our heads. Their starry marvels are conceived as a silent language in which the whole world day by day may read of a Creator; the extended sky is pictured as the tent of a hero, and this hero is the Sun, who, forever at his best, runs his daily course, scattering the mighty heat which no corner of the earth can escape. Passing to the next verse we find ourselves without any warning in a totally different set of ideas.

Unity of Contrast and Antithesis Psalm xix

> The law of the LORD is perfect, restoring the soul:
> The testimony of the LORD is sure, making wise the simple:
> The precepts of the LORD are right, rejoicing the heart:
> The commandment of the LORD is pure, enlightening the eyes.
> The fear of the LORD is clean, enduring for ever:
> The judgements of the LORD are true, and righteous altogether.

With topics so different, and no sign of any links to connect them, what has become of the Higher Unity? The answer is that it is to be looked for in this very absence of transition: we have here a literary effect which may be called the Unity of Contrast or Antithesis. The point of the poem may be summed up as the equal adoration side by side of the physical and the moral law. No literary device could make the equality of the two so forcible as this simple placing of them side by side without a word of explanation.

No doubt this is a matter in which difference of opinion arises; and its discussion is of importance as going down to fundamental principles of literary criticism. It is urged, by those who speak with the highest authority, that the disparity between the two parts of this nineteenth

Disputed unity of Psalm xix

psalm is too great to be covered by any unity of idea; that we are therefore driven to the supposition that the connection of these two pieces of literature has been effected by those through whose hands the Hebrew Scriptures have passed on their way to us. The contention is further supported by the plea that these two sections of the nineteenth psalm differ in more than subject-matter: they represent literary styles that are totally different, styles moreover that are seen upon a wide survey of Biblical literature to distinguish respectively an early and a late literary period.

I do not dispute these allegations. But in resisting the inference derived from them I would commence by deprecating the confusion so commonly made — if not by the critics themselves, yet by a large proportion of their readers — between two things which should be kept entirely separate: the confusion between literary unity and unity of authorship. Indeed, if I may widen the discussion for a moment, I should like to express the opinion that the whole study of literature is placed at a disadvantage by the intrusion into it of quite a distinct thing — the study of authors. A piece of literature is apt to be put before us as a *performance* of some author: we are expected to examine it with a view to applauding or censuring this author; we are minutely informed as to the circumstances under which he did his work; one production of his is associated with companion productions, as if the main *raison d'être* of them all was to enable us to form an estimate of the man who produced them. All this may be good in itself; but it is not the study of literature. Authors of books may in themselves be as well worthy our attention as statesmen or commercial magnates; but no one confuses Constitutional History with biographies of politicians, or Political Economy with the business histories of particular firms. And I believe that the study of literature will never reach its proper level until it is realised that literature is an entity in itself, as well as a function of the individuals who contributed to it; that it has a development and critical principles

Questions of authorship not an essential part of literary study

of its own, to be considered independently of any questions affecting the performance of particular authors.

To return to the case immediately before us. It might seem a self-evident contention that the assignment of different ages to different parts of the nineteenth psalm implied diversity of authorship. I would rather say that we are separated from the literature in question by an interval so wide as to raise a doubt whether the term 'authorship' in application to the lyric poetry of the Bible be not altogether an anachronism. *Authorship in application to Biblical poetry*

We live in the age of books; not only so, but we have travelled so far into this book age that we have forgotten the times when literature was affected by anything else than our habits of written composition. Yet the study of Comparative Literature reveals everywhere a period of literary activity long preceding the earliest book; a floating poetry destined to influence periods much later than its own, yet preserved only by oral tradition without any aid from writing, while the processes of its composition have been regulated entirely by the phenomena of spoken literature. However widely apart we may date the different parts of the Bible, yet the whole approaches much more closely the influences of this early spoken poetry than the modern literatures from which we draw our ideas.

It is precisely in the matter of this relationship between literature and 'authors' that the difference between early and late poetry is most apparent. The change which the ages have brought about in our conception of authorship is not unlike the change that has come over our conception of land. Our late civilisation takes for granted the idea of individual ownership of land. But we know that to primitive society this idea was unthinkable: land belonged to the community, and all that individuals could have would be rights over the land. Similarly we associate a book with an individual author; we sacredly guard the written book as his property; if the author alters it it becomes a new 'edition,' while if the author be dead the form of the book is fixed forever and no one may touch it. But for the floating literature of spoken poetry composition was in the hands of a class of bards and minstrels, or, shall we say, of priests and sacred singers; what each individual produced was regarded as common property, which his brethren used without any sense of indebtedness. In using one another's compositions they revised and altered them, until each delivery of a poem might make a fresh 'edition'; and thus the composition of any poem was a growth extending through generation after generation, and the united product of many minds.

Now the psalms of the Bible were the product of individual poets, but of poets living in periods when the influences of floating literature were largely felt in determining habits of composition. And this must be borne in mind in every discussion of the subject. It is common to speak of David's 'writing' a psalm: the phrase is full of misleading associations. We cannot even assume that writing, though used for many purposes, was in David's time applied to the preservation of poetical productions; but we may be quite certain that the early psalmists did not, like nineteenth century poets, think with pen in hand. Are we again to suppose that Hebrew poets when they composed a psalm entered it at some Stationers' Hall, with all rights reserved? We know the very opposite: the authors of our psalms would send their poems "to the Chief Musician upon stringed instruments," or to "the Sons of Korah." That is to say, these Biblical psalms when composed were committed to the custody of a body of minstrels or sacred singers, and so may be expected to present the phenomena of oral poetry in addition to the features of individual authorship. Thus the psalms of the Bible in their composition unite the advantages that belong to early and to late poetry: the psalm as it leaves the original poet is not a fixed thing, it is only just started on a career of life in the hands of living performers, through whom it can draw to itself the best thoughts of the ages through which it is to pass. These later modifications may be merely matters of phraseology or greater fulness of diction; they may be distinct additions, like the final verses of the fifty-first psalm, which make a poem of personal penitence serve also as an expression of national humiliation. Or they may even amount to such a transformation as the nineteenth psalm seems to have undergone, when the original song of the heavens, touching an age of enthusiasm for the law, inspired the thought that what the Sun is to the world without, God's law is to the world within. If we assume David to be the 'author' of the first six verses, then no one has a better right than David to be considered the 'author' of the fresh thoughts his words have inspired. Or the original song might be considered the 'author' of the additions it has begotten in the minds of those who have used it. But it would be still better to say that the whole idea of 'authorship' is a conception proper to modern literature, and can do nothing but mislead when applied to the wider literary phenomena of the Bible.

But I am comparatively indifferent as to whether the reader does or does not accept this conclusion with reference to the authorship of the poem. What I am concerned to insist upon is that diversity of authorship — if such there be — is no bar to the literary unity of the nineteenth psalm. This consideration again *[Diversity of authorship not inconsistent with literary unity]* demands the wider conception of literature that belongs to antiquity. Let an illustration be permitted. If a man enquires as to the building of some modern dwelling-house, he will probably be able to learn the year in which it was built and the name of the architect. It will be different if he applies his investigation to some great cathedral. The original architect of the cathedral himself completed (we will suppose) the choir and transepts, and built them in the Early English style. Then the work stood still for several generations ; when the nave was added the whole style of architecture had changed. The west front has been added later still, and reflects details of a later age. But the original architect did not think it necessary to pull down the whole of the church his cathedral was superseding ; and hence we find a beautiful Norman doorway in the middle of the Early English portion of the building. And the sexton takes the visitor down to the crypt and shows him fragments of a yet earlier Saxon church that had stood on the same spot. Here, then, we have a building that displays five different architectural styles, the product of five different ages: do we call such a building five cathedrals or one cathedral? The psalms have the artistic range of the cathedral, not of the mere dwelling-house; they reflect the literary architecture of the many ages down which they have travelled, and are often seen to have absorbed into themselves 'oracles' yet older than the date of their first composition. But with the psalm, as with the cathedral, none of these circumstances need militate against the artistic unity of the whole.

The literary unity, then, of this nineteenth psalm becomes a question of the ideas underlying its two parts, and of the mode in which these ideas are brought together. For the ideas themselves, the union in one thought of the physical and the moral universe has appealed to many minds. It is as old as Zoroaster:

He who first planned that these skies should be clothed with lights,
He by his wisdom is creator of Righteousness, wherewith to support the best
    mind.[1]

The philosopher Kant, again, was wont to speak of the two perpetual wonders, the starry heavens above and the moral law within. And a still closer association of the two ideas has inspired a line of Wordsworth, who says, addressing Duty:

Thou dost preserve the stars from wrong;
And the most ancient heavens through Thee are fresh and strong.

That the two worlds should in the Biblical poem be placed side by side without further comment is surely intelligible to our æsthetic sense. Art in general recognises the simple contrast and antithesis. But more than that, the very section of art we are considering — the psalms of

Other examples of the Unity of Antithesis

---

[1] Yasna xxxi. 9. I am indebted for this parallel to Rev. J. Hope Moulton, Fellow of King's College, Cambridge.

the Bible — give us other examples of this same poetic device. A closely analogous case is the thirty-sixth psalm, which devotes four verses to a picture of character [Psalm xxxvi] so utterly corrupt that evil has become a law unto itself; and then abruptly, without connecting links, sets against the dark background of supreme evil a supreme good — a loving-kindness as wide as the heavens, a righteousness as high as the mountains, judgments as profound as the sea, bounty as diffused as the light.[1] Again, among the 'Songs of Ascents' is found a short lyric, the thought of which would be obscure [Psalm cxxvii] did we not recognise in it one of these antithetic contrasts between two types of life — the life of anxious toil and the quiet home life — made effective by the simple juxtaposition of the two descriptions.

Strophe

Except the LORD build the house,
They labour in vain that build it:
Except the LORD keep the city,
The watchman waketh but in vain.
It is vain for you that ye rise up early,
And so late take rest,
And eat the bread of toil.

Antistrophe

So he giveth unto his beloved sleep.
Lo, children are an heritage of the LORD:
And the fruit of the womb is his reward.
As arrows in the hand of a mighty man,
So are the children of youth.
Happy is the man that hath his quiver full of them:
They shall not be ashamed when they speak with their enemies
 in the gate.

Our examination, then, of this nineteenth psalm, when once disturbing questions of authorship are laid aside, reveals a connection

[1] The parallelism of form between this and the nineteenth psalm is close: besides the main point (of antithesis without connecting links) there is in both the culmination of the whole in prayer.

of thought which is both impressive in itself, and also an addition to the types of Higher Unity under which Biblical lyrics can be classified.

In treating this general matter of the Higher Unity it is necessary to mention what may be called the Unity of Aggregation. This can be brought out best by the aid of illustrations. If the reader examines the *Book of Proverbs* and, discarding the numbering of chapters which has no literary significance, seeks to divide it into the literary compositions of which it is made up, he will be struck with the different relations in which successive verses stand to one another in different parts of the book. Let him, for example, read the last five verses of the twenty-fifth chapter.

Unity of Aggregation

Proverbs xxv. 24-28

> It is better to dwell in the corner of the housetop,
> Than with a contentious woman in a wide house.
>
> *⁎⁎*
>
> As cold waters to a thirsty soul,
> So is good news from a far country.
>
> *⁎⁎*
>
> As a troubled fountain, and a corrupted spring,
> So is a righteous man that giveth way before the wicked.
>
> *⁎⁎*
>
> It is not good to eat much honey:
> So for men to search out their own glory is not glory.
>
> *⁎⁎*
>
> He whose spirit is without restraint
> Is like a city that is broken down and hath no wall.

Nothing is plainer than that we have here five entirely distinct compositions; all that the "men of Hezekiah" have done is to collect them. Next, let the reader take four verses that follow one another in the twenty-sixth chapter.

> The sluggard saith, There is a lion in the way; *Proverbs xxvi. 13-16*
> A lion is in the streets.
>
> *
>
> As the door turneth upon its hinges,
> So doth the sluggard upon his bed.
>
> *
>
> The sluggard burieth his hand in the dish;
> It wearieth him to bring it again to his mouth.
>
> *
>
> The sluggard is wiser in his own conceit
> Than seven men that can render a reason.

Here again we have entirely separate sayings, but they are all sayings on the subject of the sluggard. The " men of Hezekiah " have not merely collected, they have in this instance arranged their matter. For completeness let the reader turn to an entirely different part of the book, and read (say) the first five verses of chapter six. *Proverbs vi. 1-5*

> My son, if thou art become surety for thy neighbour,
> If thou hast stricken thy hands for a stranger,
> Thou art snared with the words of thy mouth,
> Thou art taken with the words of thy mouth.
> Do this now, my son, and deliver thyself,
> Seeing thou art come into the hand of thy neighbour;
> Go, humble thyself, and importune thy neighbour.
> Give not sleep to thine eyes, nor slumber to thine eyelids.
> Deliver thyself as a roe from the hand of the hunter,
> And as a bird from the hand of the fowler.

Here it is clear that we have no collection of distinct sayings, but a single composition with an organic unity of its own. The sacred literature is thus found to include both what in modern phraseology are called original compositions, and also collections of separate brief compositions put together with or without arrangement. The shorter sayings are obvious in the *Book of Proverbs*. But at the proper place we shall see that they belong equally to other departments of Biblical literature: that Prophecy includes short prophetic utterances collected together as well as longer discourses, and that even a lyric composition may be constructed of separate lyrics in combination. Many mistakes of interpretation may be avoided by recognising the Unity of Aggregation.

One more consideration will complete our classification of the different forms that may be assumed by the Higher Unity in the literary compositions of the Bible. It will sometimes happen that the connection binding the different parts of a poem into a unity is to be looked for, not in the poem itself, but in the external use made of it. A notable example is the twenty-fourth psalm. Any one reading this psalm with a view to catching its general drift and connection will be struck with a break between its sixth and seventh verses, at which point there is a change both of form and matter so considerable as inevitably to raise the doubt whether the whole psalm can be a single composition. The difficulty is met by identifying the poem with a particular ceremonial, into the different parts of which the two halves of the psalm fit like a key into the wards of a lock.

Unity of External Circumstances

Psalm xxiv

This ceremonial was the bringing of the Ark to Jerusalem. There is perhaps no single day in the far distance of antiquity which we are able to follow with such minuteness as this central day of King David's career; and in a later chapter we shall see that all the songs composed for the festival can be recovered. The twenty-fourth psalm represents the words of the processional march from the House of Obed-Edom to the Gates of Jerusalem. There seem to have been two points in this march at which the instruments of fir wood, harps, psalteries, timbrels, castanets and cymbals gave place to vocal celebration. The first was when the procession halted at the foot of the high hill on which the city stood: and here it is that the first six verses of the psalm have their fitness. After a burst of adoration to the Creator of the world — one of the perfectly general ascriptions of praise with which psalms so often commence — the special anthem proceeds as follows:

> Who shall ascend into the hill of the LORD?
> And who shall stand in his holy place?
>> He that hath clean hands, and a pure heart;
>> Who hath not lifted up his soul unto vanity,
>> And hath not sworn deceitfully.
> He shall receive a blessing from the LORD,
> And righteousness from the God of his salvation.
> This is the generation of them that seek after him,
> That seek thy face, O God of Jacob.

The identification of these words with the occasion to which I am referring becomes the stronger through something which illustrates what has been said above as to the nature of Hebrew poetry, and how its composition did not fix it in one form, as our writing does, but left it scope to adapt itself in the mouths of the singers who preserved it to changes of thought or circumstances. We have a variant to the anthem just cited: this is the fifteenth psalm, and a comparison of the two poems is highly instructive.

> LORD, who shall sojourn in thy tabernacle?   *Psalm xv*
> Who shall dwell in thy holy hill?
>> He that walketh uprightly, and worketh righteousness,
>> And speaketh truth in his heart.
>> He that slandereth not with his tongue,
>> Nor doeth evil to his friend,
>> Nor taketh up a reproach against his neighbour.
>> In whose eyes a reprobate is despised;
>> But he honoureth them that fear the LORD.
>> He that sweareth to his own hurt, and changeth not.
>> He that putteth not out his money to usury,
>> Nor taketh reward against the innocent.
> He that doeth these things shall never be moved.

That these are varying forms of one poem is obvious; in both the same character for the worshipper of Jehovah is conveyed in the same form of lyric question and answer. The differences between them are two. The fifteenth psalm is much fuller in its description, and yet this fulness is no more than the working out into detail of what the other psalm had suggested. Again, there is a striking variation in the wording of the opening verse. The twenty-fourth psalm asks, "Who shall *ascend* into the hill of the LORD," the fifteenth psalm phrases the question, "Who shall *sojourn*." This exactly tallies with the view here presented of the two poems. The one is an anthem for a specific occasion, and to the circumstances of that occasion — the procession halting at the foot of the hill — the phrase is exactly relevant, "Who shall ascend." But when this description of the worshipper of Jehovah is divorced from the proceedings of that particular day, and passes into general use, there is no longer any point in the word *ascend*, and a general term, *sojourn*, is substituted. And it is equally natural that the brief suggestive sketch should be found where the thought comes as a single detail in a long ceremonial, but that when the fragment passes into use as an independent hymn the thought should expand and gather fulness and devotional beauty.

The other emphatic point in the march was when the procession drew up opposite the gates of the city: this gives us the second part of the twenty-fourth psalm. Two considerations should be carefully remembered by the reader. One of these is the nature of the day's festival. It was not a dedication of a temple, but an inauguration of a city. The tent in which David placed the Ark was clearly regarded by him as a mere temporary convenience; the task on which his whole heart was bent was to bring the Ark to the city of David. This Jerusalem was an ancient stronghold of the Jebusites; to capture it had been David's greatest achievement; he wished to turn it into the metropolis of the military monarchy in which he, as the representative of Jehovah, was the principal figure: there could then be no fitter form of inauguration than to transfer to the newly captured city the sacred Symbol with the fullest military honours. The psalm realises all this by its formal call upon the city gates to open. But a second point must be noted before the anthem becomes fully intelligible. The historical account of the ceremonial gives striking prominence to a particular title of the Divine Being — the LORD OF HOSTS: the

II Sam. vi

narrative opens by speaking of "the Ark of God which is called by the Name, even the name of the LORD of hosts"; it ends by saying that David, in dismissing the people to their homes, blessed them "in the name of the LORD of hosts." It is clear that this title made a sort of watchword to the day's proceedings. With the full circumstances before us let us follow this second section of the psalm. The procession has halted opposite the massive porch of the time-worn fortress, and in full military form summons it to open its gates.

> Lift up your heads, O ye gates;
> And be ye lift up, ye ancient doors:
> And the King of glory shall come in.

Warders answer from within:

> Who is the King of glory?

By the simplest of poetic devices the anthem keeps back for a time the great Name, and answers with other titles of Jehovah.

> The LORD strong and mighty,
> The LORD mighty in battle.

The watchword has not been spoken, and the gates refuse to open. The summons must be repeated.

> Lift up your heads, O ye gates;
> Yea, lift them up, ye ancient doors:
> And the King of glory shall come in.

A second time is heard the challenge from within:

> Who is this King of glory?

At last the great Name is spoken:

> THE LORD OF HOSTS,
> He is the King of glory!

At this word the gates roll back, the procession enters, and Jehovah has taken possession of his city.

It appears then that the two sections of the twenty-fourth psalm fit in with two points in the procession of the Ark to Jerusalem: the halt at the foot of the hill, and the climax in front of the gates. The psalm finds its unity in the external circumstances of its first production.

Enough has now been said on the subject of this Higher Unity, the bond by which different parts of a composition are woven together into a single whole. We have seen that to look for such unity is a foremost condition of literary appreciation; and that this applies to the literature of the Bible, notwithstanding difficulties thrown in our way by mediæval methods of printing or reading the Sacred Scriptures. We have seen, on the other hand, that in searching for the unity of any particular poem we must not force interpretation through some preconceived idea of poetic connection, but must be prepared to find the Higher Unity assuming various forms. We have surveyed some of these forms: Simple Unity, Unity of. Transition, Unity of Antithesis, Unity of Aggregation, Unity of External Circumstances. In each case the nature of the unity must be gathered from an examination of the particular composition, and a comparison of it with other compositions of a similar kind.

CHAPTER IV

CLASSIFICATION OF LITERARY FORMS

My purpose in Book First is to arrive at a general classification of such literary forms as Epic, Lyric, Philosophy, and others, which can in succeeding books be one by one applied to the literature of the Bible. Preceding chapters have been occupied in clearing the ground; starting from structural analysis they have advanced through lower unities of literary form to that higher unity by which a literary work is grasped as a whole. It is only when a reader has accustomed himself to thinking of a poem (or prose composition) as a whole that he is in a position to take the further step of recognising the form such a composition assumes. In the present chapter we are prepared to consider briefly the general notion underlying such terms as Epic, Lyric, and the like, when these terms are used of universal literature; and then to note a few of the special features that broadly distinguish Hebrew literature. *[The Higher Unity and distinctions of literary form]*

Let the reader firmly fix four ideas in his mind, as what may be called the four Cardinal Points of Literature. Two of these are given by the antithesis Description and Presentation. When an incident is described to us, the words are throughout the words of the author. When it is presented, the author himself nowhere appears, but he leaves us to hear the words of those personages who actually took part in the incident, perhaps to see their doings; we become spectators, and the circumstances are made to present themselves before us. *[The four Cardinal Points of Literature]* *[Description and Presentation]*

Homer and Milton give us literature of description; for presentation the most complete illustration is Shakespeare, in whose pages all varieties of mankind are speaking and moving, but the poet himself is never heard.

The other two ideas are conveyed by the words Poetry and Prose. It is impossible to use other terms; and yet about these there is an unfortunate ambiguity, owing to the exigences of language which have imposed a double duty on the word 'prose': it is antithetic to 'poetry' and it is also antithetic to 'verse.' No doubt there is a good deal in common between these two usages of the word: Poetry is mostly conveyed in verse, and Prose literature in the style called prose. But the terms must be used with a cautious recollection that Poetry is sometimes cast in the form of prose — notably, we shall see, in the Bible; while in the earlier stages of literary history verse has often been utilised for works of science and philosophy which would later have been thrown into a prose form. The conception we are at present seeking will be best grasped if we translate the Greek word 'poetry' into its Latin equivalent, 'creative literature'; it assists also to remember the old English usage by which a poet was called a 'maker.' The idea underlying these words is that the poet makes something, creates, adds to the sum of existences; whereas the antithetic literature of Prose has only to discuss what already exists. When Homer has sung and Euripides exhibited plays the world is richer by an Achilles and an Alcestis. It makes no difference whether, as an historic fact, the Greek warrior and the Queen of Pheræ ever existed, or whether they are pure figments of the imagination, or whether they existed but behaved quite differently from what the poem and the play suggest: to our poetic sense the Homeric Achilles and the Euripidean Alcestis are as real as the Cæsar of history. On the contrary, the literature of Prose moves only in the region limited by facts; history and philosophy have to deal only with what actually has existence, accurately describing things, or bringing out the relations between one thing and another.

Poetry and Prose

These four ideas, Description and Presentation, Poetry, and Prose, I have called the four Cardinal Points of Literature: they are to be regarded, not as divisions or classes into which literary works may be divided, but as so many different directions in which literary activity may move. But to understand this movement a fifth conception must be added as a starting-point for such activity. The starting-point of literature is found in what is technically called the Ballad Dance. The study of Comparative Literature reveals that wherever literature arises spontaneously its earliest form is a combination of verse, music, and imitative gesture. Whether it be a story, or an uplifting of the heart in worship, or a burst of popular frolic, the expression of these will be in rhythmic words, which are chanted to a tune with or without instrumental accompaniment, and further emphasised by expressive gestures of the whole body such as have come to be denominated 'dancing.' Hebrew literature was no exception. Of course, the actual contents of our Bibles are far removed from such primitive productions. But some portions of Sacred Scripture are early enough not to have lost the triple form with which poetry started. Thus we are expressly informed that the Song of Moses and Miriam was accompanied with timbrel music and dances; even when the bringing of the Ark to Jerusalem called forth such lofty strains of poetry we have a full description of the orchestra with which that poetry was accompanied, and we know how David himself "danced with all his might" in its performance. *(margin: Primitive literary form: the Ballad Dance; Exodus xv. 20; II. Sam. vi. 5, 14-16)*

If then the reader keeps in his mind this starting-point of literature in the Ballad Dance, and also the four directions in which its impulses are likely to carry it, he will be able to lay down as in a chart the great forms which literature assumes as it develops. On the side of Poetry three great types of literature arise, which on examination are found to reflect the three elements — verse, music, dancing — combined by primitive poetry in one. Epic is a branch thrown *(margin: Fundamental Forms for Literature in general)*

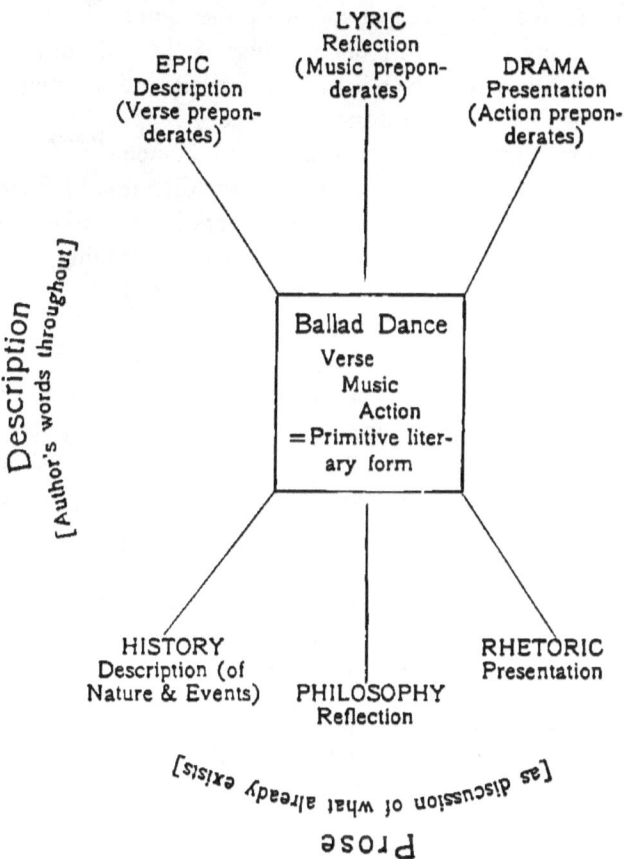

off on the side of Description, for it consists in the narration of a poetic story; the name 'Epic,' which literally means 'speech,' is seen by comparison with the other names to imply that in this branch verse is the only one of the three original elements which is essential, music and dancing being for epic poetry mere accessories that soon disappeared. Over against this Epic a second branch of creative literature is found pointing in the direction of Presentation; and its name, Drama, implies that here the imitative gesture of the ballad dance has predominated over everything else, for 'Drama' is 'acted poetry.' The remaining constituent of primitive literature, music, is suggested by the name of the third great division of poetry — Lyric, and all the devices of musical art find their analogies in the movement of lyric poetry. As Epic was concerned with Description, and Drama with Presentation, so Lyric has a special function which at the same time mediates between the other two. It may be described by the term Reflection or Meditation; by this meditative function lyric poetry can — as its position on our chart would suggest — pass at any moment into epic or dramatic without losing its own distinctive character. To illustrate: let us take up (say) the ninth psalm at the eleventh verse.

<blockquote>
Sing praises to the LORD, which dwelleth in Zion:
Declare among the people his doings.
For he that maketh inquisition for blood remembereth them:
He forgetteth not the cry of the poor.
</blockquote>

We have struck this lyric at a point where the poet is reflecting; but in the next verse the meditation has become dramatic, for we are allowed to hear the very cries of the poor who have been spoken of.

<blockquote>
"Have mercy upon me, O LORD;
Behold my affliction which I suffer of them that hate me,
Thou that liftest me up from the gates of death;
That I may shew forth all thy praise:
In the gates of the daughter of Zion,
I will rejoice in thy salvation."
</blockquote>

As the lyric form has thus changed quite naturally into a momentary drama, so in the verse that follows it is found to have passed into epic description.

> The nations are sunk down in the pit that they made:
> In the net which they hid is their own foot taken.

Biblical lyrics illustrate more fully than any others this essentially central character of lyric poetry and its power of absorbing the other forms.

Analogous to the three great types of Poetry we have three main divisions of literature on its side of Prose. Epic has its counterpart in History. The word history has for its range the whole field of positive description: 'Natural History' is the description of external nature, and 'History' without any qualifying adjective is the description of events.

History

On the other side the prose analogue of Drama is Rhetoric; for the orator differs from others who use prose in the prominence he gives to presentation. To the famous orator Demosthenes is attributed the saying that the first element of oratory is action, and the second element action, and the third action: the meaning of this is that an orator must above all things *be an actor;* he must be able to identify himself with his cause as an actor presents a part. Lastly, as Lyric was reflective poetry, the corresponding form of prose literature is Philosophy, which is no more than organised reflection. And as Lyric was found to occupy a central position on the side of poetry, so that it could dip at intervals into Epic and Drama, an analogous power attaches to Philosophy, which can extend in the direction of Description when it takes the form of scientific observation, and on the other side can advance almost to the bounds of Rhetoric in the form of exposition.

Rhetoric

Philosophy

We have thus, starting from first principles, arrived at a conception of the six main divisions of literary form. But these six forms must be understood as merely general notions, drawn from a comparative survey of literature as a whole. Just as the 'elements' into which the chemist analyses matter are seldom found in nature separate and distinct, but almost always in combination, so in the actual literatures of the world it will be an exceptional case if any particular work is found to exemplify one of the six forms we have been discussing, without any admixture of the rest.

Literary works seldom confined to a single form

We are to review the various forms as they appear in the Bible. But first I will draw attention to three points which, in the most general survey, distinguish Biblical literature from the other great literatures of the world, and affect its relation to the elements of literary form just surveyed.

Distinguishing features of Hebrew Literature

The first distinguishing characteristic of Hebrew literature is that it has not developed a separate and distinct Drama; although, as if to compensate for this, the dramatic impulse is found in Hebrew to invade other regions of literature, including such departments as might have seemed most impervious to it. The current finding no channel has spread and diffused itself. The reader of the Bible knows that he will find in it no acted play like the plays of Shakespeare. But on the other hand he will find lyric poems specially dramatic in tone, and in *Solomon's Song* a lyric idyl that impresses some of its readers as a complete drama. He will find, again, philosophy taking a dramatic shape. In the *Book of Job* the dramatic form reaches an intensity not exceeded in any literature; yet even here there is no independent drama, but the dramatised discussion is made to rest on a basis of epic story. What is still more surprising, the discourses of prophecy are found to be leavened by the dramatic spirit, and that most concentrated form of Hebrew prophecy, which will in this work be called the Rhapsody, is pre-eminent in the closeness with which it approaches to Drama. If such things could be made the subject of measurement, it would be safe to predict that the *mass* of dramatic material in Biblical literature would be not less than that found in other literatures where Drama is a distinct form.

1. No separate Drama but dramatic influence on other forms

A second consideration must be mentioned as separating Hebrew from other literatures. When a reader turns over the pages of the Bible, the department which will impress him most by its bulk and importance is one not included in the above classification, because it is no element of universal literature. This is the department of Prophecy. The distinction of Prophecy is not one of form but of spirit: Biblical Prophecy, in a sense that belongs to no other class of literature, presents itself as an actual Divine message. So far as form is concerned Prophecy is not distinctive but comprehensive: all types of literature are attracted towards it, and, as will be seen at the proper place, the various literary forms are fused together into a new form in the Prophetic Rhapsody.

2. Prophecy a special department of Literature

The third distinguishing feature of Hebrew literature needs fuller explanation. It has to do with the external form of verse and prose. We saw that Hebrew rests its verse system, not upon metre or rhyme, but upon parallelism of clauses. But, as a matter of universal literature, parallelism is one of the devices of prose: the rhetoric of all nations includes it. If then a particular language bases its verse upon something which is also the property of prose, it is an inevitable consequence that in that language prose and verse will overlap: and such is the case with Biblical literature. I do not of course mean that the verse literature of the Bible taken as a whole could be confused with the Biblical literature of prose. What could be further from prose than the *Book of Psalms?* and what could be further from verse than the *Books of Chronicles?* But while in their extremes they are totally different, yet there is a middle region of Biblical style in which verse and prose meet: a high parallelism in which transition can be rapidly made from the one to the other, or even the effects of the two can seem to be combined. It is this overlapping of verse and prose which constitutes the third distinctive feature of Hebrew literature.

3. Overlapping of Verse and Prose

I am the more particular upon this point, because it is one

which I think has not received sufficient attention. The combination of verse and prose to which I am alluding is not the fact that, in such a book as *Jeremiah*, some compositions are found to be verse and some prose. Nor am I referring merely to the literary effect of a transition in the same composition from a passage of prose to a passage of verse; such transitions belong to many literatures, and are markedly characteristic of Shakespeare in his later plays. The union of verse and prose can in Biblical literature be more intimate still: what in another language we should have to call a system of verse — for example, the analysis of a single stanza — will in the Hebrew be found to combine prose with verse into a common system.

A clear grasp of this overlapping of verse and prose is necessary for the appreciation of Hebrew literature. To gain it may require some effort of mind on the part of those who have formed their ideas in literatures of a different kind. The English reader, for example, is accustomed to a verse founded on metrical considerations or rhyme — things foreign to prose; when he hears of verse approaching prose the phrase is likely to suggest to him weakness and inefficiency. Any such suggestion becomes inapplicable in the case of a language where parallelism makes a common ground between the highest poetry and the highest rhetoric. It is clear, on the contrary, that the literary resources of Hebrew are increased by the feature we are discussing. Hebrew has the power possessed by other languages of producing literary effect with changes from the one form of expression to the other. But it has also a power all its own of maintaining (so to speak) a watershed of high parallelism, from which it can dip towards verse or prose with the utmost subtlety, or can combine in one the delight in freedom, which is the spirit of prose, with a sense of rhythm, which is the foundation of verse.

    I am about to bring forward illustrations, but I must preface them with one general remark. It will be seen in the extracts cited that certain passages are printed as prose which are usually

[marginal note: This an addition to the resources of style]

represented to be lines of verse; and the question may arise, what is the criterion for deciding such points. I would answer that the matter cannot be determined simply by examining the passages themselves and the relation of successive clauses, seeing that parallelism is common ground between verse and rhetoric prose. Where is the parallelism of clauses carried further than in the speeches of Moses as they appear in the *Book of Deuteronomy*, especially at such a point of the book as the eighth chapter? Yet no one would break up such speeches into lines of verse, because the general drift and spirit of the whole makes it clear that they constitute not poetry but oratory. So with regard to the citations from prophecy that are to be given, it is necessary, besides examining the individual clauses, to study the extract as a whole, and the way its different parts hang together; when this is done, it will often appear that a passage, which in itself would make good verse, will in its relation to the whole be better represented to the eye and ear as prose. To use the terms I distinguished when speaking on the general subject of structure, the analysis of prophetic style must be dominated by the higher and not the lower parallelism.

<small>Examples of the Compound Style</small>

<small>Amos i. 3–ii</small> My first illustration is from the prophecy of *Amos*, a book which will impress the most casual reader with the prominence in it of structural beauty.

> Thus saith the LORD:
> For three transgressions of Damascus,
> Yea, for four,
> I will not turn away the punishment thereof;
> because they have threshed Gilead with threshing instruments of iron:
> But I will send a fire into the house of Hazael,
> And it shall devour the palaces of Ben-hadad.
> And I will break the bar of Damascus, and cut off the inhabitant from the valley of Aven, and him that holdeth the sceptre from the house of Eden: and the people of Syria shall go into captivity unto Kir, saith the LORD.

Thus saith the LORD:
> For three transgressions of Gaza,
> Yea, for four,
> I will not turn away the punishment thereof;
because they carried away captive the whole people, to deliver them up to Edom:
> But I will send a fire on the wall of Gaza,
> And it shall devour the palaces thereof:
and I will cut off the inhabitant from Ashdod, and him that holdeth the sceptre from Ashkelon; and I will turn mine hand against Ekron, and the remnant of the Philistines shall perish, saith the LORD God.

Thus saith the LORD:
> For three transgressions of Tyre,
> Yea, for four,
> I will not turn away the punishment thereof;
because they delivered up the whole people to Edom, and remembered not the brotherly covenant:
> But I will send a fire on the wall of Tyre,
> And it shall devour the palaces thereof.

Thus saith the LORD:
> For three transgressions of Edom,
> Yea, for four,
> I will not turn away the punishment thereof;
because he did pursue his brother with the sword, and did cast off all pity, and his anger did tear perpetually, and he kept his wrath for ever:
> But I will send a fire upon Teman,
> And it shall devour the palaces of Bozrah.

Thus saith the LORD:
> For three transgressions of the children of Ammon,
> Yea, for four,
> I will not turn away the punishment thereof;
because they have ripped up the women with child of Gilead, that they might enlarge their border:
> But I will kindle a fire in the wall of Rabbah,
> And it shall devour the palaces thereof,
with shouting in the day of battle, with a tempest in the day of the whirlwind: and their king shall go away into captivity, he and his princes together, saith the LORD.

Thus saith the Lord:
 For three transgressions of Moab,
 Yea, for four,
 I will not turn away the punishment thereof;
because he burned the bones of the king of Edom into lime:
 But I will send a fire upon Moab,
 And it shall devour the palaces of Kerioth;
and Moab shall die with tumult, with shouting, and with the sound of the trumpet; and I will cut off the judge from the midst thereof, and will slay all the princes thereof with him, saith the Lord.

Thus saith the Lord:
 For three transgressions of Judah,
 Yea, for four,
 I will not turn away the punishment thereof;
because they have rejected the law of the Lord, and have not kept his statutes, and their lies have caused them to err, after the which their fathers did walk:
 But I will send a fire upon Judah,
 And it shall devour the palaces of Jerusalem.

Thus saith the Lord:
 For three transgressions of Israel,
 Yea, for four,
 I will not turn away the punishment thereof;
because they have sold the righteous for silver, and the needy for a pair of shoes: that pant after the dust of the earth on the head of the poor, and turn aside the way of the meek: and a man and his father will go unto the same maid, to profane my holy name: and they lay themselves down beside every altar upon clothes taken in pledge, and in the house of their God they drink the wine of such as have been fined. Yet destroyed I the Amorite before them, whose height was like the height of the cedars, and he was strong as the oaks; yet I destroyed his fruit from above, and his roots from beneath. Also I brought you up out of the land of Egypt, and led you forty years in the wilderness, to possess the land of the Amorite. And I raised up of your sons for prophets, and of your young men for Nazirites. Is it not even thus, O ye children of Israel? saith the Lord. But ye gave the Nazirites wine to drink; and commanded the prophets, saying, Prophesy not.
 Behold I will press you in your place,
 As a cart presseth that is full of sheaves.

> And flight shall perish from the swift,
> And the strong shall not strengthen his force,
> Neither shall the mighty deliver himself:
> Neither shall he stand that handleth the bow;
> And he that is swift of foot shall not deliver himself:
> Neither shall he that rideth the horse deliver himself:
> And he that is courageous among the mighty
> Shall flee away naked in that day,
> Saith the LORD.

If we examine this portion of *Amos* in the spirit of the lower parallelism, we must admit that the passages here printed as prose could be broken up into verses, most of them without straining. But the higher parallelism constructs the whole passage on an extremely simple plan: this prophecy against eight peoples is made up of common formulæ expressing ideal transgressions and ideal dooms, together with particular descriptions of actual sins and actual sufferings. It is surely in keeping with such a general plan that the formulæ and ideal portions should be found to be in verse, and the particular descriptions in prose. Moreover, when we examine the denunciation of Israel, the final climax up to which all the rest leads, we find that it is just here that the description is most difficult to compel into the form of verse: if this goes best as prose then the parts correlated with it should be prose also. Finally, if we look at the whole for a moment simply as a work of art, we must be struck with the superb elasticity of style which Hebrew obtains from a power of combining verse and prose in the same way that the oratorio combines recitative with timed music. The speaker can at any moment suspend rhythm in order to penetrate with the unfettered simplicity of prose into every detail of realism, sure of being able to recover when he pleases the rhythmic march, and the strong tone of idealisation.

My second illustration goes further than the first in the direction of artistic elaborateness, and is proportionately more open to difference of opinion. It is the famous passage in which Joel conveys the approach of the mystic destruction. [Joel ii. 1-11]

> Blow ye the trumpet in Zion,
> And sound an alarm in my holy mountain;
> Let all the inhabitants of the land tremble:

for the Day of the LORD cometh, for it is nigh at hand; a day of darkness and gloominess, a day of clouds and thick darkness, as the dawn spread upon the mountains; a great people and a strong, there hath not been ever the like, neither shall be any more after them, even to the years of many generations!

> A fire devoureth before them;
> And behind them a flame burneth:
> The land is as the garden of Eden before them,
> And behind them a desolate wilderness!

Yea, and none hath escaped them. The appearance of them is as the appearance of horses; and as horsemen, so do they run. Like the noise of chariots on the tops of the mountains do they leap, like the noise of a flame of fire that devoureth the stubble, as a strong people set in battle array.

> At their presence the peoples are in anguish:
> All faces are waxed pale:
> They run like mighty men;
> They climb the wall like men of war;
> And they march every one on his ways.

And they break not their ranks: neither doth one thrust another; they march every one in his path: and they burst through the weapons, and break not off their course.

> They leap upon the city;
> They run upon the wall;
> They climb up into the houses;
> They enter in at the windows like a thief.
> The earth quaketh before them;
> The heavens tremble:
> The sun and the moon are darkened,
> And the stars withdraw their shining:

and the LORD uttereth his voice before his army; for his camp is very great; for he is strong that executeth his word: for the Day of the LORD is great and very terrible; and who can abide it?

At first sight the reader might be surprised to see treated as prose language so full of fire and rhythm. But we have seen that this by itself is an unsafe criterion: the line is a very fine one that separates between the rhythm of universal rhetoric and the rhythm of Hebrew verse. The only safe guide is the structure of the whole passage. One point in the above arrangement is obvious — it yields the favourite Hebrew effect of augmenting: when the passages of verse are examined it will be seen that the first consists of three lines, the second of four, the third of five, the climax of a much larger number. But the more important question is, whether the breaks suggested between prose and verse coincide with any change in the spirit of the whole. The passage is dominated by one idea — the sense of mysterious approach. The prophecy of Joel, starting from a plague of locusts, idealises this into destruction as a general notion, and so finely is this idealisation executed that associations of locusts and of destruction in general mingle together until they leave on our minds nothing but a sense of awful mystery. Keeping then this idea of mystic approach before us, let us examine the sections of the whole passage. The opening verses are simply an alarm : a trumpet crash and quivering nerves. Then prose puts the meaning of the alarm, as it might be interpreted by rumour : it must be the Day of Jehovah breaking, with blackness for its light of dawn: a 'people' coming, the like of which has never been seen. With the return to verse we have advanced from hearing to seeing : but the first glance pictures the army of destruction only by its effects — the beauty before it, the destruction and burning where it has passed. A second glance analyses in prose the destroying force : like the words of one trying to make out something in the distance, we hear minglings of the appearance of horses with the sounds of chariots and flames. Another stage of advance is made by a simple contrast in verse — the pale terror of the helpless victims, and the energy of the destroying march. But no sooner is the word 'march' introduced than prose proceeds to analyse the march, with the riddling suggestions of locusts underlying the descriptions of unbroken ranks, and the pouring through opposing weapons. At last the goal of the city is reached, and in a string of abrupt verses we have the irresistible invasion from every side until the whole earth is darkened and rocking with a universal destruction. Then a yet higher climax is made when prose brings out the power that has been behind the whole judgment—it is indeed Jehovah whose word has been thus strongly executed: and who shall abide his terrible day! The structural law of the whole stands out clear: continually augmenting stanzas of verse paint the objective scene, and prose interposes between them to analyse and interpret each.

But to fully appreciate this feature of Biblical style the reader ought to watch it as it appears upon a more extended scale. I shall therefore conclude by citing the *Book of Zephaniah* in full. The structural plan of this prophecy is equally simple and impressive. It is prose broken by snatches of verse. Upon examination, the prose is found to be a continuous discourse conveying the denunciatory message of Deity; the verse passages are interruptions of lyric comment at emphatic points.

<small>Book of Zephaniah</small>

THE WORD OF THE LORD

which came unto

ZEPHANIAH

the son of Cushi, the son of Gedaliah,
the son of Amariah, the son of Hezekiah,
in the days of Josiah the son of Amon,
king of Judah.

I will utterly consume all things from off the face of the ground, saith the LORD. I will consume man and beast; I will consume the fowls of the heaven, and the fishes of the sea, and the stumbling-blocks with the wicked; and I will cut off man from off the face of the ground, saith the LORD. And I will stretch out mine hand upon Judah, and upon all the inhabitants of Jerusalem; and I will cut off the remnant of Baal from this place, and the name of the Chemarim with the priests; and them that worship the host of heaven upon the house-tops; and them that worship, which swear to the LORD and swear by Malcam; and them that are turned back from following the LORD; and those that have not sought the LORD, nor inquired after him.

> Hold thy peace at the presence of the Lord GOD:
> For the Day of the LORD is at hand:
> For the LORD hath prepared a sacrifice,
> He hath sanctified his guests!

And it shall come to pass in the day of the LORD's sacrifice, that I will punish the princes, and the king's sons, and all such as are clothed with foreign apparel. And in that day I will punish all those that leap over the threshold, which fill their master's house with violence and deceit. And in that day, saith the LORD, there shall be the noise of a cry from the fish gate, and an howling from the second quarter, and a great crashing from the hills.

> Howl, ye inhabitants of Maktesh,
> For all the people of Canaan are undone:
> All they that were laden with silver are cut off.

And it shall come to pass at that time, that I will search Jerusalem with candles; and I will punish the men that are settled on their lees, that say in their heart, The LORD will not do good, neither will he do evil. And their wealth shall become a spoil, and their houses a desolation; yea, they shall build houses, but shall not inhabit them; and they shall plant vineyards, but shall not drink the wine thereof.

> The great Day of the LORD is near:
> It is near and hasteth greatly!
> Even the voice of the Day of the LORD;
> The mighty man crieth there bitterly!

> That Day is a day of wrath,
> A day of trouble and distress,
> A day of wasteness and desolation,
> A day of darkness and gloominess,
> A day of clouds and thick darkness,
> A day of the trumpet and alarm
> Against the fenced cities,
> And against the high battlements!

And I will bring distress upon men, that they shall walk like blind men, because they have sinned against the LORD: and their blood shall be poured out as dust, and their flesh as dung. Neither their silver nor their gold shall be able to deliver them in the day of the LORD's wrath; but the whole land shall be devoured by the fire of his

jealousy: for he shall make an end, yea, a terrible end, of all them
that dwell in the land.

    Gather yourselves together, yea, gather together,
    O nation that hath no shame;
        Before the decree bring forth,
        Before the day pass as the chaff,
        Before the fierce anger of the LORD come upon you,
    Before the Day of the LORD'S Anger come upon you.

    Seek ye the LORD, all ye meek of the earth,
    Which have wrought his judgement;
        Seek righteousness,
        Seek meekness:
        It may be ye shall be hid
    In the Day of the LORD'S Anger.

For Gaza shall be forsaken, and Ashkelon a desolation: they shall drive
out Ashdod at the noonday, and Ekron shall be rooted up.

    Woe unto the inhabitants of the sea coast,
    The nation of the Cherethites!

The word of the LORD is against you, O Canaan, the land of the
Philistines; I will destroy thee that there shall be no inhabitant. And
the sea coast shall be pastures, with cottages for shepherds and folds
for flocks. And the coast shall be for the remnant of the house of
Judah; they shall feed their flocks thereupon: in the houses of Ashkelon shall they lie down in the evening; for the LORD their God shall
visit them, and bring again their captivity. I have heard the reproach
of Moab, and the revilings of the children of Ammon, wherewith they
have reproached my people, and magnified themselves against their
border. Therefore as I live, saith the LORD of hosts, the God of Israel,
Surely Moab shall be as Sodom, and the children of Ammon as Gomorrah, a possession of nettles, and saltpits, and a perpetual desolation:
the residue of my people shall spoil them, and the remnant of my
nation shall inherit them. This shall they have for their pride, because
they have reproached and magnified themselves against the people of
the LORD of hosts. The LORD will be terrible unto them: for he will
famish all the gods of the earth: and men shall worship him, every one
from his place, even all the isles of the nations. Ye Ethiopians also,
ye shall be slain by my sword. And he will stretch out his hand
against the north, and destroy Assyria; and will make Nineveh a

desolation, and dry like the wilderness. And herds shall lie down in the midst of her, all the beasts of the nations: both the pelican and the porcupine shall lodge in the chapiters thereof: their voice shall sing in the windows; desolation shall be in the thresholds: for he hath laid bare the cedar work.

>This is the joyous city,
>   That dwelt carelessly,
>   That said in her heart, I am,
>   And there is none else beside me:
>How is she become a desolation,
>A place for beasts to lie down in!
>Every one that passeth by her shall hiss,
>And wag his hand.

>Woe to her that is rebellious and polluted,
>To the oppressing city!
>   She obeyed not the voice;
>   She received not correction;
>   She trusted not in the LORD;
>   She drew not near to her God.
>   Her princes in the midst of her are roaring lions;
>   Her judges are evening wolves;
>   They leave nothing till the morrow.
>   Her prophets are light and treacherous persons:
>   Her priests have profaned the sanctuary,
>   They have done violence to the law.
>The LORD in the midst of her is righteous;
>He will not do iniquity;
>Every morning doth he bring his judgement to light,
>He faileth not;
>But the unjust knoweth no shame.

I have cut off nations, their battlements are desolate; I have made their streets waste, that none passeth by; their cities are destroyed, so that there is no man, that there is none inhabitant. I said, Surely thou wilt fear me, thou wilt receive correction; so her dwelling should not be cut off, according to all that I have appointed concerning her: but they rose early and corrupted all their doings. Therefore wait ye for me, saith the LORD, until the day that I rise up to the prey: for my determination is to gather the nations, that I may assemble the

kingdoms, to pour upon them mine indignation, even all my fierce anger; for all the earth shall be devoured with the fire of my jealousy.
For then will I turn to the peoples a pure language, that they may all call upon the name of the LORD, to serve him with one consent. From beyond the rivers of Ethiopia my suppliants, even the daughter of my dispersed, shall bring mine offering. In that day shalt thou not be ashamed for all thy doings, wherein thou hast transgressed against me: for then I will take away out of the midst of thee thy proudly exulting ones, and thou shalt no more be haughty in my holy mountain. But I will leave in the midst of thee an afflicted and poor people, and they shall trust in the name of the LORD. The remnant of Israel shall not do iniquity, nor speak lies; neither shall a deceitful tongue be found in their mouth: for they shall feed and lie down, and none shall make them afraid.

>Sing, O daughter of Zion; shout, O Israel;
>Be glad and rejoice with all the heart,
>O daughter of Jerusalem.

>The LORD hath taken away thy judgements,
>He hath cast out thine enemy:
>>The king of Israel,
>>Even the LORD, is in the midst of thee:
>Thou shalt not fear evil any more.

>In that day it shall be said to Jerusalem, Fear thou not:
>O Zion, let not thine hands be slack.
>>The LORD thy God is in the midst of thee,
>>A mighty one who will save:
>He will rejoice over thee with joy,
>He will rest in his love,
>He will joy over thee with singing.

I will gather them that sorrow for the solemn assembly, who were of thee: to whom the burden upon her was a reproach. Behold, at that time I will deal with all them that afflict thee: and I will save her that halteth, and gather her that was driven away; and I will make them a praise and a name, whose shame hath been in all the earth. At that time will I bring you in, and at that time will I gather you: for I will make you a name and a praise among all the peoples of the earth, when I bring again your captivity before your eyes, saith the LORD.

Book Second

LYRIC POETRY OF THE BIBLE

Chapter		Page
V.	The Biblical Ode	127
VI.	Occasional Poetry, Elegies, and Liturgical Psalms	153
VII.	Dramatic Lyrics and Lyrics of Meditation	174
VIII.	Lyric Idyl: 'Solomon's Song'	194

CHAPTER V

THE BIBLICAL ODE

The Ode cannot be exactly defined. Etymologically the word is equivalent to 'song'; usage seems to have given it the sense of song *par excellence*: the lyric poetry that is furthest removed from the ordinary speech, and nearest to pure music. If 'flight' be the regular image for the movement of lyric poetry, then the Ode is the song that can soar highest and remain longest on the wing. Speaking generally, we may say that it is distinguished from other lyrics by greater elaboration, and (so to speak) structural consciousness. Such a literary form will be discussed best by particular examples, and a commentary upon the Odes of the Bible will introduce us to lyric modes of movement in general. *The Ode*

It is natural to commence with *Deborah's Song.* This is the most elaborate of Biblical odes, and it exercised considerable influence upon succeeding poetry. There is another circumstance which makes it particularly valuable to the literary student. It is a narrative poem, and the story it narrates is in the previous chapter of *Judges* given in the form of history. A careful comparison of the fourth and fifth chapters of that book will enable us to study the differences between lyric narrative and narrative as it appears in history. *Deborah's Song Judges v*

Few portions of the Old Testament are more familiar, or more frequently discussed, than the incidents that enter into *Deborah's Song.* Yet I think there are important elements in the story which are by no means generally understood. The first point that I will put amounts to no more than a conjecture. The history opens by saying that Israel fell under the dominion of Jabin king of Canaan, and that he "mightily oppressed" them for twenty years. Though the *Book of Judges* is full of similar subjugations of Israel, that particular phrase is nowhere else used; the suggestion is that there was something different in kind between the tyranny of Jabin and Sisera and other tyrannies. May it be that <u>this oppression was of an indescribable nature</u>, affecting person as well as property, — <u>such wanton violence</u> as appears in a later chapter of *Judges* to have brought all Israel in arms against a city of Benjamin? If this conjecture were adopted, it would give significance to the striking phrase used by the song to describe the misery of the oppression, — that "the highways were unoccupied and the travellers walked through byways." It would explain how it was that the tyranny was borne without resistance until "a mother in Israel" roused the people against it. It would further enable us to understand how a prophetess could exult in the strange decree of Providence by which the instrument of a cruel and lustful tyranny met his doom at the hands of a woman.

My next point is a matter of certainty. It is the relation to the story of Heber the Kenite, the husband of Jael. The Kenites were a tribe who had joined Israel in the wilderness; they had become a part of the chosen nation in all respects except one, — that they still retained their life in tents, when the Israelites had settled down in villages and towns. But we are told in one verse of the narrative that there was peace between the oppressing tyrant and the house of Heber the Kenite; another verse tells us how Heber had separated himself from the other Kenites, and "pitched his tent as far as the oak in Zaanannim, which is by Kedesh," that is, close to the muster ground of Barak; and the verse that follows says, *"And they told* Sisera that Barak the son of Abinoam was gone up to mount Tabor." Though the phrasing in this last verse is general, yet when the three verses are taken together the significance is clear enough : that Heber the Kenite was a spy in the pay of Jabin and Sisera, and that he had shifted his tent for no reason but to keep a watch upon the movements of Israel, and report them to the enemy. But there would seem to have been one in his tent who had a heart to feel with the mothers of Israel ; as a sheikh's wife Jael may have been unable to hinder her husband's plans, but when the turn of events had come, and Sisera approached her as a fugitive, there was a sudden opportunity before her to strike a blow on the side which she had never deserted. Of course her act remains a treacherous violation of hospitality. But it makes some difference to our estimate of her that it was treachery done to redress her husband's treachery on the opposite side.

It is worth while, again, to make clear the military situation. Jabin's power lay in his "nine hundred chariots of iron" : against such a force the half armed infantry of Israel would be almost useless. Their only hope lay in a surprise ; and Barak's plan seems to have been to arrange a quiet muster of separate tribes moving towards the high ground by Kedesh, from which they might watch for a favourable moment and make a rapid descent. This was frustrated by the treachery of Heber, and Sisera, forewarned, poured his full forces on to the plain of Esdraelon, which afforded the best possible ground for the evolutions of chariots. Humanly speaking, there was no hope for the Israelites. What changed the situation we learn from a phrase of the song : "the stars in their courses fought against Sisera." In other words, a thunderstorm and its torrents of rain produced the effect often described by travellers in Palestine : in an astonishingly brief period the river Kishon would overflow, and the whole plain be flooded ; in the verses of the song we can almost hear the horses plunging about in the morass. This made it v. 22
possible for the whole of the formidable army to be exterminated in a single day. This further explains the bitterness of the curse denounced on Meroz — some city of Israel on the line of

the enemy's retreat: where everything depended on destroying the army before they could extricate themselves from the mud, even hesitation might amount to the blackest treachery.

With the incident thus fully before us we are in a position to make our comparison of the two narratives. In the history of the fourth chapter, as we might expect, we find the narrative connected and continuous. It commences by describing the oppression; it proceeds to tell how Deborah arose and called for resistance; it gives with some minuteness the negotiations by which Deborah secured Barak for her commander-in-chief. We next hear of the muster at Kedesh; the treachery of Heber is then implied rather than directly stated. The battle follows, and the utter rout; then the history becomes detailed as it deals with the remarkable circumstance of the assassination of Sisera by Jael.

Historic and Lyric Narrative

When we turn to the song, we seem to find this connectedness and continuity of narrative avoided, and the story touched only in selected parts. I am tempted to convey the difference by an illustration. A man watches some architectural mass, like the Church of St. Mark at Venice, in the changing light of evening. As long as full daylight is in the sky he sees clearly the vivid colouring, and the architectural details, and the numerous gilded points and spiracles with which the whole is crowned. With the waning light he loses the colour; then the carving and relief sinks into a uniform surface. He seems to be losing the whole, until a point is reached when there is just enough light left to catch the gilded crosses and spiracles: then instead of being lost the whole edifice has come back to him in an outline of luminous points. This seems to me to afford an analogue for lyric narrative. The daylight view, in which the whole surface is visible without break, represents the continuity of the history; we lose that in the song, but there the story comes to us in a selection of points every one of which is luminous. First, the oppression is painted by two picturesque strokes: the deserted highways, the vain search for weapons. All the negotia-

Lyric device of Concentration

tions between Deborah and Barak are omitted, and the next point of narrative is the muster, made luminous by the enumeration of the tribes that refused, and the tribes that came zealously, and the tribe that changed its mind. Nothing more follows until we reach the battle and rout, all brought out in a few bold strokes — kings coming to fight, the stars fighting against them; horses plunging in the flooded plain; the sudden bitterness when Meroz proves unequal to the crisis. In the matter of the assassination even the history was detailed. But here again there was a logical connectedness in the details: the warrior arriving, making provision against surprise, and then submitting to sleep and so to murder. But in the lyric we leap from the hospitable matron to the murderess taking the nail and hammer; what remains is so vivid that we can count the blows and watch the writhings, while the purely imaginary detail of the warrior's household waiting his return is drawn out at full length. This *concentration* of a whole story into a few luminous details gives us our first note of lyric movement.

A second distinguishing feature of the song is the way in which the narrative is delayed or broken by refrains, or by what are called 'apostrophés,' that is, passages in which the singers 'turn aside' from the story to address heaven, or the bystanders, or one another. Three lines of refrain, four of prelude, and a long apostrophe to God, are interposed before the narrative even commences. Then when the desolation of the country under Jabin's oppression has been told, there is a break, filled up by the refrain recurring in an enlarged form. When the mustering of the tribes is reached, after a single line there is an abrupt departure from the narrative, and the singers occupy a quatrain with cheering one another on to their task. It is clear that these digressions are part of the artistic setting to the story. When water flows on smoothly without any check it may be a useful canal or drain; but the poetic brook must have its course delayed by many a winding, and interrupted by the rocks over which it foams. We may then add *interruption* to the devices of lyric movement.

<small>Lyric device of Interruption</small>

132   LYRIC POETRY OF THE BIBLE

A third feature of the song lies upon the surface: its structure
is such as to imply the *antiphonal* performance in which one
singer or set of singers is answered by another. I
must dissent however from the usual arrangement
which divides *Deborah's Song* as between solo and
chorus. It seems clear that the nature of the antiphony is given
by the first verse of the chapter — "Then sang Deborah and
Barak": not that the two individuals sang a duet, but the ode
would be performed by a Chorus of Women with Deborah leading
them, and a Chorus of Men led by Barak. When the poem is
structurally examined in the light of this suggestion, not only do
the divisions easily present themselves, but a number of coinci-
dences confirm the suggestion. Thus the Men lead off with a
description — in the rhythm of elegy — of the oppression;
Deborah and the Women break in (with a return to ordinary rhythm) at the words, "I Deborah arose." When the singers
bid publish the tidings of victory, the Men call to those
that ride or walk by the way, or sit on carpets as public
officials, — that is, they call to men; the answering Chorus of
Women would spread the news "in the places of drawing
water," the natural spots where women would gather and
chat. In another passage, an apostrophe of four lines, there is
one couplet of the Men cheering on Deborah, and another
of the Women cheering on Barak. The mustering of the
tribes divides itself line by line: if the first line be given to the
Women, as relating to Ephraim the locality of Deborah,
the fourth line falls to the Men and it mentions Zebulun,
the tribe of Barak; the next line (of the Women) connects Issachar
with Deborah, and the line that follows (and would fall to the Men)
connects the same tribe with Barak. Then, in the climax,
the Men elaborately picture the actual murder of Sisera,
and the Women add the feminine touch of the mother and her
ladies awaiting the dead warrior's return. It is hardly
necessary to dilate upon the artistic effect of a narrative
thus given to us from one side and another alternately. One

Antiphonal per-
formance

v. 6

10

11

12

14

24

28

single antiphonal effect may be instanced. The great pastoral tribe of Reuben was amongst the defaulters. This is brought out by the Men first painting Reuben's 'resolves'; then the Women interpose a sarcastic question as to inaction; then the Men repeat their former couplet with the change of a single word to express Reuben's prudent second thoughts. Finally, the antiphonal effect is varied by the passages in which the two choruses sing together. This is especially powerful at the close, where, after the story itself has been drawn out by the two bodies of singers to its last detail, there is a sudden break, and both choruses unite in the apostrophe, "So perish all thine enemies, O LORD!"

15-16

DEBORAH'S SONG

REFRAIN

Men.   For that the leaders took the lead in Israel —
Women.   For that the people offered themselves willingly —
Tutti.   Bless ye the LORD!

PRELUDE

Men.   Hear, O ye kings —
Women.   Give ear, O ye princes —
Men.   I, even I, will sing unto the LORD —
Women.   I will sing praise to the LORD, the God of Israel.

APOSTROPHE

Tutti.   Lord, when thou wentest forth out of Seir,
           When thou marchedst out of the field of Edom,
           The earth trembled, the heavens also dropped,
           Yea, the clouds dropped water.
           The mountains flowed down at the presence of the LORD,
           Even yon Sinai at the presence of the LORD, the God of Israel.

I. THE DESOLATION

Men.   In the days of Shamgar the son of Anath,
           In the days of Jael,
           The highways were unoccupied,
               And the travellers walked through byways;
           The rulers ceased in Israel,
               They ceased —

Women.	Until that I, Deborah, arose,
	That I arose a mother in Israel.
	They chose new gods;
	Then was war in the gates:
	Was there a shield or spear seen
	Among forty thousand in Israel?

REFRAIN ENLARGED

Men.	*My heart is toward the governors of Israel—*
Women.	*Ye that offered yourselves willingly among the people—*
Tutti.	*Bless ye the LORD!*
Men.	Tell of it, ye that ride on white asses,
	Ye that sit on rich carpets,
	And ye that walk by the way:—
Women.	Far from the noise of archers,
	In the places of drawing water:—
Tutti.	There shall they rehearse the righteous acts of the LORD,
	Even the righteous acts of his rule in Israel.

II. THE MUSTER

Tutti.	Then the people of the LORD went down to the gates —
(Men.	Awake, awake, Deborah,
	Awake, awake, utter a song:—
Women.	Arise, Barak,
	And lead thy captivity captive, thou son of Abinoam.)
Tutti.	Then came down a remnant of the nobles,
	The people of the LORD came down for me against the mighty.
Women.	Out of Ephraim came down they whose root is in Amalek—
Men.	After thee, Benjamin, among thy peoples—
Women.	Out of Machir came down governors—
Men.	And out of Zebulun they that handle the marshal's staff—
Women.	And the princes of Issachar were with Deborah—
Men.	As was Issachar, so was Barak:
Tutti.	Into the valley they rushed down at his feet.
Men.	By the watercourses of Reuben
	There were great resolves of heart.
Women.	Why satest thou among the sheepfolds,
	To hear the pipings for the flocks?
Men.	At the watercourses of Reuben
	There were great searchings of heart!

Women. Gilead abode beyond Jordan —
Men. And Dan, why did he remain in ships? —
Women. Asher sat still at the haven of the sea,
And abode by his creeks.
Men. Zebulun was a people that jeoparded their lives unto the death,
And Naphtali, upon the high places of the field.

III. THE BATTLE AND ROUT

Strophe

Men. The kings came and fought;
Then fought the kings of Canaan,
In Taanach by the waters of Megiddo : —
They took no gain of money!

Antistrophe

Women. They fought from heaven,
The stars in their courses fought against Sisera.
The river Kishon swept them away, —
That ancient river, the river Kishon!

Strophe

Men. O my soul, march on with strength!
Then did the horsehoofs stamp
By reason of the pransings,
The pransings of their strong ones.

Antistrophe

Women. Curse ye, Meroz, said the angel of the LORD,
Curse ye bitterly the inhabitants thereof;
Because they came not to the help of the LORD,
To the help of the LORD against the mighty!

IV. THE RETRIBUTION

Strophe

Men. Blessed above women shall Jael be,
The wife of Heber the Kenite,
Blessed shall she be above women in the tent!
He asked water, and she gave him milk;
She brought him butter in a lordly dish.

> She put her hand to the nail,
> And her right hand to the workman's hammer;
> And with the hammer she smote Sisera.
> She smote through his head,
> Yea, she pierced and struck through his temples.
> At her feet he bowed, he fell, he lay:
> At her feet he bowed, he fell:
> Where he bowed, there he fell down dead!
>
> *Antistrophe*
>
> *Women.* Through the window she looked forth, and cried,
> The mother of Sisera, through the lattice,
> "Why is his chariot so long in coming?
> Why tarry the wheels of his chariots?"
> Her wise ladies answered her,
> Yea, she returned answer to herself,
> "Have they not found,
> Have they not divided the spoil?
> A damsel, two damsels to every man;
> To Sisera a spoil of divers colours,
> A spoil of divers colours of embroidery,
> Of divers colours of embroidery on both sides,
> On the necks of the spoil?"
>
> APOSTROPHE
>
> *Tutti.* So let all thine enemies perish, O LORD:
> But let them that love him
> Be as the sun when he goeth forth in his might!

The ode most nearly resembling this of Deborah is the *Song of Moses and Miriam* at the Red Sea. Here again the mode of performance is exactly indicated. The first verse says, "Then sang Moses and the children of Israel this song"; the twentieth verse adds: "And Miriam, the prophetess, the sister of Aaron, took a timbrel in her hand; and all the women went out after her with timbrels and with dances. And Miriam answered them, Sing ye to the LORD, for he hath triumphed gloriously; the horse and his rider hath he thrown into the sea." The natural interpretation of these

Song of Moses and Miriam Exodus xv

verses taken together is that the words last quoted are a refrain, and to be sung by Miriam and the Women; while the body of the Song was for Moses and the Men. The refrain would be repeated at the close of each stanza. The structure suggests a prelude and three stanzas, each of which commences with an apostrophe to God, and then deals with the subject of the deliverance. A further examination of these strophes reveals the lyric device of *augmenting*, mentioned in a previous chapter; not only do the successive strophes in- Lyric device of Augmenting crease in the number of their lines, but they bring out the incident with more and more fulness. The first merely refers to the event: the hosts cast into the sea and sinking like a stone. The second stanza becomes a picture full of powerful details: floods standing on heaps and depths congealed, the enemy already counting his spoils, the single blast of wind, and the sinking like lead. But when the incident is touched by the third strophe we have, not details, but consequences. The event is stretched to take in all that will follow from it: the guiding through the wilderness thus wonderfully opened to them, the terror falling upon the inhabitants of Canaan and the kings that lie in the way, the bringing in and planting in the mountain of inheritance — all poetically realised in the moment of this the first step. To describe the movement of the whole ode we may say that the prelude introduces the great deliverance with a shock that is like a plunge, and the augmenting strophes follow like ripples widening to the furthest bound that imagination can go.

SONG OF MOSES AND MIRIAM

PRELUDE

Men and Women. } *I will sing unto the LORD, for he hath triumphed gloriously;*
The horse and his rider hath he thrown into the sea.
The LORD is my strength and song,
And he is become my salvation:
This is my God, and I will praise him;
My father's God, and I will exalt him.

I

Men.   The LORD is a man of war:
          The LORD is his name.
          Pharaoh's chariots and his host hath he cast into the sea:
          And his chosen captains are sunk in the Red Sea.
          The deeps cover them:
          They went down into the depths like a stone.

Women. *Sing ye to the LORD, for he hath triumphed gloriously;*
          The horse and his rider hath he thrown into the sea.

II

Men.   Thy right hand, O LORD, is glorious in power,
          Thy right hand, O LORD, dasheth in pieces the enemy.
          And in the greatness of thine excellency thou overthrowest them
              that rise up against thee:
          Thou sendest forth thy wrath, it consumeth them as stubble.
          And with the blast of thy nostrils the waters were piled up,
          The floods stood upright as an heap;
          The deeps were congealed in the heart of the sea.
          The enemy said,
          I will pursue, I will overtake, I will divide the spoil:
          My lust shall be satisfied upon them;
          I will draw my sword, my hand shall destroy them.
          Thou didst blow with thy wind, the sea covered them:
          They sank as lead in the mighty waters.

Women. *Sing ye to the LORD, for he hath triumphed gloriously;*
          The horse and his rider hath he thrown into the sea.

III

Men.   Who is like unto thee, O LORD, among the gods?
          Who is like thee, glorious in holiness,
          Fearful in praises, doing wonders?
          Thou stretchedst out thy right hand,
          The earth swallowed them.
          Thou in thy mercy hast led the people which thou hast redeemed:
          Thou hast guided them in thy strength to thy holy habitation.
          The peoples have heard, they tremble:
          Pangs have taken hold on the inhabitants of Philistia.
          Then were the dukes of Edom amazed;
          The mighty men of Moab, trembling taketh hold upon them:

THE BIBLICAL ODE

<blockquote>
All the inhabitants of Canaan are melted away.
Terror and dread falleth upon them;
By the greatness of thine arm they are as still as a stone;
Till thy people pass over, O LORD,
Till the people pass over, which thou hast purchased.
Thou shalt bring them in, and plant them in the mountain of thine inheritance,
The place, O LORD, which thou hast made for thee to dwell in,
The sanctuary, O LORD, which thy hands have established.
The LORD shall reign for ever and ever.
</blockquote>

Women. *Sing ye to the LORD, for he hath triumphed gloriously;*
The horse and his rider hath he thrown into the sea.

The ode next to be considered is amongst the most powerful of all sacred lyrics; but totally unlike the two already reviewed. It is the seventy-eighth psalm. *[Psalm lxxviii]* As to its subject, it is sufficient at this point to say that it is a survey of the history of Israel, leading up to the call of Judah to be the Lord's people now that Northern Israel has fallen away. The form of the ode gives a type of lyric movement different from any we have yet seen, but one specially characteristic of Biblical poetry, and we shall meet with it again and again. It may be called the *pendulum movement:* the course of thought in a poem seems to swing backwards and forwards between two ideas or two phases of a subject. *[Pendulum Movement]* The psalm has an unusually long prelude. It is a common device in music to prepare the way for some great theme *[1–8]* by a succession of trumpet tones, the reiteration of which keeps the mind in a state of expectation that helps to emphasise the theme when it comes. By a similar effect in this prelude the psalmist announces a law, a parable, sayings of old, traditions from fathers to be told to children, that they may tell it to the next generation, that these may set their hopes in God, and not be, as their fathers, a rebellious generation whose spirit was not stedfast with God. The phrase "not stedfast" seems the point leading to the regular movement of the poem and its alternating stanzas. The thought sways throughout the rest of the ode between two ideas: on one hand we see bursts of Divine Energy in behalf of Israel; on the other hand we have the dead weight of human dulness and frailty by which the Divine purposes are frustrated. First, a short stanza puts the defection of Northern Israel under the metaphor of battalions deserting on the field of battle: "so the children of Ephraim" deserted the covenant and forgat God's wondrous works. At the words "wondrous works" the pendulum of movement swings to the other side; we have an outburst of Divine Energy, the energy of Deliverance. We hear how he piled up the waters of the Red Sea in a heap; how the fire led them by night and the cloud by day; how the dry rock was cloven and poured out streams with the full flow of a river. But it is in vain (the movement has swung back): the delivered people are found intent upon their appetites, and the doubts which a life of appetite engenders.

9-11, Frailty
12-16, Divine Energy
17-20, Frailty

> Can God prepare a table in the wilderness?
> Behold, he smote the rock, that waters gushed out,
> And streams overflowed;
> Can he give bread also?
> Will he provide flesh for his people?

We are thus brought to another turn in the movement, and there is a burst of Divine Energy, this time the energy of Judgment. The rush of verses suggests the scornful ease with which the skies are bidden to open and rain down manna, the winds are guided so that they rain flesh as dust and winged fowl as the sand of the seas; then, before the people have time to be satiated, the Wrath is slaying amongst them, so close comes the punishment upon the lust. But judgment, like mercy, has no permanent hold upon the unstedfast people; the movement has swung back, as the history settles down to a wearisome iteration of sinning, repenting and sinning, of dissembling repentance and compassionate forgiveness.

21-31, Divine Energy
32-42, Frailty

> For all this they sinned still,
> And believed not in his wondrous works.
> Therefore their days did he consume in vanity,
> And their years in terror.
> When he slew them, then they inquired after him:
> And they returned and sought God early;
> And they remembered that God was their rock,
> And the Most High God their redeemer.
> But they flattered him with their mouth,
> And lied unto him with their tongue.
> For their heart was not stedfast with him,
> Neither were they faithful in his covenant.
> But he, being full of compassion, forgave their iniquity,
> And destroyed them not:
> Yea, many a time turned he his anger away,
> And did not stir up all his wrath.
> And he remembered that they were but flesh;
> A wind that passeth away, and cometh not again.
> How oft did they rebel against him in the wilderness,
> And grieve him in the desert!
> And they turned again and tempted God,
> And provoked the Holy One of Israel.
> They remembered not his hand,
> Nor the day when he redeemed them from the adversary.

This phrase is the signal for another turn in the movement, and the following strophe is filled with the Divine Energy of Redemption. It displays before us, as in a finished picture, side by side the judgments falling on the enemy *43-55, Divine Energy* and the tenderness bestowed upon Israel; how wrath, indignation, and trouble, a band of angels of evil, make a path for God's anger, as plagues strike the land of Egypt and pestilence preys upon its people; while Israel is guided like a flock of sheep through the wilderness, and brought into the mountain land of their inheritance. All this is lost upon them: we have returned to the theme of frailty and unstedfastness as we see the people in their land of prom- *56-64, Frailty* ise settling down to the worship of the high places, until God comes to greatly abhor Israel. And as he silently forsakes them gradually their strength and glory depart; violence cuts off the youth, the maidens have no marriage-song, the very priests fall by the sword, and their widows make no lamentation. Suddenly the movement of the ode swings round for the last time.

<small>65-72, Divine Energy</small>

> Then the LORD awaked as one out of sleep,
> Like a mighty man that shouteth by reason of wine.

With one stroke the enemy is thrust back for ever; and then the final burst of Divine Energy is seen in a New Call: as before the whole nation of Israel had been called out from the whole world to become a peculiar people to Jehovah, so now he passes over Joseph and Ephraim, and chooses the tribe of Judah; he takes David from the sheepfolds to be their shepherd; and the unstedfastness which has reigned throughout the ode finds a final contrast in the Sanctuary which he builds like the heights,

> Like the earth which he hath established for ever.

This seventy-eighth psalm is one of four which I have ventured to group together under the title of 'National Anthems.' True, they are very different from what in modern times are called by that name; but the difference tallies with differences of circumstances. With us a National Anthem may well be a simple and brief lyric, for probably the nation is constituted a nation by some elementary consideration of race or habitat. But Israel had been called out of its original land, had been led from one part of the world to another, had been constituted the chosen people of God by a long course of Providential discipline. It is natural therefore that the National Hymn of such a people should take the form of a review of their history and relation to God. It is just such a review which makes the common ground between the four psalms; and when we examine their differences the results both confirm the classification, and explain further how it comes that Israel should have four National Anthems and not one. We have

<small>National Anthems</small>

seen that the seventy-eighth psalm is characterised by a continuous alternation between God's achievements for his people and their persistent ingratitude and sin, and that it ends with the final rejection of Ephraim and the call to Judah. It is thus fitted to be the National Anthem of Southern Israel when the kingdom of the ten tribes has been overthrown and destroyed. The psalm most nearly resembling this is the hundred and sixth: not only general drift, but many of its phases seem echoes of the seventy-eighth psalm. But the pendulum structure is almost lost by the preponderance of one side of the thought; from first to last it is sin and rebellion which dominates the poem, and the history is carried on to the final fall.

Psalm lxxviii — Anthem of Southern Israel

Psalm cvi — Anthem of the Captivity

> He made them also to be pitied
> Of all those that carried them captives.
> Save us, O LORD our God,
> And gather us from among the nations,
> To give thanks unto thy holy name,
> And to triumph in thy praise.

Thus this hundred and sixth psalm would seem to be the Hymn of Southern Israel modified so as to make it the Anthem of the Captivity. There is a great difference when we come to the historic survey which makes the hundred and fifth psalm. Here all trace of an alternation between God's work and Israel's sin is gone. And the history is carried just as far as the conquest of Canaan and no farther.

Psalm cv — Anthem of the Undivided Nation in Canaan

> And he gave them the lands of the nations;
> And they took the labour of the peoples in possession.

This of itself would suggest that we have here the Anthem of the undivided nation in the promised land; and the suggestion is confirmed by the wording of the reference to the covenant:

> Saying, "Unto thee will I give the land of Canaan,
> The lot of your inheritance:"
> When they were but a few men in number;
> Yea, very few, and sojourners in it.

It is natural in the moment of conquest to go back to the old sojourn in the land. And similar considerations explain the large amount of space given in this song to Joseph, the individual through whom Israel departed out of Canaan and went down into Egypt. The fourth psalm of the group, the hundred and thirty-sixth, is marked off from all the rest by the primitive character of its structure: the second line of each couplet is the refrain,

<small>16-22</small>

<small>Psalm cxxxvi
Anthem of the
Nation in the
Wilderness</small>

> For his mercy endureth for ever.

The whole poem is of the simplest type. Its history never reaches Canaan, but prominence is given to Sihon king of the Amorites, and Og king of Bashan, and it is their land which is made a heritage for Israel. Clearly this is the National Anthem of the people in the wilderness; and in this light the final theme of praise —

> He giveth food to all flesh —

becomes more than a commonplace; it is a reference to the miraculous feeding of the people in the desert. The peculiar circumstances of the people of Israel, then, have sufficiently explained why we should have four National Anthems in these four historic psalms: the simple rhythmic Hymn of the Wilderness, the Hymn of the whole nation in Canaan with its unbroken exultation, the Hymn of Southern Judah after the fall of the north, swaying evenly between Divine manifestations and national sin, and the Hymn of the Captivity, in which all is swallowed up in the idea of national unfaithfulness.

The sixty-eighth psalm, notwithstanding the difficulty of its details, impresses every reader with the vigour of its movement. Historians differ widely as to its exact occasion; but all that is necessary is to identify it with some procession to the sanctuary on Mount Zion. Its spirit is throughout that of a Processional Ode. In structure it is made up of a prelude and three elaborate strophes. The prelude is a general cry of triumph: God rising up and

<small>Psalm lxviii
Processional
Ode</small>

<small>1-6</small>

his enemies vanishing like smoke. But even here there is a hint of procession in the verse which speaks of a high way for him that rideth through the deserts. Hebrew poetry, whatever its immediate subject may be, is apt to preface this by a reference to God's original deliverance of his people and their journey to the promised land. The first strophe is devoted to this topic; and such is the sweep of its concentrated movement that the whole past history of Israel resolves itself into a procession of Jehovah from Sinai to Zion. In one verse we have the mountains trembling amid the giving of the Law; in the next we read of the rain of manna strengthening the weary wanderers. Then we come to the era of fighting that intervenes between the wilderness life and the land of promise, the whole era appearing as but two moments:

7-18

> The Lord giveth the word [of command]:
> The women that publish the tidings [of victory] are a great host.

The various victories are picturesquely suggested by snatches of the old triumph-songs (of which we of course know nothing but these snatches).

> "Kings of armies flee, they flee,
> And she that tarrieth at home divideth the spoil"—
>
> "Will ye lie among the sheepfolds?"—
>
> "As the wings of a dove covered with silver,
> And her pinions with yellow gold"—
>
> "When the Almighty scattered kings therein,
> It was as when it snoweth in Zalmon"—

In the real history generations intervened between the occupation of the eastern table-lands and the final conquest of Zion, but in the sweep of this ode the two periods are brought together, and the mountain of Bashan looks askance at the mountain God has chosen for his abode. And as a final climax to the history, Jehovah ascends into the sanctuary with his thousands of chariots

146   LYRIC POETRY OF THE BIBLE

and leads captivity captive. In the second strophe the point of
view changes from the past to the present: God appears
as "the Lord who daily beareth our burden." And here
the actual procession of the day is pictured — "the goings of my
God, my king, into the sanctuary": how singers go before, minstrels follow after, and the tribes are represented in their due rank.

19-27

The third strophe surveys the glorious future; but here
again the dominant spirit of the poem appears, and the
whole future becomes a procession of kings and peoples coming
with tribute to the temple at Jerusalem, the rear brought up by
the remote Ethiopia stretching out its hands to God. Thus this
Processional Ode has reflected the spirit of the occasion it celebrates upon all time, and made the past, the present, and the
future appear before us as a series of vast processions.

28-35

Four odes may be taken together from their similarity of matter
and form. Their purpose is not so much narrative as the realisation of an idea. In structure each has a closely
related prelude and close, while the body of the
ode is one continuous outburst. One of the four is David's Song
of Deliverance analysed in a previous chapter.[1]
Akin to this is the Song of Moses in *Deuteronomy*.
Its subject is announced by the prelude as God
the immovable Rock, in contrast with the Israel that has been
unfaithful and changeable. Such a subject is naturally
developed by the mode of alternation — the pendulum
structure we have traced in another ode. The first phase of the
poem brings out how the LORD's portion is his people,
lingering upon the thought with images, first of tenderness, then of immeasurable bounty. The turning point comes as
Jeshurun waxes fat and kicks, and this second phase
presents Israel provoking Jehovah with new gods that
came up but yesterday, which their fathers had not known.
The movement swings back to the unswerving nature of
God, now seen in judgments that set all nature on fire

Songs in Ode form

**Song of Moses
Deuteronomy
xxxii**

1-5

6-14

15-18

19-27

[1] Above, page 83.

and stop short only of absolute destruction. Another turning point is made as the poet breaks in to cry out at the folly and blindness of the people, and the loathly gods to which they have given the preference. By a bold transition this last description is made to cause revulsion in the mind of God himself, who thinks with complacency on the vengeance he yet has in his storehouse, and the poem reaches its final phase in exhibiting God as using this vengeance on the side of his erring people when they have sunk to their last extremity. ₂₈₋₃₃ ₃₄₋₄₃

The other two odes of the group have this in common, that the prelude and close express subjective feelings of the poet, while the rest of the ode presents objective phenomena. The twenty-ninth psalm is the Ode of the Thunderstorm. The body of the ode has "the Voice of Jehovah" for its refrain; it is the realisation of a thunderstorm, rising in the waters to the north, passing overhead with every form of violence, and dying away over the wilderness to the south, until all nature has again become a hymn of praise to its Maker. In the prelude the poet, as if awed by the approaching manifestation of God, calls upon all creatures to worship. In the close he expresses the sense of protection that has been with him; his God presided over the floods from which the tempest arose, and he will be king for ever. By an exquisite touch of detail, the last note in this song of thunder is the word 'peace.' The 'Prayer of Habakkuk' is a similar ode on a much larger scale. Here is no thunderstorm, but a whole universe racked with terrors as the Almighty comes to judgment. The prelude and close present the tumult of emotions in the prophet's own heart. Though the interposition of God is on his side, yet he cannot restrain himself from joining in the universal trembling. At the same time he confides in God; and yet again there is a third train of emotion where the prophet is astonished at his own confidence, that he should be at rest, waiting for the day of trouble: at rest—

Psalm xxix
Song of the Thunderstorm

Prayer of Habakkuk (chapter iii)

148 LYRIC POETRY OF THE BIBLE

> For though the fig tree shall not blossom,
> Neither shall fruit be in the vines;
> The labour of the olive shall fail,
> And the fields shall yield no meat;
> The flock shall be cut off from the fold,
> And there shall be no herd in the stalls:
> Yet I will rejoice in the LORD,
> I will joy in the God of my salvation.

There remains a group of Odes on set Themes. The hundred and seventh psalm is the Ode of the Redeemed.

Odes on Themes

When its prelude has called upon "the redeemed of the LORD" to praise him, the regular movement of the ode begins. First we have the strophic[1] structure already described in a previous chapter; four stanzas with double refrains, each

Ode of the Redeemed Psalm cvii

stanza putting some particular type of distress, with its cry to God for help and its song of deliverance. But when this has been fully worked out the movement of the poem is not exhausted. The structure entirely changes, and the pendulum movement comes in. A series of alternations, like the diminuendo and crescendo of the musician, present the God of the Redeemed as a God that brings low and builds up again.

> He turneth rivers into a wilderness,
> And watersprings into a thirsty ground,
> A fruitful land into a salt desert,
> For the wickedness of them that dwell therein.

> He turneth a wilderness into a pool of water,
> And a dry land into watersprings.
> And there he maketh the hungry to dwell,
> That they may prepare a city of habitation;
> And sow fields, and plant vineyards,
> And get them fruits of increase.
> He blesseth them also so that they are multiplied greatly;
> And he suffereth not their cattle to decrease.

---

[1] Above, page 65.

Again they are minished and bowed down
Through oppression, trouble, and sorrow.
He poureth contempt upon princes,
And causeth them to wander in the waste, where there is no way.

Yet setteth he the needy on high from affliction,
And maketh him families like a flock.
The upright shall see it, and be glad;
And all iniquity shall stop her mouth.

The Ode on the Covenant (Psalm eighty-nine) is transparently clear in its language; it needs mention only because of the peculiarity of its structure. It seems strange to find an ode, the prelude of which announces a song of God's mercies and their eternal faithfulness, ending with a long wail over the anointed of the Lord as rejected and forsaken. At first we are tempted to think of this final section as outside the unity of the poem, the addition of some later age. But a close examination of the structure makes it possible to include the elegy within the ode. We have seen that interruption is amongst the devices of lyric movement. There is an example of this on an extensive scale in the earlier part of this psalm: no sooner has the Divine message of the Covenant been announced in four lines, than a break occurs —

Ode on the Covenant Psalm lxxxix

And the heavens shall praise thy wonders, O LORD —

The style wholly changes, and an outburst of exultation is carried on for twenty-nine lines, making one of the loftiest strains of adoration in the whole psalter. The second strophe returns to the subject of the Covenant in an elaborate vision, to which succeeds the section of sorrow and complaint. The symmetry then of the whole poem suggests that the change to lamentation is an interruption of the second strophe as the burst of exultation was an interruption of the first.

19-37

Two odes — one on the Messiah, the other an ode of Judgment — resemble one another in their general form; in each a Divine monologue is prefaced by a scenic introduction. The second psalm opens with the busy schemes of earthly rulers against the LORD's anointed, while up in the heavens Jehovah mocks them and sets up HIS KING on Zion. Then, either in the words of this Messiah or in the words of the psalmist, the Divine decree is given, and the kings are called upon to submit while there is time. The same general form appears on a larger scale in the fiftieth psalm. The whole world has been summoned to the bar of God; the prelude brings out the scene dramatically, in the words of God's people, who are awaiting, with exultation, the opening of this High Court.

Ode on the Messiah Psalm ii

Ode of Judgment Psalm l

> "Out of Zion, the perfection of beauty,
> God hath shined forth.
> Our God cometh, and shall not keep silence:
> A fire devoureth before him,
> And it is very tempestuous round about him."

All are assembled, the 'saints of God' on one side, and the wicked opposite to them; only the heavens themselves are left to be spectators in this Act of Justice. From this point the structure becomes antistrophic. First, God addresses his faithful people: he has not come to exact of them more sacrifices or take more of their bullocks and he-goats; it is by their cries to him in trouble and their thanksgiving when deliverance has come that they can truly glorify their God. In the antistrophe God turns to the wicked: how have they dared to join in his worship, while they were partakers in evil and crime? It is he who ordereth his conversation aright that shall see the salvation of God.

Finally we have two companion odes in the hundred and third and hundred and fourth psalms. Not only are these poems united by their structure — the common enveloping refrain, "Bless the LORD, O my soul" — but in subject-matter the two are so related that neither can be fully appreciated unless it is read in connection with the

Companion Odes: Psalm ciii, the World within

other. The subjects which make the two parts of the nineteenth psalm are here again found in association: the World within and the World without are the themes of these companion poems. In the hundred and third psalm the poet, immediately after the opening refrain, calls upon all that is within him to offer grateful praise; and when the benefits which call for this gratitude are enumerated they are found to be such benefits as affect the individual, personal, spiritual life.

> Who forgiveth all thine iniquities;
> Who healeth all thy diseases;
> Who redeemeth thy life from destruction;
> Who crowneth thee with lovingkindness and tender mercies:
> Who satisfieth thy mouth with good things;
> So that thy youth is renewed like the eagle.

God's dealings with Israel are referred to only as a revelation of his ways; and the revelation is of a kind that the individual life needs: compassion for the erring, a mercy as high as heaven is above the earth, a father pitying his children, a God knowing man's frame to be but dust; the revelation of a righteousness descending to children's children, while individual lives of men are but the grass-seed blown away by the wind. Then for its climax this hymn of the spiritual life rises to spiritual creatures: angels that excel in strength, hosts of the LORD that are ministers of his pleasure in all places of his dominion.

The hundred and fourth psalm starts at once with the external universe. This is presented as the tabernacle in which God dwells: its tent-pole reaches from the waters that are below to the waters that are above the firmament; the heavens are the stretched curtains of that tent; the winds are his messengers, and light is but the garment in which he veils himself from our gaze. God appears as the Creator of this universe: at a signal from him the curtain of the chaotic deep was withdrawn, and the world resolved itself into an orderly vicissitude of mountain and valley and stream, of fowl

and Psalm civ, the World without

singing among branches that overhang the waters where wild asses quench their thirst, of earth sending up grass for cattle, and bread that gives man strength, and wine and oil to gladden his spirits. The same Creator has ordained the seasons by which his world is governed, and his sun makes the alternation between night in which the beasts roam after their prey, and day when man can go forth to his work. When the wonders of the sea have been added to the wonders of land, all is ready for the climax thought: The universe is one, and God is its soul. All creatures wait upon Him.

>   Thou openest thine hand,
>   They are satisfied with good;
>   Thou hidest thy face,
>   They are troubled;
>   Thou gatherest in their breath,
>   They die,
>   And return to their dust;
>   Thou sendest forth thy spirit,
>   They are created,
>   And thou renewest the face of the ground.

When God has been thus exalted as supreme over the world of spirit within us, and the world of the universe without, even the poetry of the Bible may be said to have reached its climax.

CHAPTER VI

OCCASIONAL POETRY, ELEGIES, AND LITURGICAL PSALMS

THE subject of the present chapter covers something like a hundred different pieces of literature. Comment on individual poems becomes impossible; they can be treated only in classes.[1]

Occasional Poetry has been illustrated in its most elaborate form by the Song of Deborah and other odes. In the case of the psalms, to connect these with the occasions that called them forth usually involves historical discussions such as are outside the scope of the present work. But there are three psalms which few will hesitate to attach to the crisis of Sennacherib's invasion. The marvellous incident of that critical period is presented in no obscure language.

Occasional Poetry

Sennacherib's invasion

> The stouthearted are spoiled, they have slept their sleep;
> And none of the men of might have found their hands.
> At thy rebuke, O God of Jacob,
> Both chariot and horse are cast into a dead sleep.

Psalm lxxvi. 5 and 2 (margin)

We see a passionate outburst of renewed love to Zion now that the oppression of the siege is lifted from the people; they walk round the city; they count the towers and bulwarks, as if to make sure that all are really safe. They hail her as beautiful in elevation, joy of the whole world, lair from which the Lion of Judah darts upon his prey; the river

xlviii. 12, 2

---

[1] The Table of Lyric Poetry in Appendix II will give the psalms falling under each designation.

154   LYRIC POETRY OF THE BIBLE

of peace holds her in its arms unmoved while all around is tossing
in tumult. And the abrupt concentration to which
xlvi. 4   Hebrew sentences lend themselves presents the
whole crisis in the fewest possible words :

xlvi. 6   The nations raged, the kingdoms were moved:
             He uttered his voice, the earth melted.

There is an earlier occasion in Hebrew history with which, as
I have before remarked, much of Biblical poetry connects itself.
The inauguration   This is the inauguration of Jerusalem by King
of Jerusalem   David. It is not difficult to read the historic
II Samuel vi   account of the day in the *Book of Samuel* and fit
the songs into their proper places.

>   And David went and brought up the ark of God from the house of
>   Obed-Edom into the city of David with joy. And it was so, that
>   when they that bare the ark of the LORD had gone six paces, he sacri-
>   ficed an ox and a fatling. And David danced before the LORD with
>   all his might; and David was girded with a linen ephod. [*Here comes
>   Psalm xxx.*] So David and all the house of Israel *brought up* the ark
>   of the LORD with shouting, and with the sound of the trumpet.
>   [*At the foot of the ascent comes Psalm xxiv. 1–6; at the top, the mili-
>   tary piece, Psalm xxiv. 7–10.*] . . . And they brought in the ark of
>   the LORD, and set it in its place, in the midst of the tent that David
>   had pitched for it: and David offered burnt offerings and peace offer-
>   ings before the LORD. [*Here comes Psalm cxxxii. 1–9.*] . . . So all
>   the people departed every one to his house. Then David returned to
>   bless his household. [*Here comes Psalm ci.*]

David commenced this festal day with the utmost trepidation,
on account of the terrible death of Uzzah, which had interrupted
his former attempt to bring the ark to Jerusalem. The first few
paces of the present procession are sufficient to show that the
Divine ban is removed; there is a halt and an offering of thanksgiving, and a lyric hymn of joy. The thirtieth
Psalm xxx   psalm, connected by its traditional title with this
particular day, fits exactly into such a situation. It breathes a
sense of escape from death; it tells how David in his prosperity

had felt himself a strong mountain that should never be moved; how the Divine face was suddenly hidden and he was plunged in trouble; how he mourned and prayed, and now his mourning is turned into this dance of joy: the weeping has but been a guest lodging for the night, but the favour of God will be a friend for a lifetime.

The procession continues, and I have in a former chapter [1] dealt with the anthem at the foot of the hill, and the summons to the city to receive the Lord of Hosts. The city is entered, and the ark is brought into the tabernacle where it was to remain for a time. Here fresh sacrifices are offered; and there could be no more suitable anthem to accompany such sacrifices than the earlier part [2] of the hundred and thirty-second psalm. It Psalm cxxxii. recites David's passionate vow to enjoy no rest 1-9 until he had found a tabernacle for the Most High. The verses that follow seem a riddle until they are explained by the search for the ark in its temporary resting-places amid the solitude of the hill country. Then follow the ceremonial words:

> Arise, O LORD, into thy resting place;
> Thou, and the ark of thy strength.

The proceedings of the day do not yet terminate. The people are dismissed, but David returns "to bless his household." The hundred and first psalm gives us just the blessing required: a vow of mercy and judgment for the Psalm ci speaker himself, for his household, and for the administration of his kingdom. The final line which speaks of cutting off the workers of iniquity "from the CITY OF THE LORD" comes with new force when we recollect that it was only on that day that the old fortress of the Jebusites and stronghold of evil had been transferred to the service of another Deity and formally inaugurated as the City of Jehovah.

---

[1] Above, pages 100-104.
[2] Verses 10-18 are the addition made for the Dedication Festival of Solomon's Temple.

The natural history of the Elegy seems to be as follows. It is based on the primitive Wail or Dirge; owing to the existence of a class of professional mourners this early attains maturity as a form of literature with metrical and other distinctiveness. Its characteristics pass over into other forms of literature by two different routes. On the one hand the metre of the Elegy, being amongst early forms one of the most perfect for expressing strong emotion, comes in time to be used for emotional strains that are not mournful; thus the student of Classical literature is familiar with the fact that the 'elegiac metre' is regularly used for love poems, and can even travel so far from its original conception as to express encomium. Again, we are able in Hebrew prophecy to see how the form of the Elegy is used *ironically* in the 'taunt-songs.' It appears then that evolutionary considerations warrant us in classing together three literary forms so different as the Elegy, the Denunciation, and the Encomium.

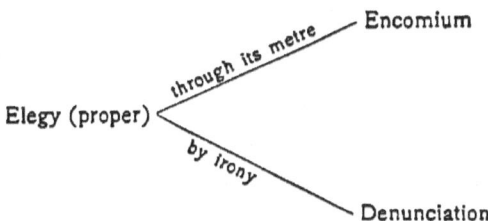

There is a curious parallelism between the Hebrew rhythm of elegy and that of Greek and Latin poetry, which is composed of the ordinary hexameter followed by the shorter pentameter. In Hebrew the elegiac rhythm is the ordinary couplet with the second member weakened, by being either shortened or left destitute of antithesis or parallelism, so much so that the two are usually printed as a single line with a cæsura.

Marginalia: The Elegy; Elegiac rhythm

He hath fenced me about that I cannot go forth; he hath made my chain heavy.

The difference of this from the ordinary rhythm is well seen in the transition from one to the other already cited as an effect in *Deborah's Song.*

> In the days of Shamgar the son of Anath,
>   In the days of Jael,
> The highways were unoccupied,
>   And the travellers walked through byways;
> The rulers ceased in Israel,
>   They ceased —
> Until that I, Deborah, arose,
> That I arose a mother in Israel.
> They chose new gods;
> Then was war in the gates:
> Was there a shield or spear seen
> Among forty thousand in Israel?

But the widespread use of this elegiac rhythm in Biblical literature is lost to the English reader, since none of the accepted versions keep it up in their translation.[1] The loss is greatest in the elaborate elegy entitled the *Lamentations of Jeremiah*, which is a highly artificial composition [sidenote: Lamentations of Jeremiah] built up on the principle of elegiac rhythm and a curious alphabetical succession of verses. The great blot upon the Revised Version of our Bible is the absence of any attempt to represent the acrostic structure which affects these as so many other Hebrew poems. The pathos of individual passages in the *Lamentations* is obvious enough; but the literary form of the whole must be given up for the present as inaccessible to the English reader.[2]

There are elegies amongst the most familiar poems of the psalter. One is the song of the captives weeping by the rivers of

---

[1] For a systematic treatment of the whole subject, see an article by Karl Budde in the *New Review,* March, 1893.

[2] In *The Psalms by Four Friends,* or the abridged edition of it as the Psalter in the Golden Treasury Series (Macmillan & Co.), the acrostic effect is maintained throughout; and the *Book of Lamentations* is given in full (in the second edition of the larger work).

Babylon, hanging their harps upon the willows at the thought of singing the songs of Zion in a strange land; until the wail hardens into an ecstasy of hatred as they long for one who will take the little ones of the oppressor and dash them against the ground. Another tells the evil done to the sanctuary by the enemy, how they behaved as men that lifted up axes upon a thicket of trees, how the carved work is broken down with hatchet and hammers, and fire has converted the sacred pile into a profane ruin. Another is made distinctive by the sustained image of the Vine brought out of Egypt, with nations cast out to make room for it; it had taken deep root until mountains were covered by its shadow and its branches reached to the River and the Sea; but now its fences are thrown down, and the beasts out of the wood can ravage it, nay, it is cut down and burned with fire. And no Biblical elegy is more impressive than the earliest of them all, the lamentation of David over Saul and Jonathan, preserved by its connection with archery meetings founded in honour of Jonathan. The simple pathos of this song is familiar to all. It is worth while also to note the structural beauty of the augmenting refrain: at the opening of the elegy it is, *How are the mighty fallen;* when the stanzas special to Saul are completed it has become, *How are the mighty fallen in the midst of the battle;* at the end of the final section expressing the poet's tender love for Jonathan the refrain has grown to a full couplet—

> How are the mighty fallen,
> And the weapons of war perished!

These are Elegies proper; but Elegies of Denunciation have a prominent place in the psalter. Indeed, the imprecatory passages that occur in several of the psalms are a difficulty with many readers, who feel that such violence of passion is out of harmony with the spirit of the psalter as a whole.

> Let them be as chaff before the wind,   Psalm xxxv. 5
> And the angel of the LORD driving them on.
> Let their way be dark and slippery,
> And the angel of the LORD pursuing them.

But for this, and for the much more extended imprecation of the hundred and ninth psalm, an important principle of interpretation is found in the different attitude of ancient and modern literature to abstract and concrete. We in modern times are quite accustomed to feel enthusiasm for the abstract thing we call 'a cause'; with the ancient world it was necessary for the cause to be embodied in a concrete party, if it was to win devotion or the reverse. Though this principle has less application in Biblical than in other literatures of antiquity, yet it obtains there to some extent. When the psalmist's hatred of evil men has once been translated into the form of hatred against evil, it will be felt that the passages cannot be too strongly worded.

The class of lyrical Encomia can be well illustrated by the Salutation to Zion, which constitutes the eighty-seventh psalm. Glorious things, cries the poet to Zion, are   Encomia Psalm lxxxvii spoken of thee: and in the fourth verse presents Zion as speaking for herself.

> "I will make mention of Rahab and Babylon
> As among them that know me:
> Behold Philistia, and Tyre, with Ethiopia;
> This one was born there."

And the poet adds his testimony: yea, it shall be said of Zion that this and that great nation owns her for a mother; not of course by natural descent, but in the Lord's spiritual register they shall be inscribed as daughters of Zion. And the final verse, in the spirit of the sixty-eighth psalm, pictures the procession of the nations, proclaiming with minstrelsy and dance that they draw their springs from Mount Zion. The psalm has been well summed up by Professor Cheyne as "the Church of Israel expanding into the Church Universal."

A large proportion of the psalter is made by the Liturgical Psalms, which are clearly designed for public worship. In literary characteristics they may be regarded as the converse of the species with which this chapter opened: occasional poetry has matter already provided for it, and the matter begets the emotion; in the other case the set emotion is taken for granted and looks for matter to sustain it. The Liturgical Psalms are mainly hymns of praise: the varied forms assumed by such hymns the reader may study from the Table in the Appendix. The student of literature can only marvel at their richness and the height at which their exultation is sustained. One variety may be called Hallelujahs: these (in typical cases) have the ejaculation from which they are named at the opening and close, while all that comes between is maintained at the same high pitch. Scarcely different from these are what have been called Accession Hymns: here the exclamation, "The LORD reigneth," is the keynote of the whole. I apply the term Festal Hymns to psalms which breathe the general spirit of a high feast day, though they may not fit themselves to any particular ceremonial. In Votive Hymns an individual comes to mingle his vow with the general thanksgiving; even the Songs of Hannah and of Mary, however personal the strain with which they start, yet before the end seem to merge this in praise that is of universal application. To all these must be added the Benedictions, such as the people bestow upon their king, or the poet upon the bridegroom and bride of some royal wedding; these are clearly distinguished from the encomia mentioned above by the tone of ritual worship that runs through them.

<small>Liturgical Psalms</small>

<small>Varieties of Liturgical Psalms</small>

Most of these liturgical psalms are characterised by a simplicity that is beyond analysis. The spirit of praise once aroused is kept alive by reiteration, or by enumeration of details.

<small>Their literary characteristics</small>

cxlviii. 7   Praise the LORD from the earth,
            Ye dragons, and all deeps:
            Fire and hail, snow and vapour;

> Stormy wind, fulfilling his word:
> Mountains and all hills;
> Fruitful trees and all cedars;
> Beasts and all cattle;
> Creeping things and flying fowl:
> Kings of the earth and all peoples;
> Princes and all judges of the earth:
> Both young men and maidens;
> Old men and children:
> Let them praise the name of the LORD.

Sometimes the reiteration takes a more fanciful form. Not to speak of the acrostic structure, which obtains here as in so many other departments of Hebrew poetry, we find a beautiful bit of imitative sound in the ninety-third psalm.

> The floods have lifted up, O LORD,
> The floods have lifted up their voice;
> The floods lift up their roaring:
> Above the voices of many waters,
> The mighty breakers of the sea,
> The LORD on high is mighty.

Poetic imagery is found here as everywhere in Biblical poetry; especially the favourite Hebrew image of external nature in excitement: the sea roars, the field leaps, the trees of the wood sing for joy, as Jehovah comes to judgment.

But these ritual psalms reach their most characteristic form when they are antiphonal in structure. Antiphonal performance may be assumed in the case of all; but there are some cases in which the whole form and succession of thought imply a designation for more than one set of performers. I will take a fully developed type in the hundred and eighteenth psalm. The reader will appreciate the illustration the better if he first reads the hundred and sixteenth psalm. The two poems are almost identical in thought and situation; in each case an individual is returning thanks for deliverance apparently from sickness. But in one case there is nothing

Ritual psalms with antiphonal structure

to break the flow of individual speech; in the other psalm the sequence of verses clearly suggests a solo and two distinct choruses. At the beginning the Worshipper is approaching the Temple with an Escort of Friends; later on a second Chorus of Priests must be added.

PSALM CXVIII

The Worshipper and his Escort approach the Temple.

Tutti.	O give thanks unto the LORD; for he is good:
	For his mercy endureth for ever.
Worshipper.	Let Israel now say—
Escort.	That his mercy endureth for ever.
Worshipper.	Let the house of Aaron now say—
Escort.	That his mercy endureth for ever.
Worshipper.	Let them now that fear the LORD say—
Escort.	That his mercy endureth for ever.
Worshipper.	Out of my distress I called upon the LORD:
	The LORD answered me, and set me in a large place.
	The LORD is on my side; I will not fear:
	What can man do unto me?
	The LORD is on my side among them that help me:
	Therefore shall I see my desire upon them that hate me.
Escort.	It is better to trust in the LORD
	Than to put confidence in man;
	It is better to trust in the LORD
	Than to put confidence in princes.
Worshipper.	All nations compassed me about:
Escort.	In the name of the LORD I will cut them off!
Worshipper.	They compassed me about;
	Yea, they compassed me about:
Escort.	In the name of the LORD I will cut them off!
Worshipper.	They compassed me about like bees;
	They are quenched as the fire of thorns:
Escort.	In the name of the LORD I will cut them off!
Worshipper.	Thou didst thrust sore at me that I might fall:
	But the LORD helped me.

	The LORD is my strength and song;

                The LORD is my strength and song;
                And he is become my salvation.
                The voice of rejoicing and salvation is in the tents of the righteous:
                The right hand of the LORD doeth valiantly.
Escort.   The right hand of the LORD is exalted:
                The right hand of the LORD doeth valiantly.
Worshipper. I shall not die, but live,
                And declare the works of the LORD.
                The LORD hath chastened me sore:
                But he hath not given me over unto death.
                Open to me the gates of righteousness:
                I will enter into them,
                I will give thanks unto the LORD.

                The Temple gates open and disclose a Chorus of Priests.

Priests.   This is the Gate of the LORD:
                The righteous shall enter into it.

Worshipper. I will give thanks unto thee, for thou hast answered me,
                And art become my salvation.
                The stone which the builders rejected
                Is become the head of the corner.
Escort.   This is the LORD's doing;
                It is marvellous in our eyes.
                This is the day which the LORD hath made;
                We will rejoice and be glad in it.
                Save now, we beseech thee, O LORD:
                O LORD, we beseech thee, send now prosperity.

                The Worshipper enters the Temple: the Escort prepare to retire.
Priests (to the Worshipper).
                Blessed be he that entereth in the name of the LORD!
        (to the Escort, retiring).
                We have blessed you out of the house of the LORD!

Priests.   The LORD is God, and he hath given us light:
                Bind the sacrifice with cords, even unto the horns of the altar.
Worshipper. Thou art my God, and I will give thanks unto thee:
                Thou art my God, I will exalt thee.
Tutti.   O give thanks unto the LORD; for he is good;
                For his mercy endureth for ever.

So far the liturgical psalms we have reviewed have been composed wholly in one tone, that of praise. But it belongs to Liturgy, that is, to Divine Service, to unite many moods of the soul in one exercise, to mingle penitence with praise, confession of faith with supplication. There are certain psalms which seem to show a similar mingling of moods, — psalms which a close analysis will separate altogether from the personal monologues filled with variations of individual experience, and which must be classified with the poetry of public worship. The explanation is that in such cases we have a complete liturgy within the limits of a single psalm.

<small>Liturgies (unity of aggregation)</small>

The characteristics I am describing distinguish one of the most impressive psalms in the whole Bible; and the discussion of this psalm illustrates the important bearing of such considerations upon interpretation. The sixty-fifth psalm will be pronounced by one commentator a harvest thanksgiving; another will see in it praise for forgiveness of national sin. But such explanations are incomplete, and leave great part of the poem without significance. Nor is the matter much mended when the two theories are combined. All such interpretation assumes for the psalm a type of unity which it does not contain. In discussing the higher unity I mentioned, among other types, the unity of aggregation. The sixty-fifth psalm is bound together by this bond; not that we have in it the aggregation of different compositions, such as we saw in the selections from the *Book of Proverbs;* but the parts of this psalm bring up in succession different moods of the soul, disconnected from one another, yet mingling as they do mingle in any elaborate act of worship.

<small>Psalm lxv a Liturgy of Praise</small>

PSALM LXV

<small>thanksgiving</small>   Praise waiteth for thee, O God, in Zion:
        And unto thee shall the vow be performed.

                    *

<small>prayer</small>   O thou that hearest prayer,
        Unto thee shall all flesh come.

                    *

Iniquities prevail against me: *penitence*
As for our transgressions, thou shalt purge them away.

*

Blessed is the man whom thou choosest,   *devotion*
    And causest to approach unto thee,
    That he may dwell in thy courts:
We shall be satisfied with the goodness of thy house,
    The holy place of thy temple.

*

By terrible things thou wilt answer us in righteousness,   *judgment*
    O God of our salvation:
    Thou that art the confidence of all the ends of the earth,
    And of them that are afar off upon the sea:
Which by his strength setteth fast the mountains;
    Being girded about with might:
Which stilleth the roaring of the seas,
    The roaring of their waves,
    And the tumult of the peoples.
They also that dwell in the uttermost parts are afraid at thy tokens:
Thou makest the outgoings of the morning and evening to rejoice.

*

Thou visitest the earth, and waterest it: *adoration*
    Thou greatly enrichest it,
    The river of God is full of water:
Thou providest them corn, when thou hast so prepared the earth;
Thou waterest her furrows abundantly,
Thou settlest the ridges thereof,
Thou makest it soft with showers,
Thou blessest the springing thereof,
Thou crownest the year with thy goodness:
    And thy paths drop fatness,
    They drop upon the pastures of the wilderness,
    And the hills are girded with joy,
    The pastures are clothed with flocks:
The valleys also are covered over with corn:
They shout for joy, they also sing.

When, without any preconceived idea of unity, the psalm is examined with a view to tracing the actual connection of its different parts, it is thus found to bring before us in succession all the elements of public worship. One verse is an ejaculation of thanksgiving, the next a simple prayer, the next a simple expression of penitence. Then follow words of devotion, describing the devout life by the image so regularly used for it in the psalms — the dwelling in God's house. Another theme of worship then finds elaborate expression; that which in modern phraseology would be called God's Providence, while the Hebrew worshipper would describe it as Judgment, or "the answer in righteousness." And the whole terminates with adoration to the God of Nature. This last outburst does not simply touch the harvest, but passes to and fro between agricultural and pastoral scenery: between the changing year of agriculture — from the first ploughing to the crowning harvest — and the dropping of 'God's paths,' the rain-clouds, upon the pasture lands, until both sides of external nature are united in a shout and hymn of joy.

> The hills are girded with joy,
> The pastures are clothed with flocks;
> The valleys also are covered over with corn;
> They shout for joy, they also sing.

The different sections of the psalm have no connection one with the other, but they are all parts of a whole, just as entirely separate sentences of confession, of praise, of supplication, are in our modern liturgies bound together into a single office for matins or evensong.

All liturgy resolves itself into three parts: acts of praise and thanksgiving, acts of prayer — the term being used to cover both supplication and devotion — and acts of faith. The first two raise no difficulty; the language of praise and prayer is the same in all ages. But when we come to acts of faith, these in modern liturgies differ so widely from their counterparts in the psalter that it requires an effort to recognise the analogy of the two. In the liturgies familiar to the modern reader the main acts of faith are the 'Creeds,' which are formal statements of theological truth. It is true that the rubric

Biblical and modern liturgies

of a creed may direct that it shall be 'sung,' and, as a matter of liturgiological theory, the Creed is regarded as the Church's joyous celebration of its belief. But when the creeds of modern liturgies are examined as pieces of literature it must be admitted that their formal clauses, their technical phraseology, and their design in some cases to settle controversies, remove them to a wide distance from lyric poetry. In the worship of the psalter, on the other hand, we have to deal with a people whose creed was a creed of a single article, and that article might be summed up in the single word 'Judgment.' This expressive word in the mouth of a Hebrew poet implies an absolute belief in the supremacy of God, and, as a consequence from this, in the vindication of good against evil. To declare such belief, to call for judgment, to passionately identify himself with such vindication of the cause of good, — this makes the act of faith which the worshipper of the Biblical psalter is continually mingling with his prayer and praise.

These lyrical creeds in the psalms will be found to take very different forms. Sometimes such an act of faith is couched in the simplest parallel or antithetic sentences: *Lyrical creeds*

> The eyes of the LORD are toward the righteous,   xxxiv. 15
> And his ears are open unto their cry.
> The face of the LORD is against them that do evil,
> To cut off the remembrance of them from the earth.

Or it may take a gnomic form:

> God hath spoken once,   lxii. 11
> Twice have I heard this;
>   That power belongeth unto God:
>   Also unto thee, O Lord, belongeth mercy:
> For thou renderest to every man according to his work.

Or it may be argumentative:

> He that planted the ear, shall he not hear?   xciv. 9
> He that formed the eye, shall he not see?
> He that instructeth the nations, shall he not correct?

The appeal to God's judgment may take the shape of a challenge.

iv. 2   O ye sons of men, how long shall my glory be turned into dishonour?
 How long will ye love vanity, and seek after falsehood?
 But know that the LORD hath set apart him that is godly for himself:
 The LORD will hear when I call unto him.

Even a personal vindication, like Job's oath of clearing, or the precisely similar passage in the seventh psalm, may be classed as an act of faith, for it amounts to taking sides in the struggle of Good and Evil.

vii. 3   O LORD my God, if I have done this ;
 If there be iniquity in my hands ;
 If I have rewarded evil unto him that was at peace with me;
 Yea, I have delivered him that without cause was mine adversary:
  Let the enemy pursue my soul, and overtake it ;
  Yea, let him tread my life down to the earth,
  And lay my glory in the dust!

Such are the lyrical confessions of faith which mingle with supplication and adoration, with thanksgiving, penitence for sin, and yearnings after the devout life, to make the liturgies of the psalter. With just those transitions which the instinct of modern devotion would express by changes of posture, — from standing to kneeling, and the like, — these poems of worship break a long prayer by a short ascription of praise, or pass from penitence to general prayer through a brief recital of confidence in God's justice. We have seen at full length a psalm which in the main is a song of faith and adoration, but which leads up to these by briefer representation of the other elements of worship. It may be well to take another example. The eighty-sixth psalm, viewed

A Liturgy of Supplication   as a whole, is a litany or supplication ; but the prayer with which it opens and closes is interrupted in the middle by a declaration of the Divine supremacy, and also by a personal thanksgiving, and these two interruptions are themselves separated by a brief ejaculation of devotion.

PSALM LXXXVI

Bow down thine ear, O LORD,   supplication
    And answer me ;
    For I am poor and needy.
Preserve my soul,
    For I am godly :
    O thou my God,
Save thy servant that trusteth in thee.

Be merciful unto me, O LORD;
    For unto thee do I cry all the day long :
Rejoice the soul of thy servant;
    For unto thee, O LORD, do I lift up my soul.
For thou, LORD, art good,
    And ready to forgive,
And plenteous in mercy unto all them that call upon thee.

Give ear, O LORD, unto my prayer;
    And hearken unto the voice of my supplications :
In the day of my trouble I will call upon thee,
    For thou wilt answer me.

*

There is none like unto thee among the gods, O LORD;   faith
Neither are there any works like unto thy works.
All nations whom thou hast made
    Shall come and worship before thee, O LORD;
    And they shall glorify thy name.
For thou art great, and doest wondrous things :
Thou art God alone.

*

Teach me thy way, O LORD; I will walk in thy truth :   devotion
Unite my heart to fear thy name.

*

I will praise thee, O LORD my God, with my whole heart;   thanks-
And I will glorify thy name for evermore.   giving
For great is thy mercy toward me;
And thou hast delivered my soul from the lowest pit.

*

supplication
    O God, the proud are risen up against me,
    And the congregation of violent men
        Have sought after my soul,
        And have not set thee before them.
    But thou, O LORD, art a God full of compassion,
        And gracious,
        Slow to anger,
    And plenteous in mercy and truth.
    O turn unto me, and have mercy upon me;
        Give thy strength unto thy servant,
        And save the son of thine handmaid.
    Show me a token for good;
        That they which hate me may see it,
        And be ashamed,
    Because thou, LORD, hast holpen me, and comforted me.

Before passing away from the subject of this chapter it is necessary to notice a portion of the *Book of Psalms* which is occupied, not with single compositions, but with a collection of similar poems, a psalter within a psalter.

The Songs of Ascents: Psalms cxx-cxxxiv

Fifteen psalms in succession have the common title, 'Songs of Ascents'; the Authorised Version renders it 'Songs of Degrees,' a translation of the word in the Vulgate which has by others been rendered 'Gradual Psalms.'[1] The literal meaning of the expression is 'Songs of the goings up.' What is the significance of this enigmatic phrase? Two theories on this point are worthy of special consideration. One is conveyed by giving the poems the title of 'Pilgrim Songs'; that is, songs of the Pilgrims going up to Jerusalem for the great feasts. The other connects them with the Return of the Captives from Babylon to Jerusalem.

The difficulty of the question is much reduced when we recollect that the title, whatever its meaning may be, expresses the purpose of the *collection*, not of the composition of any particular psalm. If we think of our modern hymn-books, we shall see that

---

[1] Armfield's *Gradual Psalms* (Hayes) contains an interesting theory of the title, connecting it on the authority of the Talmud with the part of the Temple in which these psalms would be performed.

a phrase may be apposite as a title for the whole book, and yet might have little significance if applied to the interpretation of single hymns in the collection. Keeping this consideration before us, we may find it not difficult to combine the two theories mentioned above.

Some of these Songs of Ascents associate themselves readily with the Captivity and Return. The singer of the one hundred and twentieth psalm speaks from amidst an atmosphere of turbulence and treachery, and describes himself, either really or figuratively, as living in the distant regions of Meshech and Kedar. Psalm one hundred and twenty-three seems to take local colour from some oriental empire: as the eyes of *slaves* follow their masters to anticipate every wish, so the poet would be observant of his God. The poem that follows presents Israel as just escaped like a bird out of the snare of the fowler: if Jehovah had not been on his side the foe would have swallowed him up. The hundred and twenty-sixth psalm is peculiar. It opens with the words: cxxvi

> When the LORD turned again the captivity of Zion,
> We were like unto them that dream.

And yet at the fourth verse comes the prayer:

> Turn again our captivity, O LORD,
> As the streams in the South.
> They that sow in tears shall reap in joy.

The simplest explanation of this is to connect it with the Return from Babylon. That return took place in many instalments, separated by long intervals. This psalm would seem to be a hymn of those remaining in exile when the first migration had started: they exult in the change of fortune which has at last visited their nation, and they long for their own share in the happy deliverance; meanwhile they give themselves up to patience and hope. The period of the Exile fits well with the hundred and twenty-ninth psalm, which presents Israel as a martyr, and cries execration upon those that hate Zion. And while the *De profundis* of the following psalm gives expression to national penitence in any age, yet it could at no time be so appropriate as during the Captivity.

On the other hand, the hundred and twenty-first psalm, of which the keynote is "The LORD thy keeper," seems a most appropriate marching hymn for the companies of pilgrims journeying to the yearly feasts; and its opening words, "I will lift up mine eyes unto the hills," might connect it with the first sight of the environs of the sacred city. The psalm that follows would just fit in with the next stage: "Our feet are standing within thy gates, O Jerusalem." The hundred and twenty-fifth psalm is made up of thoughts suggested by the sight of the Holy City: the massive Mount Zion is a symbol of the security of those who trust in its God; the mountains enclosing Jerusalem are like the Lord's protection thrown around his people; the territory so safely walled in is a pledge that the empire of evil shall not invade the lot of the righteous. Moreover, these companies of pilgrims were family parties, as an incident of the New Testament reminds us: hence the hundred and twenty-seventh psalm (cited elsewhere[1]) contrasting the life of busy care with the peaceful family life, or the next, which associates family joys with the blessing out of Zion, or the hundred and thirty-first, which draws from child life a conception of personal and national humble-mindedness, or again the hundred and thirty-third, which celebrates the unity of brethren. The two poems of the collection that have yet to be mentioned connect themselves directly with the Temple: one (the hundred and thirty-second) is the Dedication hymn of David and Solomon, and the other makes an appropriate close to the collection in the form of a brief exchange of greetings between the retiring worshippers and the Night Watch remaining on guard.

The psalms, individually considered, then, suggest a twofold origin; the combination of both types in a common collection is not difficult to understand. Either the 'Songs of the goings up' was at first the title for poems of the Captivity and Return, and

[1] Above, page 97.

this little psalter came to be increased by the songs of pilgrimages to the second Temple; or, more probably, the old traditionary Pilgrim Songs made the first collection, and its contents were doubled by that great pilgrimage beside which all others were commonplace. In any case the 'Songs of Ascents' are a series of hymns impressing every reader with their strong resemblance to one another; and they are the quintessence of all that is most attractive, and most unanalysable, in sacred lyrics.

CHAPTER VII

DRAMATIC LYRICS AND LYRICS OF MEDITATION

Dramatic Lyrics

I WISH to recall two points touched upon in earlier chapters of this work. In our general survey of literary classification we saw that, in the nature of things, lyric poetry holds an intermediate position between epic and drama; that thus, without wandering far from its proper path of meditation, a lyric poem can at one moment contain purely epic description, at another moment present a detail dramatically. Again, we saw it as a distinction of Hebrew literature that it has no completely separate drama, but that dramatic form appears as a considerable modifying force in other departments of its poetry. We are now to see how this dramatic form invades the department of lyric poetry, until it is possible for even so short a lyric as a psalm to be in essence a complete drama.

The simplest way of making this point clear will be to put side by side certain poems exhibiting different stages of advance from lyric to drama. Let the reader first compare carefully Psalms seventy-seven and one hundred and forty-three. The situation in the two is identical: a sufferer seeks to gain fortitude in his trouble by meditating on the wonderful doings of God. And to some extent the matter of one psalm echoes that of the other: in particular, where one poem simply speaks of finding comfort in old memories the other recites these memories at full length. As regards the form, however, in which the thoughts are conveyed to us, the two poems will be found to represent different degrees of proximity to dramatic presentation.

PSALM LXXVII

I will cry unto God with my voice; *Monody mingling*
Even unto God with my voice, *description with*
And he will give ear unto me. *presentation*
In the day of my trouble I sought the Lord:
My hand was stretched out in the night, and slacked not;
My soul refused to be comforted.
I remember God, and am disquieted:
I complain, and my spirit is overwhelmed.
Thou holdest mine eyes watching:
I am so troubled that I cannot speak.
I have considered the days of old,
The years of ancient times.
I call to remembrance my song in the night:
I commune with mine own heart;
And my spirit made diligent search.
 "Will the LORD cast off for ever?
 And will he be favourable no more?
 Is his mercy clean gone for ever?
 Doth his promise fail for evermore?
 Hath God forgotten to be gracious?
 Hath he in anger shut up his tender mercies?"
And I said, "This is my infirmity;
But I will remember the years of the right hand of the Most High.
I will make mention of the deeds of the LORD;
For I will remember thy wonders of old.
I will meditate also upon all thy work,
And muse on thy doings.
 Thy way, O God, is in holiness:
 Who is a great god like unto God?
 Thou art the God that doest wonders:
 Thou hast made known thy strength among the peoples.
 Thou hast with thine arm redeemed thy people,
 The sons of Jacob and Joseph.
 The waters saw thee, O God;
 The waters saw thee, they were afraid:
 The depths also trembled.
 The clouds poured out water;
 The skies sent out a sound:
 Thine arrows also went abroad;

The voice of thy thunder was in the whirlwind;
The lightnings lightened the world:
The earth trembled and shook.
Thy way was in the sea,
And thy paths in the great waters,
And thy footsteps were not known.
Thou leddest thy people like a flock,
By the hand of Moses and Aaron."

This poem so far resembles drama that it is a monody: instead of an author speaking about some one else, we have the actual subject of the experience speaking in his own person. But with this dramatic element mingles a great deal of the description that belongs to epic; the sufferer *narrates* how he was troubled, and how he set himself to think; though the actual words of his thinking are given, yet they are prefaced by the formula "And I said —." In the next illustration all such narration disappears, and the situation is brought out in the cries and other utterances that made a part of it; we have a present experience, and not a narration of something that is past.

Monody presenting a single dramatic situation

PSALM CXLIII

Hear my prayer, O LORD; give ear to my supplications:
In thy faithfulness answer me, and in thy righteousness.
And enter not into judgement with thy servant;
For in thy sight shall no man living be justified.
For the enemy hath persecuted my soul;
He hath smitten my life down to the ground:
He hath made me to dwell in dark places,
As those that have been long dead.
Therefore is my spirit overwhelmed within me;
My heart within me is desolate.
    I remember the days of old;
    I meditate on all thy doings:
    I muse on the work of thy hands.
    I spread forth my hands unto thee:
    My soul thirsteth after thee, as a weary land.
Make haste to answer me, O LORD; my spirit faileth:
Hide not thy face from me;

Lest I become like them that go down into the pit.
Cause me to hear thy lovingkindness in the morning;
   For in thee do I trust.
Cause me to know the way wherein I should walk;
   For I lift up my soul unto thee.
Deliver me, O LORD, from mine enemies:
   I flee unto thee to hide me.
Teach me to do thy will;
   For thou art my God:
   Thy spirit is good;
Lead me in the land of uprightness.
Quicken me, O LORD, for thy name's sake:
In thy righteousness bring my soul out of trouble.
And in thy lovingkindness cut off mine enemies,
And destroy all them that afflict my soul;
   For I am thy servant.

Here then we have pure presentation of an experience; there is no element of the poem that is not dramatic. Yet it is not drama but only a dramatic situation; to make it complete drama would necessitate a *change* from one situation to a different one, which is the essence of dramatic movement and plot. This requisite is supplied in the case of the sixth psalm, in which again we hear a sufferer complaining and praying, but before the psalm ends deliverance has come, and complaint is converted into rejoicing.

Complete Dramatic Lyric (change of situation)

PSALM VI

O LORD, rebuke me not in thine anger,
Neither chasten me in thy hot displeasure.
Have mercy upon me, O LORD;
   For I am withered away:
O LORD, heal me;
   For my bones are vexed.
My soul also is sore vexed:
And thou, O LORD, how long?
Return, O LORD, deliver my soul:
Save me for thy lovingkindness' sake.
For in death there is no remembrance of thee:

> In Sheol who shall give thee thanks?
> I am weary with my groaning;
> Every night make I my bed to swim;
> I water my couch with my tears.
> Mine eye wasteth away because of grief;
> It waxeth old because of all mine adversaries.
>
> Depart from me, all ye workers of iniquity;
> For the LORD hath heard the voice of my weeping.
> The LORD hath heard my supplication;
> The LORD will receive my prayer.
> All mine enemies shall be ashamed and sore vexed:
> They shall turn back, they shall be ashamed suddenly.

In this case we have a monody free from any admixture of description, and the monody presents a sufferer undergoing, as he speaks it, the change his words describe: an experience is acted before us, and we thus have a lyric poem that is a complete drama.

This presentation of trouble passing dramatically into relief belongs to psalm after psalm of the Bible; from the Table of Biblical Lyrics in the Appendix they can be studied as a literary species in themselves. In a former chapter was reviewed a notable example of it, the hundred and thirty-ninth psalm: there the dread of the Divine omniscience with which the poem opens becomes changed into a loving recognition of its supporting efficacy, and the transition is made at the very centre and turning-point of the lyric movement. The dramatic transition can be intensified by its abruptness. The psalm that commences with the cry,

Other examples

Psalms cxxxix, xxii, lvii

> My God, my God, why hast thou forsaken me?

and carries into detail the self-picturing of a God-forsaken heart, makes its change from despair to rapture in the middle of a sentence.

> Deliver my soul from the sword;
> My darling from the power of the dog;
> Save me from the lion's mouth —
> — Yea, from the horns of the wild-oxen thou hast answered me!

A similar abruptness marks the turning-point of the fifty-seventh psalm, which further has a refrain to bind closer its two halves; the words —

> Be thou exalted, O God, above the heavens;
> Let thy glory be above all the earth! —

when they occur the first time must be understood as an expression of resignation; when they come again they catch from the surrounding verses the tone of unfettered exultation. And perhaps the most complete illustration of this literary form is to be found in the third psalm. Here the usual change from distress to happiness appears to coincide with a variation in external surroundings between night and morning; brief as the poem is, it amounts to a miniature drama in two scenes.

Psalm iii

PSALM III

NIGHT

LORD, how are mine adversaries increased!
Many are they that rise up against me.
Many there be which say of my soul,
"There is no help for him in God."
But thou, O LORD, art a shield about me;
My glory, and the lifter up of mine head.
I cry unto the LORD with my voice,
And he answereth me out of his holy hill.

MORNING

I laid me down and slept;
I awaked; for the LORD sustaineth me.
I will not be afraid of ten thousands of the people,
That have set themselves against me round about.
Arise, O LORD; save me, O my God:
For thou hast smitten all mine enemies upon the cheek bone;
Thou hast broken the teeth of the wicked.
Salvation belongeth unto the LORD:
Thy blessing be upon thy people.

The term Dramatic Lyrics will cover another class of poems, which have a great literary interest, and are specially characteristic of the psalter. These contain two dramatic transitions instead of one; yet they present only a single moment. They open with a song of deliverance. Then the action passes backward in time to the trouble from which the speaker has been delivered; and this is presented dramatically in the actual words it evoked, as if the sufferer were quoting from himself. Then the poem returns to the point at which it started, and the triumph is renewed. The great illustration of this type is the twenty-seventh psalm.

Lyrics with Double dramatic Change

PSALM XXVII

opening triumph

The LORD is my light and my salvation; whom shall I fear?
The LORD is the strength of my life; of whom shall I be afraid?
When evil-doers came upon me to eat up my flesh,
Even mine adversaries and my foes, they stumbled and fell.
Though an host should encamp against me,
My heart shall not fear:
Though war should rise against me,
Even then will I be confident.
One thing have I asked of the LORD, that will I seek after:
That I may dwell in the house of the LORD all the days of my life,
To behold the beauty of the LORD, and to inquire in his temple.
For in the day of trouble he shall keep me secretly in his pavilion:
In the covert of his tabernacle shall he hide me;
He shall lift me up upon a rock.
And now shall mine head be lifted up above mine enemies round about me;
And I will offer in his tabernacle sacrifices of joy;
I will sing, yea, I will sing praises unto the LORD.

retrogression to the time of trouble

"Hear, O LORD, when I cry with my voice:
Have mercy also upon me, and answer me.
When thou saidst, 'Seek ye my face;' my heart said unto thee,
'Thy face, LORD, will I seek.'
Hide not thy face from me;
Put not thy servant away in anger:

> Thou hast been my help;
> Cast me not off, neither forsake me, O God of my salvation,
> For my father and my mother have forsaken me,
> But the LORD will take me up.
> Teach me thy way, O LORD,
> And lead me in a plain path,
> Because of mine enemies.
> Deliver me not over unto the will of mine adversaries:
> For false witnesses are risen up against me,
> And such as breathe out cruelty" —
>
> I had fainted, unless I had believed to see the goodness of   *return to*
>   the LORD   *triumph*
> In the land of the living.
> Wait on the LORD:
> Be strong, and let thine heart take courage;
> Yea, wait thou on the LORD.

There is no mistaking the sense of deliverance animating the opening section; this strain is abruptly resumed at the close; what then is more natural than to connect the intervening verses with the trouble to which the deliverance relates? No difficulty would have been felt had the middle verses of the poem been prefaced by the formula, "And I said —." But the omission of such introduction makes the whole more vivid and dramatic: it is like a substitution of direct speech for oblique. Some of those who do not recognise the structure I have described deal with the difficulties of the poem by dividing it, and insist that at verse seven a different psalm commences, the two having been made one by editors or transcribers. But it is difficult to see what there is in favour of such an explanation. No external evidence is suggested. No motive appears for thus putting together what, to the ordinary reader, seems separated by such a break. Moreover, the theory does not really solve the difficulty, since the transition from verse twelve to the close is as abrupt as the transition from verse six to verse seven. On the other hand, by the explanation here suggested, the breaks become part of the dramatic effect of the whole; and the psalm, instead of being treated as something accidental and exceptional, becomes one of a class of psalms which have as their common structure this double dramatic change.[1]

I have space for only one more of this class of dramatic lyrics; one that shows an interesting variation on the common type.

Psalm lxxxv The eighty-fifth psalm celebrates the deliverance of the nation from captivity. It has the usual opening triumph; it passes like the rest to the prayer in trouble; then, instead of a sudden return to the first tone, it has a transition stage, in which the poet pauses to wait for the answer to his nation's prayer;[2] the answer comes, and the final section is a burst of joy in which the recovered fatherland is beheld with a glory of transfiguration upon it.

PSALM LXXXV

opening triumph
LORD, thou hast been favourable unto thy land:
Thou hast brought back the captivity of Jacob,
Thou hast forgiven the iniquity of thy people,
Thou hast covered all their sin,
Thou hast taken away all thy wrath,
Thou hast turned thyself from the fierceness of thine anger.

---

[1] Besides the two described in the text the class includes *Psalm* cviii: its first five verses express the triumph, verses 6–12 are the prayer of the trouble [compare *Psalm* lx, where these very verses make part of the prayer on the occasion of the defeat that seems to have preceded the victory].—Again there is *Psalm* cxliv: it starts with ecstatic sense of deliverance; then verses 3–8 go back to the previous trouble, expressing the sufferer's confidence in God and scorn of the foe; from verse 9 to the end is the 'new song' inspired by the deliverance, the line of thought being obscured only by verse 11, which is however merely the repetition of the refrain (compare verses 7, 8) *parenthetically*, a common device in lyric poetry.

Psalm ix-x [which the acrostic structure shows to be a single poem] represents the same structural form *duplicated:* ix. 1-12, triumph; 13, 14, dramatic prayer of trouble; 15-20, return to triumph; x. 1-13, recurrence to dramatic prayer of trouble; 14-18, final resumption of triumph.

Psalm xxxi exhibits a similar duplication applied to the dramatic lyric with single change [1-6 trouble, 7-8 deliverance, 9-18 trouble, 19-24 deliverance]. Compare with both these last examples the pendulum movement (above, page 139).

[2] Compare the similar pause in *Habakkuk* ii. 1, and *Psalm* lxix. 22-9.

> "Turn us, O God of our salvation,   *retrogres-*
> And cause thine indignation toward us to cease.   *sion to*
> Wilt thou be angry with us forever?   *time of*
> Wilt thou draw out thine anger to all generations?   *trouble*
> Wilt thou not quicken us again,
> That thy people may rejoice in thee?
> Shew us thy mercy, O LORD,
> And grant us thy salvation."
>
> I will hear what God the LORD will speak: *transition-*
> For he will speak peace unto his people,   *al stage*
> And to his saints,
> But let them not turn again to folly.
>
> Surely his salvation is nigh them that fear him,   *return to*
> That glory may dwell in our land.   *triumph*
> Mercy and truth are met together;
> Righteousness and peace have kissed each other.
> Truth springeth out of the earth;
> And righteousness hath looked down from heaven.
> Yea, the LORD shall give that which is good;
> And our land shall yield her increase.
> Righteousness shall go before him;
> And shall make his footsteps a way to walk in.

Prayers, Meditations, and Monodies of Experience form a body of lyric poems considerable in amount, and familiar to the devotional reader. They call for little treatment in the present work, since their literary form is transparently simple. There are a few exceptions to this simplicity. In this section must be reckoned that *tour-de-force* of meditative ingenuity, the one hundred and nineteenth psalm. It is made up of no less than a hundred and seventy-six sayings, disposed on an acrostic arrangement, and bound together by the common feature that each verse contains some synonym for that which is the topic of the whole — the LAW. The beauty of the psalm is, however, largely lost to us by the neglect in our English versions of the alphabetical links.[1]

Prayers, Meditations, and Monodies of Experience

Psalm cxix

[1] See note on page 157.

One more poem may be mentioned. The fifty-third psalm is
a Meditation on Judgment of an elaborate type;
its transitions and fluctuations of form make it a
rhapsody in miniature. It opens with the much quoted line:

Psalm liii

> The fool hath said in his heart, There is no God!

It is hardly necessary to explain that this line does not predicate folly of the atheist; it has the converse meaning of ascribing atheism to the fool. It goes on to portray the 'fool,' or man of vicious life, as human nature gone bad and become 'filthy,' like rotten fruit. Then — perhaps with a faint reminiscence of Abraham and the destruction of Sodom — it calls up before our mind the picture of a Divine inspection of earth, and suggests the result that "not one" righteous man is to be found. Upon this follows the Divine surprise:

> Have the workers of iniquity no knowledge?
> Who eat up my people as they eat bread,
> And call not upon God.

A very dramatic stroke marks the next verse. It has been said that magnetic disturbances in the sun produce tempests on the earth: this might serve as an illustration for the subtle connection hinted here, whereby the wave of surprise that passes over the bosom of Deity becomes felt upon earth as a mysterious panic, striking the evil without visible cause, while the oppressed people of God catch the spirit of triumph and defiance.

> There were they in great fear, where no fear was:
> For God hath scattered the bones of him that encampeth against thee;
> Thou hast put them to shame, because God hath rejected them.

Here the psalm ends. But a postscript[1] seems to have been added by some age that looked in vain for the promised interposition of omnipotence: would that the salvation of Israel were indeed come out of Zion! The deliverance of the captive people of God would be such a triumph as has been pictured.

---

[1] Compare *Psalm* li; and possibly *Psalms* xxv, cxxx, xxxi. As to *Psalm* lxxxix, see page 149.

Last among our divisions of lyric poetry comes the type most familiar to the modern reader, the class of poems on set themes. The Bible, in common with a good deal of ancient literature, is at a disadvantage in regard to this kind of poetry, from the fact that its manuscripts do not furnish titles to such psalms. The reader who has not made the experiment would have little idea how much may be lost to modern lyrics if they be read without the author's titles. In the absence of these some prominent phrase at the commencement is apt to usurp the place of title, and often to give a false suggestion as to the drift of the whole. In the tables which make the Appendix to this work I have made it a point, wherever the particular class of literature admits of it, to affix such titles as may be collected from a careful study of the unity. *[margin: Psalms on Themes]*

Given the theme, the modes in which it is developed by the lyrics of the psalter do not differ from those of modern poetry. A topic may be sustained and kept before the mind by repetition, or multiplication of details. The psalm which might have for its title "The LORD thy Keeper," owes no small part of its effect to the reiteration of this word 'keep' in verse after verse. The psalm which proclaims "Man the Viceroy of God" sustains the thought in part by an enumeration of the orders of nature over which man has been made ruler. Or, to take another example, the "Hymn on God's House" (Psalm eighty-four) is a cluster of the thoughts which in the mind of a pious Israelite would be roused by the pilgrimages to Jerusalem. As the season of the feasts comes round, body and soul seem filled with a yearning after the courts of the LORD; the mystic force which in Spring leads the swallow to seek a nest for her young becomes to the worshipper the attraction that draws him towards his true home beside the altars of his God. Happiest they whose employment, however lowly, keeps them all the year round in the Temple service. Next happy are those *[margin: Repetition as a mode of lyric development; Psalm cxxi; Psalm viii; Psalm lxxxiv; 2-3; 4-5]* whose one passion in life are the sacred pilgrimages: the road to Zion runs through their heart. Imagination dwells on the happy journeys: on the lonely spots of the route converted into gaiety by the throng of travellers, like a desert's momentary flourishing beneath the brief spring showers; on the climbing of height after height, each a stage nearer the sacred goal; on Mount Zion itself, and the anointed people bowing before its God and Shield, and feeling streams of grace and glory descending upon it. A day in God's courts is more than a thousand days of life's routine.[1]

<small>6-7</small>

Imagery belongs to all kinds of lyric poetry alike. One remark may be made as to the use of it by the poets of the psalter. It is characteristic of them to crowd their images together in rapid succession; and such quick play of imagery sometimes is made to interchange with the development of a single image in full detail. I will give two illustrations of such interchange.

<small>Imagery as a mode of lyric development</small>

In the opening verses of the twenty-seventh psalm the images are so crowded together that there is danger of our losing them through their very exuberance. When all the suggestions lurking in word and phrase are pressed, the whole passage seems to call up visions of danger chasing one another as through the changes of a dream. The poet is desperately threading his way through pitchy blackness, with pitfalls all around him — when a sudden light shines, and all is clear: the LORD is that light. He is back again in the thick of his perils, he has actually stumbled — when he is suddenly caught up and supported: in that salvation he sees the LORD. Now he is being chased by the foe, and they are gaining upon him — when a stronghold unseen before opens its gates to him and he is safe: JEHOVAH is that stronghold of life, and of whom in future need he be afraid?

<small>Psalm xxvii. 1-6</small>

[1] I understand verses 8-12 as the actual prayer of the pilgrims, now arrived in the Temple, interrupted by the parenthesis of verse 10. Such a parenthetic interruption is highly characteristic of lyric triumph: a closely parallel case is *Judges* v. 12. See the arrangement of Deborah's Song, above, page 134.

The scene has changed and the crowd of his adversaries and foes, with dream-like horror taking the shape of beasts of prey, are rushing upon him; there is no escape, and already he can see the sharp teeth — when, lo, they stumble over hidden pitfalls and disappear from view:

> When evil-doers came upon me to eat up my flesh,
> Even mine adversaries and my foes, they stumbled and fell.

He is now in a solitary tower and countless hosts beleaguer him on all sides, yet he feels no doubt or fear; now an ambush of a whole army suddenly rises out of the ground, but he can only wonder how it comes that no tremor shakes him.

> Though an host should encamp against me,
> My heart shall not fear:
> Though war should rise against me,
> Even then will I be confident.

The various images have flitted past us like a succession of dream changes as the waking point is neared. And a transition like that from the fitful visions of sleep to the steady light of waking comes over the psalm as the poet passes on to the "one thing" he has desired of the LORD: this all-sufficing aspiration is for a life-long dwelling in the house of the LORD, in happy round of meditation and service, on a rock of security far above the disturbance of peril and trouble. This psalm then has illustrated the change from a rapid succession of images to a single sustained metaphor.

A similar transition, but in reverse order, marks the twenty-third psalm. This opens with the peaceful imagery of pastoral life drawn out to its furthest detail. *Psalm xxiii*

> The LORD is my shepherd; I shall not want.
> He maketh me to lie down in green pastures:
> He leadeth me beside the still waters.
> He restoreth my soul:
> He guideth me in the paths of righteousness for his name's sake.
> Yea, though I walk through the valley of the shadow of death,
> I will fear no evil; for thou art with me:
> Thy rod and thy staff, they comfort me.

Then the break comes, and a quick succession of varying images passes before us. In one line the image is that of a siege, and the poet is pressed by hunger — when, lo, a mystic table is before him, and the enemy looks on helpless and amazed. In the next line he is a festal guest, the sweet perfume is poured over him, and the wine of abundance is by his side. Again the imagery changes, and he sees goodness and mercy following him in his journeyings through life, as the streams of water followed the Israelites in the wilderness. Once more the thought changes to the Temple: other men may make their occasional pilgrimages, but he will be a dweller in the house of the LORD for ever.

An important topic for the expository critic is Concealed Imagery. It is possible for a metaphorical idea to be sustained throughout the whole of a poem or lengthy passage, and yet not to be embodied in distinct words; the image must be collected from a variety of indirect references, while to miss it is to lack the key to the whole. Such Concealed Imagery will explain some of the most difficult parts of the Bible.

Concealed Imagery

It has been, for example, well suggested that the idea underlying the eighty-second psalm is that of a hierarchy of world-rulers, such as the 'Sons of God' mentioned in the prologue to *Job*. We see in the latter poem how one of them can interfere in the guidance of human events, always of course with the Divine permission; and the suggestion of the plural is that there are many. It is supposed by Professor Cheyne that a scene like the prologue to *Job* underlies this eighty-second psalm, the 'gods,' 'sons of the Most High,' being such spiritual world-rulers; that it is these, and not earthly judges, who are the objects of the Divine remonstrance, and they are held responsible for the corruption of mankind which they have failed to prevent. Only upon such a supposition does the conclusion become intelligible.

Psalm lxxxii

I said, Ye are gods,
And all of you sons of the Most High:
Nevertheless ye shall die like men,
And fall like one of the princes.

The supernatural Powers who have neglected their office are threatened with degradation to the rank of men with the doom of mortality.[1]

No doubt the suggestion of Concealed Imagery is an uncertain weapon of interpretation, and one which leaves much room for the fancy of an individual expositor. It is therefore with diffidence that I suggest the application of it [Psalm xc] to a poem which is amongst the most familiar psalms of the psalter, but which leaves on my own mind an impression different from that ordinarily associated with it. To many readers the ninetieth psalm is known as part of the Service for the Burial of the Dead: it comes therefore to be connected with thoughts of gloom and bereavement. But the language justifying that use of it is confined to one part of the psalm; when the whole is studied it is found to take a wider range. If the total play of thought and details of imagery in this poem be put together, the resultant appears to me to fit in with a Hymn of Mountain Sunrise.

Let the reader fix in his imagination the mountain scenery that would surround one who has made his dwelling-place in the deserts of the Holy Land. He has awoke in the midst of a dreadful solitude, with the break of day at hand. Monotony of rocky landscape stretches in every direction; here are heaps of shingle and crumbling dust, there deep clefts wrapped in blackest shadow; the scantiest vegetation may be seen in the crannies, or shows greener at the margin of the torrent that rushes down by his side. He watches through the last phase of the night, and feels the solemn mystery attaching to these impalpable changes of time, and the passage of day into day. The sun rises, and the stony desert becomes a mirror to reflect its brilliance; soon the light has penetrated to the lowest depth of every cleft, and the landscape glows like a furnace; the grass by the torrent's side, which had bloomed for a moment in the morning freshness, has already begun

---

[1] The same image will be found to underlie the fifty-eighth psalm (see marginal readings of R. V.).

to droop and wither. But the dominant sensation is still the unbroken solitude of his mountain dwelling, which has thus watched day pass into day without change since the very foundation of the world. Suddenly his thoughts rise to a higher plane in the contemplation of a vaster changelessness, which has been a home for Israel, and has endured through a succession, not of day into day, nor generation into generation, but of everlasting into everlasting.

> Lord, thou hast been our dwelling place
> In all generations.
> Before the mountains were brought forth,
> Or ever thou hadst formed the earth and the world,
> Even from everlasting to everlasting, thou art God.

It is an eternity like this that makes divisions of time and succession of human generations appear so feeble; the thought of them can find vent only in a chain of images drawn from all that is around the poet. God turns man "into crumbling dust," *verse 3 (margin)* like the débris he sees before him; a thousand years in his sight are but "as yesterday when it passeth" into to-day, as the watch of the night he had felt so *verse 4 (margin)* brief; the generations of men rush past like this torrent flood by his side; they drop as lightly as sleep fell from him when the dawn awoke him; they are like the grass beside the torrent flood, which he had just seen bloom in the *verse 5* morning's freshness, and which is already withering in the glare of the day. Verily the Divine anger is a scorching sun which lays bare all iniquity, which pours light upon the most secret sins as this sun's rays are illuminating the *verses 7-8* deep clefts that were so dark in the shadows of morning. And under wrath like this the "days of our years" are being brought to an end — "like a tale that is told." This striking phrase has been traditionally understood as comparing human life to a story, — in itself an exquisite idea. But, in the absence of any indication from the original (for the Hebrew word is obscure), surely the context obliges us to understand the other sense of the word 'tale': the years pass as swiftly as if they were but being counted — one, two, three, four, . . . up to seventy; or if it be eighty, yet the ten years so proudly achieved are ten years of labour and sorrow. But this meditation on swiftly passing years is suddenly brought to a noble climax:

> So teach us to number our days,
> That we may get us an heart of wisdom.

Now the whole spirit of the psalm changes, and another class of associations come to the front: the freshness of morning, and its irresistible suggestion of repentance and a new start, of casting trouble and affliction behind like the night that is past, and looking to the future as a day of glory.

> Return, O LORD; how long?
> And let it repent thee concerning thy servants.
> O satisfy us in the morning with thy mercy;
> That we may rejoice and be glad all our days.
> Make us glad according to the days wherein thou hast afflicted us,
> And the years wherein we have seen evil.

The thought is carried forward with the concealed image of sunrise and day beneath it. The work which God works for his people shall "appear" — like the sun mounting above the horizon, and so "the beauty of the LORD their God shall be upon them." And a final association with morning — the zest for work it brings — closes the psalm:

> Establish thou the work of our hands upon us;
> Yea, the work of our hands, establish thou it.

The psalm is thus seen to be made up of three sections. The last gives a prominent place to the phrase "in the morning," and is filled with morning thoughts of repentance, of change from a dark past to a bright future, of beauty shed upon God's people from above, of security for the work of the hands. The middle section has the one thought of succession — succession of days, of generations; and this is in one verse expressly associated with the image of yesterday passing into to-day. Through both these sections, then, the idea of morning is present. The first section brings forward mountains and the framework of earth as enduring things to be contrasted with the greater eternity of their Creator; while all the images used are such as would form part of a mountain landscape. When the whole poem is put together, then, it will seem that, while its subject is "Life as a passing Day," the setting of the thought is the concealed imagery of a mountain sunrise.

We have thus considered imagery, repetition, enumeration, as modes by which a theme can be developed in lyric poetry. There is one other mode, simpler still: that of Contrast. Previous chapters have alluded to the contrast of the Heavens above and the Law within which makes the subject of the nineteenth psalm; and again to the Supreme Evil and the Supreme Good which stand contrasted in the thirty-sixth. But it seems specially appropriate in this work, and at this point of it, to mention the first psalm, which stands as preface to the whole lyrical poetry of Scripture. It celebrates the man,

Contrast as a mode of development

Psalm i

> Whose delight is
> In the Law of the LORD:
> And in his Law
> Doth he meditate day and night.

No one will understand the word 'Law' in its narrow modern sense; when fully weighed, the expression 'the Law of the LORD' will seem not very different from what is conveyed to a modern ear by the term 'Sacred Scriptures.' The first psalm may be said to bestow a blessing on the literary study of the Bible. The thought of this prefatory psalm is worked out by Contrast. The theme is stated in the form of a contrast; the Meditative Life is made antithetical to another type of life, not necessarily vicious, but one that looks in other directions than the Law of the LORD for the counsels by which it shall walk: — in modern phraseology, the Worldly Life. This double theme is illustrated by an exquisite piece of contrasted imagery. The Worldly Life is compared to "the Chaff which the wind driveth away": airy, not ungraceful motion of that which is mere outside without substance, carried round by forces from without. Over against this is set the rooted Tree, drawing perpetual sustenance from the water streams, moving harmoniously through its season of leafage and fruit. Then the contrast is carried forward to that which is the dominant thought of Biblical poetry — 'the judgment.' There is no denunciation or detailed prophecy; but the psalmist is assured that the empty life "shall not stand in the judgment." And on the other hand, no particular blessing is invoked upon "the way of the righteous": it is enough that "the LORD knoweth it."

CHAPTER VIII

LYRIC IDYL: 'SOLOMON'S SONG'

THE poem which is the subject of the present chapter affords a good illustration of the principle underlying this work, — that clear knowledge of the outer literary form is an essential for a thorough grasp of the matter and spirit of literature. That *Solomon's Song* is dialogue of a dramatic character, with a story underlying it, must be recognised by all; but when we go beyond this we find commentators divided, one set holding the poem to be a drama, the other an idyl. Those who consider it a drama are in substantial agreement as to its plot: that the Shulammite is wooed by King Solomon with offers of regal splendour, that she remains faithful to her humbler Shepherd lover, that in the end King Solomon gives way and the faithful lovers are united. The other interpretation, as followed in this chapter, identifies Solomon himself with the humble lover. The whole story now becomes this: that King Solomon, visiting his vineyard upon Mount Lebanon, comes by surprise upon the fair Shulammite maiden; she flees from him, and he visits her disguised as a Shepherd and wins her love; then he comes in state to claim her as his queen; they are being wedded in the Royal Palace when the poem opens. Now, whichever of these interpretations be correct, it is clear that the technical question as between drama and idyl involves a fundamental difference in the story of the poem.

I believe that the divergence of interpretation in the present case is largely due to the fact that, while Drama is a thing familiar to all, few have considered the extent to which the development of Lyric Idyl can be carried.[1] It may be admitted at once that the traditional masters of the Idyl, such as Theocritus and Virgil, have given us nothing that in dramatic elaborateness approaches *Solomon's Song*. But the fine arts are all one family, and the development which may stop short in pure poetry may be carried forward in the sister art of music. Speaking roughly, we may say that the difference between Drama and Lyric Idyl is the difference between Opera and Oratorio; and most of the peculiar structural features of *Solomon's Song* are such as will be readily intelligible to the student of dramatic music.

Distinction of Lyric Idyl from Drama

It is necessary to see exactly what is involved in the difference between the dramatic form and the form of lyric idyl. In the first place, it is inevitable in drama that the order of incidents should tally with the order of speeches representing them. In narrating a story, it is easy to mention a catastrophe and then go back in time to the circumstances which brought that catastrophe about. But drama is pure presentation, and its action can never go back; hence the necessity in Ancient Tragedy, which dramatised only the end of a story, of lyric choral odes to bring out by narrative important incidents that happened earlier than the opening scene. In a lyric idyl, on the contrary, the story is not acted, but assumed and alluded to; and allusion can be made to the different parts of the story in any order. A pure dramatisation of a love story would begin (say) with the first meeting of the lovers, would proceed with the cir-

(1) Incidents may be alluded to in any order

---

[1] The word 'Idyl' is diminutive of the Greek *eidē*, the term for the various *forms* of poetry. Thus the Idyl did not appear in our table of Literary Forms, because it may be a slighter variation of any of them: the slightness being traditionally supposed to consist in the nature of the subject matter,—personal love, domestic life, etc. As an interesting example of the traditional conception appearing in modern art, it may be pointed out that Wagner's *Siegfried* is an elaborate and massive musical drama: but when the composer takes the themes of this opera and interweaves them with an old cradle song to make a birthday serenade to his wife in honour of their infant son, he calls it the *Siegfried Idyl*.— In the Bible *Ruth* is an Epic Idyl, *Solomon's Song* a Lyric Idyl.

cumstances of their growing intimacy, and end with their marriage. But the series of idyls making *Solomon's Song* commences with the wedding day, goes back to the day of betrothal and reminiscences of the courtship, and then goes forward to what in modern parlance might be called the close of the honeymoon.

Again, in a drama every speech must be referred to personal speakers, either an individual or a Chorus. But lyric poetry, in addition to these, can make use of a Reciting Chorus, which is impersonal, and merely the author's device for carrying on the story in the parts not represented dramatically. Thus in Mendelssohn's *Elijah*, the Chorus is sometimes personal, as where it presents the Priests of Baal crying, "O Baal, hear us"; in other cases it is impersonal, as where it is used to describe the fire falling from heaven, or to point the moral in the chorale, "Cast thy burden upon the Lord." So in the present case, we have both a personal Chorus of Daughters of Jerusalem who escort the Bride, and a merely abstract Chorus used to describe the journey of Solomon in his state chariot. Another consideration is worth mentioning in this connection. Every speech in a drama must be spoken in a definite place or 'scene': but this Reciting Chorus is, on the contrary, used as a device for suggesting transition from one scene to another.

(2) the Reciting Chorus

As a third feature of the Lyric Idyl may be mentioned the refrains. Refrains in lyric poetry always may be, and usually are, parenthetic; they must not be attached to their context, but referred to the poem as a whole. A simple modern ballad will narrate a story, — how, for example, the spectre of a lover comes to claim his mistress, how she responds to his summons, and is borne to a distant land, where she is found dead on his tomb. The verses containing this narrative will be continually interrupted by the refrain:

(3) parenthetic refrains

— Sing hey, sing ho, the linden tree —

These words have no point in relation to the sentences to which they are attached, but very likely interrupt their grammatical construction. On the other hand, the idea of the wind singing through the trees makes an effective background to be kept present in the mind through the whole of a story of weird incident. Such refrains may be compared to the musical accompaniment heard continuing the strains of a song during the intervals between the spoken verses. In the present case there are three refrains which, wherever they occur, must be separated from the dialogue. In their subject they are just suited to keep before us the general spirit of the whole poem. In one, there is a call upon all to leave the lovers to their repose.

> *I adjure you, O daughters of Jerusalem,*
> *By the roes, and by the hinds of the field,*
> *That ye stir not up, nor awaken love,*
> *Until it please.*

ii. 7: compare iii. 5 and viii. 4

The second is, in its various forms, the mutual pledge.

> *My beloved is mine, and I am his:*
> *He feedeth his flock among the lilies.*

ii. 16: compare vi. 3 and vii. 10

The third is the summons to embrace.

> *Until the day break, and the shadows flee away,*
> *Turn, my beloved, and be thou like a roe or a young hart*
> *Upon the mountains of separation.*

ii. 17: compare iv. 6 and viii. 14

Love strains like these are the essence of the whole poem, and are naturally used to separate the idyls from one another, or mark the natural divisions of each.

I have yet to mention something specially characteristic of this poem, which is readily intelligible as a feature of a lyric idyl. We find incidents conveyed dramatically by dialogue which, nevertheless, cannot be part of the scene in which they occur, but must, at that point, (4) dramatised reminiscences
be a reminiscence. Such an effect may be called a Dramatised Reminiscence. Thus it is part of the story as here interpreted that Solomon, when the Shulammite damsel had fled from him at

his first appearance, continued his suit to her in the disguise of a Shepherd. She wonders who this stranger is, so different from the shepherds she knows.

i. 7
> Tell me, O thou whom my soul loveth,
> Where thou feedest thy flock,
> Where thou makest it to rest at noon:
> For why should I be as one that wandereth
> Beside the flocks of thy companions?

He of course seeks to evade her scrutiny by a vague answer.

i. 8
> If thou know not, O thou fairest among women,
> Go thy way forth by the footsteps of the flock,
> And feed thy kids beside the shepherds' tents.

Such a detail in itself is natural enough in a love story. But the point of the present suggestion is that the position of the speeches just quoted — in the wedding scene — is perfectly intelligible. It is natural that the Shulammite, when for the first time she beholds her royal lover in the splendour of his palace, should allude to her former attempt to penetrate his disguise. And it is equally natural that the allusion should take the form of recalling the actual words used by each: they are merely quoting their former selves, a thing which we have already seen as a tendency of the dramatic lyrics in the psalter.[1] Or, to take another instance, it is natural for the king in his musings on his bride to recall the moment of their first meeting. The sudden surprise of the courtly escort at the rustic maiden's beauty is conveyed in the form of a speech.

vi. 10
> Who is she that looketh forth as the morning,
> Fair as the moon,
> Pure as the sun,
> Terrible as an army with banners?

Her startled feelings as the royal cortege surprised her are expressed as if they had been spoken.

[1] See above, page 180.

>I went down into the garden of nuts,   vi. 11
>To see the green plants of the valley,
>To see whether the vine budded,
>And the pomegranates were in flower.
>Or ever I was aware, my soul set me
>Among the chariots of my princely people.

It is natural to follow up this with the cry to the damsel to stop.

>Return, return, O Shulammite;   vi. 13
>Return, return, that we may look upon thee.

Then will be expressed her uneasiness at the gaze, whether spoken at the time or not.

>Why will ye look upon the Shulammite;
>As upon the dance of Mahanaim?

All this is not a dialogue taking place at point of the poem where the words occur, but the form of dialogue thrown over the sensation of an emphatic moment, recalled as a reminiscence by the king in the midst of his meditations on his queen. It belongs naturally to the free movement of lyric poetry between meditation and dramatic presentation; and resembles the common device in narrative of a sudden change from indirect to direct narration.[1]

Keeping these points of literary form before us, we may follow the poem as a Suite of seven Idyls. The first presents the Wedding Day, its personages being the King, the Bride, and her escort, the Chorus of Daughters of Jerusalem. It opens with the decisive moment of the ceremony when the Bride is being lifted over the threshold; it proceeds with the conversation inside the palace; then we have the procession from the banqueting house to the bridal chamber; and the closing refrain leaves the lovers to their repose.

Solomon's Song as a Suite of Seven Idyls

i. 1–ii. 7

---

[1] The Dramatised Reminiscence may be conveniently represented to the eye by inverted commas.

The second idyl is given up to the Bride's Reminiscences. She recalls a visit of her lover in the fair springtide, and how they were interrupted. She tells a happy dream of seeking her lover abroad and finding him. And these two reminiscences are separated by refrains.

ii. 8-iii. 5

The third idyl goes back to the Day of Betrothal. The Reciting Chorus describe the journey of King Solomon in his chariot of state. He has already won the Shulammite's love, but now he is to throw off his disguise and claim her as his queen. His outpourings of love follow, and her acceptance; then the Chorus which opened this third idyl closes it by invoking a blessing on the happy pair.

iii. 6-v. 1

The fourth in this 'song of songs' is occupied with a troubled Dream of the Bride. She fancies her beloved comes to her door in the night; she delays but a moment to adjust her dress and dip her fingers in the myrrh, and by that moment's waiting she loses him, and wanders in vain to find him. By an exquisite touch of dream change she finds herself (in her dream) accosting the Chorus of Daughters of Jerusalem, and in dialogue with them discusses the beauty of her lover, until the loss with which this fourth song began is forgotten in the triumphant refrain of the close.

v. 2-vi. 3

The fifth idyl belongs to the royal Bridegroom. Its opening and close are musings on the beauty of his bride; the two parts are separated by the dramatised reminiscence of the first moment of their meeting.

vi. 4-vii. 9

The last two songs introduce a beautiful piece of simple human nature. The Bride amid the splendour of the palace longs for her home on Lebanon, and in the sixth song persuades her husband to journey to this place where their love was first pledged. Accordingly, the scene of the last idyl has changed to Lebanon. A few words of the Reciting Chorus bring out the arrival of the pair;—the words sound like a brief echo from their description of the former journey made in state. Renewal of love follows in this the Bride's home. Then

vii. 10-viii. 4 and viii. 5-14

comes a very natural touch: the Bride, in this spot where she grew up from infancy, recalls the riddling speeches her Brothers used to make to her when she was too young to understand the mysteries of love. She then makes a fresh surrender of her heart, with a quaint conceit founded on the circumstance that her husband is (in modern phrase) the 'landlord' of this home of herself and brothers. The voices are heard of the Escort approaching to conduct them back; so with a final embrace the poem closes.

I am about to cite the whole poem with an arrangement intended to make it easy for the general reader to follow. One more prefatory remark is necessary. This is a poem of pure conjugal love.

> There are threescore queens,
>   And fourscore concubines,
>   And virgins without number:
> My dove, my undefiled is but one.

Nevertheless, a reader who is not prepared for it may be startled by the amatory warmth of the phraseology. Partly this is due to the more passionate nature of oriental peoples. But partly it connects itself with the symbolism of Hebrew poetry, which enables it to take liberties impossible to our direct western speech. There is a famous passage at the close of *Ecclesiastes* which makes the disagreeable symptoms of old age graceful by throwing over them a symbolic veil. The same treatment in the poem under consideration softens the warmth of amatory speech. The enraptured gaze of the Bridegroom bending over his Bride at the feast is disguised as a "banner of love" waving over her. The sweet surrender of the maiden to her spouse is symbolically put: *(ii. 4)*

> They made me keeper of the vineyards; *(i. 6)*
> But mine own vineyard have I not kept!

She does not in plain terms clasp her lover to her bosom, but the refrain bids him to be as a roe "on the mountains of separation." The Bible consecrates everything it touches; *(ii. 17)* and the fact is not without significance that the great Honeymoon Song of all literature should be given to us in the Sacred Scriptures.

[marginalia: Amatory language]

THE SONG OF SONGS

i. 1-ii. 7

Idyl I

THE WEDDING DAY

1

Outside the Palace

The Bridal Procession approaches: the Royal Bridegroom leading the Bride, followed by an Attendant Chorus of Daughters of Jerusalem

THE BRIDE

Let him kiss me with the kisses of his mouth:
   For thy love is better than wine;
   Thine ointments have a goodly fragrance;
   Thy name is as ointment poured forth:
Therefore do the virgins love thee.

A pause is made at the threshold of the Palace

THE BRIDE (*to the Bridegroom*)

Draw me —

ATTENDANT CHORUS

We will run after thee.

The Bridegroom lifts the Bride across the threshold

THE BRIDE

The king hath brought me into his chambers.

ATTENDANT CHORUS.

We will be glad and rejoice in thee,
We will make mention of thy love more than of wine.

THE BRIDE

In uprightness do they love thee.

2

Inside the Palace

The Bride addresses her Attendant Chorus

THE BRIDE

I am black, but comely,
O ye daughters of Jerusalem,
As the tents of Kedar,
As the curtains of Solomon.
Look not upon me, because I am swarthy,
Because the sun hath scorched me.
My mother's sons were incensed against me,
They made me keeper of the vineyards;
But mine own vineyard have I not kept!

The Bride and Bridegroom converse: Dramatised Reminiscence of their Courtship: how she sought to penetrate his disguise and he answered mysteriously

"THE BRIDE

"Tell me, O thou whom my soul loveth,
"Where thou feedest thy flock,
"Where thou makest it to rest at noon:
"For why should I be as one that wandereth
"Beside the flocks of thy companions?"

"THE BRIDEGROOM

"If thou know not, O thou fairest among women,
"Go thy way forth by the footsteps of the flock,
"And feed thy kids beside the shepherds' tents."

3

The Procession from the Banqueting House to the Bridal Chamber

THE BRIDEGROOM

I have compared thee, O my love,
To a steed in Pharaoh's chariots.
Thy cheeks are comely with plaits of hair,
Thy neck with strings of jewels.
We will make thee plaits of gold
With studs of silver.

The Bride

While the king sat at his table,
My spikenard sent forth its fragrance.
My beloved is unto me as a bundle of myrrh,
That lieth betwixt my breasts.
My beloved is unto me as a cluster of henna-flowers
In the vineyards of En-gedi.

The Bridegroom

Behold, thou art fair, my love; behold, thou art fair;
Thine eyes are as doves.

The Bride

Behold, thou art fair, my beloved, yea, pleasant:
Also our couch is green.
The beams of our house are cedars,
And our rafters are firs.
I am a rose of Sharon,
A lily of the valleys.

The Bridegroom

As a lily among thorns,
So is my love among the daughters.

The Bride

As the apple tree among the trees of the wood,
So is my beloved among the sons.
I sat down under his shadow with great delight,
And his fruit was sweet to my taste.
He brought me to the banqueting house,
And his banner over me was love.
Stay ye me with raisins, comfort me with apples:
For I am sick of love.
Let his left hand be under my head,
And his right hand embrace me.

REFRAIN

*I adjure you, O daughters of Jerusalem,
By the roes, and by the hinds of the field,
That ye stir not up, nor awaken love,
Until it please.*

Idyl II

THE BRIDE'S REMINISCENCES OF THE COURTSHIP

1

How her lover came to her in the Springtide, and they were interrupted

The Bride

The voice of my beloved! behold, he cometh,
Leaping upon the mountains, skipping upon the hills.
My beloved is like a roe or a young hart:
Behold, he standeth behind our wall,
He looketh in at the windows,
He sheweth himself through the lattice.
My beloved spake, and said unto me,

" Rise up,
    My love,
    My fair one,
And come away.
For, lo, the winter is past,
The rain is over and gone;
The flowers appear on the earth;
The time of the singing of birds is come,
And the voice of the turtle is heard in our land;
The fig tree ripeneth her green figs,
And the vines are in blossom,
They give forth their fragrance.
    Arise,
    My love,
    My fair one,
And come away.
O my dove,
That art in the clefts of the rock,
In the covert of the steep place,
Let me see thy countenance,
    Let me hear thy voice;
    For sweet is thy voice,
And thy countenance is comely."

VOICES OF THE BROTHERS (*heard interrupting*)

"Take us the foxes,
"The little foxes that spoil the vineyards;
"For our vineyards are in blossom."

REFRAINS

*My beloved is mine, and I am his:
He feedeth his flock among the lilies.*

*Until the day break, and the shadows flee away,
Turn, my beloved, and be thou like a roe or a young hart
Upon the mountains of separation.*

2

Her happy Dream of seeking him abroad and finding him

By night, on my bed,
    I sought him whom my soul loveth:
    I sought him, but I found him not.
I said, I will rise now, and go about the city,
In the streets and in the broad ways,
    I will seek him whom my soul loveth:
    I sought him, but I found him not.
The watchmen that go about the city found me:
To whom I said, Saw ye him whom my soul loveth?
It was but a little that I passed from them,
    When I found him whom my soul loveth:
    I held him, and would not let him go,
Until I had brought him into my mother's house,
And into the chamber of her that conceived me.

REFRAIN

*I adjure you, O daughters of Jerusalem,
By the roes, and by the hinds of the field,
That ye stir not up, nor awaken love,
Until it please.*

Idyl III

THE DAY OF BETROTHAL

iii. 6–v. 1

1

King Solomon comes in State

Reciting Chorus

Who is this that cometh up out of the wilderness
Like pillars of smoke,
Perfumed with myrrh and frankincense,
With all powders of the merchant?
    Behold, it is the litter of Solomon;
    Threescore mighty men are about it,
    Of the mighty men of Israel.
    They all handle the sword, and are expert in war:
    Every man hath his sword upon his thigh,
    Because of fear in the night.

    King Solomon made himself a palanquin
    Of the wood of Lebanon.
    He made the pillars thereof of silver,
    The bottom thereof of gold,
    The seat of it of purple,
    The midst thereof being inlaid with love from the daughters of
        Jerusalem.
Go forth, O ye daughters of Zion, and behold King Solomon,
With the crown wherewith his mother hath crowned him
In the day of his espousals,
And in the day of the gladness of his heart.

2

King Solomon pours forth his love to the Shulammite damsel

King Solomon

Behold, thou art fair, my love; behold, thou art fair;
Thine eyes are as doves behind thy veil:
Thy hair is as a flock of goats,

    That lie along the side of Mount Gilead.
Thy teeth are like a flock of ewes that are newly shorn,
    Which are come up from the washing;
    Whereof every one hath twins,
    And none is bereaved among them.
Thy lips are like a thread of scarlet,
And thy mouth is comely.
Thy temples are like a piece of a pomegranate
    Behind thy veil.
Thy neck is like the tower of David builded for an armoury,
    Whereon there hang a thousand bucklers,
    All the shields of the mighty men.
Thy two breasts are like two fawns that are twins of a roe,
    Which feed among the lilies.

REFRAIN

Until the day break, and the shadows flee away,
I will get me to the mountain of myrrh,
And to the hill of frankincense.

3

King Solomon (under the symbolic expression of an enclosed garden) proposes marriage to the Shulammite damsel, and she (using the same symbolism) accepts

KING SOLOMON

Thou art all fair, my love;
And there is no spot in thee.
Come with me from Lebanon, my bride,
With me from Lebanon:
Go from the top of Amana,
From the top of Senir and Hermon,
From the lions' dens,
From the mountains of the leopards.
Thou hast ravished my heart, my sister, my bride;
Thou hast ravished my heart
    With one look from thine eyes,
    With one chain of thy neck.
How fair is thy love, my sister, my bride!

How much better is thy love than wine!
And the smell of thine ointments than all manner of spices!
Thy lips, O my bride, drop as the honeycomb:
Honey and milk are under thy tongue;
And the smell of thy garments is like the smell of Lebanon.

A garden shut up is my sister, my bride;
    A spring shut up,
    A fountain sealed.
Thy shoots are an orchard of pomegranates,
    With precious fruits;
    Henna with spikenard plants,
    Spikenard and saffron,
    Calamus and cinnamon, with all trees of frankincense,
    Myrrh and aloes, with all the chief spices.
Thou art a fountain of gardens,
    A well of living waters,
    And flowing streams from Lebanon.

The Shulammite

Awake, O north wind; and come, thou south;
Blow upon my garden, that the spices thereof may flow out.
Let my beloved come into his garden,
And eat his precious fruits.

King Solomon

I am come into my garden, my sister, my bride:
    I have gathered my myrrh with my spice;
    I have eaten my honeycomb with my honey;
    I have drunk my wine with my milk.

Reciting Chorus

Eat, O friends;
Drink, yea, drink abundantly of love!

Idyl IV

THE BRIDE'S TROUBLED DREAM

Her troubled Dream that her beloved came to her at night, and by a moment's delay she lost him

The Bride

I was asleep, but my heart waked:
It is the voice of my beloved that knocketh, saying,

"Open to me,
  My sister, my love,
  My dove, my undefiled:
For my head is filled with dew,
My locks with the drops of the night."

I have put off my coat; how shall I put it on?
I have washed my feet; how shall I defile them?

My beloved put in his hand by the hole of the door,
And my heart was moved for him.
I rose up to open to my beloved;
And my hands dropped with myrrh,
And my fingers with liquid myrrh,
Upon the handles of the bolt.
I opened to my beloved;
But my beloved had withdrawn himself and was gone.
My soul had failed me when he spake:
I sought him, but I could not find him;
I called him, but he gave me no answer.
The watchmen that go about the city found me,
They smote me, they wounded me;
The keepers of the walls took away my veil from me.

(In her Dream she finds herself accosting a Chorus of Daughters of Jerusalem)

I adjure you, O daughters of Jerusalem,
  If ye find my beloved,
That ye tell him, that I am sick of love.

Chorus

What is thy beloved more than another beloved,
    O thou fairest among women?
What is thy beloved more than another beloved,
    That thou dost so adjure us?

The Bride

My beloved is white and ruddy,
The chiefest among ten thousand.
    His head is as the most fine gold,
    His locks are bushy, and black as a raven.
    His eyes are like doves beside the water brooks;
    Washed with milk, and fitly set.
    His cheeks are as a bed of spices, as banks of sweet herbs:
    His lips are as lilies, dropping liquid myrrh.
    His hands are as rings of gold set with beryl:
    His body is as ivory work overlaid with sapphires.
    His legs are as pillars of marble, set upon sockets of fine gold:
    His aspect is like Lebanon, excellent as the cedars.
    His mouth is most sweet: yea, he is altogether lovely.
This is my beloved, and this is my friend,
O daughters of Jerusalem.

Chorus

Whither is thy beloved gone,
    O thou fairest among women?
Whither hath thy beloved turned him,
    That we may seek him with thee?

The Bride

My beloved is gone down to his garden,
    To the beds of spices,
To feed in the gardens,
    And to gather lilies.

REFRAIN

I am my beloved's, and my beloved is mine:
He feedeth his flock among the lilies.

Idyl V

vi. 4–vii. 9   THE KING'S MEDITATION ON HIS BRIDE

1

The King muses on her Beauty

THE KING

Thou art beautiful, O my love, as Tirzah,
   Comely as Jerusalem,
   Terrible as an army with banners.
Turn away thine eyes from me,
For they have overcome me.
Thy hair is as a flock of goats
   That lie along the side of Gilead.
Thy teeth are like a flock of ewes,
   Which are come up from the washing;
   Whereof every one hath twins,
   And none is bereaved among them.
Thy temples are like a piece of a pomegranate
   Behind thy veil.
There are threescore queens,
   And fourscore concubines,
   And virgins without number:
My dove, my undefiled, is but one;
   She is the only one of her mother;
   She is the pure one of her that bare her.
The daughters saw her, and called her blessed;
Yea, the queens and the concubines, and they praised her.

2

The Surprise of the first meeting. A dramatised Reminiscence

"THE ROYAL PARTY"

" Who is she that looketh forth as the morning,
" Fair as the moon,
" Pure as the sun,
" Terrible as an army with banners?"

"The Shulammite

"I went down into the garden of nuts,
"To see the green plants of the valley,
"To see whether the vine budded,
"And the pomegranates were in flower.
"Or ever I was aware, my soul set me
"Among the chariots of my princely people."

"The Royal Party

"Return, return, O Shulammite;
"Return, return, that we may look upon thee."

"The Shulammite

"Why will ye look upon the Shulammite,
"As upon the dance of Mahanaim?"

3

The King continues to muse upon his Bride's Beauty

The King

How beautiful are thy feet in sandals, O prince's daughter!
The joints of thy thighs are like jewels,
The work of the hands of a cunning workman.
Thy navel is like a round goblet,
   Wherein no mingled wine is wanting:
Thy belly is like an heap of wheat
   Set about with lilies.
Thy two breasts are like two fawns that are twins of a roe.
Thy neck is like the tower of ivory;
Thine eyes as the pools in Heshbon, by the gate of Bath-rabbim;
Thy nose is like the tower of Lebanon which looketh toward Damascus.
Thine head upon thee is like Carmel,
And the hair of thine head like purple;
The king is held captive in the tresses thereof.
How fair and how pleasant art thou,
O love, for delights!

This thy stature is like to a palm tree,
And thy breasts to clusters of grapes.
I said, I will climb up into the palm tree,
I will take hold of the branches thereof:
Let thy breasts be as clusters of the vine,
And the smell of thy breath like apples;
And thy mouth like the best wine,
That goeth down smoothly for my beloved,
Gliding through the lips of those that are asleep.

REFRAIN

*I am my beloved's,
And his desire is toward me.*

vii. 10-viii. 4

Idyl VI

THE BRIDE'S LONGING FOR HER HOME ON LEBANON

THE BRIDE

Come, my beloved, let us go forth into the field;
Let us lodge in the villages.
Let us get up early to the vineyards;
Let us see whether the vine hath budded,
    And the tender grape appear,
    And the pomegranates be in flower:
There will I give thee my love.
The mandrakes give forth fragrance,
And at our doors are all manner of precious fruits,
    New and old,
    Which I have laid up for thee, O my beloved.

Oh, that thou wert as my brother,
That sucked the breasts of my mother!
When I should find thee without, I would kiss thee;
Yea, and none would despise me.
I would lead thee, and bring thee into my mother's house,
  That thou mightest instruct me.
I would cause thee to drink of spiced wine,
  Of the juice of my pomegranate.
His left hand should be under my head,
And his right hand should embrace me.

Refrain

*I adjure you, O daughters of Jerusalem,
That ye stir not up, nor awaken love,
Until it please.*

Idyl VII

viii. 5-14

THE RENEWAL OF LOVE IN THE VINEYARD OF LEBANON

I

The arrival

Reciting Chorus

Who is this that cometh up from the wilderness,
Leaning upon her beloved?

King Solomon

Under the apple tree I awakened thee:
There thy mother was in travail with thee,
There was she in travail that brought thee forth.

The Bride

Set me as a seal upon thine heart,
    As a seal upon thine arm:
For love is strong as death;
    Jealousy is cruel as the grave:
The flashes thereof are flashes of fire,
    A very flame of the LORD.
Many waters cannot quench love,
    Neither can the floods drown it:
If a man would give all the substance of his house for love,
    It would utterly be contemned.

2

The Bride recalls the riddling speeches of her Brothers when she was a child: she understands them now

The Bride

" We have a little sister,
" And she hath no breasts:
" What shall we do for our sister
" In the day when she shall be spoken for?
" If she be a wall,
" We will build upon her a turret of silver:
" And if she be a door,
" We will inclose her with boards of cedar."
I was a wall, and my breasts like the towers thereof:
Then was I in his eyes as one that found peace.

3

The Bride renews her vows to her husband in this the home of her childhood: Solomon shall be the landlord of her heart as he is the landlord of her home

The Bride

Solomon had a vineyard at Baal-hamon;
    He let out the vineyard unto keepers;
    Everyone for the fruit thereof was to bring a thousand pieces of silver.
My vineyard, which is mine, is before me:
    Thou, O Solomon, shalt have the thousand,
    And those that keep the fruit thereof two hundred.

The Escort heard approaching to conduct them back from Lebanon: a final embrace

King Solomon

Thou that dwellest in the gardens,
The companions hearken for thy voice:
Cause me to hear it.

The Bride

Make haste, my beloved,
And be thou like to a roe or to a young hart
Upon the mountains of spices.

BOOK THIRD

BIBLICAL HISTORY AND EPIC

CHAPTER	PAGE
IX. EPIC POETRY OF THE BIBLE	221
X. BIBLICAL HISTORY IN ITS RELATIONS WITH BIBLICAL EPIC	244

CHAPTER IX

EPIC POETRY OF THE BIBLE

It has often been said that there is no Epic Poetry in the Bible. This opinion seems to me to be founded on a double mistake. In part it is a relic of a discarded system of criticism that did much to distort the study of literature, and at one time went to the extent of pronouncing Shakespeare no dramatist:—the criticism which assumed the masterpieces of Greek and Latin literature to be the only literary standards. Of course, those who have formed their conception of Epic solely on the *Iliad* and *Odyssey* will look in vain for poems resembling these in the Bible. Again, in many minds epic poetry is associated with fiction; and to classify any portion of Sacred Scripture as epic will to such persons appear a mode of saying that it is untrue. But this is an entire misapprehension of the term. It is one thing to say that creative poetry is not, like history and philosophy, tied to reality; it is quite another thing to say that its matter may not be real. Creative poetry is a treatment which can be applied alike to fact, to idealised fact, and to purely imaginative matter.

In our examination of fundamental literary forms,[1] we found that the term 'Epic' implied just two things: narrative, in contrast with dramatic presentation, and creative treatment, in contradistinction to discussion. Now more than half the Bible consists of narrative. The question, then, of Epic Poetry in the Bible narrows itself to this: whether the whole of Biblical narrative is to be classified as

The question of Epic Poetry in the Bible

---

[1] Above, page 109.

history, or does any part of it make just that appeal to our emotions and artistic sense which is made by the epic poems of secular literature? Let a reader set himself to read continuously the *Book of Genesis*. He will feel that different parts of what he is reading affect his literary sense in different ways. At one time he finds himself traversing long genealogical lists, or noting brief accounts of migrations; he moves through generations or centuries of time in a few verses. He reaches (suppose) the name of Joseph: and at once all is changed. Ten lengthy chapters — in bulk equal to one-fifth of the whole *Book of Genesis* — centre around this one man and his relations with his brethren. From the beginning a striking personality begins to emerge, which even in childhood divides the household between envy and doting affection, which makes itself felt in captivity and even in prison. In the background we get glimpses of varied life — scattered settlements of shepherds, merchant caravans, palace life in the empire of Egypt. Mutation of fortune, which plays so large a part in story, is represented by the change which in a single day takes Joseph from prison to set him next to the throne; and throughout the movement of events the supernatural interest of dreams and their mystical revelations has been hovering. When among the crowds that come from distant lands to ask corn from this Egyptian potentate Joseph's own brethren stand before him, recognised but not recognising, then we have just one of those ironic situations which make the masterstrokes of plot. And no invented plot could draw more out of such a situation than we get in this piece of history, with the long-sustained perplexities in which the Egyptian minister involves his family, not for the purpose of some subtle revenge, but to prolong the strange situation in which he finds himself placed, and the conflict of emotions in his breast between natural affection and sense of wrong. At last Joseph breaks down in the part he is playing, and has to sob out that he is their brother; and when the excitement has had time to subside, the train of events settles

The distinction of Epic and History illustrated from Genesis

to a sedate conclusion in the picturesque migration of the sons of Israel into Egypt, and the patriarchal blessing bestowed on Pharaoh himself. We continue our reading, and find ourselves tracing, in bare outline, economic changes comprised in a verse or two which needed generations of time to be accomplished in fact. It is impossible for any one, reading with his literary sense awakened, not to feel the difference of kind between the account of Joseph and his Brethren and other portions of the *Book of Genesis* preceding and following it : this is the difference between Epic and History. Joseph, it is true, is an important historic personage, and it is no novel that we have been reviewing. But a single chapter would have been sufficient to present the sons of Jacob as a link in the chain of history; what more there is in the narrative must be credited to interest of story. The exact classification of this portion of *Genesis* is expressed by the term 'Epic Incident'; it is an Incident because it is a portion of the history; it is Epic because the treatment of it touches the imagination and emotions in the regular way of creative poetry.

The historical books of the Bible are full of such Epic Incidents. But they are merged in the history of which they are a part, without anything to mark them off from the surrounding matter which is purely historic. I must not be thought to insist upon trifles if I recommend the student — with the aid of the Tables in the Appendix to this work,[1] or otherwise — to pencil off in his Revised Version the epic matter, and to write in the margin a title to each portion. I believe that an important factor in literary appreciation is the expectant attitude of the reader; and one who has, in the way I suggest, adjusted his mental focus from the outset, will be in a specially favourable situation for feeling the epic richness of Sacred Scripture.

When we turn to survey the field of Biblical Epic, one phenomenon attracts our attention at once, as being unique, **No Verse Epic in** yet not difficult to understand. In secular litera- **the Bible** ture the most famous epics are in verse. In the Bible there is no

[1] Tables II, III.

verse narrative.[1] But we have seen that the distinction of prose and verse is not at all coincident with the distinction between poetry and its antithesis. Again, we have seen that it is one of the distinguishing features of Hebrew that its verse and prose systems overlap. When these two considerations are put together, it will appear a natural thing that the epic incidents which are scattered through the historical books should gravitate to the literary form of the history in which they constitute a minor part.

But though the Bible has no Verse Epic, it contains illustrations of the interesting literary form that may be called the Mixed Epic, in which a story is conveyed in prose, but has the power of breaking into verse at suitable points.[2] The grand example of this Mixed Epic is the Story of Balaam.

Mixed Epic

The Old Testament is specially interesting where it lifts the veil which separates the Chosen People from the rest of the world, and allows us to see worshippers of Jehovah outside the ranks of the Israelites. Such was Balaam. But he seems to have been a light shining in a dark place: surrounded by those who could not understand the worship of an invisible God, yet felt the atmosphere of spiritual power that Balaam carried about with him, and came to look upon it with awe, as a thing to be dreaded or to be secured on their own side. Such a conception of Balaam had been formed by Balak, king of Moab: "I know that he whom thou blessest is blessed, and he whom thou cursest is cursed." He bethinks him of the prophet when confronted with a new danger threatening his kingdom: danger from a people moving through the desert at once prolific and highly organised, threatening to swallow up the Moabites "as the ox licketh up the grass of the

The Story of Balaam Numbers xxii-xxiv

---

[1] Of course, in the lyric narratives of Chapter V the narrative is not being told or conveyed, but assumed and meditated on.

[2] In early literature of story this form had a wide range. See a note on the 'cantifables' in Mr. Jacobs's *English Fairy Tales*, page 240. In modern poetry this form is admirably represented by William Morris's *Roots of the Mountains* and *House of the Wolfings*.

field." So Balak sends an embassy of princes to Balaam, "with the rewards of divination in their hand." The central interest of this, as of most epics, is the personality of its hero. The character of Balaam seems to be summed up in calling him a man of compromise in spiritual matters. Perfectly sincere in his worship of Jehovah, he nevertheless desires to keep in touch with those who can only translate his spiritual religion into gross and material conceptions. He has laid down for himself a compromise: he will never be unfaithful to a distinct Divine word, — and in fact to this he never is unfaithful, — but where not prohibited he will go as far as he can with the world about him, and make all he can out of them. This is the man to whom the embassy of Balak comes. He lodges the Moabite princes with oriental hospitality; and in the darkness of the night he gives himself up to the spiritual influences from which he is wont to seek guidance. The revelation comes, apparently in the form of dream; and on the morrow Balaam dismisses his visitors without hesitation: his God will not suffer him to obey the summons.

To Balak all this seems no more than a diviner's artifice to increase his consequence. He accordingly sends a second embassy, more princes and more honourable, with an urgent message and unbounded offers. Balaam receives this second embassy with noble words, which his subsequent conduct showed to be no idle boast: "If Balak would give me his house full of silver and gold, I cannot go beyond the word of the LORD my God, to do less or more." But he lodges the ambassadors for the night. Whether or not his spirit was clouded by the prospects held out to him, the revelation of that night's dream appeared to wear an air of compromise: he would accompany the embassy, but with the distinct understanding that he should speak only as his God should direct him.

So we have the famous journey of Balaam to Moab. Mystic hindrances stop his way, until he would fain turn back. But from the lips of the angel he receives the words of his own compromise: he must go, but speak only as he is bidden. At a border city the king of Moab meets the prophet, and chides him for his delay. But Balaam is strong in the line of action he has laid down for himself: "Lo, I am come unto thee: have I now any power at all to speak anything? the word that God putteth in my mouth that shall I speak." Nevertheless he will go as far as he can: by his direction the preliminary ritual is commenced, the seven altars erected, and the seven bullocks and rams offered in due form by the princes of Moab. Balaam himself ascends "a bare height" to be alone in communion with his God, while the king and princes stand by the altars; and from the high ground where all this is taking place the whole length and breadth of the Israelitish encampment is visible in the desert below. Amid the influences of the solitude and the spectacle beneath him Balaam feels the rush of inspiration coming upon him; in the simple phrase of Scripture, God "put a word in his mouth." He returns to confront the king and princes; and at this point the prose of narrative gives place to the rhythmic verse which is to convey the Divine message.

> From Aram hath Balak brought me,
> The king of Moab from the mountains of the East:
> "Come, curse me Jacob,
> And come, defy Israel."
>
> How shall I curse, whom God hath not cursed?
> And how shall I defy, whom the LORD hath not defied?
> For from the top of the rocks I see him,
> And from the hills I behold him:
> Lo, it is a people that dwell alone,
> And shall not be reckoned among the nations.
> Who can count the dust of Jacob,
> Or number the fourth part of Israel?
> Let me die the death of the righteous,
> And let my last end be like his!

The king and princes are overwhelmed with confusion: the prophet summoned to curse has altogether blessed the enemy! But Balaam calmly answers, "Must I not take heed to speak that which the LORD putteth in my mouth?"

To Balak only one explanation seems possible: the prophet in his ecstatic state has been overawed by the vastness of the enemy's forces. The desired end must be secured by cunning. Balaam shall be taken to a point from which only a corner of the Israelitish camp is visible; enough, according to magic lore, to lodge a curse upon, but too small to affect the beholder's nerves. The man of compromise goes as far as he can with popular superstition; he accompanies the king and his suite to the heights of Pisgah, he gives orders for the renewal of the sacrifices, and himself goes apart, with some faint idea of persuading Jehovah into returning an oracle in conformity with his prophet's material interests. But no sooner is Balaam alone with his God than the unreality of the whole proceeding makes itself felt by him; his soul is strung up to its true level as he returns to face the Moabites. A second time the poem breaks from prose into verse.

> Rise up, Balak, and hear;
> Hearken unto me, thou son of Zippor:
>
> God is not a man, that he should lie;
> Neither the son of man, that he should repent:
> Hath he said, and shall he not do it?
> Or hath he spoken, and shall he not make it good?
> Behold, I have received commandment to bless:
> And he hath blessed, and I cannot reverse it.
> He hath not beheld iniquity in Jacob,
> Neither hath he seen perverseness in Israel:
> The LORD his God is with him,
> And the shout of a king is among them.
> God bringeth them forth out of Egypt;
> He hath as it were the strength of the wild-ox.
> Surely there is no enchantment against Jacob,
> Neither is there any divination against Israel:
> At the due season shall it be said of Jacob and of Israel,
> What hath God wrought!
> Behold, the people riseth up as a lioness,
> And as a lion doth he lift himself up:
> He shall not lie down until he eat of the prey,
> And drink the blood of the slain.

"Neither curse them at all, nor bless them at all!" But Balaam has only one answer: all that the LORD speaketh he must do.

At all hazards another attempt must be made. Even Balak has begun to understand that there is some real power restraining Balaam; but if the prophet will accompany him to a third point of view, "peradventure it will please God" that the enemy shall be cursed from thence. The instinct of compromise carries Balaam to this third ceremony, but he has no heart to play his ignoble part to its conclusion. He does not, as before, go aside to meditate his answer, but listlessly turns his face towards the wilderness. It happens that from where he is standing his eye just catches the long lines of tents stretching, row after row, with the regularity that distinguished the highly organised Israelites from the tumultuous hordes of desert nomads. The divine principle of order sinks deep in Balaam's soul, and inspires his song as he turns to face for a third time the king and princes of Moab.

> Balaam the son of Beor saith,
> And the man whose eye is opened saith:
> He saith, which heareth the words of God,
> Which seeth the vision of the Almighty,
> Falling down, and having his eyes open:
>
> How goodly are thy tents, O Jacob,
> Thy tabernacles, O Israel!
> As valleys are they spread forth,
> As gardens by the river side,
> As lign-aloes which the LORD hath planted,
> As cedar trees beside the waters.
> Water shall flow from his buckets,
> And his seed shall be in many waters,
> And his king shall be higher than Agag,
> And his kingdom shall be exalted.
> God bringeth him forth out of Egypt;
> He hath as it were the strength of the wild-ox:
> He shall eat up the nations his adversaries,
> And shall break their bones in pieces,
> And smite them through with his arrows.
> He couched, he lay down as a lion,

And as a lioness; who shall rouse him up?
Blessed be every one that blesseth thee,
And cursed be every one that curseth thee.

The Moabite king storms with rage and disappointment, and dismisses the prophet with a sneer: "The LORD hath kept thee back from honour." But instead of quailing before the royal indignation, Balaam forces Balak to endure another outpouring of prophetic inspiration, as he beholds a star arising out of Jacob, before which Moab shall be smitten, and the sons of tumult shall be broken down; his eye traverses the horizon and sees one people after another involved in the coming destruction; not the Kenites in their rocks, nor Amalek first of nations, shall be able to resist.

Alas, who shall live when God doeth this?

Then Balaam returns to his country, and the Epic of Balaam is concluded. But Balaam does not disappear from the history; and we learn how the man of compromise was caught in the meshes of his own compromising spirit.[1] At some time when the spiritual enlightenment was not upon him he brought himself to give the counsel that the people, who were too strong to be conquered by force, might yet be undermined by lust. Lustful intercourse led in its turn to war; and the name of Balaam the son of Beor appears in the list of the slain.

Apart from the question of prose or verse as its medium of expression, Epic Poetry may be classified according to degrees of organic completeness.[2] In secular literature there are, from this point of view, three forms of epic. There is the simple, isolated story, usually called a 'Ballad.' Then there is the 'Cycle' or aggregation of separate stories attributed to the same hero: an Achilles cycle, or Ulysses cycle. Finally there is the weaving of a multiplicity of incident into one organic plot, as when the genius of an individual poet makes out of the Achilles cycle an *Iliad*, or out of the cycle

Classification of Epic Poetry

[1] Compare *Numbers* xxxi. 8, *Revelation* ii. 14.
[2] Compare throughout Table III in Appendix II.

of Ulysses an *Odyssey*. It is to the last only that the term 'Epic' is usually applied. Biblical Epic exhibits analogies to all three types. The simple independent Story is exemplified by such an incident as that of Cain and Abel in primitive history, or in later history by the Story of Gideon or Jephthah. Again, great part of *Genesis* is occupied with Cycles of Stories attaching to the names of the great patriarchs, — an Abraham cycle, a cycle of Jacob, and others. And the Story of Joseph and his Brethren has already been used to illustrate the complete Epic History, with its wide reach of incidents bound together into one organic whole.

(1) **Epic Stories**
(2) **Epic Cycles**
(3) **Epic Histories**

The most elaborate of these Epic Histories is the *Book of Esther*. This, in addition to every other element of interest, has what may be called a double plot: two distinct trains of events, centring around Esther herself and Mordecai respectively, are woven together into a complex story. The opening of the book plunges us into the life and manners of an oriental empire, with its hundred and twenty-seven provinces of varying races and speech, its government by irresponsible despotism, and its court etiquette, the violation of which is punishable with death. We have a picture of festivities on a scale proportionate to the empire itself — pageantry lasting half a year, and for climax a continuous feast of seven days. The king's drunken impulse to send for Queen Vashti to appear before his lords, her refusal and solemn deposition from the throne, and the elaborate preparations for choosing a successor which end in the elevation to the crown of a Jewish maiden Esther, are detailed with minuteness. The general effect of this introductory part is to make an oriental atmosphere for the reader's mind, by which he is the better able to appreciate all that follows.

The Book of Esther

The movement of the story begins with the mention of Haman. Despotism is never so despotic as when it takes a private subject and elevates him to its own rank, demanding for him, by no title but that of royal favour, the homage which is paid to the king by prescriptive right. Such elevation was accorded by Ahasuerus to Haman: and the whole empire obediently bowed down. A single individual was found to resist: the Jew Mordecai, who had made his kinswoman and adopted daughter a queen, but for himself was content to watch over her from a distance, as one of those who sat in the king's gate. Officials of the court sought in vain to move Mordecai, and at last had to make his stubborn resistance known to Haman. The offended favourite " thought scorn to lay hands on Mordecai himself": nothing less would satisfy his oriental spirit of vengeance than to destroy the whole people to which Mordecai belonged throughout the empire of Ahasuerus. To make the destruction more dramatic, a day is chosen by lot for simultaneous slaughter. To the king Haman uses two arguments: the diversity of the Jews in laws and customs from all other peoples, and the treasure of silver he will himself pay into the king's treasury if his petition be granted. But Haman is at the height of favour with the king, who bids him take the people and the silver too. The complex machinery of the empire is set in motion, and despatches sent in every direction. Then, we are told, " the king and Haman sat down to drink, but the city of Shushan was perplexed."

We have been following one side of the story; but the other centre of interest, Queen Esther, is involved in the conspiracy thus set on foot; and the mourning of Mordecai and the city soon makes the Queen aware of the peril hanging over her people, for whom there seems to be no help but through herself. There is something very attractive to the imagination in the situation in which Esther is thus placed. The strongest and most mature of men will feel his nature tasked to its depths by a summons to rest his life and all upon a single crisis. But such a summons comes in this case to a girl, in beauty found fairest after an empire has been searched, in the first flush of her youth, with life just opening before her as a vista of softness and luxury. Her momentary hesitation only makes her seem more human. But when the extremity of the crisis is urged upon her, with the suggestion that she may have come to the kingdom for such a time as this, she nerves herself to her task. First she gives herself up to fasting and prayer; then, with all signs of fear suppressed, she presents herself in full splendour of beauty and royal state before the king, well knowing that she may incur thereby the penalty of death. For a moment the fate of her nation and herself trembles in the balance: then the sceptre is held out to her and the perilous moment is past. Here it is that the character of Esther begins to come out. It might well have been expected that, in the reaction from personal danger, Esther might have at once cast herself before the king, and with sobs and cries told the affliction of her people. This is probably what Mordecai meant her to do. But a girl has been raised up to save her people, and she must do it in her own girlish way; and accordingly, when she is asked her petition and request unto the half of the kingdom, the answer reveals no court intrigue, but a simple childlike invitation that the king and Haman may come to a banquet that she will prepare. Ahasuerus is delighted: he had deposed Vashti for refusing his summons to an orgie, her successor is one to risk her life on an invitation to a banquet. The enemy is disarmed from suspicion. But, more than all this, Esther knows well that she has to fight against the whole power of Haman and the king with no weapon but that of her own beauty: instinct makes her realise that she must give that beauty full opportunity to make itself felt.

The banquet takes place, with the king and Haman as the sole guests. Though she had been crowned as the fairest in the kingdom, yet for thirty days before this the charms of Esther had been entirely forgotten by the royal voluptuary amid other distractions of pleasure. Now the dominion of beauty can make its sway prevail over Ahasuerus, and at the end of the feast he again asks his Queen what is her petition and request. But Esther is strong enough to wait, and make surety yet more sure. She begs therefore for a second banquet on the morrow with the same two guests, and by that time she will have a boon to ask. Haman leaves the palace at the height of blind security. In the gate his spirits feel a rebuff at the sight of the unbending Mordecai: a first speck of shadow upon his horizon of fortune. He hurries home, and in family council details his accumulated honours and his one drop of bitterness. They bid him build a gallows fifty cubits high, and ask Mordecai's life at once without waiting for the slower fate of his nation.

Two days and the night that separates them make up the period of crisis for this story of Esther. The turning-point of the whole is found in the words: "On that night could not the king sleep." They read to the restless king the chronicles of his kingdom; and the particular passage details how a conspiracy against his life was revealed by one Mordecai, a Jew. Ahasuerus enquires what honour has been done to this Mordecai in recompense; and hearing that nothing has been done, the king will take up the matter at once. Haman is entering in the early morning to beg the life of the Jew, who refuses to bow down before him, when the king shouts to him from his bed the question, "What shall be done unto the man whom the king delighteth to honour?" It is impossible for Haman to understand this otherwise than as a salutation to himself; and in reply advises a royal progress with a chief prince to proclaim before the fortunate man the king's purpose to honour him. He is bidden to carry out his advice without omission of a single article upon Mordecai. So bitterly has nemesis swung round upon him that Haman is forced with his own lips to proclaim the honours of his hated foe. And when, after the ordeal is over, he rushes home to his family council for comfort, here, where he feels most secure, he is forced to see the shadow of doom deepening over him; for his wife and councillors make answer:

> If Mordecai, before whom thou hast begun to fall, be of the seed of the Jews, thou shalt not prevail against him, but shalt surely fall before him.

But before he has time to ponder these words the royal escort summons him to Esther's banquet.

The second banquet intensifies the effect of the first, and Ahasuerus is completely under the spell of Esther's beauty when, for the third time, he asks her to name her petition and request. The youthful queen has been all this time holding a crisis of history in her delicate fingers. Now she lets the thunderbolt fall. Her petition is her own life, and the life of her people, sold, to the king's damage, by "this wicked Haman." The stricken favourite grovels before the king's burst of fury, and is seeking the injured Jewess as an intercessor, when he is hurried away to the gallows he had prepared for Mordecai. The crisis is past, and Mordecai is elevated to the dignity from which his foe had fallen. But there is still the decree against the Jews throughout the empire, enrolled among the laws of the Medes and Persians that cannot be altered, and the date of their doom is steadily advancing. Mordecai's plan is to send another decree after the first, to the effect that the Jews on the day appointed shall have full power to defend themselves. So when the day of fate arrives, this is the situation throughout the hundred and twenty-seven provinces of the empire: on one side are the enemies of the Jews armed with the king's irreversible decree to massacre them; on the other side are the Jews armed with the king's irreversible decree to defend themselves; and the satraps and princes of the provinces will know which side to take in the fray now that a Jew is minister of the empire. It becomes a day of slaughter for the enemies of the Jews throughout the provinces and the royal city; and our last sight of Esther reveals her as a beautiful incarnation of vengeance, petitioning for another day of slaughter. But this is the passing excitement of the crisis, the passionate justice of one trained in the law of retaliation. When the ordinary current of events is resumed, a feast is instituted throughout the villages and towns of the Jews, in which they are to send portions one to another and gifts to the poor, as they commemorate their nation saved from destruction by the wisdom of Mordecai and the beauty of Esther.

So far the literature we have treated has been Epic Poetry in the strictest sense. There are, however, two other types to be noted. The Idyl is not a distinct literary form, but a modification of other forms; and the Bible contains an Epic Idyl as well as a Lyric Idyl.[1]   *Modifications of Epic*
Again, the great department of Prophecy has one branch which is specially connected with Epic Poetry.

If the chief distinction of the Idyl be its subject matter of love and domestic life, then in all literature there is no more typical Idyl than the *Book of Ruth*. Following the *Book of Judges*, which has been filled with bloodshed   *Epic Idyl: The Book of Ruth*
and violence and the heroism of the sterner virtues, it comes upon us like a benediction of peace. It contains no trace of war or high politics; the disasters of its story are the troubles of family life — exile, bereavement, poverty; while its grand incidents are no more than the yearly festivities of country life, and the formal transfers of property that must go on although kingdoms rise and fall.

The thread running through the whole, and binding the parts together, is found in a magnetic personality such as may exist in the quietest life, leaving no achievements behind it, yet in its time swaying all who approach it. Elimelech the husband, and his two sons, are no more than names to us; it is Naomi who is remembered in Bethlehem when the family have been long in exile; and when she returns, the whole of the rural city is moved at the thought of the 'Pleasant One' — the famous beauty of former years — come back again. Naomi herself feels the bitter irony of a name that speaks of attractiveness: "Call me not Naomi, call me Mara, for the Almighty hath dealt very bitterly with me." Three waves of trouble had passed over her since she had wedded the husband of her youth. First came famine: Elimelech's land would yield no living, and husband, wife, and two youthful sons had to migrate into the land of Moab, where exile meant not only change of climate and people, but isolation in religion, with wor-

[1] See above, note on page 195.

shippers of strange gods all around. There they continued to live until Elimelech died, and Naomi was left alone to watch over her growing sons. She must, moreover, in this land of strangers find wives for these youths ; for to live over again in posterity was the only immortality to which in their daily thoughts the families of Israel would give much heed. Ten years of such life was allowed to Naomi, and then the third blow came with the loss of her two sons, one after another, while no children had yet been born to continue their line. Broken by misfortunes, and with no link now to bind her to her Moabitish home, Naomi sets out to return to the land of Judah. Her daughters-in-law, though of foreign race, yet have felt the spell of her attraction, and would fain accompany her ; but she will not involve their young lives in the dark fate which heaven seems to have marked out for herself : " It grieveth me much for your sakes, for the hand of the LORD is gone forth against me." Situations like this make the dividing points of character ; and a contrast of character is fully depicted to us in the simple verse : " And Orpah kissed her mother-in-law ; but Ruth clave unto her." The strong and sweet Naomi has bound to herself another character like her own, with a bond no trouble can break ; and the musical speech of Ruth has descended to us as the formula of personal devotion for all time.

> Intreat me not to leave thee, and to return from following after thee : for whither thou goest, I will go ; and where thou lodgest, I will lodge : thy people shall be my people, and thy God my God : where thou diest, will I die, and there will I be buried : the LORD do so to me, and more also, if aught but death part thee and me.

So the ageing Naomi and her Moabite daughter-in-law return to Bethlehem, and, after creating a momentary flutter of excitement, settle down to a life of obscure poverty, with the added bitterness to Naomi of seeing the family estate in the hands of others.

Now the interest of the idyl changes to the picturing of popular manners and customs. We have before us all the bustle and excitement of wheat and barley harvest in an agricultural community: the progress of the reapers, and the maidens gleaning behind them, the common meal in the heat of the day, the master coming down to look on and exchanging greetings with his people. We see the stranger shyly joining the gleaners, the story of her faithfulness known to all from the humblest reaper to Boaz himself. With a strange charm there come to us across the gulf of centuries the delicate attentions shown to Ruth by all, the little contrivances by which she is made to glean plentifully without knowing who has befriended her, the place of honour accorded her at the meal. No detail of social life is too petty for the idyl, not even the way in which Ruth eats her portion of food till she is sufficed, and what she leaves she brings to her lonely mother-in-law at home. The gloomy day of Naomi's life is to have light at eventide, and the first gleam of that light is the name of the master who has been so hospitable: Boaz is recognised as one near of kin, and Naomi rallies herself to the task of seeking a resting-place for the loving Ruth.

More manners and customs follow, and those of the quaintest. Ruth follows exactly the instructions of Naomi in going through the strange ritual by which she must claim the wealthy and powerful landowner as next of kin. The story is not too short to prevent our catching the tenderness with which Boaz shields the stranger from the breath of gossip, nor the refined courtesy by which he treats the great service asked of him as a favour done to himself: "Blessed be thou of the LORD, my daughter: thou hast showed more kindness in the latter end than at the beginning, inasmuch as thou followedst not young men, whether poor or rich." The scene changes to give us the minutiæ of legal procedure in the gate of the city; and here again contrast of character appears, between the nameless kinsman who is ready to do everything that is just, and Boaz, who will go further and be generous. So, with all formalities, the land of Elimelech is redeemed, and Boaz takes Ruth to wife, in order that, according to the interesting Hebrew law, the child born to them may be considered to have revived the line of his grandfather. The long delayed happiness of Naomi becomes full as the women of the city move in procession to lay the new-born babe in her bosom, and sing to her how his name shall be famous in Israel: "and he shall be unto thee a restorer of life, and a nourisher of thine old age: for thy daughter-in-law, which loveth thee, which is better to thee than seven sons, hath borne him." And the simple Idyl in its last words joins itself on to the main stream of history by telling that this new-born Obed was the father of Jesse, and Jesse was the father of King David himself.

It remains to point out that Biblical Prophecy, including as it does all literary forms, has one branch which is in character epic. The Greater and Minor Prophets, whose books of prophecy occupy so large a proportion of the Old Testament, all date from a period not earlier than the reign of Jeroboam the Second. Yet before that period, from the time of Samuel if not earlier, prophets played a great part in the history of Israel and Judah. No name in the roll of prophets will seem higher than that of Elijah: yet the Bible contains no 'Book of the Prophet Elijah.' These earlier prophets did not write their prophecy; they lived it. It was conveyed in action, and its only representation in literature is the narrative of that action. A fit name then for such literature is 'Epic Prophecy.'

Epic Prophecy

(1) Prophetic Stories

This Epic Prophecy exhibits all the three types of Epic. Of the isolated Prophetic Story there can be no better illustration than the Story of Balaam, already treated in full. Prophetic Cycles are connected with the names of Elisha and of Daniel. The former is particularly well marked, occupying seven successive chapters with fourteen stories, disconnected from one another, but all having Elisha for hero. The element of miracle is common to them all. Some seem to have no point beyond this interest of miracle: such are the Story of the Mocking Children, of the Feeding of a hundred men, of the Axe-head that swam. Others are deeply interesting pictures of life,

(2) Prophetic Cycles

Cycle of Elisha
II Kings ii-viii

like the Story of Naaman and Gehazi, or the Siege of Samaria. One of these is so impressive in the suggestiveness of its miraculous details, and the lofty plane of morality to which its conclusion rises, that I cannot forbear from citing it in full as the very ideal of Prophetic Story.

The Expedition to arrest Elisha

Now the king of Syria warred against Israel; and he took counsel with his servants, saying, In such and such a place shall be my camp. And the man of God sent unto the king of Israel, saying, Beware that thou pass not such a place; for thither the Syrians are coming down. And the king of Israel sent to the place which the man of God had told him and warned him of; and he saved himself there, not once nor twice. And the heart of the king of Syria was sore troubled for this thing; and he called his servants, and said unto them, Will ye not show me which of us is for the king of Israel? And one of his servants said, Nay, my lord, O king: but Elisha, the prophet that is in Israel, telleth the king of Israel the words that thou speakest in thy bedchamber. And he said, Go and see where he is, that I may send and fetch him. And it was told him, saying, Behold, he is in Dothan. Therefore sent he thither horses, and chariots, and a great host: and they came by night, and compassed the city about. And when the servant of the man of God was risen early, and gone forth, behold, an host with horses and chariots was round about the city. And his servant said unto him, Alas! my master, how shall we do? And he answered, Fear not: for they that be with us are more than they that be with them. And Elisha prayed, and said, LORD, I pray thee, open his eyes, that he may see. And the LORD opened the eyes of the young man; and he saw: and, behold, the mountain was full of horses and chariots of fire round about Elisha. And when they came down to him, Elisha prayed unto the LORD, and said, Smite this people, I pray thee, with blindness. And he smote them with blindness according to the word of Elisha. And Elisha said unto them, This is not the way, neither is this the city: follow me, and I will bring you to the man whom ye seek. And he led them to Samaria. And it came to pass, when they were come into Samaria, that Elisha said, LORD, open the eyes of these men, that they may see. And the LORD opened their eyes, and they saw; and, behold, they were in the midst of Samaria. And the king of Israel said unto Elisha, when he saw them,

My father, shall I smite them? shall I smite them? And he answered, Thou shalt not smite them: wouldest thou smite those whom thou hast taken captive with thy sword and with thy bow? set bread and water before them, that they may eat and drink, and go to their master. And he prepared great provision for them: and when they had eaten and drunk, he sent them away, and they went to their master. And the bands of Syria came no more into the land of Israel.

There is a third type of Epic Prophecy analogous to the Epic Histories which combine a multiplicity of incidents into an organic whole. The Bible contains two such Prophetic Epics, connected with the two names of Elijah the Tishbite and Jonah.

(3) Prophetic Epics

The *Book of Jonah* is contained amongst the books of the Minor Prophets, yet every reader feels how different it is from all the rest. Nahum and Jonah alike received a commission to denounce Nineveh: Nahum gives us the usual prophetic discourse; the other book contains no discourse, but describes the actions of Jonah precisely as certain chapters in the *Book of Kings* describe the actions of Elijah. There is another peculiarity of Jonah. With other prophets to hear is to obey. But the *Book of Jonah* narrates the rebellion of the prophet against the Divine mandate even more fully than it describes his obedience. If such a narrative is correctly described as Epic Prophecy it will follow that the resistance of Jonah, no less than his obedience, will contain the revelation which it is the province of Prophecy to impart. This seems to be the key to the interpretation of the book.

The Book of Jonah

The prophecy opens with the command to go to Nineveh and denounce it. "But Jonah rose up to flee unto Tarshish from the presence of the LORD." In picturesque detail we have the embarking at Joppa, the "great wind hurled into the sea," the terror of the mariners, each calling on his god. Jonah, waked from sleep, recognises the power of Jehovah pursuing him, and humbly bows to his fate. However reluctantly, the mariners are at last driven to cast him overboard. While for them the storm ceases,

Jonah is miraculously swallowed up — the detail of the miracle is of no significance — and in no less miraculous manner restored. The first part of the book ends with his song of thanksgiving.

This series of incidents contains a revelation that may seem elementary to us, but was unquestionably needed by the times of the prophet. I have before had occasion to speak of the primitive conception of Deity by which a god was regarded as a territorial being, whose power was limited by the region in which he was worshipped. That this conception extended to the age of Jonah is clear from a verse in the *Book of Kings*, which tells how the servants of the king of Syria [I Kings xx. 23] said of the Israelites, "Their god is a god of the hills; therefore they were stronger than we: but let us fight against them in the plain, and surely we shall be stronger than they." In this prophecy the same notion appears in the way the mariners — no doubt varying in race and country — call each upon his god; it appears still more strikingly in the accession of terror brought to them amid the tossing of the waves by Jonah's saying that his God was the creator of land *and sea*. Nay, the same idea is seen to have affected the prophet himself. No doubt Jonah was blessed with a higher revelation of God. But the history of all religions makes it plain that the acceptance of a higher conception does not so far obliterate older conceptions but that they can influence conduct at times. And it is clear that the old notion of God as the God of a particular land was moving Jonah's purposes when he set out for the far west "from the presence of Jehovah." Waking to the tempest, he recognised Jehovah's power as extending through heaven, and the sea, and the dry land; and the double miracle wrought upon himself of judgment and deliverance brought this revelation to its climax.

The narrative continues. A second commission is immediately obeyed, and Jonah journeys through the vast city, crying, "Yet forty days, and Nineveh shall be overthrown." Like an account of some infection spreading through a great centre of population reads the description of the city of Nineveh repenting in sackcloth and with "mighty cries." The repentance is genuine, is accepted by God, and the destruction does not come. Jonah is "displeased exceedingly." It is to be noted that this displeasure of Jonah is no mere ebullition of temper. With the impulsive sincerity of his character he lays his complaint before God; and it seems to be with some hope of having moved Jehovah from his purpose of mercy that Jonah makes his booth, and sits watching "till he might see what would become of the city." Burned by the sun without and prophetic anger within, Jonah is suddenly aware of a 'gourd-plant' which with swift growth has shot up to screen him, and he comes to love it for its beauty and grateful shadow. In a single night a worm gnaws the gourd, and by morning it is withered and fallen. Soon su'try wind and direct blaze of sun drive Jonah to physical exhaustion; more than that, "he does well to be angry": the lovely gourd smitten by the foul worm seems to him a blot on God's providence. Then comes the Divine message.

> Thou hast had pity on the gourd, for the which thou hast not laboured, neither madest it grow; which came up in a night, and perished in a night: and should not I have pity on Nineveh, that great city; wherein are more than six score thousand persons that cannot discern between their right hand and their left hand; and also much cattle?

What is the prophetic revelation underlying this latter part of the book? Not, as some would have it, the lovingkindness of Jehovah and his forgiveness of the repentant: for this Jonah expressly declares he has known from the first. But this glorious mercy of Jehovah the prophet had conceived as the heritage of the Hebrew people; he watches with indignation its extension to the heathen. As in the earlier part of the prophecy he was led to see that Divine power was not confined to the land of Israel, but that the dominion of Jehovah extended over the universe, so now he is to be taught that the supremacy of mercy over judgment is an attribute of God in which all races may feel that they have an interest. There is more than this.

iv. 2

Even Jonah would not have challenged the authority of God to forgive Nineveh; only he claimed for himself the right to dissociate himself from such mercy: he did well to be angry. To entwine his affections about the simplest work of creation — a plant, and then to wound those affections by roughly destroying it: this was the object lesson by means of which the prophet was to be admitted into the commencement of communion with the worldwide sympathy of Deity. To raise men's thoughts from the narrow conception of a local god to the vision of an Omnipotence exercising dominion over the universe; then to extend to the whole human race the supremacy of mercy over judgment, alike in the attributes of God and the sympathy of man: these are the points of prophetic revelation conveyed in the Epic of *Jonah*.

CHAPTER X

BIBLICAL HISTORY IN ITS RELATIONS WITH BIBLICAL EPIC

IN the wider treatment of literature, which includes questions of authorship and discussion of subject matter, the historical books of the Bible present many and great difficulties.

Various Types of History represented in the Bible

A small space only need be allotted to them in the present work, the field of which is limited to the characteristics of Scriptural literature as it stands, apart from any further enquiry as to how it has grown into what we find it. If we except the *Book of Deuteronomy*, which is best classified otherwise, narrative extends without break from *Genesis* to *Esther* in the Old Testament, and in the New Testament from *St. Matthew* to *Acts*. The sole question for the present chapter is, How many of the various forms that History may assume are represented in this succession of historical works?

The name *Genesis* is suggestive of the character of the book to which it is a title: it is Primitive History. It covers the ages

Primitive History Book of Genesis

preceding the appearance of the Chosen People as a nation. Eleven of its chapters deal with the first beginnings of the world; the rest is occupied with the succession of the patriarchs Abraham, Isaac, Jacob, Joseph. At the close of *Genesis* the seed of Abraham is still treated as a large family; when the history is resumed in the fol-

Exodus i. 9

lowing book the Egyptians pronounce the Children of Israel a people more and mightier than themselves. The character of this Primitive History may be described as an historic framework enclosing epic incidents. The epic element has been dealt with in the last chapter: *Genesis* contains single epic stories, such as the flood, cycles of stories attaching to the successive patriarchs, and a single complete epic history in the Story of Joseph and his Brethren. The framework of history is made up of genealogies, annals, and connective matter of various kinds. As part of this connective matter we have certain incidents which are clearly introduced for some historic purpose. Thus incidents connecting Abimelech and Abraham, and again Abimelech and Isaac, are related with a view to explain the naming of Beersheba and other ancient wells. Similarly the story of Canaan's father, and the story of Lot's daughters are designed to account for the mutual relations of great world families. Such Historic Incidents are easily distinguishable from the Epic Incidents of which the interest lies in the story itself. xxi. 22-34; xxvi

ix. 20-9; xix. 30-8

Following this Primitive History of *Genesis*, three books describe the Migration of the Nation up to the arrival at the Land of Promise. These three books may be classified together as Constitutional History. They are in the nature of things different in kind from what that term generally suggests. Other peoples have gradually elaborated their constitution out of original popular customs and modifications by specific enactment. But the Chosen Nation of Israel is governed directly by God, and its only Constitutional History is the successive revelations of the Law. Such history will of course include certain incidents, leading up to these revelations or intimately associated with them; as where the visit of Jethro leads to the institution of subordinate judges, or factions and rebellions issue in fresh confirmation of the authority wielded by Moses or the priesthood as Jehovah's representatives. Besides these incidents, the opening of this section of history assumes creative form in the great Epic of the Ten Plagues; and near its conclusion is found the Epic Story of Balaam. The natural divisions of this Constitutional History are

Constitutional History
Books of Exodus, Leviticus, Numbers

three: eighteen chapters of *Exodus* describe the slavery in Egypt, the deliverance, and the journey to Sinai; the rest of *Exodus* and the whole of *Leviticus* are occupied with the general constitution of the nation at Sinai; and the *Book of Numbers* traces the march from Sinai and the thirty-eight years wandering in the wilderness.

We pass to another period, which is represented in the literature by yet another type of history. The Chosen Nation in its various efforts towards secular government is pictured in the *Books of Joshua* and *Judges* and the *First Book of Samuel*.[1] The *Book of Joshua* narrates the conquest of Canaan and division of the conquered country. The book that follows indicates an age of sporadic attempts at government by 'Judges,' who from time to time rise up and succeed in commanding a more or less wide obedience; in the intervals between such Judges there is nothing but local government, or, in the language of Scripture, every man does that which is right in his own eyes. In this book, however, is to be found the first idea of that monarchical rule which was eventually to assimilate Israel to other nations. After the great deliverance wrought by Gideon he is invited to become king, but refuses: "I will not rule over you, neither shall my son rule over you: the LORD shall rule over you." After Gideon's death another and less worthy son allowed himself to be crowned king by the men of Shechem; feud and civil war followed until this king and his party had exterminated one another. The demand for a secular king does not reappear until the movement which ended in the appointment by Divine permission of Saul. But before this took place another power had emerged for the control of the Israelite people: in Samuel the 'Judge' gradually grew into the 'Prophet,' and all through the subsequent age of secular kings there were never wanting prophets to represent the old theocracy of the Chosen People. All these considerations confirm the description of this epoch as a period of transition and tentative rule.

Incidental History
Joshua, Judges,
I Samuel

viii. 22

viii. 33-ix

[1] The exact division should come at the end of the first chapter of *II Samuel*.

The history in the three books is properly described as Incidental History. Nearly the whole of it consists in Epic Incidents: whether the separate Stories of the Judges, or Cycles of Stories relating to Joshua, to Samson, to Samuel and Saul. In the latter part the Feud of Saul and David appears as one of the most extended of Epics. The historic framework binding these epic portions together is often of the slightest description, no more than a linking of one incident to another. The most considerable parts of such connective matter   i-iii. 6 are the summary with which the *Book of Judges* opens, and the geographical chapters in *Joshua* which make a sort of Canaanite Doomsday Book.   xiii-xxii

The accession of King David marks the settlement of the monarchy; the period extending from this point to the Captivity is narrated in the second book of *Samuel* and the   Regular History two books of *Kings*. First we have the reigns of II Samuel, I and David and Solomon over a united people; then II Kings comes the schism of the nation and the continuance of the kingdoms of Judah and Israel side by side; finally, after the fall of the northern kingdom, the history of Judah by itself is carried on to its close. The narrative in these three books may be described as Regular History. It is a systematic account of successive reigns. There is formal arrangement of the matter: in the earlier part public policy is to a large extent separated from court life,[1] while later on the respective kings of Judah and Israel are kept as nearly parallel as the nature of the case permits. Lists of officials from time to time add an element of documentary history; and there is constant reference to authorities, the Chronicles of the Kings of Israel and Judah, and others. Incidents are narrated historically, that is, in proportion to the bearing of each on the general course of events. There is, however, in the early part one considerable Epic, the Feud between David's Sons and the Revolt of Absalom; and to this may be added the *Book of Esther*, which, however, falls outside the period, and is a story of the Captivity.

---

[1] Chapters ix-xx of *II Samuel* centre around court life.

The place occupied in the other sections of history by Epic Incidents is in this last section mainly represented by Epic Prophecy: in the stories of individual prophets like Nathan and Abijah, and the more extended narratives connected with Elijah and Elisha, the theocratic side of Israel's government finds representation.

There remain in the Old Testament the books of *Chronicles*, *Ezra*, and *Nehemiah*. These make a series that covers the period treated in the last section, and carries it forward as far as the return of the Exiles to Jerusalem. But the history in this series is entirely changed in character: it is distinguished by the prominence of documents, genealogies, statistics; the narrative appears to consist in excerpts from the other books of the Bible and from authorities distinct from these. What is more important, the whole is dominated by a definite purpose: the matter is abridged, amplified, arranged, with reference to its bearing on the Jewish Church, as that Church was restored after the exile. It is thus Ecclesiastical History.

Ecclesiastical History Chronicles, Ezra, Nehemiah

The distinctness of this Ecclesiastical History from the Regular History which appeals generally to our sense of record is best illustrated by taking a particular incident for comparison. I have before had occasion to refer to the inauguration of Jerusalem by King David; it will be instructive to note how this is treated in *Chronicles* and in *Samuel*.

II SAMUEL	I CHRONICLES
	xiii. 1–4 David's proposal to the Assembly in the matter of the Ark: with the special mention of priests and Levites.
vi. 1–12 (*a*) The Assembly, and first attempt to bring up the Ark, ending in the death of Uzzah, the leaving of the Ark in the house of Obed-Edom, and the blessing on the house of Obed-Edom.	5–14 The same matter as in the corresponding section of *Samuel*: considerable verbal agreement, with some difference of names, etc.

	xv. 1-24 David's recognition that none but the Levites should bear the Ark — long lists of appointments both for the bearing and the musical performance.
vi. 12 (*b*)-19 (*a*) The procession of the Ark — David's part in it — Michal's displeasure — the inauguration carried to the point of a dole to the assembly.	xv. 25-xvi. 3 Substantial agreement with the corresponding section of *Samuel* — but fuller musical details.
	xvi. 4-42 Appointment, apparently dating from this festival, of a *regular* ministry before the Ark: names of officials and citation of (leading) songs used.
vi. 19 (*b*)-20 (*a*) Return home of the people and of David.	xvi. 43 Exactly as in *Samuel*.
vi. 20 (*b*)-23 Sequel of Michal's displeasure.	

Thus, the substance of the narrative is common to both accounts, with variation in unimportant details, and an amount of verbal agreement sufficient to show that the author of the later work had the earlier before him, or else that both used a common authority. But the account in *Chronicles* has additions which bring out the ecclesiastical purpose of its history: there is the explanation of Uzzah's death as owing to the neglect of the Levitical privileges, the appointments made in consequence of this, and the full detail of musical arrangements. Again, when the common narrative has been brought down to all but its last detail, it is, in *Chronicles*, interrupted by a lengthy account of a general ministry dating from this day of inauguration; then the final detail of the common narrative is added. On the other hand, the only section of the story of *Samuel* which has no counterpart in *Chronicles* is the domestic incident of Michal's remonstrance with the king, in which Ecclesiastical History would have no concern.

The Ecclesiastical History of the Jewish Church in the Old Testament has in the New Testament a counterpart in the historical works connected with the foundation of Christianity. In a literary classification what is the position to be assigned to the Four Gospels? Though they are a part of Ecclesiastical History, yet they are not histories. How far they are from being biographies is seen by the difficulty which modern writers, with the Gospels before them, find in constructing a satisfactory biography of Jesus Christ. It might seem more plausible to associate them with the department of Prophecy, since we have seen that prophetic literature is concerned both with the discourses of the prophets and with their actions. But the difference between the Gospels and Prophecy is greater than the resemblance. The personal position of Jesus in the history of the Gospels is not that of a prophet. Though the function of prophets is to convey a Divine message, yet prophetic literature is made not so much by the message as by the discourse which enforces it: Jesus Christ, on the contrary, speaks throughout the Gospels with the authority that commands and enacts, not with the appeal inviting to a doctrine other than his own. The conclusion we are led to is that the Gospels must be classified by themselves, as a specific literary form. The description of this form is that they are Authoritative Statements of the Acts and Words of Christ. As in the machinery of public life we have *protocols* reciting with authority facts or documents upon which political action is to be founded, so the authors of the Gospels drew up, and the early Church accepted, what were, not in themselves books of law, but the best authorities for the Acts and Words of their Founder, to which the Church looked for its supreme law. And this technical description is borne out by the language of the Preface to *St. Luke*.

The Four Gospels

> Forasmuch as many have taken in hand to draw up a narrative concerning those matters which have been fulfilled among us, even as they delivered them unto us, which from the beginning were eyewitnesses and ministers of the word, it seemed good to me also, having traced

the course of all things accurately from the first, to write unto thee in order, most excellent Theophilus; that thou mightest know the certainty concerning the things wherein thou wast instructed.

If this be a correct description from the literary standpoint of the Four Gospels, then it will be seen that the remaining book of *Acts* must be referred to the same classification. It is indeed announced as a continuation of St. Luke's Gospel; and in character it is an Authoritative Statement of the Proceedings of the Apostles, in the early stages of founding the Church, and opening it to the whole Gentile world. This characterisation of the book will appear in its title, if the wording of the title be translated out of technical into familiar language. The 'Apostles' are so called because they have received a certain 'commission' from their Master; the 'Acts of the Apostles' are the 'Proceedings of the Commissioners.' This description again exactly tallies with the plan and arrangement of the book. If *Acts* be regarded as ordinary history, it will seem strange that the personages and places which dominate the earlier part are in the latter part almost forgotten; moreover, the history seems to end abruptly just where it might be expected to become specially full. But the terms of the 'commission' are that the Apostles are to make disciples of all nations, beginning at Jerusalem. The book that is to narrate the execution of this commission deals in full detail with the start made at Jerusalem. The rest of it has for its purpose to bring out the successive enlargements of the area in which the Church is at work. The first grand enlargement is the admission of Gentiles; and this is voluminously treated in the account of St. Peter's Vision, of the Council settling difficulties between the Jews and the Gentile converts, above all, in the rise of the Apostle who is to devote himself specially to this work. It is natural that from this point the history should mainly concern itself with St. Paul. Another miraculous Vision marks a further enlargement, where the Gospel is carried from Asia to Europe. And a series of providential circumstances, not less wonderful

The Acts of the Apostles

xvi. 9

than a vision, are narrated at length from their importance in bringing the Apostle of the Gentiles to Rome. When the work of making disciples has thus been carried from Jerusalem to the city which is the metropolis of all nations, the terms of the commission have been fully executed: what remains may be left to the history which is not authoritative.

xxi. 17-xxviii

These are the various types of history represented in Scripture. In conclusion I would say that those who desire to appreciate these narrative books as literature, apart from the historical problems they raise, will do well to see that they read, not in 'chapters,' but in portions that are fixed by literary considerations; taking in a book at a sitting, or if not, something which makes a natural division of a book. It is the purpose of the tables in the Appendix to this work to assist such reading; and I suggest that a student should, by a little use of the pencil in the margin of his Revised Version, do that for Biblical History which in any other history would be done for him by the printer.

Book Fourth

THE PHILOSOPHY OF THE BIBLE, OR WISDOM LITERATURE

Chapter		Page
XI.	Forms of Wisdom Literature .	. 255
XII.	The Sacred Books of Wisdom .	. 284
XIII.	'The Wisdom of Solomon'	. 305

CHAPTER XI

FORMS OF WISDOM LITERATURE

THIS fourth book is reserved for the Philosophy of the Bible; that is to say, for the wide range of Scriptural literature which is the counterpart of our modern Philosophy and Science. These two names, however, are scarcely to be found in the sacred writings; the literature we are to consider is, in the Bible itself, uniformly designated 'Wisdom.' The word is suggestive of one, if not both, the main distinctions which separate Biblical Philosophy from modern thought. If it be not pressing the word too far, there is a picturesqueness in the name 'Wisdom' that harmonises with the picturesqueness of form never absent from Scriptural literature of thought. Modern works of science confine themselves strictly to severe prose style. But the literature of Wisdom borrows often the form of lyric, and sometimes even of dramatic poetry, and where it is furthest removed from these, it still leaves the impression of attaching as much consequence to the artistic form as to the thought. More important than this is the suggestion in the name 'Wisdom' that its literature will have a practical bearing on human conduct. A great part of such writings is made up of specific observations or precepts in matters of social and family life, of business management, public policy, and general self-government. And where such works as *Ecclesiastes* or the *Wisdom of Solomon*[1] are occupied in

'Wisdom' Literature

---

[1] I assume throughout this part of my subject the Apocryphal books of *Wisdom of Solomon* and *Ecclesiasticus*. The distinction implied in the word 'Apocryphal' is one of theology: according to the Anglican formula, "the Church doth read [them]

interpreting history, or reading the riddle of life, they make it clear that the argument is followed with a constant reference to the bearing of the whole on conduct. It is only when comparison is made with the kindred department of Prophecy that we see the right of Wisdom literature to be classified under the head of Philosophy, the organ of reflection. Prophecy also is concerned with conduct; but it starts always with a Divine message, on which all that it contains is based. Of course Wisdom is in harmony with the revelation contained in Law and Prophecy, but it never appeals to it. The sayings of the Wise come to us only as the result of their own reflections, in combination with the general tradition of Wisdom.

The present chapter is occupied with the various literary forms in which this Wisdom literature of the Bible and Apocrypha is conveyed to us. The two chapters that follow will treat the separate Books of Wisdom as they stand.

Varieties of Wisdom Literature

The starting-point for this whole class of literature is the Proverb. There were two sources of Hebrew proverbs: Folk-lore, and the sayings of the Wise Men. The popular proverbs that float from mouth to mouth appear only by accident in the Bible. "Out of the wicked cometh forth wickedness" is an ancient saying hurled by David at Saul, in the wilderness of Engedi, when Saul's groundless suspicions of him had just been exposed. "Is Saul also among the prophets?" is a proverb that has descended from those days to our own.

The Proverb

Popular Proverbs

One form of popular proverb was the Riddle; and, just as great part of the intercourse between the Wise — between Solomon and Hiram, or Solomon and the Queen of Sheba — consisted in hard questions to be interpreted, so popular festivities made opportunities for the guessing

Riddles

---

for example of life and instruction of manners; but yet doth it not apply them to establish any doctrine." As doctrinal questions are excluded from this work, the distinction does not here apply. The two books are of the highest literary interest.

of riddles. One cycle or 'game of riddles' has been preserved complete in the *Book of Judges*. It connects itself naturally with Samson, whose magnificent frame and redundant high spirits make him the nearest approach in the [Judges xv] Bible to a humorous personage. Samson, it will be recollected, loved a woman of the Philistines, and after asking her hand through his father went down to Timnah to the wedding feast. The feast lasted a week, during which the hero had to endure the company of thirty guests from the Philistine people he hated and despised. Denied the vent of physical violence, his irritation took the form of a wager: the amount, thirty linen garments and thirty changes of raiment; the subject of contention, that the Philistines would not guess his riddle. The wager was accepted and the riddle put forth.

> Out of the eater came forth meat,
> And out of the strong came forth sweetness.

According to modern notions of riddles, Samson was not playing fairly, for his question involved information exclusively his own. On his walks to and fro between his home and the home of the bride he had one day met a young lion; the lion roared at him, and Samson, by a sudden impulse, was led to seize the brute with his bare hands and tear it in pieces; the next time he passed he found a cluster of bees settled in the torn carcase of the lion, and actually tasted their honey: this strange conjunction was the foundation of his riddle. But the Philistine guests, in their turn, could violate fair play; they brought pressure upon the bride, and she coaxed the secret out of her lover. At the end of the seven days the Philistines came to answer the riddle; and their answer, like the original question, makes a single couplet:

> What is sweeter than honey?
> And what is stronger than a lion?

Samson turns upon them with a repartee couched in the same form:

> If ye had not ploughed with my heifer,
> Ye had not found out my riddle.

Samson, with his usual grim humour, slew thirty Philistines, and sent their raiment in payment of the wager; then went home in dudgeon, and left the bride, who was soon appropriated by another husband.

But it is with the second type of proverbs that we are mainly concerned. The single couplet, which we have just noted in connection with popular riddles, is the root of the forms taken by the sayings of the Wise Men.[1] Such a proverb may be defined as a unit of thought in a unit of form.

The Unit Proverb

These Unit Proverbs exhibit two varieties. In one type the thought is conveyed in a single line, and the other line of the couplet is supplementary. The single line contains all that philosophic reflection requires; but the sense of form, even in the simplest Wisdom literature, is so strong that the thought must be filled out to the dimensions of the received pattern before it can obtain currency as a proverb.

> He that is slow to anger is better than the mighty,
> And he that ruleth his spirit than he that taketh a city.
>
> ***
>
> The heart knoweth its own bitterness;
> And a stranger doth not intermeddle with its joy.

The supplement in these two examples is a parallel to the main thought, or its converse. Where the essence of the proverb is deep or obscure, the supplementary line comes to interpret it.

> The fruit of the righteous is a tree of life;
> And he that is wise winneth souls.

How can fruit be a tree? The supplement interprets of the wise life which is the fruit of righteous endeavour, and which has an attractive force on all around, bringing forth in them lives of like righteousness. The supplement may precede the thought:—

---

[1] The triplet is not entirely absent even from such elementary anthologies as that constituting the second book of our Biblical *Proverbs* (e.g. xix. 7, 23; compare xxiv. 27). There is an interesting form of unit proverb that can be read either as a couplet or triplet: examples are *Proverbs* x. 26; and especially xxv. 3, 12, 20; xxvi. 1, 3, etc.

> The LORD hath made everything for its own end:
> Yea, even the wicked for the day of evil.

The point of this proverb is clearly that the wicked exist for the purpose of being destroyed: the statement is made the fuller by the reminder that everything has its purpose. Two proverbs may be made out of the same thought with different supplements.

> Though hand join in hand, the evil man shall not be unpunished:
> But the seed of the righteous shall be delivered.
>
> *⁎*
>
> Everyone that is proud in heart is an abomination to the LORD.
> Though hand join in hand, he shall not be unpunished.

In the other variety of Unit Proverb there is no room for supplementary matter: the thought, which is the essence of the saying, requires the whole of the proverb for its expression, and is distributed through the two lines of the couplet.

> It is naught, it is naught, saith the buyer:
> But when he is gone his way, then he boasteth.
>
> *⁎*
>
> He kisseth the lips
> That giveth a right answer.

To this variety belong the large class of proverbs which are founded on a comparison.

> As vinegar to the teeth, and as smoke to the eyes,
> So is the sluggard to them that send him.
>
> *⁎*
>
> A rebuke entereth deeper into one that hath understanding
> Than an hundred stripes into a fool.
>
> *⁎*
>
> Seven days are the days of mourning for the dead;
> But for a fool and an ungodly man, all the days of his life.
>
> *⁎*
>
> The fining pot is for silver, and the furnace for gold,
> And a man is tried by his praise.

It appears, then, that the parallel couplet, which we have seen as the most elementary type of Hebrew verse, is also the fixed form for the Unit Proverb of Philosophy, a department that naturally belongs to prose. The Unit Proverb thus makes a meeting-point for prose and verse. The Wisdom literature, developing from this as germ, takes two directions, and for every poetic form which it throws off a corresponding form of prose is to be found. This will be best conveyed by a table.

The Unit Proverb as the germ of Wisdom Literature

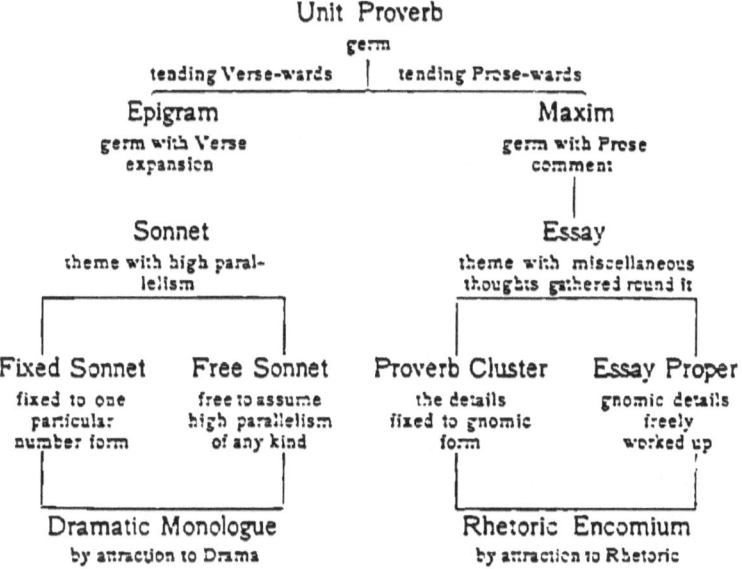

On the side of verse, we have first the Epigram. It will be remembered that the epigrams of antiquity did not necessarily exhibit the pointedness of expression and flash of wit which modern literature associates with the name. A Greek epigram needed nothing more than the concise expression of a complete thought within the limits of a few couplets. The Hebrew epigrams may be said to be more pointed than the Greek, since each has buried in it one of these 'gnomes'

The Epigram

or unit proverbs. The distinction of the Epigram is that two of its lines (not necessarily consecutive) will be found to constitute a gnomic germ, of which the rest is the expansion. In the examples to be quoted these lines will be distinguished by italics.[1]

A Chaplet of Instruction

My son, hear the instruction of thy father,
And forsake not the law of thy mother:
For they shall be a chaplet of grace unto thy head,
And chains about thy neck.

※

The Fall of the Righteous and the Wicked

Lay not wait, O wicked man, against the habitation of the righteous;
Spoil not his resting place:
For a righteous man falleth seven times, and riseth up again:
But the wicked are overthrown by calamity.

※

The Fool's Friends

The fool will say, "I have no friend,
And I have no thanks for my good deeds;
And they that eat my bread are of evil tongue."
How oft, and of how many, shall he be laughed to scorn!

In each case the lines italicised would stand alone as a unit proverb. In the first example a second proverb is added to support the first. In the other two cases, each line of the germ saying is followed by another line enforcing or interpreting it. It will be seen that the germ proverb need not be at the commencement; in the example that follows it comes at the end.

Gluttony

Hear thou, my son, and be wise,
And guard thy heart in the way.
Be not among winebibbers;
Among gluttonous eaters of flesh:
For the drunkard and the glutton shall come to poverty,
And drowsiness shall clothe a man with rags.

---

[1] References to the examples in this chapter are omitted, as the Epigrams, Essays, etc., are cited by their titles in the table of Appendix II.

To make longer epigrams, we find the first line of a unit proverb buttressed by a parallel line, while to the second a full explanation is appended.

Hospitality of the Evil Eye

Eat thou not the bread of him that hath an evil eye,
Neither desire thou his dainties:
 For as one that reckoneth within himself, so is he
 Eat and drink, saith he to thee,
 But his heart is not with thee.
 The morsel which thou hast eaten shalt thou vomit up,
 And lose thy sweet words.

_{*}

Wisdom and Honey

My son, eat thou honey, for it is good;
And the honeycomb, which is sweet to thy taste;
 So shalt thou know wisdom to be unto thy soul:
 If thou hast found it, then shall there be a reward,
 And thy hope shall not be cut off.

More elaborate in structure is the epigram of Lemuel's mother: first, each line of the germ proverb is supported by a parallel line, then each has a whole quatrain antithetical to it.

Kings and Wine

It is not for kings, O Lemuel, it is not for kings to drink wine,
Nor for princes to say, Where is strong drink?
 Lest they drink, and forget the law,
 And pervert the judgement of any that is afflicted.
Give strong drink unto him that is ready to perish,
And wine unto the bitter in soul:
 Let him drink, and forget his poverty,
 And remember his misery no more.
  Open thy mouth for the dumb,
  In the cause of all such as are left desolate.
  Open thy mouth, judge righteously,
  And minister judgement to the poor and needy.

Exactly corresponding to these Epigrams in verse we find, on the prose side, compositions that will here be called Maxims.[1] Their form is that of a text with a comment; a germ proverb (or the essential words of it) is merged in what is a prose expansion of the same.

Maxims

> *Wisdom is as good as an inheritance:* yea, more excellent is it for them that see the sun. For wisdom is a defence, even as money is a defence: but the excellency of knowledge is, that wisdom preserveth the life of him that hath it.
>
> *⁎⁎⁎*
>
> *Make not merry in much luxury; neither be tied to the expense thereof.* Be not made a beggar by banqueting upon borrowing when thou hast nothing in thy purse. A workman that is a drunkard shall not become rich.
>
> *⁎⁎⁎*
>
> *The words of a wise man's mouth are gracious; but the lips of a fool will swallow up himself.* The beginning of the words of his mouth is foolishness: and the end of his talk is mischievous madness. A fool also multiplieth words: yet man knoweth not what shall be; and that which shall be after him, who can tell him?

These are among the shorter maxims; longer examples are to be found in the book of *Ecclesiastes*.

> *Two are better than one;* because they have a good reward for their labour. For if they fall, one will lift up his fellow: but woe to him that is alone when he falleth, and hath not another to lift him up. Again, if two lie together, then they have warmth: but how can one be warm alone? And if a man prevail against him that is alone, two shall withstand him; and a threefold cord is not quickly broken.

---

[1] I am not aware of any English term that exactly describes the class of compositions here brought forward. The word 'maxim' in English is used loosely. Mr. Joseph Jacobs in his (Golden Treasury) edition of Gracian contends, not without reason, that the term has a special application to sayings which are practical and not meditative. At the same time the 'maxims' he is editing have a closer resemblance to this form of text and comment than anything outside Biblical Wisdom.

As with the epigram, the text is not necessarily at the commencement, but may be absorbed into the body of the maxim.

> Speak not one against another, brethren. *He that speaketh against a brother*, or judgeth his brother, *speaketh against the law*, and judgeth the law: but if thou judgest the law, thou art not a doer of the law, but a judge. One only is the lawgiver and judge, even he who is able to save and to destroy: but who art thou that judgest thy neighbour?

The germ of this maxim is the paradox, "*He that speaketh against a brother speaketh against the law*"; and it illustrates how much thought can be packed into one of these gnomic sentences. The Apostle is writing to those whose reverence for 'the law' had amounted to a superstition; and it is one of the underlying ideas of the whole epistle that the Christian's 'liberty' is, not a laxer, but a higher law. In this saying the writer lays down that one who is censorious against another is impugning his brother's liberty of action, is therefore impugning that which the new dispensation has made the highest law.

Continuing to follow the prose side of our table, we are brought to that which may be considered the most important of the forms assumed by Wisdom literature — the Essay. The

The Essay

word has been used somewhat loosely in modern speech, but it essentially implies two things: first, a composition professing only a fragmentary treatment of a subject; and secondly, that the details of this composition need have no mutual bond except their relevancy to the topic which stands as title of the Essay. If more than this goes to any composition — if, for example, there is methodical arrangement or formal investigation — then the name 'treatise' would be more proper; the Essay is bound to nothing beyond miscellaneous thoughts collected around a common theme. This description applies to the Essays of the Bible and Apocrypha; but upon these a further characteristic is stamped by their gnomic origin. Indeed, it becomes necessary to recognise a type of composition which makes a half-way stage

between the Proverb and the Essay. This we shall call the
'Proverb Cluster': a number of proverbs (including maxims and epigrams) are collected together around a common theme, each retaining its independence and fixed gnomic form. To make an Essay, the component parts are freely worked together into a new style, though the Wisdom Essays continually suggest their gnomic origin, and often a considerable number of their sentences will stand as independent proverbs. *Proverb Clusters*

We are able, in the literature which has come down to us, to watch the process by which Essays have been evolved out of Proverbs. I propose to bring this out by placing side by side three compositions; the matter of the three is largely the same, and it is clear that the later authors have borrowed from the earlier; in form, they represent three stages in the development of the Essay. *Development of Essays out of Proverbs*

On the Government of the Tongue

Winnow not with every wind, and walk not in every path: thus doeth the sinner that hath a double tongue.

Be stedfast in thy understanding; and let thy word be one.

Be swift to hear; and with patience make thine answer.

If thou hast understanding, answer thy neighbour; and if not, let thy hand be upon thy mouth.

Glory and dishonour is in talk: and the tongue of a man is his fall.

Be not called a whisperer; and lie not in wait with thy tongue: for upon the thief there is shame, and an evil condemnation upon him that hath a double tongue.

In a great matter and in a small, be not ignorant; and instead of a friend become not an enemy; for an evil name shall inherit shame and reproach: even so shall the sinner that hath a double tongue.

The above is plainly a Proverb Cluster: each paragraph is an independent saying, which has a bearing upon the general subject, but no bond with the other paragraphs; any one of these could be removed without the unity of the whole being affected. In the extract which next follows, consecutive sentences have fused together into connectedness of thought: but there still remain a considerable number of them which make complete proverbs, and some of these could be cut out without damage to the rest.

On the Tongue

If thou blow a spark, it shall burn; if thou spit upon it, it shall be quenched: and both these shall come out of thy mouth. Curse the whisperer and double-tongued: for he hath destroyed many that were at peace. A third person's tongue hath shaken many, and dispersed them from nation to nation; and it hath pulled down strong cities, and overthrown the houses of great men. A third person's tongue hath cast out brave women and deprived them of their labours. He that hearkeneth unto it shall not find rest, nor shall he dwell quietly. The stroke of a whip maketh a mark in the flesh; but the stroke of a tongue will break bones. Many have fallen by the edge of the sword: yet not so many as they that have fallen because of the tongue. Happy is he that is sheltered from it, that hath not passed through the wrath thereof; that hath not drawn its yoke, and hath not been bound with its bands. For the yoke thereof is a yoke of iron, and the bands thereof are bands of brass. The death thereof is an evil death; and Hades were better than it. It shall not have rule over godly men; and they shall not be burned in its flame. They that forsake the Lord shall fall into it, and it shall burn among them, and shall not be quenched: it shall be sent forth upon them as a lion; and as a leopard it shall destroy them. Look that thou hedge thy possession about with thorns; bind up thy silver and thy gold: and make a weight and a balance for thy words: and make a door and a bar for thy mouth. Take heed lest thou slip therein: lest thou fall before one that lieth in wait.

The difference between this passage and that which follows is only one of degree. When the same topic is presented by St. James, we find connectedness of thought reigning throughout, and the free flow of Essay style has prevailed completely over the independence of sentences that belong to proverbs: only here and there the turn of a sentence reminds us of the gnomic origin of this class of Essay.

The Responsibility of Speech

Be not many teachers, my brethren, knowing that we shall receive heavier judgement. For in many things we all stumble. If any stumbleth not in word, the same is a perfect man, able to bridle the whole body also. Now if we put the horses' bridles into their mouths, that they may obey us, we turn about their whole body also. Behold, the ships also, though they are so great, and are driven by rough winds, are yet turned about by a very small rudder, whither the impulse of the steersman willeth. So the tongue also is a little member, and boasteth great things. Behold, how much wood is kindled by how small a fire! And the tongue is a fire: the world of iniquity among our members is the tongue, which defileth the whole body, and setteth on fire the wheel of nature, and is set on fire by hell. For every kind of beasts and birds, of creeping things and things in the sea, is tamed, and hath been tamed by mankind: but the tongue can no man tame; it is a restless evil, it is full of deadly poison. Therewith bless we the Lord and Father; and therewith curse we men, which are made after the likeness of God: out of the same mouth cometh forth blessing and cursing. My brethren, these things ought not so to be. Doth the fountain send forth from the same opening sweet water and bitter? can a fig tree, my brethren, yield olives, or a vine figs? Neither can salt water yield sweet.

There is a whole literature of essays in the Wisdom books of the Bible and the Apocrypha. They are not essays in the more modern sense which the English reader associates with the name of Lord Macaulay: but they rather *Wisdom Essays* represent the oldest type of such compositions, to which contributions were made by Bacon and by Montaigne, by Feltham and by the author of the *Microcosmography*. Indeed, there can be no doubt that these writers (Montaigne excepted) owed largely to the influence of *Ecclesiasticus* and kindred books the sententiousness of their style and the asyndeton of their sentences. But in the case of these essays the same difficulty confronts the literary reader which has been pointed out in reference to other departments. In the form in which our Bibles are presented to us the separate essays are allowed to run together without break, and the titles so essential to this kind of writing are wholly wanting. I have endeavoured to meet this difficulty by indicating in the Appendix[1] to this work the separate essays, and suggesting appropriate titles. And here, as elsewhere, I would advise the reader to mark such divisions and titles in his Bible and Apocrypha, before he attempts to appreciate the literary character of these compositions.

At this point I can do nothing but illustrate. Of the shorter essays a good specimen is that of *Ecclesiasticus* on Gossip.

On Gossip

He that is hasty to trust is lightminded; and he that sinneth shall offend against his own soul. He that maketh merry in his heart shall be condemned; and he that hateth talk hath the less wickedness. Never repeat what is told thee, and thou shalt fare never the worse. Whether it be of friend or foe, tell it not; and if thou canst without sin, reveal not the matter; for he hath heard thee and observed thee, and when the time cometh he will hate thee. Hast thou heard a word? let it die with thee: be of good courage, it will not burst thee. A fool will travail in pain with a word, as a woman in labour with a child. As an arrow that sticketh in the flesh of the thigh, so is a word in a fool's belly. Reprove a friend; it may be he did it not; and if he did it, that he may do it no more. Reprove thy neighbour; it may be he said it not; and if he hath said it, that he may not say it again. Reprove a friend, for many times there is slander: and trust not every word. There is one that slippeth, and not from the heart: and who is he that hath not sinned with his tongue? Reprove thy neighbour before thou threaten him; and give place to the law of the Most High.

This essay is one of those in which gnomic verses abound. In the next they are rare, and the whole essay strikes a higher key.

Prosperity and Adversity are from the Lord

There is one that toileth, and laboureth, and maketh haste, and is so much the more behind. There is one that is sluggish, and hath need of help, lacking in strength, and that aboundeth in poverty; and the eyes of the Lord looked upon him for good, and he set him up from his low estate, and lifted up his head; and many marvelled at him. Good things and evil, life and death,

---

[1] See *Ecclesiastes, Ecclesiasticus, Wisdom, St. James,* in the Literary Index (Appendix I); or the Table of Wisdom Literature in Appendix II.

poverty and riches, are from the Lord. The gift of the Lord remaineth with the godly, and his good pleasure shall prosper for ever. There is that waxeth rich by his wariness and pinching, and this is the portion of his reward: when he saith, I have found rest, and now will I eat of my goods; yet he knoweth not what time shall pass, and he shall leave them to others, and die. Be stedfast in thy covenant, and be conversant therein, and wax old in thy work. Marvel not at the works of a sinner; but trust the Lord, and abide in thy labour: for it is an easy thing in the sight of the Lord swiftly on the sudden to make a poor man rich. The blessing of the Lord is in the reward of the godly; and in an hour that cometh swiftly he maketh his blessing to flourish. Say not, what use is there of me? and what from henceforth shall my good things be? Say not, I have sufficient, and from henceforth what harm shall happen unto me? In the day of good things there is a forgetfulness of evil things; and in the day of evil things a man will not remember things that are good. For it is an easy thing in the sight of the Lord to reward a man in the day of death according to his ways. The affliction of an hour causeth forgetfulness of delight; and in the last end of a man is the revelation of his deeds. Call no man blessed before his death; and a man shall be known in his children.

I follow this with one of the longer essays, one marked also by a greater variety of style.

On Counsel and Counsellors

Every counsellor extolleth counsel; but there is that counselleth for himself. Let thy soul beware of a counsellor, and know thou before what is his interest (for he will counsel for himself); lest he cast the lot upon thee, and say unto thee, Thy way is good: and he will stand over against thee, to see what shall befall thee. Take not counsel with one that looketh askance at thee; and hide thy counsel from such as are jealous of thee. Take not counsel with a woman about her rival; neither with a coward about war; nor with a merchant about exchange; nor with a buyer about selling; nor with an envious man about thankfulness; nor with an unmerciful man about kindliness; nor with a sluggard about any kind of work; nor with a hireling in thy house about finishing his work; nor with an idle servant about much business: give not heed to these in any matter of counsel. But rather be continually with a godly man, whom thou shalt have known to be a keeper of the commandments, who in his soul is as thine own soul, and who will grieve with thee, if thou shalt miscarry. And make the counsel of thy heart to stand; for there is none more faithful unto thee than it. For a man's soul is sometime wont to bring him tidings, more than seven watchmen that sit on high on a watch-tower. And above all this entreat the Most High, that he may direct thy way in truth. Let reason be the beginning of every work, and let counsel go before every action.

As a token of the changing of the heart, four manner of things do rise up, good and evil, life and death; and that which ruleth over them continually is the tongue. There is one that is shrewd and the instructor of many, and yet is unprofitable to his own soul. There is one that is subtle in words, and is hated; he shall be destitute of all food: for grace was not given him from the Lord; because he is deprived of all wisdom. There is one that is wise to his own soul; and the fruits of his understanding are trustworthy in the mouth. A wise man will instruct his own people; and the fruits of his understanding are trustworthy. A wise man shall be filled with blessing; and all they that see him shall call him happy. The life of man is numbered by days; and the days of Israel are innumerable: the wise man shall inherit confidence among his people, and his name shall live for ever.

The second paragraph of this essay has an obscurity which is rare in Wisdom literature. The line of thought seems to be as follows. Man's whole experience for good or evil depends upon the direction of his purposes; and a force continually influencing these purposes is the speech of his fellowmen. Hence the importance of marking the character of those who counsel. One type has the power of imparting instruction, but no morale to make the instruction worth having: for all his wisdom he is unprofitable to his own soul. One is false in speech, and so wholly hateful. A third has his wisdom bounded by selfishness; but what he is willing to speak will be worth marking. The truly wise will have not only wisdom but also the desire to impart it to his fellow-countrymen; his blessedness will be as much beyond that of the other as a nation is wider and more lasting than an individual.

As a final example, I cite an essay of St. James, to show how wide-reaching a treatment of how profound a subject can be compressed within the narrow limits of this fragmentary form of composition.

FORMS OF WISDOM LITERATURE 271

On the Sources of the Evil and the Good in Man

Blessed is the man that endureth temptation: for when he hath been approved, he shall receive the crown of life, which the Lord promised to them that love him. Let no man say when he is tempted, I am tempted of God: for God cannot be tempted with evil, and he himself tempteth no man: but each man is tempted, when he is drawn away by his own lust, and enticed. Then the lust when it hath conceived, beareth sin; and the sin, when it is full-grown, bringeth forth death. Be not deceived, my beloved brethren.

Every good gift and every perfect boon is from above, coming down from the Father of lights, with whom can be no variation, neither shadow that is cast by turning. Of his own will he brought us forth by the word of truth, that we should be a kind of first-fruits of his creatures. Know ye this, my beloved brethren; but let every man be swift to hear, slow to speak; slow to wrath, — for the wrath of man worketh not the righteousness of God. Wherefore putting away all filthiness and overflowing of wickedness, receive with meekness the inborn word, which is able to save your souls. But be ye doers of the word, and not hearers only, deluding your own selves. For if any one is a hearer of the word, and not a doer, he is like unto a man beholding his natural face in a mirror: for he beholdeth himself, and goeth away, and straightway forgetteth what manner of man he was. But he that looketh into the perfect law, the law of liberty, and so continueth, being not a hearer that forgetteth, but a doer that worketh, this man shall be blessed in his doing. If any man thinketh himself to be religious, while he bridleth not his tongue but deceiveth his heart, this man's religion is vain. Pure religion and undefiled before our God and Father is this, to visit the fatherless and widows in their affliction, and to keep himself unspotted from the world.

It would be difficult to find elsewhere so complete and harmonious a theory stated in so brief a space. The question is of the origin of the Evil and Good within us. The author strikes the keynote of Temptation — the struggle in us between ∙Evil and Good. Echoing a saying of *Ecclesiasticus*, he warns us against the delusion that temptation to evil could come from God. The true origin of evil he illustrates by the image of childbirth: it is the fruit of a union between the individual

<small>Ecclus. xv. 11</small>

man — that is, man's Will[1] — and his Lust; only when these have consented together is evil born, and such a union is not a marriage, but a seduction. The germ of evil thus accounted for, the Apostle proceeds to its further development; and this he explains by the same image of childbirth, carried on to a second generation. Turning, then, to the question of Good, St. James continues the imagery of childbirth; a union is hinted at between "The Will of God" and "The Word of Truth," as a result of which there exists in each individual an "inborn word" as the germ of Good. As with Evil, so here the writer proceeds to the development of such a germ, and this occupies the larger part of the essay. The imagery changes to that of listening: laying aside obstacles such as wrath, malice, filthiness, we are with patience and acuteness of attention, to listen for the word within us. But one more condition is essential: that the truth in proportion as it is caught must be carried into action. To enforce this principle, the remarkable illustration of a mirror is used: truth that is seen without being acted upon is compared to a reflection in a glass that vanishes as soon as the face is turned away. But how is this image to be carried on to express the man who lives the truth he sees? Such a man will behold truth reflected in the mirror of his action: but, in accordance with one of the main ideas of his epistle, St. James puts it, not as action according to law, but action according to the Christian liberty, which is the highest form of law. With practical examples the essay concludes.

I now turn back to the verse side of Wisdom literature. Here we find a class of compositions, which, like the Essay, are made up of miscellaneous thoughts gathered around a common theme. Their poetic form is evidenced in the fact that, not only are they composed of rhythmic lines, but also their parts are bound together by high parallelism — the parallelism, that is, which links not single verses only but masses

The Sonnet:

---

[1] The wording of the corresponding section in the second paragraph (verse 15 of St. James) justifies its interpretation.

of lines, or again, not adjacent lines, but portions of a composition widely separated.[1] This characteristic can be best conveyed by illustration.

On Evil Company

>My son, if sinners entice thee,
>   Consent thou not.
>If they say, "Come with us,
>Let us lay wait for blood,
>Let us lurk privily for the innocent without cause;
>Let us swallow them up alive as Sheol,
>And whole, as those that go down into the pit;
>We shall find all precious substance,
>We shall fill our houses with spoil;
>Thou shalt cast thy lot among us;
>We will all have one purse:"
>   My son, walk not thou in the way with them;
>   Refrain thy foot from their path:
>   For their feet run to evil,
>   And they make haste to shed blood.
>   For in vain is the net spread,
>   In the eyes of any bird;
>   And these lay wait for their own blood,
>   They lurk privily for their own lives.
>   So are the ways of every one that is greedy of gain;
>   It taketh away the life of the owners thereof.

The eye catches that the whole of this poem, after the opening couplet, falls into two blocks of lines; upon examination it will be found that the block of lines indented to the left are all of them expansions of the first line of the opening couplet, "My son, if sinners entice thee," and the block of lines indented to the right are expansions of the second line of the couplet, "Consent thou not." Thus it appears that precisely the same parallelism which unites the two opening lines into a couplet of verse is found to bind the divisions of the poem itself into a whole. This is a simple instance of the higher parallelism.

What is the proper name for this class of compositions? To

---

[1] Above, Chapter II, pages 74-5, and Appendix III.

me it appears that their position in relation to universal literature is expressed by calling them 'Sonnets.' No doubt they present one palpable difference from the poems we are accustomed to designate by that name: they are not, like Italian and English sonnets, constructed of exactly fourteen lines each. But is this limitation to fourteen lines the essential of the Sonnet, or is it only a matter of prescriptive usage? I would contend that if the Sonnet is to rank as a leading poetic type in universal literature its principle must be deeper. The true distinction of the Sonnet, like that of the Fugue in music, is that it reverses the usual order of things, and presents us with matter adapting itself to external form. The form that obtains in our modern poetry is the arrangement in fourteen lines; accordingly, the thought of our sonnets must be sufficient to fill out the fourteen lines, it must not be too wide to be compressed into that space; further (in the Italian sonnet) the logical connection of the thoughts must be such as will fit in with the division of the fourteen lines into a set of eight and a set of six. Now it is impossible to read the Biblical poems under discussion without feeling that here too we have thought adapting itself to form; not, of course, to any particular number of lines, but to elaboration of parallelism of some kind. To generalise, we may say that wherever thought runs into poetic moulds we have the spirit of the Sonnet; it belongs to the individuality of different literatures to decide whether only one mould shall be used, or more than one. Already we have seen a difference of type between the strict Italian sonnet with its division into eight and six, and the English sonnets which may observe or ignore that division. Hebrew poetry multiplies that difference by allowing free variety of forms, yet still leaving in its sonnets the literary impression of matter fitting itself to form.

Difference between Hebrew and English Sonnets

These Wisdom poems fall into two distinct types. The first may be called the Fixed Sonnet: it is fixed, not to one particular number of lines, but to the working out of a number form indicated in the opening verses.

The Fixed Sonnet

Little and Wise

There be four things which are little upon the earth,
    But they are exceeding wise:
The ants are a people not strong,
    Yet they provide their meat in the summer;
The conies are but a feeble folk,
    Yet make they their houses in the rocks;
The locusts have no king,
    Yet go they forth all of them by bands;
The lizard thou canst seize with thy hands,
    Yet is she in kings' palaces.

***

What Wisdom loves and hates

In three things I was beautified,
And stood up beautiful before the Lord and men:
    The concord of brethren,
    And friendship of neighbours,
And a woman and her husband that walk together in agreement.

But three sorts of men my soul hateth,
And I am greatly offended at their life:
    A poor man that is haughty,
    A rich man that is a liar,
And an old man that is an adulterer lacking understanding.

The number form is usually reached by a progression.

The Unsatisfied

The horseleach hath two daughters, called Give, Give;
    There are three things that are never satisfied,
        Yea, four that say not, Enough:
The grave;
And the barren womb;
The earth that is not satisfied with water;
And the fire that saith not, Enough.

***

Wonders

There be three things which are too wonderful for me,
Yea, four which I know not:
    The way of an eagle in the air;
    The way of a serpent upon a rock;
    The way of a ship in the midst of the sea;
And the way of a man with a maid.

*_**

The Golden Mean

Two things have I asked of thee;
Deny me not three[1] before I die:
Remove far from me vanity and lies;
    Give me neither poverty nor riches;
        Feed me with the food that is needful for me:
            Lest I be full, and deny thee, and say, Who is the LORD?
    Or lest I be poor and steal,
And use profanely the name of my God.

*_**

The Love of the Lord

There be nine things that I have thought of,
And in mine heart counted happy;
And the tenth I will utter with my tongue:
A man that hath joy of his children;
    A man that liveth and looketh upon the fall of his enemies;
        Happy is he that dwelleth with a wife of understanding;
And he that hath not slipped with his tongue;
    And he that hath not served a man that is unworthy of him;
        Happy is he that hath found prudence;
And he that discourseth in the ears of them that listen;
    How great is he that hath found Wisdom!
        Yet is there none above him that feareth the Lord.

The Love[2] of the Lord passeth all things:
He that holdeth it, to whom shall he be likened?

---

[1] This has obviously slipped out of the line [A. V. and R. V. of *Proverbs* xxx. 7 read 'them'], otherwise the sonnet would name 'two' things and enumerate 'three.'

[2] This is the reading of A. V. to *Ecclus.* xxv. 11: the R. V., no doubt on better textual authority, reads 'fear,' which destroys the form of the Sonnet. The emendation comes under the principle laid down above, page 57, note.

The other type of Sonnet is free to adopt high parallelism of any kind. A simple example was cited above, in which the lines fell into two blocks, one block of lines parallel with the first, the other of lines parallel with the second line of the couplet text. In the Sonnet that follows the lines seem to alternate irregularly: but upon examination it will appear that all on the left deal with the commandment, and those on the right with its reward.

The Free Sonnet

The Commandment and its Reward

My son, forget not my law;
But let thine heart keep my commandments:
    For length of days, and years of life,
    And peace, shall they add to thee.
Let not mercy and truth forsake thee;
Bind them about thy neck:
Write them upon the table of thine heart:
    So shalt thou find favour and good understanding
    In the sight of God and man.
Trust in the LORD with all thine heart,
And lean not upon thine own understanding:
In all thy ways acknowledge him,
    And he shall direct thy paths.
Be not wise in thine own eyes:
Fear the LORD and depart from evil:
    It shall be health to thy navel.
    And marrow to thy bones.
Honour the LORD with thy substance,
And with the first fruits of all thine increase:
    So shall thy barns be filled with plenty,
    And thy fats shall overflow with new wine.

More elaborate in structure is the Sonnet on Intoxication. It has the general form of an enigma: six short lines contain six questions, the common answer to which makes a single couplet of longer lines. Then these two parts are doubled, and their order reversed: the couplet is expanded into a quatrain, after which the ideas of the six opening lines are emphasised in six couplets.

On Intoxication

Who hath woe?
Who hath sorrow?
Who hath contentions?
Who hath complaining?
Who hath wounds without cause?
Who hath redness of eyes?
They that tarry long at the wine;
They that go to seek out mixed wine.

Look not thou upon the wine
When it is red,
When it giveth its colour in the cup,
When it goeth down smoothly:
　At the last it biteth like a serpent,
　　And stingeth like an adder.
　Thine eyes shall behold strange things,
　　And thine heart shall utter froward things.
　Yea, thou shalt be as he that lieth down in the midst of the sea,
　　Or as he that lieth upon the top of a mast.
"They have stricken me,
　And I was not hurt;
They have beaten me,
　And I felt it not;
When shall I awake?
　I will seek it yet again."

This single sonnet has illustrated two leading devices of sonnet form — reversing the order of parts, and augmenting. I add two more poems, illustrating each of these devices respectively, and further interesting from their thought and tone.

On the Unsearchableness of God

I have wearied myself, O God,
I have wearied myself, O God,
And am consumed:
For I am more brutish than any man,
And have not the understanding of a man:
And I have not learned wisdom,
Neither have I the knowledge of the Holy One.

Who hath ascended up into heaven, and descended?
Who hath gathered the wind in his fists?
Who hath bound the waters in his garment?
Who hath established all the ends of the earth?
> What is his name,
> And what is his son's name,
> If thou knowest?

If we may intrude upon the spiritual beauty of this poem by technical analysis, it is to point out how three short lines grow into four long, and then, by reverse process, four long sink into three short. In the example that follows form and thought are clearly working together. A quatrain of apprehension answered by a triplet of prayer augments into a double quatrain of apprehension answered by a double triplet of prayer. Such structural augmenting means spiritual intensification.

Watchfulness of Lips and Heart

Who shall set a watch over my mouth,
And a seal of shrewdness upon my lips,
That I fall not from it,
And that my tongue destroy me not?
> O Lord, Father and Master of my life,
> Abandon me not to their counsel:
> Suffer me not to fall by them.

Who will set scourges over my thought,
And a discipline of wisdom over my heart;
That they spare me not for mine ignorances,
And my heart pass not by their sins:
That my ignorances be not multiplied,
And my sins abound not;
And I shall fall before mine adversaries,
And mine enemy rejoice over me?
> O Lord,
> Father and God of my life,
> Give me not a proud look,
> And turn away concupiscence from me.
> Let not greediness and chambering overtake me,
> And give me not over to a shameless mind.

Before passing away from this class of composition, we may note that, as we saw in the case of the Essay, so the development of the Sonnet out of the Proverb can be illustrated in all its parts. One example is singularly complete. We are able to go back to an original germ preserved in another poem.

Development of Sonnets out of Proverbs

> For the drunkard and the glutton shall come to poverty,
> And drowsiness shall clothe a man with rags.

The thought of this unit proverb, namely, the second line which connects together drowsiness and rags, has grown into an epigram.

Epigram on the Sluggard

> "Yet a little sleep, a little slumber,
> A little folding of the hands to sleep":
> So shall thy poverty come as a robber;
> And thy want as an armed man.

We may judge that this epigram belonged to the extensive floating literature of proverbs, from the fact of its appearing in two distinct poems. These poems are sonnets, belonging, of course, to the age of individual poets; the two work from distinct points of view to the above epigram as their climax.

Sonnet on the Field of the Slothful

> I went by the field of the slothful,
> And by the vineyard of the man void of understanding;
> And, lo, it was all grown over with thorns,
> The face thereof was covered with nettles,
> And the stone wall thereof was broken down.
> Then I beheld, and considered well:
> I saw, and received instruction.
> "Yet a little sleep, a little slumber,
> A little folding of the hands to sleep":
> So shall thy poverty come as a robber;
> And thy want as an armed man.

**

Sonnet on the Sluggard

Go to the ant, thou sluggard;
Consider her ways, and be wise:
　Which having no chief,
　Overseer, or ruler,
　Provideth her meat in the summer,
　And gathereth her food in the harvest.
How long wilt thou sleep, O sluggard?
When wilt thou arise out of thy sleep?
　"Yet a little sleep, a little slumber,
　A little folding of the hands to sleep":
So shall thy poverty come as a robber,
And thy want as an armed man.

It remains to note, in conclusion, that Wisdom literature, on both its sides of verse and prose, is attracted by other literary departments, and compound forms arise. Prose Philosophy feels the attraction of Rhetoric, and we get as a result the Rhetoric Encomium. The name conveys the character of the composition; a writer sets himself formally to the task of praising Wisdom, or the works of the Lord, and the style has rhetorical flow rather than gnomic sententiousness. Indeed, these compositions are usually considered poems. But I have pointed out more than once, in connection with the general discussion of the subject, that parallelism by itself is an insufficient criterion of verse and prose, belonging as it does to Rhetoric equally with Hebrew verse. And when the matter of these encomia is considered, it seems to me nearer to the matter of prose essays than to that of sonnets. Even as regards structure, the parallelism is sometimes broken by what will make excellent prose, but feeble verse.

The Rhetoric Encomium

Good things are created from the beginning for the good: so are evil things for sinners. The chief of all things necessary for the life of man are water, and fire, and iron, and salt, and flour of wheat, and honey, and milk, the blood of the grape, and oil, and clothing. All these things are for good to the godly; so to the sinners they shall be turned into evil.

Ecclus. xxxix. 25

If this enumeration of necessary things be placed side by side with a not dissimilar enumeration taken from a lyric ode, the rhythmic gulf which separates the two will be apparent.

> Deut. xxxii. 13
>
> And he made him to suck honey out of the rock,
> And oil out of the flinty rock;
> Butter of kine, and milk of sheep,
> With fat of lambs.
> And rams of the breed of Bashan, and goats,
> With the fat of kidneys of wheat;
> And of the blood of the grape thou drankest wine.

In any case, the Rhetoric Encomium makes one more point at which Hebrew verse and prose approach one another.

On the other hand, Wisdom is attracted by Drama, and conveys its thoughts in the form of Dramatic Monologues. Wisdom is personified: she is made to build her house, to spread her table, to speak in warning or invitation. The most elaborate poem of this type in the *Book of Proverbs* prepares the way for the monologue itself by a vivid picture of the 'Strange Woman,' laying her snares, and speaking her wiles, till the simple victim follows, like an ox going to the slaughter, to the house that is the way to the Abyss. Immediately, without a word of connection, comes the contrast.

The Dramatic Monologue

> Doth not Wisdom cry,
> And Understanding put forth her voice?
> In the top of high places by the way,
> Where the paths meet, she standeth;
> Beside the gates, at the entry of the city,
> At the coming in at the doors, she crieth aloud.

Wisdom tells of her excellent things: of her instruction that is worth more than silver, her knowledge and subtlety more valuable than rubies and gold.

> Counsel is mine, and effectual working,
> I am understanding; I have might.
> By me kings reign;
> And princes decree justice.
> By me princes rule,
> And nobles, even all the judges of the earth.

The climax comes with creative wisdom. The scientific statement of the thought would be that the structure of the universe is such as to suggest design in its Author: but here the design itself is personified, and claims to have been with the Creator from the first.

> When there were no depths, I was brought forth;
> When there were no fountains abounding with water.
> Before the mountains were settled,
> Before the hills was I brought forth:
> While as yet he had not made the earth, nor the fields,
> Nor the beginning of the dust of the world.
> When he established the heavens, I was there:
> When he set a circle upon the face of the deep:
> When he made firm the skies above:
> When the fountains of the deep became strong:
> When he gave to the sea its bound.
> That the waters should not transgress his commandment:
> When he marked out the foundations of the earth:
> Then I was by him, as a master workman:
> And I was daily his delight,
> Sporting always before him;
> Sporting in his habitable earth.

In personifications like this the form of Drama is borrowed to clothe the meditations of the wise. But there are dramatic monologues which go further than personification, and put certain phases of philosophic reflection into the mouth of historical or imaginary personages. These, however, will be best dealt with in the chapters describing the Books of Wisdom in which they are found.

CHAPTER XII

THE SACRED BOOKS OF WISDOM

THE various literary forms in which the philosophical thought of Scripture may be cast have been reviewed: it remains to consider the Books of Wisdom as they stand.

The first of these is entitled *The Proverbs*. In technical form it may be described as a Miscellany in Five Books: the five-fold division of this work (and of *Ecclesiasticus*) being as well marked as in the *Book of Psalms*. The first book is made up of nine chapters. This is a portion of Scripture dear to every reader: for literary charm no part of the Bible is more impressive. I must, however, express dissent from the received view that the nine chapters make one continuous poem. The view seems to rest upon such considerations as these: the uniqueness in character of this section; the way in which it serves as prologue to what follows; the fact of its being cast in the form of a father's counsels to a son; while some have claimed to trace in it a regular progression of thought. The unique character of these chapters is sufficiently explained by the preponderance in them of one type of poem: out of twenty-two free sonnets and dramatic monologues eighteen are to be found in this section of *Proverbs*, and only four outside it.[1] Again: the chapters cannot be called a prologue in the sense of an introduction making reference to the rest of the work; on the other hand, it would be quite natural for the

The Proverbs: a miscellany in five books

First Book i-ix

---

[1] Throughout the chapter compare *Proverbs*, etc., in the Literary Index (Appendix I).

editor of the collection to place first poems treating Wisdom as a whole, and after these the proverbs that deal with more particular themes. As to the formula ' My Son,' it may be remarked that in considerable portions of the nine chapters it is absent,[1] portions apparently containing independent poems, one of which is addressed to a sluggard; where such a formula does occur it varies between ' My Son ' and ' My Sons,' which suggests its general character. When it is further seen that elsewhere the formula is found, rarely in unit proverbs, but commonly in the longer compositions of this kind,[2] there will be no difficulty in understanding why it should appear so often in this part of the book which is made up of long poems. In any case, the recurrence of the expression ' My Son ' is no more an evidence of connectedness, than would the recurrence from a modern pulpit Sunday after Sunday of the expression ' My Brethren ' prove that the preacher's successive sermons made a unity. The supposed progression of thought is rejected by many of those who accept the unity of the chapters; it can be traced only by supposing passages to be interpolations that do not fit in with it. But the idea must be pronounced impossible, if for no other reason, on the ground of repetitions and redundancies. That the theme of Wisdom and the Strange Woman, after being brought to a magnificent climax in the seventh and eighth chapters, should be treated again in brief studies in the ninth chapter, is entirely inconsistent with a continuous poem, though natural enough in that which is a collection of similar compositions.

This first section of *Proverbs* then, like the other sections, is miscellaneous in character. It is a series of poems that would be fairly described by the title, ' Sonnets on Wisdom.' In some [3] the name does not occur, but Wisdom is set off by kindred or by contrasting ideas. One sonnet exhibits the company of the evil

---

[1] i. 20–33; vi. 6–11, 12–19; ix. 1–6, 7–9, 10–12, 13–18.
[2] In unit proverbs I have only observed it twice (*Prov.* xxvii. 11 and *Ecclus.* vii. 3). It occurs in epigrams (*Prov.* xxiii. 15; xxiv. 13) and often in the essays and proverb clusters of *Ecclus.* (iv. 1; vi. 18; x. 28; xiv. 11; etc.). Compare the use of ' My Children ' (*Ecclus.* xli. 14) and ' Young Man ' (*Eccles.* xi. 9).
[3] Compare the titles of the sonnets, etc., in the Appendix.

as laying snares for their own lives; another contrasts the path of the wicked with the path of the righteous shining on from dawn to perfect day; others denounce the vices that Wisdom would hate. In the greater part of the poems Wisdom is celebrated directly: appearing as a gracious personality speaking her winning invitations, in contrast with the 'strange woman' that lures fools to their death; or as the great prize in view the sight of which is to make even chastening endurable; or as the 'principal thing' coming down from venerable tradition. In some places this Wisdom narrows to the prudence that takes alarm at the idea of suretiship for another, or the diligence that hates the sluggard. But elsewhere it gradually widens its scope, from the caution checking a personal impulse to sin, till it gathers into itself all subtlety and discretion, the knowledge of the counsellor and the justice of the great, and appears at last as the universal principle that has made the strength and beauty of the whole universe, playmate of the Creator from the earliest birth of time.

The second book has for its title: 'The Proverbs of Solomon,' and is by far the largest of the sections. Except that two triplets[1]
Second Book x-xxii. 16 have somehow crept into it, this whole book is a mass of unit proverbs. No attempt has been made to arrange them; in the fullest sense of the word the second book is a miscellany. The third book is a Gnomic
Third Book xxii. 17-xxiv Epistle. Its introduction makes clear that it is delivered in writing, and on the application of a delegate who represents others beside himself: the suggestion is of the intercourse that prevailed between Wise Men at a distance, such as Solomon and Hiram of Tyre.

> Incline thine ear, and hear the words of the wise, and apply thine heart unto my knowledge; for it is a pleasant thing if thou keep them within thee, if they be established together upon thy lips. That thy trust may be in the LORD, I have made them known to thee this day, even to thee. Have not I written unto thee excellent things of counsels and knowledge; to make thee know the certainty of the words of truth, that thou mayest carry back words of truth to them that send thee?

[1] xix. 7 and 23.

At the end of it there is a postscript commencing, "These also are sayings of the wise "— an addition, presumably, by an editor, not by the writer of the epistle. The epistle and postscript are mainly made up of epigrams; though there are two sonnets, and a few unit proverbs.[1]

The next book is described by its title as 'Proverbs of Solomon' copied out by the 'Men of Hezekiah.' When this is compared with the second book there is a noticeable difference. Unit proverbs still preponderate, but with these mingle epigrams; and the occurrence of a few proverb clusters shows that between the dates of the two collections the idea of arrangement, as well as expansion, has come in. One item in this fourth book should be noted as distinct from anything else preserved in Wisdom literature: it seems to be a Folk Song of Good Husbandry.

Fourth Book xxv-xxix

    Be thou diligent to know the state of thy flocks,   xxvii. 23-7
    And look well to thy herds:
        For riches are not for ever;
        And doth the crown endure unto all generations?
    The hay is carried,
    And the tender grass sheweth itself,
    And the herbs of the mountains are gathered in.
        The lambs are for thy clothing,
        And the goats are the price of the field:
        And there will be goat's milk enough for thy food,
        For the food of thy household;
        And maintenance for thy maidens.

The last book is made up of shorter collections: the sayings of Agur, chiefly fixed or number sonnets; the epigrams of Lemuel's mother; and the famous poem on the Virtuous Woman, which in the original is an acrostic.

Fifth Book xxx-xxxi

To the whole collection is prefixed what, in modern phraseology, might be called an elaborate title-page.

---

[1] Compare throughout the chapter the analysis of the books in the Appendix.

THE PROVERBS OF SOLOMON

The Son of David, King of Israel

To know wisdom and instruction;
To discern the words of understanding;
To receive instruction in wise dealing,
In righteousness and judgement and equity:
To give subtilty to the simple,
To the young man knowledge and discretion:
That the wise man may hear, and increase in learning;
And that the man of understanding may attain unto sound counsels:
To understand a proverb, and a figure;
The words of the wise, and their dark sayings.

Title-Page i. 1-6

This title-page is not meant to describe the whole contents of the collection as proverbs of Solomon; else, why should the title 'Proverbs of Solomon' be repeated at the head of particular sections? The prominence of this expression in the general title may be explained in one of two ways. The longest section may have given its name to the whole: a thing quite familiar to us in modern literature. But when we observe the contents of the sections specifically designated 'Proverbs of Solomon,' and see the preponderance in them of one kind of saying, the suggestion must occur that the phrase is the description of a type: and this Solomonian Proverb would seem to include the unit proverb and the brief epigrams.

The Book of Proverbs as a whole

If, then, we survey the *Book of Proverbs* as a whole, we find it a miscellany comprising various literary types, from the germ proverb to the elaborate sonnet or dramatic monologue; what arrangement there is, is based on the kind of composition, or has reference to author or compiler. The philosophic attitude reflected in the book is that of disconnected observations; there is no attempt to combine observations into a system. The correlation of all things, which is the instinctive aim of modern philosophy, has not at this period come to be treated with analytic reflection; it is on the other hand passionately adored under the name of 'Wisdom.'

The next work for our consideration is *The Wisdom of Jesus the son of Sirach*, which has curiously come to be known familiarly by the title, *Ecclesiasticus*: that is, a book to be read in churches, as distinguished from a book of canonical authority. Like *Proverbs*, this work is a miscellany, and all forms of Wisdom literature are represented in it. The difference of the two might fairly be described by saying that they represent, in general impression, the poetic side of Wisdom and its rhetoric side respectively; what sonnets and dramatic monologues are to *Proverbs*, that essays and rhetoric encomia are to *Ecclesiasticus*. The work falls naturally into five books; the dividing points being made by the emergence of the author's personality, and his celebration, not of particular themes, but of Wisdom and the works of God as a whole. The first book starts from an account of the author by his grandson, followed by a sonnet on Wisdom. At the opening of the second book the author's preface is interwoven into an encomium on Wisdom. "Wisdom," cries the author, "shall praise herself."

<small>Ecclesiasticus: a miscellany in five books</small>

<small>Prefaces to the several books</small>

<small>xxiv. 1</small>

> I came forth from the mouth of the Most High, and covered the earth as a mist. I dwelt in high places, and my throne is in the pillar of the cloud. Alone I compassed the circuit of heaven, and walked in the depth of the abyss. In the waves of the sea, and in all the earth, and in every people and nation, I got a possession. With all these I sought rest; and in whose inheritance shall I lodge? So the Creator of all things gave me a commandment; and he that created me made my tabernacle to rest, and said, Let thy tabernacle be in Jacob, and thine inheritance in Israel.

Wisdom dwells upon her exaltation and beauty, and on the fulness of her riches; then the author speaks to identify these riches with the law of the Lord, from whom came the abundance of Wisdom.

> The first man knew her not perfectly; and in like manner the last hath not traced her out. For her thoughts are filled from the sea, and her counsels from the great deep. And I came out as a stream

from a river, and as a conduit into a garden. I said, I will water my garden, and will water abundantly my garden bed; and lo, my stream became a river, and my river became a sea. I will yet bring instruction to light as the morning, and will make them to shine forth afar off.

In this quaint and beautiful figure does the author express to the reader how his materials have grown upon him, and he must add a second book to the first. The third book is opened only by a brief preface in which the author describes himself as one gleaning after grape gatherers; but in the case of the remaining two books the author appears at the commencement inviting to the praise of God's works, and so introducing what are rhetoric encomia closely bordering on hymns.

<small>xxxiii. 16-18</small>

<small>xxxix. 12 and xlii. 15</small>

In this fifth book occurs that which is the most extended of all the compositions so far noted in this department,—the Encomium on Famous Men. In the prologue the author proposes to praise those who have manifested the Lord's mighty power, whether as rulers, or counsellors, or men of learning; inventors of music and verse; or rich men living peaceably in their habitations.

<small>Encomium on Famous Men xliv-l.24</small>

There be of them, that have left a name behind them, to declare their praises. And some there be which have no memorial; who are perished as though they had not been, and are become as though they had not been born; and their children after them. But these were men of mercy whose righteous deeds have not been forgotten. With their seed shall remain continually a good inheritance; their children are within the covenants. Their seed standeth fast, and their children for their sakes. Their seed shall remain for ever, and their glory shall not be blotted out. Their bodies were buried in peace, and their name liveth to all generations; peoples will declare their wisdom, and the congregation telleth out their praise.

In a tone of dignified panegyric he goes through the roll of Israel's great men: Enoch, Noah, the patriarchs; Moses, the man of mercy, with Aaron and the third in glory the zealous Phinehas;

Nathan, David, Solomon, Josiah of fragrant memory, until he ends with Simon whom, in all the pomp of his priestly function, he describes with the vividness of an eye-witness.

Immediately after the close of this Encomium the work ends with something that reads like the colophon of a mediæval book, made out of a number sonnet and a beatitude. *Colophon. 1. 25-9*

> With two nations is my soul vexed,
> And the third is no nation:
>   They that sit upon the mountain of Samaria,
>   ·And the Philistines,
> And the foolish people that dwelleth in Sichem.

> I have written in this book the instruction of understanding and knowledge, I Jesus, the son of Sirach, of Jerusalem, who out of his heart poured forth wisdom.

> Blessed is he that shall be exercised in these things;
>   And he that layeth them up in his heart shall become wise.
> For if he do them, he shall be strong to all things:
>   For the light of the Lord is his guide.

There is still added after this a 'Prayer of Jesus the son of Sirach,' with a confession of faith in Wisdom; from their position they may be assumed to be either the insertion of the grandson, or other editor, or else the preface to the whole book as left by its author. *li*

It is instructive to compare *Ecclesiasticus* and *Proverbs* as types of Wisdom literature. If the comparison be made of individual compositions in the two works, those of *Ecclesiasticus* will be found to show a marked advance as regards the combination of shorter into longer, which implies the extension of more limited into wider observations of life. The proverb cluster, so slenderly represented in the *Book of Proverbs*, has a considerable place in the later work; and a still larger space in it is occupied by the essay, which, we have seen, carries the aggregation of unit proverbs to a higher degree *Proverbs and Ecclesiasticus compared* of fusion. But when we look at *Ecclesiasticus* as a whole, its contents appear as miscellaneous as those of *Proverbs;* the work clearly appeals to a discursive taste, unhampered by any thought of system or arrangement; and, however elaborate the essays or sonnets may become, these have not been thought by the author inconsistent with considerable spaces left for entirely disconnected proverbs. This is the more striking from the fact that the later work is not, like *Proverbs,* a combination of different collections; it is entirely the work of a single author, who has spoken in his own person to mark the beginnings and endings of the five books: making it clear that the miscellaneous character of the work belongs to the author's conception of Philosophy, and is not the result of chance or want of care. We have thus reached a phase of thought in which systematisation begins to work upon the more fragmentary observations of life, without approaching the conception of life and the universe as a whole. Wisdom and the works of God in general are still celebrated with poetic or rhetoric fervour. The last composition, the Praise of Famous Men, shows that the conception of Wisdom has now enlarged to take in history. But this history is touched only with the tone of panegyric; and *Ecclesiasticus* thus contrasts with a later work of this department, in which we shall see history subjected to philosophic reflection and analysis.

What *Ecclesiasticus* is to the Old Testament, that the *Epistle of St. James* is to the New. We have already seen in a portion of the *Book of Proverbs* a precedent for a Wisdom Epistle; and with this conception fits the difference of tone which every reader perceives between this portion of the New Testament and all the rest. The Apostle, moreover, shows himself a deep student of *Ecclesiasticus,* the thoughts of which he frequently echoes.[1] Of course, the matter of

Gnomic Epistle of St. James

---

[1] For the Essay on the "Origin of the Evil," etc. (*St. James* i. 12–27), compare *Ecclus.* Essay on Free Will (xv. 11–20); and also *Ecclus.* v. 11 and iv. 10. — For the Essay on the "Responsibility of Speech" (*St. James* iii. 1–12) compare *Ecclus.*

the epistle has enlarged to take in Christian thought, and 'My Son' has changed into 'My Brethren.' But the form is that of *Proverbs* and *Ecclesiasticus*—a miscellany: the epistle will not yield a connected line of thought such as is traced in the writings of St. Paul, but must be read as a series of independent essays. Two of these essays have been cited in the last chapter—that on the Sources of the Evil and the Good in Man, and another on The Responsibility of Speech. Others are On Faith and Works; On Respect of Persons; On the Earthly Wisdom and the Wisdom from above; A Discourse on Judgment. And here, as in other Books of Wisdom, we find interspersed between these longer essays maxims and paradoxes entirely disconnected.

We now approach *Ecclesiastes*: most fascinating of all Wisdom literature to those who desire only to read, while it is the stumbling-block of all who have the responsibility of interpreting. Yet the difficulties and obscurities which undoubtedly attach to this work have been much aggravated by the neglect of the axiom on which I have so frequently insisted: that it is vain to search into the meaning of a work until its outer literary form has been determined. Our first duty then is to enquire into the form of *Ecclesiastes*, basing our enquiry upon the book itself, and also upon what may be expected from the analogy of other Wisdom literature.

Ecclesiastes: its form

In the first place, *Ecclesiastes*, like the other Books of Wisdom we have surveyed, contains a series of essays: the attempt to trace a continuous argument from beginning to end must be dismissed. On the other hand, the most cursory examination shows a new purpose in the thinkings of the Preacher such as is sure to affect the form of the book. We find in *Ecclesiastes*, what was so markedly absent from *Proverbs* and *Ecclesiasticus*, that reflection

---

Essay on Gossip (xix. 5-17), on the Tongue (xxviii. 12-26).—Other parallels are *Ecclus.* i. 26 and *St. James* i. 5; *Ecclus.* ii. 1-6 and *St. James* i. 12; *Ecclus.* ii. 1 and 14 and *St. James* i. 2-4; *Ecclus.* iv. 1-6, xxi. 5 with *St. James* v. 4; *Ecclus.* x. 22-24 and *St. James* ii. 1-6.—Possibly the somewhat obscure paradox in *St. James* i. 9 may be an echo of *Ecclus.* iii. 18-19.

has now been turned upon life as a whole, and particular observations have a reference to the general problem of reading the meaning of existence. Accordingly, the individual essays in this book must be expected to unite in some common drift; their mutual relation can best be expressed by borrowing — as literature so often must — a term from music, and *Ecclesiastes* may be described as a *suite* of essays. One more point needs to be insisted upon. In each collection of Wisdom literature we have found that, whatever else there might be, there was always a place for series of disconnected proverbs interspersed amongst more extended compositions. This feature is not wanting to the work under consideration: of the ten sections (to include prologue and epilogue) into which I have divided the whole,[1] three are not essays, but strings of disconnected sayings and paradoxes, more or less tinged with the tone of the author, but outside the drift of thought in the essays. The recognition of such gaps in the unity is clearly of importance to the interpretation of the whole; yet it is no more than we are bound to expect from the analogy of other Wisdom literature.

We find, then, *Ecclesiastes* to be in form a suite of independent essays, regularly disposed between a formal prologue and epilogue, concurring to present some enquiry into life as a whole, and separated at intervals by collections of the isolated sayings which had constituted the older conception of Wisdom. Our business must be to follow the thought of the separate essays, and then put our results together in order to understand the Preacher's general view of life and the universe.

The Prologue breathes the spirit of the whole in its reiteration, "Vanity of vanities, all is vanity." Philosophy has turned itself from mere observation of the details to contemplation of the whole, and in this contemplation can see no solid result; its enquiry, to use a phrase of a later essay, is a striving after wind — continuous pursuit of that which continually eludes.

Prologue
i. 2-11

[1] Compare the Literary Index in Appendix I.

> One generation goeth, and another generation cometh; and the earth abideth for ever. The sun also ariseth, and the sun goeth down, and hasteth to his place where he ariseth. The wind goeth toward the south, and turneth about unto the north; it turneth about continually in its course, and the wind returneth again to its circuits. All the rivers run into the sea, yet the sea is not full; unto the place whither the rivers go, thither they go again. All things are full of weariness; man cannot utter it: the eye is not satisfied with seeing, nor the ear filled with hearing. That which hath been is that which shall be; and that which hath been done is that which shall be done: and there is no new thing under the sun.

The writer's imagination has been overpowered by the vast "wheel of nature": the first glimpse from the outside of that interdependence of things which modern science has tracked up to the conservation of energy. In contemplation of this, life seems not a progress but a treadmill, and the human world is drawn within the tyranny of Law. The impressiveness of this prologue appears the greater when it is realised that the 'All,' which is thus pronounced 'vanity,' is precisely that which previous books would joyously celebrate under the name of 'Wisdom.' Philosophic reflection has been turned on to the sum of things, and adoration has changed to elegy.

We proceed to the first essay, and at the outset are met by an obstacle: the unfortunate misinterpretation of a single verse—a double misinterpretation—has had the effect of throwing a false colour over the whole work. The essay opens with the words: "I the Preacher was king over Israel in Jerusalem": and what follows identifies the king referred to with King Solomon. Hence readers have jumped to the conclusion that Solomon was the author of *Ecclesiastes*. The mistake is not unnatural in a modern reader, whose leading interest in a literary work is apt to be the author; but a student of Comparative Literature will see at once that these words make Solomon, not the author, but the hero of the narrative that follows. Several schools of ancient philosophy instinctively attributed to

First Essay i. 12-ii

Mistake as to Solomon's authorship of the book

the first founder all that each follower produced. In this way the whole of Plato's philosophy is given to the world, not in the form of abstract arguments by Plato himself, but in highly dramatic dialogues, in which Socrates, as main speaker, is represented in discussion with other prominent men of the age, the discussion abounding in touches of wit, scenery, and action, as artistically disposed as in the scenes of Shakespeare. No reader ever supposed that Socrates said what Plato represents him to say; but Socrates had started the impulse of thought which produced Plato, and the scholar pays reverence to his master by making him the hero of his dialogues. Another striking instance has been pointed out by a recent writer on this book:[1] that the school of Pythagoras considered the drowning of one of their number a judgment upon him because he had put forward his discovery in his own name, instead of making it part of the philosophy of Pythagoras. But there is no need to go so far for illustrations: a companion production to this *Ecclesiastes* is the *Wisdom of Solomon*, which, at a date little removed from the Christian era, makes King Solomon the speaker of all the philosophic stores of that late age. It belongs to Hebrew philosophy, we have seen, to clothe itself in poetic and dramatic form: to put into the mouth of Solomon reflections a later writer thinks fitted to his personality is no more than an extension of the dramatising treatment by which, in *Proverbs*, Wisdom was personified as the inviter to all good things. On the other hand, authorship is a question of dates; and, apart from this verse, all the indications of language, style, and matter, are found by experts to indicate a date for the book centuries later than that of Solomon. Dr. Ginsburg has pronounced it as impossible for Solomon to be the author of *Ecclesiastes*, as for Chaucer to be the writer of *Rasselas*.

The old interpretation involves a double mistake. Not only is Solomon the hero instead of the author, but he is the hero for only a fraction of the whole book. The narrative that commences with the verse under discussion extends no further than the close

[1] Article *Ecclesiastes* in Sir William Smith's Dictionary of the Bible.

of the second chapter.¹ From that point onward there is not to be found a sentence that associates itself with Solomon. And in the prologue and epilogue, where we naturally look for personal touches, there is no trace of this wise king, either in direct mention, or in circumstances into which his personality can be fitted.

The connection of Solomon, then, with the book as a whole must be abandoned; and with it must be given up the idea of finding in the unwholesome life of that monarch an explanation for the tone of *Ecclesiastes*. Solomon's place in the book is limited to a single essay, which may be entitled: Solomon's Great Experiment. The author identifies himself for the moment with this famous king, as the one individual in whom wealth, wisdom, and power met in their highest forms, and in his person the Preacher supposes himself to go through an experience designed to test all the forms of positive good in which men believe. First, he will use his resources to accumulate all kinds of pleasure, including such pleasures as wise men call follies, but he will keep all the time his reflective powers unimpaired for the purpose of testing what he enjoys.

ii. 1

> I made me great works; I builded me houses; I planted me vineyards; I made me gardens and parks, and I planted trees in them of all kinds of fruit: I made me pools of water, to water therefrom the forest where trees were reared: I bought men-servants and maidens, and had servants born in my house; also I had great possessions of herds and flocks, above all that were before me in Jerusalem: I gathered me also silver and gold, and the peculiar treasure of kings and of the provinces: I gat me men singers and women singers, and the delights of the sons of men, concubines very many. So I was great, and increased more than all that were before me in Jerusalem: also my wisdom remained with me. And whatsoever mine eyes desired I kept not from them: I withheld not my heart from any joy, for my heart rejoiced because of all my labour;

¹ Even less far than that if we assume the marginal readings of R. V. (to ii. 5, and the first of those to ii. 12); it would then extend no further than ii. 11. This would ascribe to Solomon just that part of the whole experiment which none but Solomon could have fully carried out.

and this was my portion from all my labour. Then I looked on all the works that my hands had wrought, and on the labour that I had laboured to do: and, behold, all was vanity and a striving after wind, and there was no profit under the sun.

From pleasure he turns to experiment in the field of wisdom itself and its opposite. He finds indeed that wisdom excels folly as far as light excels darkness: but he finds also that "one event" happeneth to both. There is yet a third region to be tried — labour, or as we should call it, enterprise: not the enjoyment of wealth, but its production. But this also seems to fail in the end, when the labourer must die and leave his labour to another, not knowing whether this other will prove a wise man or a fool. So the result of all this experimenting is that there is no criterion for ranking anything as higher than mere enjoyment. Is, then, this enjoyment the one reality that has stood the test of his long enquiry? Not at all: for the thought soon follows that this enjoyment is not a thing in man's power, but is itself the gift of God. The great experiment has yielded only negative results: "vanity and a striving after wind."

<small>ii. 13</small>

<small>ii. 18</small>

<small>ii. 24</small>

The second essay may be entitled: The Philosophy of Times and Seasons. A certain theory of the universe seems to be suggested, as something to satisfy the craving for an explanation of things, for which the great experiment had failed to provide. The theory is stated, examined, and rejected.

<small>Second Essay
iii-iv. 8</small>

> To everything there is a season, and a time to every purpose under the heaven: a time to be born, and a time to die; a time to plant, and a time to pluck up that which is planted; a time to kill, and a time to heal; a time to break down, and a time to build up; a time to weep, and a time to laugh; a time to mourn, and a time to dance; a time to cast away stones, and a time to gather stones together; a time to embrace, and a time to refrain from embracing; a time to seek, and a time to lose; a time to keep, and a time to cast away; a time to rend, and a time to sew; a time to keep silence, and a time to speak; a time to love, and a time to hate; a time for war, and a time for peace.

Hebrew philosophy affects artistic, and especially gnomic forms, and in the guise of this *tour de force* of enumeration is clothed a very intelligible philosophy; — indeed, that which was the unconscious theory underlying the old Wisdom, with its tendency to observe the parts, but turn no reflection upon the whole. It is a sort of practical eclecticism; a disposition to recognise differences of kind in good things without comparing them. The previous essay has sought a *summum bonum :* this suggests the idea, not *summum bonum*, but *multa bona.* Against this theory the Preacher seems to make four distinct objections. First: it is true that separate things have an interest of their own. But it iii. 9-11
is also true that God has implanted in men's hearts a conception of the universal underlying these particulars; so that it is no longer possible to enjoy these without thinking of their bearing on the whole; while to discover this last all man's powers are insufficient.

> He hath made everything beautiful in its time: also he hath set the world in their heart, yet so that man cannot find out the work that God hath done from the beginning even to the end.

Again: it is true that there is nothing better than to enjoy. But it is also true that this enjoyment is the gift of God, and in granting it God will act upon principles as fixed iii. 12-15
as fate, and no effort will change him. Yet again: the 'seasons' of things are not observed; wickedness is seen in the place of judgment. A flash of thought suggests to the iii. 16-22
Preacher that hereafter there may be a righting of these wrongs. A second flash rejects the idea: what guarantee of an hereafter has man more than the beasts?

> I said in mine heart, God shall judge the righteous and the wicked: for there is a time THERE for every purpose and for every work. I said in mine heart, It is because of the sons of men, that God may prove them, and that they may see that they themselves are but as beasts. For that which befalleth the sons of men befalleth beasts; even one thing befalleth them: as the one dieth, so dieth the other.

As a final objection the Preacher thinks of the things that no season can make beautiful: the oppression that is worse than death; the skill that exists at the cost of bitter competition; the isolated life that has no pleasure in its own achievements. The essay ends, like the last, in 'vanity.'

iv. 1-4

Then follows one of the sections we have been led to expect, that are occupied with isolated proverbs having no relation to the unity of the whole book. The sayings are miscellaneous, with nothing in common except that they are positive, not negative, in form. It is a section of Maxims of Life.

The fourth section is an Essay on the Vanity of Desire. It is easy to instance possession without enjoyment: a man loving silver yet never satisfied with silver; seeing goods increase, but seeing also increased those who consume them; or even riches kept by the owner of them to his own hurt. But the essay is mainly occupied with two companion pictures. One is that of a man to whom God grants riches and wealth, and at the same time the power to enjoy them: so much so that he may give little thought to his life as one happy day follows another, joy of heart coming as answer to his prayers almost before they are uttered. The other picture is of a man on whom God has bestowed without stint the same gifts, but has denied him the power to enjoy:

v. 10–vi. 12

v. 20

> I say, that an untimely birth is better than he: for it cometh in vanity, and departeth in darkness, and the name thereof is covered with darkness: moreover it hath not seen the sun nor known it; this hath rest rather than the other.

The sight of the eyes is better than the vain wandering of desire. Why should man enlarge his desires?

vi. 10-12

> Whatsoever he be, his name was given him long ago, and it is known that he is Man.

The force of these words will be abundantly evident when we recollect the tendency of ancient thought to look upon the Name of a thing as its formula of definition. Human activity is presented as energy striving against inherent limitation. Man is Fate to himself.

After another of the relief sections, occupied with miscellaneous Paradoxes of Life, we come to an important essay, **Fourth Essay** which puts the thought of the opening section from vii. 23-ix. 16 a somewhat different point of view.

> I said, I will be wise; but it was far from me. That which is is far off, and exceeding deep; who can find it out? I turned about, and my heart was set to know and to search out, and to seek wisdom and the reason of things, and to know the wickedness of folly, and foolishness which is madness.

In other words: Perhaps the problem of life is too vast to be solved, but is an *approach* to the solution possible? Accordingly, the enquirer sets himself to take what steps he can in this direction. Hence the essay may be entitled: " The Search for Wisdom with Notes by the way." The section is a long one, and in the course of it the formula, " I find," or, " All this have I seen," ushers in some particular observation presented as an instalment of the solution of life. There is no need to dwell upon the details; most of his notes are notes of disappointment. But beside these one stands out in strong contrast.

> Go thy way, eat thy bread with joy, and drink thy wine with a merry heart; for God hath already accepted thy works. Let thy garments be always white; and let not thy head lack ointment. Live joyfully with the wife whom thou lovest ix. 7 all the days of the life of thy vanity, which he hath given thee under the sun, all the days of thy vanity: for that is thy portion in life, and in thy labour wherein thou labourest under the sun.

There is another miscellaneous section, and then we reach the two final sections. These consist of an essay **Fifth Essay** followed by a sonnet. The essay presents Life as **and Sonnet** a Joy shadowed by the Judgment. The sonnet xi. 7-xii. 7 is one of the most familiar and beautiful of all Biblical poems, with its symbolic picture of old age.

Rejoice, O young man, in thy youth; and let thy heart cheer thee in the days of thy youth, and walk in the ways of thine heart, and in the sight of thine eyes: but know thou, that for all these things God will bring thee into judgement.

It is most important to avoid reading into this Old Testament Wisdom associations drawn from the New Testament. 'The judgment' is one of the dominant ideas of Hebrew literature: but it is by no means what modern Christianity understands by that term. That evil and good are inherently antagonistic, that evil is doomed to fail in the struggle with good,—this is the thought underlying the word 'judgment' in Old Testament poetry: but there is in the conception no note of time and place, no distinction even of this world and an hereafter. Thus the effect of the passage quoted is to recommend happiness, but happiness accompanied with a sense of responsibility. The very shortness of life is made by this essay a reason for putting sorrow away, and reaping to the full the bliss of living. But with this joyous youth must be united the remembrance of Him who has created it, and the familiar sonnet follows to paint the coming of the evil days, the decrepitude unfavourable alike to the realisation of happiness and to the search after God.

The Epilogue starts, like the Prologue, with the cry, "Vanity of vanities, all is vanity!" It goes on to say that the Preacher continued to pour out his stores of Wisdom, that he 'pondered and sought out' and 'set in order' many proverbs : the latter term would just describe the elaborated essays of the book, as the former expression would fit the miscellaneous sections. After a warning against multiplication of books, a conclusion is made by pronouncing the whole duty of man to be the fear of God and the keeping of his commandments, in view of the judgment into which every work will be brought.

Epilogue xii. 8-14

The separate parts have been surveyed : what is the significance of the whole? The Prologue cries, "All is vanity"; the Epilogue, "Fear God"; the Essays have the function of linking the two ideas. A twofold spirit, negative and positive, prevails through the book; it is a work of destructive criticism, with one positive thought emerging and becoming continually stronger. The supposed experiment of Solomon reduced all things to the level of enjoyment: but this enjoyment, it was added, comes from God. In the attack on eclecticism, the thought was repeated more strongly: enjoyment depends, not on the man who is to enjoy, but on God, and therefore on inexorable law. The next essay elaborately contrasted one to whom God had given wealth and the power to enjoy it, with another who had the possession without the enjoyment. In the description of the search after Wisdom, the gloomy failures were interrupted by a single picture of bright simple happiness, with the important addition that such happiness was a token that God had accepted the man's works. And the final essay occupies its whole field with the idea of joy tempered by a sense of responsibility. Devout scepticism as a background for natural happiness: this seems to sum up the whole thought of the book. Interpreters who have seen *Ecclesiastes* clouded by its supposed connection with the life of the historic Solomon have pronounced it scepticism, or hedonism, or cynicism. Cynicism it certainly is not: for its one positive conclusion is the supremacy of happiness. If it be hedonism, it is hedonism by Divine right. The Preacher cannot mention enjoyment without adding that it is God's gift; the happiness he celebrates must be 'natural,' that is, tempered by sense of responsibility and the thought of God's judgment; the means of pleasure, such as wealth and position, may be possessed by the wicked, but the power to enjoy them is God's own hall mark on the man he has accepted. Scepticism this book of *Ecclesiastes* certainly is, but it is scepticism with constant reference to God. God is recognised as the author of all things, the sole judge whose authority determines right and wrong. Nay, God is represented as himself the author of the intellectual despair that is the essence of scepticism, since he has placed the world in man's heart, yet so that man cannot find out the work that God doeth from the beginning even unto the end.

Ecclesiastes as a whole

The Bible, in the universality of its literary field, finds a place for scepticism; but it presents a scepticism that is not impious but devout, not gloomy but a ground for sober happiness and a full life.

Yet there is a point of view from which *Ecclesiastes* may be described as pessimist: at all events in compari-son with another work of Wisdom literature. The Preacher surveys life as a whole: but it is life bounded by this world. Once indeed the thought of a judgment hereafter occurs for a moment; but it is dismissed with a despair that sees man as only one of the beasts.

<small>Attitude of the book to a Future Life</small>

<small>iii. 16-21</small>

> That which befalleth the sons of men befalleth beasts; even one thing befalleth them: as the one dieth, so dieth the other; yea, they all have one breath; and man hath no pre-eminence above the beasts: for all is vanity. All go unto one place; all are of the dust, and all turn to dust again. Who knoweth the spirit of man whether it goeth upward, and the spirit of the beast whether it goeth downward to the earth?

This attitude to the future recurs again and again: every vista along which the Preacher looks for light appears bounded by death. Like the answer to a challenge, then, comes the remaining 'Book of Wisdom,' which borrows once more the dramatic form of the historic Solomon, and in his name puts forward the startling truths that God made not death, that righteousness is immortal; while it proceeds, with wonderful picturesqueness of imagination, to present the scene of the judgment hereafter, of which the Preacher had despaired. But the *Wisdom of Solomon* is so important in matter and so unique in form that it needs a chapter to itself.

CHAPTER XIII

'THE WISDOM OF SOLOMON'

THE *Wisdom of Solomon* resembles the early Books of Wisdom in clothing deep reflection with artistic and even dramatic form. It goes far beyond these in the demands it makes upon the imagination. The dramatic monologue, applied to the idea of a judgment hereafter, pre- sents an elaborate and moving picture of the wicked triumphant on earth and their terrible awakening beyond the grave. Indeed, *Wisdom* has an artistic weapon peculiarly its own, which may be called Analytic Imagination. With reverent curiosity it reads into the cautious reticence of some sacred narrative an array of imaginary details. *Exodus* speaks of a "darkness which might be felt": *Wisdom* boldly sketches all that the imprisoned Egyptians might be conceived to feel in that darkness, and the result is one of the marvels of creative literature.

<small>'Wisdom of Solomon': its form</small>

The form of the book is distinguished by another characteristic,—a product of different influences. The Apocrypha stands between our Old and New Testaments. When the writings which make the Old Testament came to a close, Hebrew literature still continued in an oral form: the vast literature of commentary which, from the time of Ezra, maintained itself and gathered volume, until, in the Christian era, it took shape in the Talmud. It would have been strange if that which made so large a part of Jewish religious life had left no trace in the written literature of the times. A slight trace may be seen in what we have called maxims, the brief compositions which take the form of texts with comments. But in the *Wisdom of Solomon* the discourses are entirely in this form of text and comment.[1] The discourses are (so to speak) *dovetailed* together, the final thought of one being akin to the text of the next. And the whole book is made up of such discourses: the strings of disconnected proverbs which in previous collections separated the longer compositions have now disappeared.

Texts with comments

In this last of the Books of Wisdom there is a curious feature of style, which may be just mentioned here, while its fuller treatment is relegated to an Appendix.[2] This is the use of Digression, not as an accidental device, but as an end in itself. What at first gives the impression of obscurity is soon recognised as an elaborate series of digressions, and digressions from those digressions, carrying the argument further and further from the original thought; in one case the dropped threads are regularly gathered up, and the argument brought back to its starting-point. When this peculiarity is combined with characteristics previously mentioned, it will be easy to understand the following as the structural form of the *Wisdom of Solomon:* A suite of five Discourses on texts, the last of which has a sevenfold illustration, at one point of which occurs a sevenfold digression.

Special use of Digressions

Passing from form to matter, we may say that this book resembles *Ecclesiastes* in the fact that it turns reflection upon the sum of things, and not merely upon details. But any such resemblance is thrown into the shade by the wide difference of *Wisdom*, both from *Ecclesiastes* and from the earlier books, in its conception of the sum of things which is to be surveyed.

Its Matter: enlarged conception of Wisdom

---

[1] The sentences which make the texts are easily distinguishable. Whereas the other sentences are closely locked together by argumentative particles, the text sentences are, in the first two discourses, independent and hortatory (i. 1, i. 12); the text of the third (vi. 12) is an independent gnomic sentence. In the last two sections the texts are the final sentences of the preceding discourses (last line of ix. 18, xi. 5), which are gnomic, and unmistakably make new departures in the argument.

[2] See Appendix IV.

In the first place, it is remarkable that in the earlier philosophy of the Bible the examination of external nature has no place. The mass of unit proverbs, and the essays arising out of these, turn upon topics of human life. If there is mention of the diligent ant, of the creatures little and wise, of the stately marchers, it is to point from them a human moral; even the Preacher describes the rain clouds pouring their fulness on the earth, or the perpetual drift of rivers to the sea, only to find in these images of fatalism. The exquisite observation which, in *Job*, speaks of the dayspring taking hold of the ends of the earth until the dull landscape has changed as clay under the seal, is the observation of the poet; and from a similar source comes the sympathy with the wild ass in its desert freedom and the war horse chafing under restraint, and the wealth of detail which builds up the pictures of behemoth and leviathan. The first book of *Proverbs* and the prefatory sections of *Ecclesiasticus* deal largely with external nature: but only as the works of the Lord which are to be magnified. Thus the son of Sirach celebrates the clear firmament, the sun bringing tidings as he goes, and the rainbow glory, only to assist the thought that the Lord made all these things; he enumerates the material things chiefly necessary for man, and proclaims that these are for good to the godly, but for sinners they shall be turned into evil; he makes a climax by the thought that this Wisdom, of which these glories are a part, has been commanded to find a tabernacle in Jacob and an inheritance in Israel. It is only in the last of the Wisdom Books that we find the analytic examination of nature for its own sake which makes the substance of modern science; and the passage which sets forth knowledge of this kind ends by claiming it as part of the universal Wisdom.

Ecclus. xxiv. 8

> For himself gave me an unerring knowledge of the things that are, to know the constitution of the world, and the operation of the elements, the beginning and end and middle of times, the alternations of the solstices and the changes of seasons, the circuits of years and the positions of stars; the natures of

vii. 17

living creatures and the ragings of wild beasts, the violences of winds and the thoughts of men, the diversities of plants and the virtues of roots: all things that are either secret or manifest I learned, for she that is the artificer of all things taught me, even Wisdom.

History, no less than nature, is conspicuous by its absence from the early Books of Wisdom. In the whole of *Proverbs* and *Ecclesiastes*,[1] and in four out of the five books of *Ecclesiasticus*, there is not a single allusion to an historic event. The fifth book of *Ecclesiasticus* is largely occupied with history; but here the introductory words—

Let us now praise famous men—

prepare us to expect, what the subsequent chapters confirm, that the writer treats history, as he treats nature, for purposes of rhetoric encomium, not of scientific reflection. On the other hand, more than half of the *Wisdom of Solomon* consists in analytic examination of history; and its conception of 'Wisdom' is enlarged to include the emergence of providential design from beneath the succession of events.

But there is a still more important widening of the field of view in the last of the Books of Wisdom. The early books, ignoring nature and history, confined their reflection to human life: but the life they surveyed was a life bounded by the grave. In *Proverbs* and *Ecclesiasticus* there is nowhere a suggestion of anything but this. In the case of *Ecclesiastes* I have drawn attention[2] to the passage in which the Preacher for a single moment entertains the thought of a judgment after death, only to fling it away and plunge into a pessimist doubt whether human life can have any ending different from that of the brutes. But in the *Wisdom of Solomon* the starting-point and foundation of the whole argument is the extension of life beyond the grave; an immortality bound up with righteousness and the redress of wrong is assumed with

---

[1] I have argued above (page 297) that Solomon's experiment in i. 2 must be understood as an imaginary incident; and similarly iv. 13-16 and ix. 13-16 are, like all the context, general statements.

[2] See above, pages 299, 304.

such certainty that it is the 'ungodly' who are presented as ignoring it.

This fact inevitably raises the question: Is the *Wisdom of Solomon* an answer to *Ecclesiastes?* In parts of *Wisdom* particular phrases and turns of expression seem to echo thoughts of the earlier book. The Preacher has cried that "the sons of men are a chance, and the beasts are a chance, and one thing befalleth them"; that man hath no "power over the day of death, and there is no discharge in that war." The ungodly of the later book reflect that by mere chance they were born, and hereafter they will be as though they had never been, and none was ever known that gave release from Hades. In *Ecclesiastes:* {Relation of Wisdom to Ecclesiastes} {iii. 19; viii. 8} {ii. 1, 2}

> The dead know not anything, neither have they any more a reward; for the memory of them is forgotten. As well their love as their hatred and their envy is now perished; neither have they any more a portion for ever in anything that is done under the sun. {ix. 5, 6}

The same strain is heard in *Wisdom:*

> And our name shall be forgotten in time, and no man shall remember our works; and our life shall pass away as the traces of a cloud, and shall be scattered as is a mist. {ii. 4}

One of the few positive thoughts of the Preacher is that Wisdom excelleth folly as far as light excelleth darkness: and the later book finds a climax for its panegyric on Wisdom in the reflection — {ii. 13}

> Being compared with light she is found to be before it; for to the light of day succeedeth night, but against wisdom evil doth not prevail. {vii. 29}

Above all, the pessimism of *Ecclesiastes* reflects that "the righteous, and the wise, and their works, are in the hand of God": that they know not what fortune he will bestow upon them and {ix. 1} are powerless to influence it. The phrase seems to be caught up by the optimist thinker —

iii. 1   The souls of the righteous are in the hand of God, and no torment shall touch them —

and this is his foundation for a picture of goodness triumphant. Such parallelisms are insufficient to prove anything as to the intention of the writer; but they certainly serve as an enhancement to the literary interest of the reader.

When we consider the matter and general argument of *Wisdom* there is more ground for considering it a veiled answer to *Ecclesiastes*. This will appear as I proceed to review the several discourses. I may here, however, premise, that the suggestion is not of any such antagonism between the two books as would imply that one was right and the other wrong. The exact attitude of *Wisdom* to *Ecclesiastes* seems to me to be that of St. Peter to St. Paul when the former says :

II Peter   In all his epistles . . . are some things hard to be understood, which
iii. 16   the ignorant and unstedfast wrest, as they do also the other scriptures, unto their own destruction.

No argument of *Ecclesiastes* is in *Wisdom* cited and attacked ; but the second discourse undoubtedly presents the ignorant and unstedfast 'wresting' the Preacher's theory of life to their own destruction.

The first discourse is on Singleness of Heart. The text is made by the opening words of the book.

> *Love righteousness, ye that be judges of the earth,*
> *Think ye of the Lord with a good mind,*
> *And in singleness of heart seek ye him.*

The comment on this text is brief and simple. But its simplicity becomes charged with keen interest if we look upon the discourse as glancing indirectly at the opening essay of *Ecclesiastes*. That essay imagined a great experiment of Solomon : how he would lay hold on folly, his heart yet guiding him with wisdom ; how he would heap together

First Discourse
i. 1-11

every form of pleasure, and withhold nothing that his eyes should desire, yet at the same time his wisdom should remain with him. The present discourse seems boldly to pronounce such an experiment impossible.

> Wisdom will not enter into a soul that deviseth evil, nor dwell in a body that is held in pledge by sin. For a holy spirit of discipline will flee deceit, and will start away from thoughts that are without understanding, and will be put to confusion when unrighteousness hath come in.

And this thought is enforced by enlarging upon the spirit of the Lord filling the world, while an ear of jealousy listens to every secret utterance.

The second is the main discourse of the whole series. It might well have for its title: Immortality and the Covenant with Death. Here is the point at which the opposition between the two Books of Wisdom is most acute. The Preacher, whichever way he turned, found death as an inevitable destiny mocking human effort. In startling contradiction to this the very text of the present discourse assumes death to be a thing of human origin.

Second Discourse i. 12-vi. 11

> *Court not death in the error of your life;*
> *Neither draw upon yourselves destruction by the works of your hands.*

All doubt about the doctrine is removed by the first words of comment: "God made not death." *Ecclesiastes*, with melancholy iteration, had insisted on joining man with the beasts in regard to his end. But the present discourse declares that all the races of creatures in the world are healthsome by creation, and that Hades has no royal dominion on earth: "for righteousness is immortal." Whence, then, has come death into the world? By invitation of the ungodly. The invitation is described as being "by their hands and their words." The ungodly life is interpreted as a covenant with death. The discourse proceeds to voice this ungodly life in a monologue which starts from the point of view of *Ecclesiastes*.

> Short and sorrowful is our life; and there is no healing when a man cometh to his end, and none was ever known that gave release from Hades; because by mere chance were we born, and hereafter we shall be as though we had never been: because the breath in our nostrils is smoke, and reason is a spark kindled by the beating of our heart, which being extinguished the body shall be turned into ashes, and the spirit shall be dispersed as thin air; and our name shall be forgotten in time, and no man shall remember our works; and our life shall pass away as the traces of a cloud, and shall be scattered as is a mist, when it is chased by the beams of the sun, and overcome by the heat thereof. For our allotted time is the passing of a shadow, and our end retreateth not; because it is fast sealed, and none turneth it back.
>
> Come therefore and let us enjoy the good things that are; and let us use the creation with all our soul as youth's possession. Let us fill ourselves with costly wine and perfumes; and let no flower of spring pass us by: let us crown ourselves with rosebuds, before they be withered: let none of us go without his share in our proud revelry: everywhere let us leave tokens of our mirth: because this is our portion, and our lot is this.

So far the train of reasoning has corresponded with the theory of life laid down in *Ecclesiastes*. But now comes an unexpected trend of thought. It will be recollected that the Preacher's momentary conception of a judgment beyond the grave, and subsequent lapse into hopelessness, came upon him when he contemplated wickedness seated in the place of judgment. As the present monologue continues, we find this wicked oppression springing naturally out of the Preacher's own conception of life.

> Let us oppress the righteous poor; let us not spare the widow, nor reverence the hairs of the old man gray for length of years. But let our strength be to us a law of righteousness; for that which is weak is found to be of no service. But let us lie in wait for the righteous man, because he is of disservice to us, and is contrary to our works, and upbraideth us with sins against the law, and layeth to our charge sins against our discipline. He professeth to have knowledge of God, and nameth himself servant of the Lord. He became to us a reproof of our thoughts. He is grievous to us even to behold, because his life is unlike other men's, and his paths are

of strange fashion. We were accounted of him as base metal, and he abstaineth from our ways as from uncleannesses. The latter end of the righteous he calleth happy; and he vaunteth that God is his father. Let us see if his words be true, and let us try what shall befall in the ending of his life. For if the righteous man is God's son, he will uphold him, and he will deliver him out of the hand of his adversaries. With outrage and torture let us put him to the test, that we may learn his gentleness, and may prove his patience under wrong. Let us condemn him to a shameful death; for he shall be visited according to his words.

The author breaks in to say how these reasoners are blinded by wickedness to the mysteries of God; and (as already pointed out) he catches at a phrase of the Preacher to turn it to an opposite use.

> The souls of the righteous are in the hand of God, and no torment shall touch them. In the eyes of the foolish they seemed to have died; and their departure was accounted to be their hurt, and their journeying away from us to be their ruin: but they are in peace. For even if in the sight of men they be punished, their hope is full of immortality; and having borne a little chastening, they shall receive great good . . . and in the time of their visitation they shall shine forth, and as sparks among stubble they shall run to and fro. They shall judge nations, and have dominion over peoples; and the Lord shall reign over them for evermore.

The picture of the ungodly reasoners is to be completed by a companion picture of the same reasoners beyond the grave. But first, with his tendency to digression, the author turns aside to glance at the rival hopes to this his hope of immortality. The substitutes for our modern conception of immortality in the minds of Old Testament worthies were two : length of days in this world, and the living over again in posterity. The author of *Wisdom* strikes at both these ideas. The multiplying brood of the ungodly is profitless : better is childlessness with virtue. As for length of days : it may well be that the life cut short is the life crowned.

> For honourable old age is not that which standeth in length of time, nor is its measure given by number of years: but understanding is gray hairs unto men, and an unspotted life is ripe old age. . . . Being

made perfect in a little while he fulfilled long years; for his soul was pleasing unto the Lord: therefore he hastened him away out of the midst of wickedness.

And now the dramatic monologue is again called into requisition to paint the amazement of the ungodly, risen from a dishonoured sojourn among the dead, to behold the righteous standing in great boldness before those who afflicted him.

This was he whom aforetime we had in derision, and made a parable of reproach: we fools accounted his life madness, and his end without honour: how was he numbered among sons of God? and how is his lot among saints? Verily we went astray from the way of truth, and the light of righteousness shined not for us, and the sun rose not for us. We took our fill of the paths of lawlessness and destruction, and we journeyed through trackless deserts, but the way of the Lord we knew not. What did our arrogancy profit us? And what good have riches and vaunting brought us? Those things all passed away as a shadow, and as a message that runneth by: as a ship passing through the billowy water, whereof, when it is gone by, there is no trace to be found, neither pathway of its keel in the billows: or as when a bird flieth through the air, no token of her passage is found, but the light wind, lashed with the stroke of her pinions, and rent asunder with the violent rush of the moving wings, is passed through, and afterwards no sign of her coming is found therein: or as when an arrow is shot at a mark, the air disparted closeth up again immediately, so that men know not where it passed through: so we also, as soon as we were born, ceased to be; and of virtue we had no sign to shew, but in our wickedness we were utterly consumed.

The author speaks in person to second this despair: the hope of the ungodly is as smoke and vanishing foam, while the righteous live for ever. Then the discourse reaches a peroration in a picture of the universe united to war against the enemies of good.

He shall take his jealousy as complete armour, and shall make the whole creation his weapons for vengeance on his enemies: he shall put on righteousness as a breastplate, and shall array himself with judgement unfeigned as with a helmet: he shall take holiness as an invincible shield, and he shall sharpen stern wrath for a sword. And the world shall go forth with him to fight against his insensate foes. Shafts of lightning shall fly with true aim, and from the clouds, as from a well drawn bow, shall they leap to the mark. And as from an engine of war shall be hurled hailstones full of wrath; the water of the sea shall be angered against them, and rivers shall sternly overwhelm them; a mighty blast shall encounter them, and as a tempest shall it winnow them away: and so shall lawlessness make all the land desolate, and their evil doing shall overturn the thrones of princes.

An appeal to Kings, as those whose responsibility is greater than that of lowly men, closes the second discourse, and prepares for the text of the third, that Wisdom is found of her seekers, nay, forestalleth them by making herself first known. This discourse is devoted to the personality of King Solomon: a personality which, as in *Ecclesiastes*, is dropped when its purpose has been served. Here in full distinctness we have a king addressing his brother kings; and a very different character is painted from that of the Preacher's Solomon. The wisest of men tells how he was mortal, like all others; moulded, like all others, in the womb; how he was born, and drew in the common air, and fell upon the kindred earth, his first voice a wail: for all men have one entrance into life, and a like departure. For this cause he had to pray for the understanding that has been given to him. And this understanding he preferred before sceptres and thrones, and riches, and health, and comeliness, and all other good things: but with this Wisdom came to him all other good things, for she is the mother and artificer of them all. Then follows the famous panegyric.

Third Discourse vi. 12-ix

> For there is in her a spirit quick of understanding, holy, alone in kind, manifold, subtil, freely moving, clear in utterance, unpolluted, distinct, unharmed, loving what is good, keen, unhindered, beneficent, loving toward man, stedfast, sure, free from care, all-powerful, all-surveying, and penetrating through all spirits that are quick of understanding, pure, most subtil: for wisdom is more mobile than any motion; yea, she pervadeth and penetrateth all things by reason of her pureness. For she is a breath of the power of God, and a clear

> effluence of the glory of the Almighty; therefore can nothing defiled find entrance into her. For she is an effulgence from everlasting light, and an unspotted mirror of the working of God, and an image of his goodness. And she, being one, hath power to do all things; and, remaining in herself, reneweth all things: and from generation to generation passing into holy souls she maketh men friends of God and prophets. For nothing doth God love save him that dwelleth with wisdom. For she is fairer than the sun, and above all the constellations of the stars: being compared with light, she is found to be before it; for to the light of day succeedeth night, but against wisdom evil doth not prevail; but she reacheth from one end of the world to the other with full strength, and ordereth all things graciously.

Such Wisdom Solomon tells how he loved from his youth, and sought to take her for his bride: with her as his spouse he would gain glory among the multitudes and honour in the sight of the elders; because of her he would have immortality, and leave behind an eternal memory; he will govern people and be courageous in war.

> When I am come into my house, I shall find rest with her; for converse with her hath no bitterness, and to live with her hath no pain, but gladness and joy.

Accordingly he pleaded with the Lord, that he would send down Wisdom out of the holy heavens and from the throne of his glory: and thus the historic prayer of Gibeon is expanded
1 Kings iii. 4
into an elaborate appeal. The concluding part of this prayer makes the transition to the important discourses which are to follow.

> For a corruptible body weigheth down the soul, and the earthly frame lieth heavy on a mind that is full of cares. And hardly do we divine the things that are on earth, and the things that are close at hand we find with labour; but the things that are in the heavens who ever yet traced out? And who ever gained knowledge of thy counsel, except thou gavest wisdom, and sentest thy holy spirit from on high? And it was thus that the ways of them which are on earth were corrected, and men were taught the things that are pleasing unto thee; and through wisdom were they saved.

These last words become the text on which the discourse that is to follow is founded.

Through wisdom were they saved.

This fourth discourse occupies a transitional position in the train of thought which connects the last three sections of the book. Without attempting to analyse all the shades of meaning and mystic senses that attach to the word 'wisdom,' it may be said that they centre around two main usages, which may be broadly distinguished as subjective and objective: the wisdom which an individual, from whatever source, receives into himself, and by which he guides his actions, and again the wisdom which underlies the sum of things. Of course the two senses are closely related: an individual is wise in personal wisdom when he brings himself into conformity with the Divine order and harmony. The final discourse will, without using the word,[1] expound wisdom in the objective sense as seen in history. The third discourse has ended with Solomon's prayer for personal wisdom. This section which intervenes deals with history, but mainly with its prominent individuals; and its use of the term 'wisdom' in an interesting manner hovers between the two senses of the word. In the opening reference to Adam —

<blockquote>
Wisdom guarded to the end the first formed father of the world, that was created alone, and delivered him out of his own transgression, and gave him strength to get dominion over all things —
</blockquote>

Fourth Discourse x-xi. 5

the first clause seems to speak of external guidance, the rest of self-discipline. It is from wisdom in the latter sense that Cain 'fell away' in his anger; but it must be wisdom as providential guidance that saved the world from the flood, guiding the righteous man's course by a poor piece of wood. Providence must be the wisdom that "knew the righteous man," Abraham: but wisdom in the other sense "preserved him blameless" unto God, and kept him strong when his heart yearned toward his child. Exter-

[1] It occurs only once (xiv. 5) in a subordinate phrase.

nal wisdom saved Lot, but it must be the wisdom within that Lot's wife 'passed by,' and became a monument of folly. It is providential wisdom that guided the fugitive Jacob, and still more clearly the same wisdom which went down into the dungeon with Joseph, and left him not till she brought him the sceptre of a kingdom. When Moses is reached, the two senses seem again to interlace:

> Wisdom delivered a holy people and a blameless seed from a nation of oppressors. She entered into the soul of a servant of the Lord, and withstood terrible kings in wonders and signs.

But as the details of the deliverance are reviewed the thought is more and more of providential guidance, until we find ourselves in the analysis of history that constitutes the final discourse.

The fifth and last section, in bulk equal to one half the book, branches off at the words:

> For by what things their foes were punished,
> By these they in their need were benefited.

This text conveys clearly the argument of the whole discourse; though (as remarked above) at one part of it there occurs a chain of digressions, carrying our thoughts from one to another of kindred topics, until the original argument is recovered and maintained to the close.[1]

Fifth Discourse xi. 5-xix

The text embodies a principle of providential government, and the discourse elaborately supports it with seven illustrations connected with the deliverance of Israel out of Egypt.

The first of the 'things' illustrating the principle is *thirst*. For the Egyptians the inexhaustible Nile turned to blood — meet judgment on those who had shed the blood of infants: while for Israel the desert rock poured out abundant streams, Israel having suffered thirst just enough to understand the torment of their enemies, and see the difference between fatherly admonition and the wrath of a stern king.

[1] See Appendix IV.

It is as the writer is commencing a second illustration that the series of digressions begins. One of these digressions puts the principle of providential government which in sec- *The Chain of* ular literature is called nemesis: by what things a *Digressions* man sinneth by these he is punished. The example *xi. 15-xvi. 1* that suggests it is the plague of vermin sent upon the Egyptians, who are vermin worshippers. This leads to a further argument on the forbearance of God in his judgments —
xi. 21-xii making the judgment assume a form that is equivalent to admonition, and convicting little by little so as to give a place for repentance: this is the forbearance of strength, and of one who loves everything that he has made. Another digression is on the folly of idolatry. There are degrees in that folly: least blamable are those who mistake *xiii. 1-xiv. 11* *and xv* the beautiful works of nature for God; next miserable are those who rest their hopes in dead things like gold or silver; but the furthest gone in folly are the Egyptians in their deifying creatures hateful and void of beauty. The scorn of the wise man closely follows the scorn of the prophet, in fancying a woodcutter cutting down a tree and carefully fashioning the best wood into useful vessels, then warming food with the refuse, and then taking the very refuse that is good for nothing and carving it in an idle hour into a god.

> For health he calleth upon that which is weak, and for life he beseecheth that which is dead, and for aid he supplicateth that which hath least experience, and for a good journey that which cannot so much as move a step, and for gaining and getting and good success of his hands he asketh ability of that which with its hands is most unable. Again, one preparing to sail, and about to journey over raging waves, calleth upon a piece of wood more rotten than the vessel that carrieth him.

The folly of idolatry leads naturally to the question of its origin. The writer insists that idolatry is a corruption, and not
xiv. 12-31 one of the things that have been from the beginning. It may have begun in the image of a lost child, or an absent king,

coming in time to be honoured with rites and worship, until stocks and stones have become invested with the incommunicable Name. With such corruption of worship has crept in corruption of morals — frantic revels, tumult, perjury, defiling of souls, confusion of sex, adultery, and wantonness: they live in a great war of ignorance, and that multitude of evils they call peace.

The digressions have occupied half of the whole discourse; the original argument is resumed with a second illustration of things which were judgments on the wicked turning to mercies on God's people. This is connected with *appetite:* the plague of vermin caused the Egyptians to loathe their necessary food, but to the Israelites were sent quails of dainty flavour when their appetite had become keen in the desert. A third illustration is founded on *noxious bites:* the bites of locusts and flies destroyed without healing the men of Egypt; whereas the rage of crooked serpents did but admonish God's people to heed his oracles, and then salvation was found for them, not indeed from that which they gazed upon, but from the Healer of all, who has authority over life and death. Once more, there is a contrast between the *rain* of hail and showers inexorable mingling with fire which destroyed the fruits of Egypt, and the rain of angels' bread from heaven on God's people in the wilderness. The contrast is worked out with minute subtlety. The elements strained their force against the unrighteous, the fire of destruction burning in the rain and flashing in the hail; while the same fire slackened in behalf of the Israelites, and, like the fire of a domestic hearth, tempered the food to every taste. Yet the manna which the fire had thus not marred melted in the first faint sunbeam, teaching men to rise early to give thanks.

xvi. 1

The fifth example gives great scope for the feature of style which I have called analytic imagination. It is the plague of darkness.

> When lawless men had supposed that they held a holy nation in their power, they themselves, prisoners·of darkness, and bound in the fetters of a long night, close kept beneath their roofs, lay exiled

from the eternal providence. For while they thought that they were
unseen in their secret sins, they were sundered one from another by
a dark curtain of forgetfulness, stricken with terrible awe, and sore
troubled by spectral forms. For neither did the dark recesses that
held them guard them from fears, but sounds rushing down rang
around them, and phantoms appeared, cheerless with unsmiling
faces. And no force of fire prevailed to give them light, neither were
the brightest flames of the stars strong enough to illumine that
gloomy night: but only there appeared to them the glimmering of a
fire self-kindled, full of fear; and in terror they deemed the things
which they saw to be worse than that sight, on which they could not
gaze. And they lay helpless, made the sport of magic art, and a
shameful rebuke of their vaunts of understanding: for they that
promised to drive away terrors and troublings from a sick soul, these
were themselves sick with a ludicrous fearfulness: for even if no
troublous thing affrighted them, yet, scared with the creepings of
vermin and hissings of serpents, they perished for very trembling, refusing even to look on the air, which could on no side be
escaped. . . . All through the night which was powerless indeed,
and which came upon them out of the recesses of powerless Hades,
all sleeping the same sleep, now were haunted with monstrous appa-
ritions, and now were paralysed by their souls' surrendering; for
fear sudden and unlooked for came upon them. So then every man,
whosoever it might be, sinking down in his place, was kept in ward
shut up in that prison which was barred not with iron: for whether
he were a husbandman, or a shepherd, or a labourer whose toils
were in the wilderness, he was overtaken, and endured that inevitable
necessity, for with one chain of darkness were they all bound.
Whether there were a whistling wind, or a melodious noise of birds
among the spreading branches, or a measured fall of water running
violently, or a harsh crashing of rocks hurled down, or the swift
course of animals bounding along unseen, or the voice of wild beasts
harshly roaring, or an echo rebounding from the hollows of the
mountains, all these things paralysed them with terror. For the
whole world beside was enlightened with clear light, and was occupied with unhindered works; while over them alone was spread a
heavy night, an image of the darkness that should afterward receive
them; but yet heavier than darkness were they unto themselves.

With such supernatural darkness is contrasted the great light
enjoyed all the while by the holy ones; and further, the burning

pillar of fire sent as convoy of their unknown journey, and kindly sun for their proud exile.

The sixth illustration reverses the order of the contrast. First is mentioned the night of deliverance to the chosen people, when sacrifice was being offered in secret, and with one consent they took upon themselves the covenant of Divine law. The fathers were already leading the sacred songs of praise when there sounded back in discord the cry of the stricken enemy.

> For while peaceful silence enwrapped all things, and night in her own swiftness was in mid course, thine all-powerful word leaped from heaven out of the royal throne, a stern warrior, into the midst of the doomed land, bearing as a sharp sword thine unfeigned commandment; and standing it filled all things with death; and while it touched the heaven it trod upon the earth.

And a picture follows of the dead thrown here and there in the tossings of troubled dreams which showed to each his doom ere the death fell on him.

Finally, death itself is amongst the things which are judgments alike and benefits. It befell the righteous to make trial of death, but only as a brief calamity; for the blameless Phinehas, bringing the weapons of his ministry, confronted the advancing wrath, and cut off the way to the living. But upon the ungodly came wrath without mercy, who by a counsel of folly pursued the fugitives, and themselves met with strange death, creation fashioning itself anew, and land rising out of the sea for the salvation of the fugitives. In the deliverance Israel thus celebrated, and the plagues of Egypt fresh in their memory, and the gifts of ambrosial food they were soon to receive, might they see all the elements, interchanging like the notes of a psaltery, conspire to magnify the people of God.

So ends the last of the Scriptural Books of Wisdom. Throughout its whole course it has returned to the tone of serene contemplation, broken only by adoration, which had distinguished all Wisdom literature except *Ecclesiastes*. The middle discourse of the series has vindicated Solomon from the morbid experiment imagined for him by the Preacher, and portrayed in his personality individual wisdom in its most kingly form. The earlier discourses have set over against the pessimist conception of a life bounded by death the optimism that is made by extending the vision into a future beyond the grave; while, in place of the Preacher's concluding strain of clinging to happiness, the opening note of the present book is, Love righteousness. And as these discourses have dealt with the future, so the concluding discourses extend the field of Wisdom to include the past, and the history of God's people has been presented as an ordered scheme of providence.

We have seen that the Philosophy of the Bible takes its rise from a floating literature of proverbs. The form of these germ proverbs is fixed to that of a single couplet; accordingly the couplet is the meeting point of verse and prose. Proverb literature develops on the one side into the poetic forms of the epigram and the sonnet, on the other side it travels prosewards in maxims and essays; but in either case Biblical Philosophy always seeks artistic form, and it is just where the thought is most elaborate that the most extended dramatic monologues are found, or the most brilliant rhetorical encomia and pictures. In matter and spirit this Biblical Philosophy is 'Wisdom': reflection associates itself with practical life. In the earlier works reflection has been directed upon life in its separate parts, and miscellanies of practical wisdom are the result: the totality of things is not a subject for theorising upon, but is approached with awe, and worshipped as a personified Wisdom. With *Ecclesiastes* we reach the point at which analysis has turned itself upon the sum of things, and there ensues a strange divorce between theory and practice: while the old miscellaneous maxims still appear, we now hear of a whole duty of man, and this is presented as a reverent happiness; but on the other hand the theory of life has started only to break down in negations, and in despair of all but God. But in the *Wisdom of Solomon* Philosophy has recovered

Review

its balance, theoretical and practical are harmonised. The principle underlying the All — an All which takes in past, present, and future — has again become Wisdom, and is again contemplated with rapture; detailed maxims of practical life have disappeared, except so far as they are items in a universal system. But this final achievement of philosophic reflection has been brought about by drawing within the field of thought something which has not been obtained from philosophy: it is the tacit assumption of a future world that has reversed the conclusions of *Ecclesiastes*. And when this final stage of Wisdom literature has been reached, the conception of 'Wisdom' itself has become so deep and so many-sided that it would be impossible to discuss it without trenching upon the deepest mysteries of Theology.

BOOK FIFTH

BIBLICAL LITERATURE OF PROPHECY

CHAPTER		PAGE
XIV.	FORMS OF PROPHETIC LITERATURE	327
XV.	FORMS OF PROPHETIC LITERATURE: THE DOOM SONG	353
XVI.	FORMS OF PROPHETIC LITERATURE: THE RHAPSODY	364
XVII.	THE RHAPSODY OF 'ZION REDEEMED' [Isa. xl-lxvi]	395
XVIII.	THE WORKS OF THE PROPHETS	417

CHAPTER XIV

FORMS OF PROPHETIC LITERATURE

WE commence in this chapter another of the grand departments of Biblical literature; and our first difficulty is its name — Prophecy. By one of those silent changes in the signification of words, which are brought about by the wear and tear of ordinary speech, this word 'Prophecy' has, for about a century, narrowed itself, in common parlance, to the sense of 'prediction'; and there are many readers of the Bible to whom the term suggests nothing more than the foretelling of the future. It is, of course, true that the Hebrew prophets dealt with the future, as they dealt with the present and the past. But the reference to future time is not the sole, nor even the chief, function of the literature we are about to survey. The *pro-* in *prophecy* is not the *pro-* that means 'before' but the *pro-* that means 'forth': Prophecy is a forth-pouring or out-pouring of discourse. That such out-pouring of discourse belongs, not only to the thing described, but also to the signification of the English word, is powerfully illustrated by the fact that a father of the Anglican Church and great master of English prose, writing in the seventeenth century a work in which he was to plead for the freedom of the English pulpit, gave to it the title: 'Liberty of Prophesying.' The true distinction of this department of Biblical literature lies in its presenting itself as the channel of an immediate Divine message: "Thus saith the Lord" is contained explicitly or implicitly in every utterance of the prophets. The essence of Prophecy then belongs to its spirit

Prophecy as a department of literature

Forms of Prophetic Literature

and matter: what more of description is needed will be given by distinguishing the various forms in which the prophetic matter can be conveyed.

The simplest form of Prophecy, and the form of most frequent occurrence, is the Prophetic Discourse: counterpart to the modern Sermon. The Divine message essential to Prophecy is not to be understood as the Discourse itself, but rather, in theory at least, as the subject or text of the Discourse, which all the rest is to explain or enforce. In this connection it is important to note a word which even in the Bible itself seems to be used as a technical term: — the word translated 'Burden,' in the titles to chapters of Prophecy, and in the text itself.[1] It would appear that this was understood of the actual Divine message, though the term was abused by false prophets as a name under which to clothe their own imaginings.

The Prophetic Discourse

(The word 'Burden')

Jeremiah xxiii. 32 — Behold, I am against them that prophesy lying dreams, saith the LORD, and do tell them, and cause my people to err by their lies, and by their vain boasting: yet I sent them not, nor commanded them; neither shall they profit this people at all, saith the LORD. And when this people, or the prophet, or a priest, shall ask thee, saying, What is the burden of the LORD? then shalt thou say unto them, What burden! I will cast you off, saith the LORD. And as for the prophet, and the priest, and the people, that shall say, The burden of the LORD, I will even punish that man and his house. Thus shall ye say every one to his neighbour, and every one to his brother, What hath the LORD answered? and, What hath the LORD spoken? And the burden of the LORD shall ye mention no more: for every man's own word is his burden, and ye pervert the words of the living God, of the LORD of hosts our God.

In the Prophetic Discourses as they have reached us, however, the text and recommendatory matter seem fused together without distinction. Such merging of a Divine message in the exhortations enforcing it may be illustrated from that which is the prototype

---

[1] The word substituted by R. V. (in titles, but not in the text) is 'Oracles': this explains the usage by a parallel term in secular literatures.

of all Prophetic Discourses, — the Ten Commandments. The versions of the Ten Commandments in *Exodus* and in *Deuteronomy*, though each is introduced with the formula, "The Lord spake . . . saying," yet differ, not verbally only, but in substance; in particular, the reason assigned for the observance of the Sabbath is entirely different in the two books. The natural explanation of this is to understand that the actual commandment inscribed on tables of stone would be limited to the imperative clause, "Thou shalt not make unto thee any graven image," "Remember the Sabbath day, to keep it holy"; in the simple commandments directed against murder or theft nothing more would be needed, but in the more spiritual commandments comment would be added by Moses, based on his general intercourse with God, and not upon the Divine words of any particular occasion. A similar intermingling of message and exhortation extends throughout the whole literature of Prophecy. And a passage in *Ezekiel* shows us that, even in the times of the prophets themselves, the rhetorical element in their discourses was coming to be regarded as a separate interest.

> Son of man, the children of thy people talk of thee by the walls and in the doors of the houses, and speak one to another, every one to his brother, saying, Come, I pray you, and hear what is the word that cometh forth from the LORD. . . . And, lo, thou art unto them as a very lovely song of one that hath a pleasant voice, and can play well on an instrument: for they hear thy words, but they do them not.
>
> <small>Ezekiel xxxiii. 30</small>

When the discourses of Prophecy are analysed as pieces of literature, we find, as we should expect, that they do not as a rule exhibit any clear structural plan, but rather contain warning, description, reflection, intermingling in a fervour of appeal. A typical discourse is that which makes the opening chapter of *Isaiah;* where the idea of children rebelling against a <small>Isaiah i</small> Divine parent, of the abject condition of the people leading them to fresh sin, of their intentness on sacrifices and neglect of righteousness, the golden hopes held out to them, the picture of universal corruption with the threat of terrible purging that shall leave no more than a small remnant, — all combine in a rush of passionate thought that has no need of logical arrangement.

There are, however, some discourses which have structural as well as other interest. The elaborate manifesto of Isaiah which follows the opening chapter commences with an ideal picture of the mountain of the Lord's house established at the head of the mountains, and all nations flowing to it to learn His ways, beating their swords into ploughshares for an era of universal peace. In the light of such a picture the prophet invites the house of Jacob to walk: and so plunges into denunciatory portrayal of corruption and idolatry, against which he places in contrast the terror of the majesty of the Lord. The general upsetting of natural relations he makes the beginning of judgment on oppression; the luxury of women he scornfully details, and threatens the nemesis that is coming upon it. From such ideas of judgment the prophet passes, by the image of a young shoot from an old tree, to the remnant of Israel that shall be again beautiful, cleansed from pollution, and blest again with the nightly fire and daily cloud of Divine guidance. So to frame a denunciation between pictures of a golden age at the beginning and end, gives an individuality of plan to this deliverance of Isaiah.

<small>Isaiah ii-iv</small>

A discourse of Ezekiel, again, has distinctiveness of form given to it by its being cast wholly in the mould of pastoral ideas and scenery. God declares Himself against the Shepherds of Israel, that feed themselves and not the sheep.

<small>Ezekiel xxxiv</small>

> Ye eat the fat, and ye clothe you with the wool, ye kill the fatlings: but ye feed not the sheep. The diseased have ye not strengthened, neither have ye healed that which was sick, neither have ye bound up that which was broken, neither have ye brought again that which was driven away, neither have ye sought that which was lost; but with force and with rigour have ye ruled over them.

Still under the name of sheep is described the loss of God's people, wandering without rescue until He shall seek them out Himself.

> As a shepherd seeketh out his flock in the day that he is among his sheep that are scattered abroad, so will I seek out my sheep; and I will deliver them out of all places whither they have been scattered in the cloudy and dark day. And I will bring them out from the peoples, and gather them from the countries, and will bring them into their own land; and I will feed them upon the mountains of Israel, by the watercourses, and in all the inhabited places of the country.

Among His other gifts, God will feed them with the 'judgment' that makes distinction between oppression and meekness.

> Seemeth it a small thing unto you to have fed upon the good pasture, but ye must tread down with your feet the residue of your pasture? and to have drunk of the clear waters, but ye must foul the residue with your feet? And as for my sheep, they eat that which ye have trodden with your feet, and they drink that which ye have fouled with your feet. Therefore thus saith the Lord GOD unto them: Behold, I, even I, will judge between the fat cattle and the lean cattle.

As usual, the prophecy works towards the thought of restoration, and a purified people amid ideal surroundings.

> And I will set up one shepherd over them, and he shall feed them, even my servant David: he shall feed them, and he shall be their shepherd. And I the LORD will be their God, and my servant David prince among them; I the LORD have spoken it. And I will make with them a covenant of peace, and will cause evil beasts to cease out of the land: and they shall dwell securely in the wilderness, and sleep in the woods. And I will make them and the places round about my hill a blessing; and I will cause the shower to come down in its season; there shall be showers of blessing. And the tree of the field shall yield its fruit, and the earth shall yield her increase, and they shall be secure in their land; and they shall know that I am the LORD, when I have broken the bars of their yoke, and have delivered them out of the hand of those that served themselves of them.

With exquisite tenderness the pastoral imagery has been maintained without a break; only in the last verse is the image dropped.

> And ye my sheep, the sheep of my pasture, are men, and I am your God, saith the Lord GOD.

In treating Lyric Poetry I spoke of the pendulum structure, or swaying of a poem in successive sections between opposite sides of a theme. This structure is very characteristic of Prophecy, especially the swaying between pictures of judgment and mercy; an interpreter should keep it constantly before his mind as a possible clue to the connection of thought in any portion of prophetic literature. I will here illustrate only with a very simple example.

Jeremiah xxx. 4-22

A discourse of Jeremiah opens with sounds of trembling and fear, a picture of Jacob in time of trouble: as if men travailed with child, every man bowed down with anguish, and all faces pale. In that day, the next paragraph declares, the yoke of slavery shall be broken from off his neck: as the servant of Jehovah he shall be brought from far-off lands of captivity to quiet and ease in his own land, while full end is made of all the oppressing nations. With the formula, "For thus saith the Lord," the next paragraph goes back to the conception of judgment: Jacob's wound is described as incurable, Jehovah has wounded him with the wound of an enemy, there is no medicine nor plaister, all the lovers of Jacob have forgotten him in his sore need. With the connective 'therefore' the discourse passes to the reverse of this picture: health restored, adversaries devoured, captivity turned, the city builded on its own heap, with glory and thanksgiving sounding out of its palaces. Thus to the instinct of Hebrew poetry this passing backwards and forwards between opposites seems to present itself as a continuously advancing train of thought.

I have said that prediction is only a secondary element of Scriptural prophecy. Still, it has its place, and occasionally a whole discourse is given up to a picture of the future. An interesting example is the last of the discourses ascribed to the prophet

Zechariah xiv

Zechariah. It describes a 'Day of the Lord' which is to come. All nations will be gathered against Jerusalem to battle; the city will be taken, and suffer the horrors of war, and half its people will go away into captivity, before the Lord appears to save. This salvation seems to echo the deliverances of past history. As the Red Sea divided to afford escape from the pursuing Egyptians, so now the Mount of Olives is cloven, and the fugitives escape through the valley. With a reminiscence of the sun and moon standing still for Joshua, we read of the succession of day and night being interrupted: at the time for evening there is still light, and the delivered people have, not day and not night, but "one day which is known unto the Lord." The nations that warred against Jerusalem are smitten with consuming plagues, the description of which recalls the curse in *Deuteronomy*. The very land shall change its surface, until Jerusalem alone stands out on high, and from its height healing waters flow on either side to the boundary sea. In Jerusalem the LORD shall reign as king over all the earth: the nations that had fought against the holy City shall go thither to worship, distant Egypt not excepted, while drought of heaven and plagues of earth shall unite to punish those who fail. A new age of holiness is thus introduced; when there is no need for traffic; when all life resolves itself into journeys to the sacred feasts; when holiness is inscribed on the bells of the horses, and the meanest pot in the Lord's house is as holy as the bowls before the altar.

From the general Prophetic Discourse a small variation brings us to Lyric Prophecy. High-strung oratory easily passes into lyric verse; the more easily in a language in which prose and verse overlap. In prophecies of all types lyrics may be interspersed. Thus we have seen in a previous chapter[1] how the *Book of Zephaniah* resolves itself into a single continuous discourse of the Divine speaker, interrupted at intervals by lyric strains of comment and application. In the course of other prophecies we come upon bursts of lyric thanksgiving, songs of triumph, or 'taunt-songs,' such as that in *Isaiah* over fallen Babylon; these taunt-songs would be seen to play a great part in prophetic literature, were it not that (as before remarked[2]) the dirge rhythm on which they are founded is missed in our current translations.

Lyric Prophecy

Isaiah xlvii

---

[1] Above, page 120.   [2] Above, page 157.

But the term 'Lyric Prophecy' is most fully applicable where a complete discourse is in this form. A striking example is found in the early chapters of *Isaiah*. Its structure is antistrophic: each of the four stanzas has an opening couplet, a closing refrain, and in the centre a quatrain that is gnomic in character, while the intervening portions of prose are exegetical of the rest. Besides this antistrophic effect, the reiteration of the refrain produces an effect of crescendo and advance from the way in which two words in it — 'this' and 'still' — gather increase of meaning with each succeeding stanza.

Isaiah
ix. 8-x. 4

DOOM OF THE NORTH

1

  The LORD sent a word into Jacob,
  And it hath lighted upon Israel.
And all the people shall know, even Ephraim and the inhabitant of Samaria, that say in pride and in stoutness of heart,
  The bricks are fallen,
    But we will build with hewn stone;
  The sycomores are cut down,
    But we will change them into cedars.
Therefore the LORD shall set up on high against him the adversaries of Rezin, and shall stir up his enemies; the Syrians before, and the Philistines behind; and they shall devour Israel with open mouth.
  For all this his anger is not turned away,
  But his hand is stretched out still!

2

  Yet the people hath not turned unto him that smote them,
  Neither have they sought the LORD of hosts.
Therefore the LORD will cut off from Israel head and tail, palm-branch and rush, in one day.
  The ancient and the honourable man,
    He is the head;
  And the prophet that teacheth lies,
    He is the tail.

For they that lead this people cause them to err; and they that are led of them are destroyed. Therefore the LORD shall not rejoice over their young men, neither shall he have compassion on their fatherless and widows: for every one is profane and an evil-doer, and every mouth speaketh folly.

    For all this his anger is not turned away,
    But his hand is stretched out *still!*

3

    For wickedness burneth as the fire;
    It devoureth the briers and thorns:
yea, it kindleth in the thickets of the forest, and they roll upward in thick clouds of smoke. Through the wrath of the LORD of hosts is the land burnt up: the people also are as the fuel of fire; no man spareth his brother.

    And one shall snatch on the right hand,
      And be hungry;
    And he shall eat on the left hand,
      And they shall not be satisfied:
they shall eat every man the flesh of his own arm: Manasseh, Ephraim; and Ephraim, Manasseh: and they together shall be against Judah.

    For all this his anger is not turned away,
    But his hand is stretched out STILL!

4

    Woe unto them that decree unrighteous decrees,
    And to the writers that write perverseness:
to turn aside the needy from judgement, and to take away the right of the poor of my people, that widows may be their spoil, and that they may make the fatherless their prey!

    And what will ye do in the day of visitation,
      And in the desolation which shall come from far?
    To whom will ye flee for help?
      And where will ye leave your glory?
They shall only bow down under the prisoners, and shall fall under the slain.

    For all this his anger is not turned away,
    But his hand is stretched out STILL!

An important division of prophetic literature is Symbolic Prophecy. If Prophecy in general is in the form of discourses, Symbolic prophecies are discourses with texts; but the texts taken by the prophets are not, like the texts of modern sermons, quotations from the sacred writings, but object-texts, that is, external things treated symbolically. Perhaps modern life has approached nearest to such Symbolic Prophecy in the 'Emblem Literature,' now forgotten, but for a century or two the chief reading of the religious world. This Emblem Literature was made up of sermons in verse with hieroglyphic texts. To take a typical case. One of Quarles's emblems represents a balance; in one scale of this balance worlds (represented conventionally by balls with cross handles) are being heaped up; the other scale contains nothing, but a mouth is seen blowing into it, and this empty scale weighs down the heaped-up worlds on the other side. This hieroglyph is the text: on the opposite page a poetic sermon works out with vigour the thought that worldly goods are less than empty breath. In the same way there is an Emblem Prophecy which has for its texts, not exactly pictures, but visible things or actions. Jeremiah is commanded to wear a linen girdle in the eyes of the people; when they have become accustomed to it he is to take the girdle off and hide it in a hole of the rock; several days after he is to show it again, marred and profitable for nothing. This is to be a text, from which he will preach how Judah, that ought to cleave to the Lord as the girdle cleaveth to the figure, shall for their sins be seen to be marred and useless. Or, again, the same prophet is led to watch the potter at work, aiming at one kind of vessel, but if the clay is marred making it at his pleasure into a vessel of a different kind: from this text he will proclaim that Israel in the hands of Jehovah is but the clay in the hands of the potter. Or, attention is called to baskets of figs standing before the Temple, figs of the best quality and figs uneatable: then is spoken the paradox that it is the captives carried away to Babylon who resemble the good figs, and the bad are those who think they have escaped by remaining in the land. An object-text in one of the discourses of Ezekiel seems to have been a map.

> The word of the LORD came unto me again, saying, Also, thou son of man, appoint thee two ways, that the sword of the king of Babylon may come; they twain shall come forth out of one land: and mark out a place, mark it out at the head of the way to the city. Thou shalt appoint a way, for the sword to come to Rabbah of the children of Ammon, and to Judah in Jerusalem the defenced. For the king of Babylon stood at the parting of the way, at the head of the two ways, to use divination: he shook the arrows to and fro, he consulted the teraphim, he looked in the liver. In his right hand was the divination for Jerusalem, to set battering rams, to open the mouth in the slaughter, to lift up the voice with shouting, to set battering rams against the gates, to cast up mounts, to build forts.

_{Ezekiel xxi. 18}

I have called the emblems texts, but they do not necessarily come at the beginning. A discourse would be specially impressive when its close was accompanied with some symbolic action. We find Jeremiah delivering a strain of unmeasured threatening and denunciation, holding all the while an earthen bottle in his hand: at the end he dashes the bottle to pieces in token of the irremediable destruction that is to come. On another occasion he sends to the captives in Babylon a written discourse foretelling the total overthrow of the oppressing city: he instructs his deputy, when he has read to the end, to bind the book to a stone and cast it into the Euphrates, emblem of the future when Babylon shall sink to rise no more.

_{Jeremiah xix. 10; li. 61-4}

Sometimes the symbolic text may be no more than a gesture. Ezekiel is to set his face towards the mountains of Israel, when he proceeds to denounce the idolatries committed on them; he is to smite with his hands and stamp with his foot as a starting-point to a picture of utter ruin. If such things as these seem too slight to constitute an emblem, it must be recollected that in all prophecy reiteration played a large part. In the case of Jonah, so far as we can tell, no discourse is given

_{Ezekiel vi. 1, 11}

him to speak, but only the cry, "Yet forty days, and Nineveh shall
(Prophetic Reiteration) be overthrown," to be repeated over and over again for a day together. And elsewhere there are suggestions of similar reiteration.

Jeremiah xiii. 12 Therefore thou shalt speak unto them this word: Thus saith the LORD, the God of Israel, Every bottle shall be filled with wine: and they shall say unto thee, Do we not know that every bottle shall be filled with wine? Then shalt thou say unto them, Thus saith the LORD, Behold, I will fill all the inhabitants of this land, even the kings that sit upon David's throne, and the priests, and the prophets, and all the inhabitants of Jerusalem with drunkenness.

The natural interpretation of this passage is that the apparent truism would be repeated by the prophet, as he moved about the city, with a persistency designedly irritating, until public impatience breaking out in questioning made a state of mind favourable for being impressed with the mystic sense of the truism. Similar reiteration may be understood in certain discourses of Ezekiel, who would ejaculate "An end, an end," or "An evil, an only evil," until curiosity had been excited, as by a riddle: such curiosity would serve to emphasise the discourse which answered to those riddling ejaculations. It is clear that words so delivered have as much objective force as a visible emblem.

Ezekiel vii. 2, 5

In other cases the symbolic action from which discourses would take their departure seems to have been sustained dumb show: the sermon would be acted first, and preached afterwards. A notable example of this is the mimic siege which formed the basis of so much of Ezekiel's prophesying.

Ezekiel iv. 1-v. 4 Thou also, son of man, take thee a tile, and lay it before thee, and pourtray upon it a city, even Jerusalem: and lay siege against it, and build forts against it, and cast up a mount against it; set camps also against it, and plant battering rams against it round about. And take thou unto thee an iron pan, and set it for a wall of iron between thee and the city: and set thy face toward it, and it shall be besieged, and thou shalt lay siege against it. This shall be a sign to the house of Israel.

> Moreover lie thou upon thy left side, and lay the iniquity of the house of Israel upon it: according to the number of the days that thou shalt lie upon it, thou shalt bear their iniquity. For I have appointed the years of their iniquity to be unto thee a number of days, even three hundred and ninety days: so shalt thou bear the iniquity of the house of Israel. And again, when thou hast accomplished these, thou shalt lie on thy right side, and shalt bear the iniquity of the house of Judah: forty days, each day for a year, have I appointed it unto thee. And thou shalt set thy face toward the siege of Jerusalem, with thine arm uncovered; and thou shalt prophesy against it. And, behold, I lay bands upon thee, and thou shalt not turn thee from one side to another, till thou hast accomplished the days of thy siege. Take thou also unto thee wheat, and barley, and beans, and lentils, and millet, and spelt, and put them in one vessel, and make thee bread thereof; according to the number of the days that thou shalt lie upon thy side, even three hundred and ninety days, shalt thou eat thereof. And thy meat which thou shalt eat shall be by weight, twenty shekels a day: from time to time shalt thou eat it. And thou shalt drink water by measure, the sixth part of an hin: from time to time shalt thou drink.

From various passages in the *Book of Ezekiel* we are able to form an idea of the mode in which such a commission would be executed. It was the custom for companies of the elders of Israel to wait upon the prophet at his house, and sit before him until "the hand of the Lord should fall upon him." [II Kings iv. 23] From the historical books we know that such visits to the prophets were periodical, belonging especially to new moons and Sabbaths; but a passage of *Ezekiel* suggests that among the exiles they took place daily. [xxiv. 18] We may suppose then that at the period in question the prophet would, for the whole time indicated in the above passage, receive the daily deputation with the same mimic siege, now taking the part of the besiegers and now of the besieged; and from this constant text he would enlarge upon the various topics of sin and judgment that each day's inspiration brought to his mind. The matter contained in the chapter that follows is no more than the general substance of the long series of discourses.

We even find a change of demeanour and manner of life, in so marked an individual as a prophet, made an emblem under which a Divine message could be conveyed. The Lord takes from Ezekiel the desire of his eyes with a stroke: yet he is neither to mourn nor weep. This loss of a beloved wife borne without signs of grief is to be a symbol of sorrows coming upon Israel that are too deep for tears. A still more painful experience is laid upon the prophet Hosea, who is commanded to take a wife from the ranks of fallen women: his family life, and the efforts of the prophet to reclaim his charge, are a living text for ministry to a people unfaithful to their God.

<small>Ezekiel xxiv. 15</small>

<small>Hosea i-iii</small>

When we consider the number and variety in prophetic literature of these object-texts—symbolic articles, symbolic gestures and ejaculations, symbolic demeanour and manner of life — we are able to see how this Emblem Prophecy has its prototype in the grand Ceremonial Worship of the Tabernacle and Temple. The Holy of Holies, the Ark of the Covenant, the Shewbread, the rites of sacrifice or of the Scapegoat, all these are perennial emblems of those ideas in Hebrew religion which are eternal and of constant application. In the same spirit Prophecy uses symbols to fulfil its function of bringing the principles of the religion to bear upon the detailed exigencies and occasional problems of public and social life. And in the light of this analogy we cease to be surprised at the minuteness with which, in such a case as Ezekiel's siege, the emblematic action is prescribed; the ceremonial teaching of the prophet is carried out with a reverent fidelity to detail as great as in the elaborated worship of the Temple itself.

The conception of a prophetic emblem develops readily into another conception of considerable importance. When a prophecy had reference to future time, and was illustrated with some symbol that was not transitory but durable, the emblem would remain to be confronted with the fulfilled prophecy, and so would vindicate the authority of the prophet. A prophetic emblem would

<small>Emblem Prophecy and the 'Sign of the Prophet'</small>

then become a 'sign of the prophet.' Jeremiah, carried by force into Egypt, consoles his fellow-captives with predictions of the conquest of Egypt by Nebuchadrezzar; he takes great stones and hides them in the mortar at the entrance of Pharaoh's palace in Tahpanhes, declaring that the conqueror "will set his throne upon these stones." Though the word is not used, yet it is clear that this emblematic action would become a 'sign' of Jeremiah's prophetic function, when the event should take place. Such 'signs' are part of the recognised machinery of prophecy. Isaiah bids Ahaz, in a certain political crisis, "Ask thee a sign of the LORD thy God; ask it either in the depth, or in the height above." When Ahaz in his panic holds back, the prophet himself volunteers the sign of a virgin conceiving and bearing a son and calling his name Immanuel: that child shall not be old enough to know good from evil before the prophet's prediction concerning the war shall be seen to be fulfilled.[1] It is to be observed, however, that the word 'sign' is also, in prophetic liter-

Jeremiah xliii. 8-13

Isaiah vii. 10

[1] In regard to the meaning of this much disputed passage, it is to be observed that the difficulties disappear if the words of the prophet be understood to apply, not to any virgin of Judah (real or idealised), but to a woman of the enemy's land. The expression 'Immanuel' occurs three times. (1) First, in the passage vii. 10-16. The situation here is that the junction of Israel with Syria has thrown the princes of Judah into a panic, and the prophet strengthens them by pouring contempt upon the enemy. So elated and confident at this moment (he says) is the enemy that a woman of their land gives her new-born child the proud name, 'God with us': but that child will soon be feeding on famine fare [that 'butter and honey' is a name for famine fare is shown by verse 22]: for before the child is old enough to distinguish good food from evil the enemy's land whose allied kings cause this panic to Judah shall be forsaken by these kings. (2) The phrase occurs a second time in viii. 5-8. This whole paragraph is addressed to the enemy, Israel; and the Assyrian, under the image of a flood, is described as overflowing the land of Israel [there is no reference to Judah except the single clause, "he shall sweep onward into Judah"]: the climax is, the flood shall fill thy land, O boaster of "God with us." (3) The third recurrence of the phrase is in viii. 10, where the false boast of Israel is claimed for Judah as a truth: lay your schemes (the prophet cries to the allied enemies) and they shall come to nought, for "God is with us." Of course this explanation relates to the *primary* interpretation of the piece of historic prophecy: it need not interfere with any theological use of the term 'Immanuel' as a *secondary* interpretation; indeed, the third passage, which claims the true 'Immanuel' for Judah, is basis enough for such interpretation.

ature, applied to what we have here called the emblem; thus
Ezekiel carrying on his siege, or refraining from
Ezekiel iv. 3; tears at his wife's death, is pronounced by the Lord
xxiv. 24   to be a 'sign' to the people. The variation between the two meanings of the word — between the 'sign' which is a symbolic illustration of the prophecy, and the 'sign' which is a miraculous vindication of the prophet — is the index of an important tendency in the attitude of the public mind towards prophecy, by which the spiritual force of prophetic utterances came to be more and more ignored, and the element of prediction and miracle grew into emphasis. So far has this tendency prevailed in the age of the New Testament that the constant and indignant complaint of Jesus Christ is against a "generation that seeketh a sign."

The Prophecy of Vision is, in its elementary form, hardly distinguished from Emblem Prophecy: the emblem
Symbolic Proph-
ecy: The   texts are merely presented in supernatural vision.
Vision   instead of being seen by the ordinary eyesight.
The books of Amos and Zechariah are full of such vision emblems. But the supreme example of them is Ezekiel's Vision of the Valley
of Dry Bones. He is carried out in the spirit of
Ezekiel xxxvii   the Lord and set down in the midst of the valley; the valley is full of bones, and lo, they are very dry. He is commanded to prophesy: and as he pours forth his speech there is thundering and earthquake; bone comes to his bone, flesh and skin cover them; from the four winds comes breath, and breathes upon the slain, and they live, and stand upon their feet, an exceeding great army. Thus impressively is elaborated, in the region of the supernatural, a symbolic text, from which Ezekiel preaches that Israel with its dead hopes shall come out of its graves, and feel the life-giving breath of the Lord.

The Vision Em-   But this elementary conception of Vision Prophecy undergoes a development similar to that traced
blem and
'Revelation'   in the last section. As the prophetic emblem, when applied to futurity, tended to change into the 'sign of the

prophet,' so the vision emblem develops into the 'Revelation,' as that word is generally understood, namely, the supernatural revelation of the future. It is worth while to distinguish three types among such Visions of Revelation. **Revelation of the Future** First, we have the case in which the vision is symbolic and supernatural, whereas the interpretation comes by natural means. The fingers of a hand writing on the wall startle Belshazzar's feast with mystic words: Daniel by his wisdom discovers the meaning, and the destruction that is about to come. In the second type an interpreter is provided by supernatural means, and the vision is given by him in direct speech. Thus Daniel, troubling over the mysteries of times and seasons, feels himself 'touched' by an angel at the time of the evening oblation, and Gabriel foretells what shall come to pass in terms that are direct, however difficult. To this second category may be referred the Calls of the Prophets: visionary scenes in which God himself appears under symbolic forms, but the commission is given to the prophet in plain language. In the third type both the vision and the interpretation are symbolic and supernatural; as where the future interchange of dynasties is conveyed to Daniel in the vision of the Four Beasts, or the vision of the Ram and the He-goat, while the significance of what he sees is explained by a personage of the vision itself.

But it is important to distinguish from this another meaning of the word 'Revelation'; we find visions that are revelations, not of the future, but of the law and pattern of things. As the one kind of vision is an extension of the **Revelation of Law and Ideal** prophetic dream, so the other has for its prototype the original revelation to Moses on the mount of the ceremonial law and the pattern of the Tabernacle. Important examples of the two types of Revelation are Ezekiel's companion visions of Jerusalem under Judgment and Jerusalem Restored, which cover no less than thirteen chapters of his **Ezekiel viii-xi and xl-xlviii** book. The two are separated, in conformity with the general arrangement of Ezekiel's writings, and their division between prophecies of judgment and of restoration; but that the two are parts of one whole is expressly said in the vision itself.

xliii. 1-8   In the first case Ezekiel is carried "in the visions of God" to Jerusalem, and beholds the Glory of the God of Israel as on the occasion of his own call. He is made to dig through the Temple wall and see idolatrous practices carried on in its chambers and precincts; agents of destruction do their work before his eyes, and he sees the city sprinkled with ashes taken from between the cherubim; he is himself called to bear a part in the work of judgment, and as he prophesies he sees one of the leaders of iniquity fall dead. All the scene so described makes up the symbol of this vision. We are not to understand that the weeping for Tammuz, or the creeping abominations, were necessarily to be seen in just the spot where Ezekiel beholds them, any more than we are to understand that Pelatiah actually died at the time when Ezekiel was under the prophetic spell. The whole is a symbolic representation of the general idolatry and desecration of the sacred city. The companion vision shows a great change from this symbolism. The same supernatural agency transports the prophet to the same spot. But what he sees is a city and temple gradually taking shape, and measured with exactness of proportions which he is commanded to store in his memory. The Glory of the God of Israel proclaims this the place of his throne for ever, and, in phrases which seem to echo *Exodus*, calls upon the house of Israel to "measure the pattern," or to receive this as "the law of the house." Then is continued the ordering of city, temple, ritual, and even division of the land of Palestine, with a minuteness which seems like the former revelation on Sinai adapted to a new dispensation. Throughout the whole nine chapters there is scarcely anything that can be called symbolic, except the conception of the living waters issuing from the Temple and flowing to fertilise the Dead Sea, on the banks of which are the never-withering trees, with their fruits renewed month by month and their leaves for healing. In the course, then, of this extended vision we are able to watch the transition from one type of revelation to another; while the symbolic is the distinction of the one, in the other the symbolic passes into the ideal. In the interpretation of Prophecy it is of the utmost importance to distinguish to which of these two types of revelation any particular vision belongs.

Symbolic Prophecy has detained us a long time; it remains to point out that, in addition to Emblem Prophecy and Vision Prophecy, it includes a third branch, — the Prophetic Parable. This is again a sermon with a symbolic text: the only difference is that the emblem is here narrated instead of being visibly presented. Such a parabolic text has its ultimate basis in the Fable of primitive literature.[1] Isaiah's Parable of the Vineyard, so favourably placed and carefully tended, yet bringing forth wild grapes, is amongst the most familiar portions of prophetic literature. The same symbol is differently used in a parable of Ezekiel, who treats the vine as one wood that is profitable for no use. This latter prophet is specially fond of parabolic discourse, and his favourite symbol seems to be that of an unfaithful spouse; in a way peculiar to himself he works out this theme with a wonderful combination of tenderness and unsparing plainness of speech. It is hardly necessary to remark upon the prominence assumed in a later age by this particular type of discourse: of the supreme Prophet of the New Testament it is said that "without a parable spake he not."

<small>Symbolic Prophecy: The Parable</small>

<small>Isaiah v</small>

<small>Ezekiel xv, xvi, xvii, xxiii</small>

Prophetic Intercourse makes a literary division that does not need lengthy discussion. The intercourse of the prophet with

---

[1] The Fable as a literary form is defined by its conveying human interest under the disguise of inferior beings. It is observable that the two specimens of the primitive Fable in Scripture (*Judges* ix. 8-15 and *II Kings* xiv. 9) are of the kind that ascribe human thoughts to things of the vegetable world. The other great division of Fables, that which puts human speech into the mouth of brutes, is not represented in the Bible, unless, as some commentators suppose, the incident of Balaam and his ass be such a Fable incorporated in the narrative.

God constitutes legitimate matter of prophecy. Besides the visions of their call to the office of prophet, both Jeremiah and Ezekiel have set forth in their books communings which do not seem intended for publication to the people. We find also Dialogues of Intercession (either standing alone, or merged in other prophecies), of which the great prototype is Abraham's intercession for Sodom.

Prophetic Intercourse: (1) with God

Again, there is the intercourse of the prophet with enquirers. From the earliest history we read of persons 'enquiring of the Lord,' and receiving oracles in reply. Thus Rebekah heard before their birth the destiny of her twin children; Saul enquiring found no answer, "by dreams, nor by Urim, nor by prophets." We find, as a regular custom, that deputations visit the prophet, and wait till inspiration falls upon him, and so receive his Response. With this is connected what may be called an artificial form of prophecy, in which there is no actual interview between the prophet and another interlocutor, but the discourse takes the form of a reply to an imaginary objection or interruption. The whole of *Malachi* seems constructed in this form of Dialectic Prophecy. Its paragraphs uniformly take a shape that may be thus represented:

(2) with enquirers

(Dialectic Prophecy)

{ A Complaint
  An interposed Objection
  The answering Discourse

In some cases the objection is duplicated, as may be illustrated by the following brief condensation :

{ Instead of honouring, the priests despise God's name.
  Wherein despise it?
  In offering polluted bread upon his altar.
  Wherein polluted?
  The Answering Discourse puts the cheapening of offerings made to the Lord, and how the ideal of the priesthood is reversed.

Once more, Prophecy includes the intercourse of the prophet with the world in general. The books narrate Incidents, like the conspiracy of his native Anathoth against Jeremiah, or the burning of his roll by the king, or the casting of Daniel into a den of lions; or Contro- *(3) with the World* versies, like that stirred up by Jeremiah's wearing the emblem of the yoke. These Incidents (illustrations of which are given in the Table of Prophecy) make an approach to the Epic Prophecy discussed in a former book. More than this, the department of Prophecy overlaps with that of History, as whole sections of the prophetic books show. What Nathan was to David, that the whole succession of greater and minor prophets were to later history. The secular kingship had its orders of officials; the order of prophets were the representatives of the higher theocracy, and their action in each crisis makes a part at once of Prophecy and History.

We find ourselves on a different literary plane when we come to Dramatic Prophecy. To constitute this a scene or situation must be presented entirely by dialogue, without any description or comment from the prophet, *Dramatic Prophecy* except so far as he may be a party to the scene. These dramatic scenes are highly interesting; but the absence in ancient literatures of any attempt to indicate the speakers in passages of dialogue has led to much obscurity and misinterpretation.

A simple illustration occurs in the *Book of Micah*, and may be entitled, 'The Lord's Controversy before the Mountains.' Jehovah calls upon the Mountains to hear his con- *Micah vi. 1-8* troversy with his people; and himself proceeds to arraign Israel, rehearsing his long-continued kindnesses, and citing Balaam as his witness to the blessings bestowed on Jacob. Then the other party to the controversy is afraid to put in an appearance.

> Wherewith shall I come before the LORD, and bow myself before the high God? shall I come before him with burnt offerings, with

calves of a year old? Will the LORD be pleased with thousands of rams, or with ten thousands of rivers of oil? Shall I give my firstborn for my transgression, the fruit of my body for the sin of my soul?

The Mountains may then be understood to pronounce judgment.

> He hath shewed thee, O man, what is good; and what doth the LORD require of thee, but to do justly, and to love mercy, and to walk humbly with thy God?

This dramatic scene is immediately followed by another somewhat more extended in form. The passage is headed: "The voice of the LORD crieth unto the city, and the man of wisdom will fear thy name." This title suggests that we have in 'the Man of Wisdom' an addition to what may be called the natural *dramatis personæ*, namely, God, the Prophet, and the offending People, which last may in this case be termed the Men of Folly. The voice of God is heard denouncing injustice, violence, and the "statutes of Omri"; wounding, humiliation, famine, are threatened, until the people of the wicked city shall become a desolation and a hissing. This interposition of Jehovah throws the wicked of the city into confusion, while the wise see in it their salvation.

[sidenote: Micah vi. 9-vii]

> *The Men of Folly.* — Woe is me! for I am as when they have gathered the summer fruits, as the grape gleanings of the vintage: there is no cluster to eat; nor first-ripe fig which my soul desired. The godly man is perished out of the earth, and there is none upright among men: they all lie in wait for blood; they hunt every man his brother with a net. Both hands are put forth for evil to do it; the prince asketh, and the judge is ready for a reward; and the great man, he uttereth the mischief of his soul: thus they weave it together. The best of them is as a brier: the straightest is as it were taken from a thorn hedge: the day of thy watchmen, even thy visitation, is come; now shall be their perplexity. Trust ye not in a friend, put ye not confidence in a guide: keep the doors of thy mouth from her that lieth in thy bosom. For the son dishonoureth the father, the daughter riseth up against her mother, the daughter-in-law against her mother-in-law; a man's enemies are the men of his own house.

The Man of Wisdom. — But as for me, I will look unto the LORD; I will wait for the God of my salvation: my God will hear me. Rejoice not against me, O mine enemy: when I fall, I shall arise; when I sit in darkness, the LORD shall be a light unto me. I will bear the indignation of the LORD, because I have sinned against him; until he plead my cause, and execute judgement for me: he will bring me forth to the light, and I shall behold his righteousness. Then mine enemy shall see it, and shame shall cover her; which said unto me, Where is the LORD thy God? Mine eyes shall behold her; now shall she be trodden down as the mire of the streets.

The voice of God is now heard in tones of comfort: it proclaims the rebuilding of the city's walls, and (after an echoing cry from the Prophet) describes marvels of restoration to equal the old wonders done in Egypt: the oppressing nations shall come creeping out of their hiding-places, trembling with fear of the Deliverer. Then the Prophet brings the scene to a conclusion.

The Prophet. — Who is a God like unto thee, that pardoneth iniquity, and passeth by the transgression of the remnant of his heritage? he retaineth not his anger forever, because he delighteth in mercy. He will turn again and have compassion upon us; he will tread our iniquities under foot: and thou wilt cast all their sins into the depths of the sea. Thou wilt perform the truth to Jacob, and the mercy to Abraham, which thou hast sworn unto our fathers from the days of old.

A slight variation from this simple dramatic type is afforded by those prophecies in which only a single speaker is presented, — God: but the alternations in the Divine mind between judgment and compassion produce all the effect of dialogue. The Divine Yearning is pictured in this way by Hosea.

God. — When Israel was a child, then I loved him, and called my son out of Egypt. —

As they called them, so they went from them: they sacrificed unto the Baalim, and burned incense to graven images. —

Hosea xi. 1-11

Yet I taught Ephraim to go; I took them on my arms; but they knew not that I healed them. I drew them with cords of a man, with bands of love; and I was to them as they that take off the yoke on their jaws, and I laid meat before them. —

He shall not return into the land of Egypt; but the Assyrian shall be his king, because they refused to return. And the sword shall fall upon his cities, and shall consume his bars, and devour them, because of their own counsels. And my people are bent to backsliding from me: though they call them to him that is on high, none at all will exalt him. —

How shall I give thee up, Ephraim? how shall I deliver thee, Israel? how shall I make thee as Admah? how shall I set thee as Zeboim? mine heart is turned within me, my compassions are kindled together. I will not execute the fierceness of mine anger, I will not return to destroy Ephraim: for I am God, and not man; the Holy One in the midst of thee: and I will not come in wrath. They shall walk after the LORD, who shall roar like a lion: for he shall roar, and the children shall come trembling from the west. They shall come trembling as a bird out of Egypt, and as a dove out of the land of Assyria: and I will make them to dwell in their houses, saith the LORD.

This alternating monologue is combined with the dialogue that involves a second speaker in a more extended composition of the same prophet. The whole may be entitled, 'A Drama of Repentance.'

Hosea xiii-xiv

God. — When Ephraim spake with trembling, he exalted himself in Israel: but when he offended in Baal, he died. And now they sin more and more, and have made them molten images of their silver, even idols according to their own understanding, all of them the work of the craftsmen: they say of them, Let the men that sacrifice kiss the calves. Therefore they shall be as the morning cloud, and as the dew that passeth early away, as the chaff that is driven with the whirlwind out of the threshing-floor, and as the smoke out of the chimney. —

Yet I am the LORD thy God from the land of Egypt; and thou knowest no god but me, and beside me there is no saviour. I did know thee in the wilderness, in the land of great drought. According to their pasture, so were they filled; they were filled, and their heart was exalted: therefore have they forgotten me. —

Therefore am I unto them as a lion: as a leopard will I watch by the way: I will meet them as a bear that is bereaved of her whelps, and will rend the caul of their heart: and there will I devour them like a lion; the wild beast shall tear them. It is thy destruction, O Israel, that thou art against me, against thy help. Where now is thy king, that he may save thee in all thy cities? and thy judges, of whom thou saidst, Give me a king and princes? I have given thee a king in mine anger, and have taken him away in my wrath. The iniquity of Ephraim is bound up; his sin is laid up in store. The sorrows of a travailing woman shall come upon him: he is an unwise son; for it is time he should not tarry in the place of the breaking forth of children. —

I will ransom them from the power of the grave; I will redeem them from death: O death, where are thy plagues? O grave, where is thy destruction? —

Repentance shall be hid from mine eyes. Though he be fruitful among his brethren, an east wind shall come, the breath of the LORD coming up from the wilderness, and his spring shall become dry, and his fountain shall be dried up: it shall spoil the treasure of all pleasant vessels. Samaria shall bear her guilt; for she hath rebelled against her God: they shall fall by the sword; their infants shall be dashed in pieces, and their women with child shall be ripped up.

Repentant Israel. — O Israel, return unto the LORD thy God; for thou hast fallen by thine iniquity. Take with you words, and return unto the LORD: say unto him, "Take away all iniquity, and receive us graciously: so will we render as bullocks the offering of our lips. Asshur shall not save us; we will not ride upon horses: neither will we say any more to the work of our hands, Ye are our gods: for in thee the fatherless findeth mercy."

God. — I will heal their backsliding, I will love them freely: for mine anger is turned away from him. I will be as the dew unto Israel: he shall blossom as the lily, and cast forth his roots as Lebanon. His branches shall spread, and his beauty shall be as the olive tree, and his smell as Lebanon. They that dwell under his shadow shall return; they shall revive as the corn, and blossom as the vine: the scent thereof shall be as the wine of Lebanon. Ephraim shall say, What have I to do any more with idols? I have answered, and will regard him: I am like a green fir tree; from me is thy fruit found.

We have thus seen the prophetic literature of the Bible assuming very various forms. Besides the simple record of intercourse with God or with the people, the prophet's message may be an elaborate discourse; the discourse may have a symbolic text, and so present the varieties of emblem, vision, and parable; the prophecy may clothe itself in lyric poetry, or it may be presented in a dramatic scene. There still remain to be mentioned two kinds of prophecy of such importance from the literary standpoint that they must be discussed in separate chapters.

CHAPTER XV

FORMS OF PROPHETIC LITERATURE: THE DOOM SONG

AMONG forms of Prophecy there is one which has a distinctiveness and prominence in the Bible, and from the literary point of view so special an interest, that it seems proper in this work to treat it in a chapter by itself. This is the Doom Song: a prophetic utterance directed against some particular city, nation, or country. The kingdoms of Israel, however unique their position in the history of mankind, yet in their own age formed part of a network of states. There were neighbour peoples, like the Philistines or Syrians, kindred races, such as Moabites, Edomites, Ammonites, the maritime powers of Tyre and Sidon, and others: all stretching like a chain between the two world empires of Egypt on the south and Assyria on the northeast. Deliverance from one of these empires formed the starting-point of Israel's history, and into the other she was destined to be absorbed; meanwhile the ceaseless fluctuations of power and of mutual relations between all these nations and empires imposed a continual foreign policy on the kingdoms of Israel and Judah. The prophets exercised influence in this foreign policy, as well as in domestic questions. And, over and above questions of temporary policy, there was the perpetual function of Israel as a nation to uphold the worship of the true God amidst nations of idolaters; and the constant witnesses to this were the prophets. One product of such prophetic ministry was this denunciatory discourse or Doom Song.

The Doom Song as a form of Prophecy

There is a remarkable passage in *Jeremiah* which may well serve as preface to a discussion of the whole subject.

XXV. 15 For thus saith the LORD, the God of Israel, unto me: Take the cup of the wine of this fury at my hand, and cause all the nations, to whom I send thee, to drink it. And they shall drink, and reel to and fro, and be mad, because of the sword that I will send among them. Then took I the cup at the LORD's hand, and made all the nations to drink, unto whom the LORD had sent me: to wit, Jerusalem, and the cities of Judah, and the kings thereof, and the princes thereof, to make them a desolation, an astonishment, an hissing, and a curse; as it is this day; Pharaoh king of Egypt, and his servants, and his princes, and all his people; and all the mingled people, and all the kings of the land of Uz, and all the kings of the land of the Philistines, and Ashkelon, and Gaza, and Ekron, and the remnant of Ashdod; Edom, and Moab, and the children of Ammon; and all the kings of Tyre, and all the kings of Sidon, and the kings of the isle which is beyond the sea; Dedan, and Tema, and Buz, and all that have the corners of their hair polled; and all the kings of Arabia, and all the kings of the mingled people that dwell in the wilderness; and all the kings of Zimri, and all the kings of Elam, and all the kings of the Medes; and all the kings of the north, far and near, one with another; and all the kingdoms of the world, which are upon the face of the earth: and the king of Sheshach shall drink after them. And thou shalt say unto them, Thus saith the LORD of hosts, the God of Israel: Drink ye, and be drunken, and spue, and fall, and rise no more, because of the sword which I will send among you. And it shall be, if they refuse to take the cup at thine hand to drink, then shalt thou say unto them, Thus saith the LORD of hosts: Ye shall surely drink. For, lo, I begin to work evil at the city which is called by my name, and should ye be utterly unpunished? Ye shall not be unpunished: for I will call for a sword upon all the inhabitants of the earth, saith the LORD of hosts. Therefore prophesy thou against them all these words, and say unto them, The LORD shall roar from on high, and utter his voice from his holy habitation; he shall mightily roar against his fold; he shall give a shout, as they that tread the grapes, against all the inhabitants of the earth. A noise shall come even to the end of the earth; for the LORD hath a controversy with the nations, he will plead with all flesh; as for the wicked, he will give them to the sword, saith the LORD.

The Doom Songs then are the pourings out of "the cup of the Lord's Fury" against particular kingdoms, such as the words of Jeremiah suggest. Their prototype is the primitive Curse on Canaan:

> Cursed be Canaan: *Genesis*
> A servant of servants shall he be unto his brethren.   ix. 25

They are indignant denunciations of idolatry and vice; prophetic pictures of doom to come in spite of all appearances to the contrary; realistic pictures of overthrow and desolation; wails as over the dead, soon changing to taunts from victims to a fallen oppressor. They have been compared to the Satires and Philippics of other literatures: and it is true that they give scope to the literary impulses which in other cases have produced these forms. But there is a wide difference of tone between the Biblical denunciation and its secular counterparts. I would rather say that the Doom Song is to the Satire what Tragedy is to Comedy; the Doom Song is to the Philippic what Poetry is to Prose.

Coming to particulars, we may note the difference between the brief, oracular, almost enigmatic utterances which seem to be the earlier forms of Doom, and the elaborate invectives of later times, upon which all the resources of literature are concentrated.

Of the earlier type there can be no better illustration than the series of three 'Oracles' which make the twenty-first chapter of *Isaiah*, and which, however obscure their historic references may be, seem by their internal resemblances to constitute a unity. Their interest lies, not so much in the events they foreshadow, as in the way they give poetic realisation to the prophetic attitude. They are bound together by underlying imagery of a prophet keeping vigil on the eastern boundary of the holy land, with his watchman still further in advance, both peering through the darkness of future history to catch the first signs of the Lord's dealing with his foes. The first oracle has its title from the "wilderness of the sea," that is, the region of Tigris and Euphrates, and brings out the fall of the empire that is the eastern boundary

The earlier or Oracular Dooms

Isaiah xxi

of the prophet's world. It has the usual mingling of prose and lyric verse: the prose puts the prophet's position of vigil, and the agitation which his vision produces in his own heart, while snatches of verse convey gleams of vision, or words of the watchman, or even the call of the Lord to the destroying foe.

1

The Oracle of the Wilderness of the Sea

As whirlwinds in the South sweep through,
   It cometh from the wilderness,
From a terrible land!
A grievous vision is declared unto me; the treacherous dealer dealeth treacherously, and the spoiler spoileth.
   "Go up, O Elam;
     Besiege, O Media;
   All the sighing thereof will I make to cease."
Therefore are my loins filled with anguish; pangs have taken hold upon me, as the pangs of a woman in travail: I am pained so that I cannot hear, I am dismayed so that I cannot see. My heart panteth, horror hath affrighted me: the twilight that I desired hath been turned into trembling unto me.
   "They prepare the table,
     They spread the carpets,
     They eat, they drink:
   Rise up, ye princes, anoint the shield."
For thus hath the LORD said unto me, Go, set a watchman; let him declare what he seeth: and when he seeth a troop, horsemen in pairs, a troop of asses, a troop of camels, he shall hearken diligently with much heed. And he cried as a lion:
   O Lord,
   I stand continually upon the watch-tower in the day-time,
     And am set in my ward whole nights:
   And, behold, here cometh a troop of men,
     Horsemen in pairs.
   And He answered and said,
     "Babylon is fallen,
     Is fallen;   [ground."
And all the graven images of her gods are broken upon the O thou my threshing, and the corn of my floor: that which I have heard from the LORD of hosts, the God of Israel, have I declared unto you.

The second oracle is not associated with any incident, but seems entirely devoted to bringing out the prophetic attitude of vigil. A voice out of the lower region of Mount Seir calls to the watchman in his wilderness station for tidings: the sentinel, as if repeating the formula of the watch, replies that the regular succession of day and night is broken by no tidings as yet, the enquirer must ask again.

2

The Oracle of Silence

One calleth unto me out of Seir;
   Watchman, what of the night?
   Watchman, what of the night?
The watchman said,
   The morning cometh,
     And also the night:
   If ye will enquire, enquire ye;
     Come ye again.

The third oracle sees another storm-cloud about to break from the north; and bids nomad peoples get ready food for the fugitives of Kedar, whom they will find before the night just beginning is over.

3

The Oracle at Evening

In the thickets at evening shall ye lodge,
O ye travelling companies of Dedanites.
Unto him that is thirsty bring ye water;
Ye inhabitants of the land of Tema,
Meet the fugitives with your bread.
For they fled away from the swords,
From the drawn sword, and from the bent bow,
And from the grievousness of war.

For thus hath the Lord said unto me, Within a year, according to the years of an hireling, and all the glory of Kedar shall fail: and the residue of the number of the archers, the mighty men of the children of Kedar, shall be few: for the LORD, the God of Israel, hath spoken it.[1]

But the larger proportion of the Doom Songs are elaborate outpourings, which hover on the borderland between rhetoric declamation and poetic imagery. The destroying enemy appears as strangers come to fan, or waters out of the north, or smoke out of the north; the country is swept with the besom of destruction, it is scattered to the four winds. In the panic fathers look not back to their children for feebleness of hands, fortresses go down before the invader as ripe figs are shaken from a tree. Babylon has been a golden cup in the Lord's hand to make the nations drunken and mad; and when the work is done Babylon is suddenly fallen and destroyed. She has been a destroying mountain, destroying all the earth: but the Lord will stretch his hand upon her, and roll her down from the rocks, and make her a burnt mountain: men shall not take of her a stone for a corner, but she shall be desolate forever. Babylon is Jehovah's 'battle-axe,' with which he will break in pieces the nations: but the 'hammer of the whole earth' is cut asunder and broken. "Moab hath been at ease from his youth, and he hath settled on his lees, and hath not been emptied from vessel to vessel, neither hath he gone into captivity: therefore his taste remaineth in him, and his scent is not changed." Therefore shall be sent to him those that pour off, and they shall empty his vessels, and break the bottles in pieces. The Assyrian was a cedar in Lebanon, with fair branches and a shadowing shroud; his top amid the clouds, till the cedars in the garden of God could not hide him; the waters nourished him, the deep made him to grow; the fowls of heaven made their nests in his boughs, and all great nations dwelt under his shadow. But he is delivered

The more elaborate Doom Songs

---

[1] It might seem at first sight that the title of the section which follows, 'The Oracle of the Valley of Vision,' should make it a part of the same series. But comparison of verses 5, 7, 8 (of xxii) will show that the 'valley of vision' is to be associated, not with the prophet's place of observation, but with the details of the blockade. The enemy had reached a point close enough to see into the city through the breaches and to be seen by the citizens: hence the panic.

into the hands of the mighty, the terrible have cut him off and left him; his branches are fallen over mountains and valleys, and his broken boughs along the watercourses; all the fowls of heaven dwell upon his ruin. When Babylon goes down hell from beneath is moved to meet him; the shades of the kings of the nations rise from their thrones to gaze at the mighty oppressor become weak like themselves. The glorious seat of empire turns to utter desolation.

> It shall never be inhabited,
> Neither shall it be dwelt in from generation to generation:
> Neither shall the Arabian pitch tent there;
> Neither shall shepherds make their flocks to lie down there.
>
> But wild beasts of the desert shall lie there;
> And their houses shall be full of doleful creatures;
> And ostriches shall dwell there,
> And satyrs shall dance there.
>
> And wolves shall cry in their castles,
> And jackals in the pleasant palaces:
> And her time is near to come,
> And her days shall not be prolonged.

Perhaps the most wide-reaching and many-sided of the Doom Songs is Ezekiel's burden, or rather succession of burdens, against the maritime metropolis of the ancient world, — the city of Tyre. God is against Tyre, and the nations shall overwhelm her like the waves of a rising sea: they shall wash down walls and towers, and even her very dust, until Tyre has become a bare rock, a place for the spreading of nets in the midst of the sea. From imagery the Song changes to picture: and in successive sentences we see Nebuchadrezzar's advance: the daughter fortresses on the confines are destroyed, mounts and battering engines are before the mother city, the very dust of his march smothers the beautiful site, at the mere sound of his horsemen and chariots the gates are shaken down; horse-hoofs deface the streets, the sword slays, the obelisks of strength are thrown down, riches spoiled, pleasant houses made rubbish

Doom of Tyre Ezekiel xxvi-xxviii

heaps: Tyre becomes a silent and bare rock, a place for the spreading of nets. Then all the princes of the sea come down from their thrones, and lay aside their robes, and strip off their broidered garments: they clothe themselves with tremblings, as they raise the wail over the renowned city, won from the sea, and the terror of all that haunt it. For God shall bring up the deep upon her, and the great waters shall cover her, and he will bring her down with them that descend into the pit, and will make her to dwell in the nether parts of the earth, in the places that are desolate of old; though she be sought for, yet shall she never be found again. Then another strain of denunciation commences, and with prolonged enumeration brings out poetically the world-wide enterprise of the wealthy port. Tyre is represented in the form of a ship, and the various races with which she has dealings make their contributions to its perfection.

> Thou, O Tyre, hast said, I am perfect in beauty. Thy borders are in the heart of the seas, thy builders have perfected thy beauty. They have made all thy planks of fir trees from Senir: they have taken cedars from Lebanon to make a mast for thee. Of the oaks of Bashan have they made thine oars; they have made thy benches of ivory inlaid in boxwood, from the isles of Kittim. Of fine linen with broidered work from Egypt was thy sail, that it might be to thee for an ensign; blue and purple from the isles of Elishah was thine awning. The inhabitants of Zidon and Arvad were thy rowers: thy wise men, O Tyre, were in thee, they were thy pilots. The ancients of Gebal and the wise men thereof were in thee thy calkers: all the ships of the sea with their mariners were in thee to occupy thy merchandise. Persia and Lud and Put were in thine army, thy men of war: they hanged the shield and helmet in thee; they set forth thy comeliness. The men of Arvad with thine army were upon thy walls round about, and the Gammadim were in thy towers: they hanged their shields upon thy walls round about; they have perfected thy beauty.

This is only a fragment of the long-sustained enumeration: for when mention is made of the merchants who traffic with this Ship of Tyre all nations of the civilised world appear, and every kind of merchandise and riches is detailed, until the successive sentences have accumulated a conception of inexhaustible wealth. Then comes the shock of change. The Ship that makes such a thing of glory in the heart of the seas suffers wreck.

> Thy rowers have brought thee into great waters: the east wind hath broken thee in the heart of the seas. Thy riches, and thy wares, thy merchandise, thy mariners, and thy pilots, thy calkers, and the occupiers of thy merchandise, and all thy men of war, that are in thee, with all thy company which is in the midst of thee, shall fall into the heart of the seas in the day of thy ruin. At the sound of the cry of thy pilots the waves shall shake.

After fresh lamentations of the sea-faring world over their chief, the tempest of denunciation glances upon the prince of Tyre, who says "he is a god, he sits in the seat of God in the heart of the seas": but he is a man, and not God, in the hand of him that woundeth him; and he shall die the death of the uncircumcised. Then the strain of denunciation gathers to a climax. Tyre sealeth up the sum, full of wisdom and perfect in beauty. Tyre was in Eden the garden of God; every precious stone was her covering; she was the cherub overshadowing the mercy seat: till unrighteousness was found in her. Multitude of traffic filled her with violence; she has been cast out as profane; fire from the midst of her has devoured her; she has been turned to ashes in the sight of all beholders; she shall exist no more.

If the burden of Ezekiel against Tyre be a typical example of this department of literature, we may take from the same prophet another Doom Song which is unique. The idea underlying it is the same thought we have already cited from Isaiah, — that of the kingdoms among the dead receiving the newly fallen empire in the gloomy underworld. The form of this burden is a Wail or Dirge. It is an extreme example of the overlapping of verse and prose which I have illustrated in so many branches of Hebrew literature: monotonous prose recitative carries on the thread of description, and is broken by strongly rhythmic lines, that leave the impression

Doom of Egypt
Ezekiel xxxii. 17-32

at once of varying and of recurring with the regularity of a refrain. I cite this Song in full, and then our notice of the literature of Doom will have been carried sufficiently far.

DOOM OF EGYPT

Son of man, wail for the multitude of Egypt, and cast them down, even her, and the daughters of the famous nations,
    Unto the nether parts of the earth,
    With them that go down into the pit.
Whom dost thou pass in beauty? go down, and be thou laid with the uncircumcised. They shall fall in the midst of them that are slain by the sword: she is delivered to the sword: draw her away and all her multitudes.

The strong among the mighty shall speak to him out of the midst of hell with them that help him:
    They are gone down,
    They lie still,
    Even the uncircumcised,
    Slain by the sword.
Asshur is there and all her company; his graves are round about him:
    All of them slain,
    Fallen by the sword:
Whose graves are set in the uttermost parts of the pit, and her company is round about her grave:
    All of them slain,
    Fallen by the sword,
    Which caused terror in the land of the living.
There is Elam and all her multitude round about her grave:
    All of them slain,
    Fallen by the sword,
    Which are gone down uncircumcised
    Into the nether parts of the earth,
    Which caused their terror in the land of the living,
and have borne their shame with them that go down to the pit. They have set her a bed in the midst of the slain with all her multitude; her graves are round about her;
    All of them uncircumcised,
    Slain by the sword;

for their terror was caused in the land of the living, and they have borne their shame with them that go down to the pit: he is put in the midst of them that be slain. There is Meshech, Tubal, and all her multitude; her graves are round about her:
> All of them uncircumcised,
> Slain by the sword;
> For they caused their terror in the land of the living.

And shall they not lie with the mighty that are fallen of the uncircumcised,
> Which are gone down to hell,
> With their weapons of war,

and have laid their swords under their heads, and their iniquities are upon their bones;
> For they were the terror of the mighty
> In the land of the living;

but thou shalt be broken in the midst of the uncircumcised, and shalt lie with them that are slain by the sword. There is Edom, her kings and all her princes, which for all their might are laid
> With them that are slain by the sword:
> They shall lie with the uncircumcised,
> And with them that go down to the pit.

There be the princes of the north, all of them, and all the Zidonians,
> Which are gone down with the slain;

for all the terror which they caused by their might they are ashamed;
> And they lie uncircumcised
> With them that are slain by the sword,
> And bear their shame
> With them that go down to the pit.

Pharaoh shall see them, and shall be comforted over all his multitude: even Pharaoh and all his army,
> Slain by the sword (saith the Lord GOD),
> For I have put his terror in the land of the living:
> And he shall be laid in the midst of the uncircumcised,
> With them that are slain by the sword:

even Pharaoh and all his multitude, saith the Lord GOD.

CHAPTER XVI

FORMS OF PROPHETIC LITERATURE: THE RHAPSODY

PROPHECY in one of its aspects may be described as the philosophy of history erected into a drama. But both the terms of this description must be understood in a special sense. Philosophy acts through its instrument of reflection when it interprets history into intelligible theory, or catches the drift of a passing crisis. But the prophets carry their scheme of faith with them into the events they observe. It is faith in that which the Old Testament expresses by the word 'Judgment': the eternal controversy between Good and Evil, between God's people and idolatrous nations, between the 'remnant' and the godless mass of Israelites; and this carries with it the correlative idea of a golden age, placed in the future and not the past, when the controversy should culminate in a Messianic reign of peace. To harmonise with this principle of Judgment the working of events is great part of the prophetic function. And, as one mode of conveying their conceptions, the prophets display the incidents themselves before our imagination working towards their goal with the realistic clearness of drama. But upon examination such prophetic compositions are found to go far beyond the machinery of dramatic literature, and to borrow from all other literary departments special modes of treatment, to be blended together into that most highly wrought and spiritual of literary forms which is here called the Rhapsody.

The Prophetic Rhapsody: General Conception

I desire to explain this in detail; but first it may be well to take an illustration. The simplest example of the form of prophecy under consideration is Habakkuk's *Rhapsody of the Chaldeans*. Its exact date is a question for historical experts; for literary interpretation it is sufficient to say that it belongs to the period when the Chaldean power first looms as a terror on the political horizon. Under such terror the first instinct of the devout would be to think of national corruption unpunished at home. But prophetic insight must go further. If the Chaldeans — a cruel, godless embodiment of might without right — were to be God's instrument of judgment, would not the instrument be far worse than that against which it was used? It is this perplexity which is presented before us by Habakkuk in dramatic dialogue.

<small>Rhapsody of the Chaldeans
Habakkuk i-ii</small>

> *The Prophet.* — O LORD, how long shall I cry, and thou wilt not hear? I cry unto thee of violence, and thou wilt not save. Why dost thou shew me iniquity, and cause me to look upon perverseness? for spoiling and violence are before me: and there is strife, and contention riseth up. Therefore the law is slacked, and judgement doth never go forth: for the wicked doth compass about the righteous; therefore judgement goeth forth perverted.
>
> *God.* — Behold ye among the nations, and regard, and wonder marvellously: for I work a work in your days, which ye will not believe though it be told you. For, lo, I raise up the Chaldeans, that bitter and hasty nation; which march through the breadth of the earth, to possess dwelling places that are not theirs. They are terrible and dreadful: their judgement and their dignity proceed from themselves. Their horses also are swifter than leopards, and are more fierce than the evening wolves; and their horsemen bear themselves proudly: yea, their horsemen come from far; they fly as an eagle that hasteth to devour. They come all of them for violence; their faces are set eagerly as the east wind; and they gather captives as the sand. Yea, he scoffeth at kings, and princes are a derision unto him: he derideth every stronghold; for he heapeth up dust, and taketh it. Then shall he sweep by as a wind, and shall pass over, and be guilty; even he whose might is his God.
>
> *The Prophet.* — Art not thou from everlasting, O LORD my God, mine Holy One? thou diest not. O LORD, thou hast ordained him for judgement; and thou, O Rock, hast established him for correction. Thou that art of purer eyes than to behold evil, and that

canst not look upon perverseness, wherefore lookest thou upon them that deal treacherously, and holdest thy peace when the wicked swalloweth up the man that is more righteous than he; and makest men as the fishes of the sea, as the creeping things, that have no ruler over them? He taketh up all of them with the angle, he catcheth them in his net, and gathereth them in his drag: therefore he rejoiceth and is glad. Therefore he sacrificeth unto his net, and burneth incense unto his drag; because by them his portion is fat, and his meat plenteous. Shall he therefore empty his net, and not spare to slay the nations continually?

The perplexity has been fully opened: the point has been reached where a solution may be looked for. Additional literary force is given to this solution by delay; there is a pause, and the prophet will retire to his watch-tower to wait the answer of God. The answer, when it comes, is ushered in by many phrases of emphasis,— it is to be written, to be made plain, the 'vision,' though it seem to tarry, is really hasting to its appointed time. What then is the Divine solution to the prophet's trouble? As so often happens in literature of this type, the central point of the whole prophecy is conveyed under the form of imagery,— in this case the imagery of intoxication. The haughty irresistibility of the Chaldean is no more than the vinous elation that goes before the tottering and falling; he is 'puffed up,' he cannot go straight, the treacherous dealing of wine has given him the haughtiness that will not abide, and the insatiable appetite of hell. Then the fall that is to come is made present to our imaginations by a sudden breaking out of the Taunt-Song of the oppressed nations over their fallen tyrant. In lyric sequence four woes are denounced, all celebrating the same theme — the pride and fall of the Chaldean, but celebrating it under four different images. The first woe puts the image of usury: Chaldean aggrandisement has been a mounting up of borrowed property, and there shall rise up suddenly those who will exact usury. In the second woe the image is of house-building: the tyrant has been building his own shame into the house he thought to

ii. 1

ii. 2

ii. 4-5

ii. 6-8

ii. 9-11

make so high above all evil; now it is finished the stone cries out of the wall and the beam out of the timber answers it. In the third woe the image changes to fortification: the deep purposes of Jehovah suffer a city to be built with blood and ramparted with iniquity, just that its burning may fill earth and sea with the light of his judgment. The fourth woe rests on the regular prophetic metaphor—the cup of the Lord's fury, handed by the Chaldean to the other nations, and drunk by the Chaldean in his turn. Then a final woe goes to the root of the whole evil: the Chaldean has been led astray by his lying idols, all covered with gold and silver, but with no breath in them. But Jehovah in his holy temple is the true teacher of the nations: let all the earth sit in silence at his feet. ii. 12-14
ii. 15-17
ii. 18-20

Simple as this prophecy is, it has exhibited all that is essential in rhapsodic literature; a problem of current history has been stated in the form of dramatic dialogue, and solved in the form of lyric song. This department of prophecy includes some of the most intricate and obscure literature in the whole Bible. But in all cases there is an enlargement of dramatic machinery by the fusion with it of other kinds of literary treatment. A similar fusion has taken place in the companion art of music; and those who are familiar with the Oratorio and the Cantata will understand how a dramatic action may be maintained, though particular movements in it are in lyric or meditative form. *The Rhapsody as an enlargement of dramatic treatment*

What exactly is the mental experience of a spectator watching a drama? He has a movement of events brought home to him, not by any narrative or explanation, but by the dialogue of the personages taking part in the incidents, assisted by changes in the scene before his eyes. The reader of prophetic drama has history presented to him as moving in the direction of Divine judgment. But the stage on which such movement takes place is nothing less than the whole universe. Its changing scenery must be conveyed to him, rarely in vision, mainly by description. It is not the description that belongs to Epic poetry and deals with incidents in the past. It is what may be called Scenic Description, such as speaks in the present tense with the vividness of one who beholds what he tells, and yet the personality of no spectator is interposed between the reader and the scene. Or it is Prophetic Description, that uses present or future indifferently: for what God, or his prophetic mouthpiece, foretells is as objectively real to the imagination as if it were visibly present. Similarly, the machinery of dialogue needs enlargement to meet the requirements of the prophetic drama. Besides actual dialogue we have the Soliloquy or Monologue, whether of the Divine Being or others; in particular, alternating monologues — say, of the righteous and wicked from opposite regions — produce a literary effect closely akin to dialogue. Another element of dialogue is the Divine Address: the omnipresence of Deity extends to those with whom he speaks, and his call to them makes them at once part of the scene. This consideration is more important than might at first be thought; we shall find the longest scene in prophecy to have no speaker but the Divine Being, whose alternate addresses to the nations and to Israel keep both present before us to the end. And in a less degree the same effect attaches to other addresses: the cries at the opening of *Joel* to various classes of society to come and weep serve to bring these classes into the scene of his poem. Again, the prophet, besides being the mouthpiece of God, remains a spectator of his own drama, and his comments, spoken to earth or heaven, form a part of the scenes. 'Voices,' again, may join in the dialogue, yet not in such a way as to make the personality of those who speak continuously present: or yet more impersonal 'Cries' may serve a temporary purpose in the drama. As an element of dialogue more abstract still we have Lyric Songs or Responses: not the Choral songs, such as closed Habakkuk's prophecy, and were spoken by the oppressed nations, but impersonal lyrics, like those used in *Zephaniah* to answer or second the announcements of Deity, or to interrupt the continuity of movement by bursts of praise or lament.

In all these ways the machinery of drama is enlarged and spiritualised to make it the vehicle of prophecy. It borrows lyric treatment and oratorical discourse; it does the work of philosophy; even that which is the antithesis of drama, description, appears in a modified form to serve a scenic purpose. And, while the constant object is dramatic realisation, the transitions in this prophetic literature from dramatic to other literary forms are so frequent and rapid that they seem, not so much to be blended, as to be fused together. If the various types of literary treatment might be supposed to be so many different colours of thought, then this prophetic drama would be the white light made by the merging of all these colours in one. The term 'drama,' then, seems to me altogether inadequate for such a specialised form of literature. A more appropriate name would be found in the 'Rhapsody,' which poetry and music alike reserve as something specially exalted and free from limitations of form.

The Prophecy of Joel makes a single *Rhapsody of the Locust Plague*. The idea of locusts, singly so insignificant, so terribly destructive in the mass, lends itself readily to poetic treatment; and the prophet, starting probably from some contemporary visitation of this kind, idealises it into mystic and awful forces of destruction, under the description of which the original idea can be dimly traced. On this as basis he works up a conception of advancing judgment: first an immediate crisis, and then the final judgment in which all nations are involved. And, like the *leit-motif* of a musical work, "the great and terrible Day of the Lord" runs through the whole as a refrain. Those who are accustomed to literary technicalities will be struck with the beautiful *movement* of this work: the seven stages into which its action falls advance regularly to a crisis, and then, as with the figure of an arch, turn round, the later corresponding to the earlier, until the final stage is seen as a reversal of the first. The accompanying

<small>Joel's Rhapsody of the Locust Plague</small>

<small>Its Movement a continuous Advance</small>

figure may convey this to the eye. [Commence to read at the bottom.]

      4. Relief and Restoration
        ii. 18-27

  3. At the last moment   5. Afterward: Israel spiritualised —
    Repentance   the Nations summoned
    ii. 12-17   to Judgment
             ii. 28-iii. 8

 2. Judgment visibly Ad-   6. Advance to the Valley
   vancing: CRISIS   of Decision: CRISIS
    ii. 1-11   iii. 9-16

1. The Land of Israel des-   7. The Holy Mountain
  olate and mourning   and eternal Peace
    i   iii. 17-21

  The prophecy opens with distress and wailing. Calls to lament bring before us old men witnessing to children and children's

<small>1. The Land of Israel desolate and mourning</small> children of devastation such as their fathers never knew; drinkers of wine awaking from their stupor to howl for the desolating, strong-toothed foe that has wasted the vine and blanched the fig tree; husbandmen howling under the shame and languishing that sits upon the crops and the trees of the field, and upon the helpless sons of men; the ministers of the altar clothing themselves with sackcloth as the meal-offering and drink-offering fails from the house of God. The different groups of mourners draw together into a solemn assembly of the whole land, crying with one voice, "Alas for the day of the LORD at hand!" and chaunting of seeds shrivelled under the clods, garners broken down, corn bowed with shame, cattle perplexed and flocks panting beside the dry watercourses and burnt pastures.

  But there is no relief: the action intensifies. A trumpet blast of alarm from the mountains darts into every trembling heart the

<small>2. Judgment visibly advancing: Crisis</small> consciousness that the Day of the Lord has come nigh! The day seems to have broken with clouds and thick darkness for the colours of its dawn; and they know that the destroying foe will be great and strong,

such as has never been known before, neither shall there be any like them. The advancing doom can just be discerned by the destruction it works: fires spreading from it in all directions: as it were the garden of Eden before it, and behind it a desolate wilderness. Straining eye and ear can dimly make out now the appearance of horses, now rattlings like chariots crossing the mountain ridges, now cracklings as of fire in stubble, now the array as of an ordered army. A nearer vision reveals pale anguish on the one side, on the other mighty warriors and an irresistible march; there is mystery in the way no ranks are broken with the inequalities of the ground, none swerves for a moment out of his place; the encountering weapons actually meet them, but the onward course has not stopped. Now the city is reached with a bound, is filled; the earth begins to quake, the heavens are all dark:— and the long-expected Voice of Jehovah brings the certainty that this is the Day of the Lord, a great and terrible day; who can abide it?

Then a surprise: for the Voice of Jehovah before his army speaks of a time yet for turning to the Lord, with weeping and fasting, with rending of the heart and not the garment, to a God who is gracious and full of compassion, slow to anger, and plenteous in mercy, one who repenteth him of the evil. And a response begins to stir among the doomed people: "Who knoweth whether he will not turn and repent, and leave a blessing behind him?" And once more, with sound of trumpet, there is a solemn assembly: all are gathered together, from the elder to the child at the breast, the bridegroom out of his chamber and the bride out of her closet: weeping priests and ministers of the altar leading the cry of "Spare thy people, O LORD." *3. At the last moment Repentance*

The turning-point of the prophecy has been reached: "Then was the LORD jealous for his land, and had pity on his people." In the words of Him with whom future and present are the same we have pictured a relief from the impending judgment: the northern army passing on to its own *4. Relief and Restoration* destruction in a desert between the seas, the land awakening to joy after fear, as pastures spring out of wilderness and the trees again yield their strength. Relief grows to restoration: the former and latter rain comes down each in its season, floors and vats overflow till the loss of locust and caterpillar has been repaired. Plenty and peace abound, with praise to the Lord for his wondrous dealings, and confidence that Israel shall be ashamed no more.

But instead of this being an end, the action of the rhapsody continues to advance. We have presented before us an 'afterward': in which there shall be a pouring out of the spirit upon the sons and daughters of Israel, until old and young, servant and handmaid, are all alike endowed with prophecy and vision. But for the nations, darkened sun and blood-stained moon, with pillars of smoke, with fire and blood, give warning in the heavens of another great and terrible Day of the Lord: a day of pleading with the nations, in the valley called after the name of judgment, for the wrongs they have done to the captives of the Lord's people. And, at the mention of living beings bartered and sold for goods, Divine description bursts into Divine remonstrance with the men of Tyre and Zidon and Philistia, for their pillage of the holy things, and their cruelty to the children of Judah and Jerusalem. And what recompense have they to make to the adversary, who shall swiftly return their recompense upon their own head?

3. Afterward: Israel spiritualised

4. The Nations summoned to Judgment

5. Advance to the Valley of Decision. Crisis

The action intensifies: like the former judgment on Israel this final doom of the nations quickens its advance, and already the cries of the coming contest are heard.

God. — Proclaim ye this among the nations; prepare war: stir up the mighty men; let all the men of war draw near, let them come up. Beat your plowshares into swords, and your pruninghooks into spears: let the weak say, I am strong.

Israel. — Haste ye, and come, all ye nations round about, and gather yourselves together: thither cause thy mighty ones to come down, O LORD.

> *God.* — Let the nations bestir themselves, and come up to the valley of Jehoshaphat: for there will I sit to judge all the nations round about.
> *God in the Celestial Host.* — Put ye in the sickle, for the harvest is ripe; come, tread ye; for the winepress is full, the fats overflow; for their wickedness is great.

The scene is before us of multitudes after multitudes in the valley of decision: the Day of the Lord is near, and this is the place of the contest. The awful crisis is veiled from us: sun and moon are dark, and the stars withdraw their shining. But from Jerusalem and Mount Zion Jehovah roars, and utters a voice under which the heavens and earth rock to and fro, all save the stronghold in which the Lord's people are held in safe refuge. The darkness clears away to reveal a final scene of Jehovah comforting his people from his holy dwelling-place in Zion. The mountains drop down sweet wine, and the hills flow with milk, and all the brooks are full of waters, while fountains from the house of the Lord carry fertility to the valleys around. Over the ruins of guilty Egypt and Edom Judah towers, an abiding habitation; and its people are washed with innocence meet for the people of the Lord that dwelleth in Zion. 7. The Holy Mountain and Eternal Peace

In this rhapsody of Joel the movement is a continuous advance, and its seven parts are seven successive stages like Acts of a drama. But I have several times had to remark upon another type of movement to which Hebrew literature shows attraction, — the pendulum movement, which alternates to and fro between two topics or scenes. This pendulum movement is specially characteristic of Prophecy. It will be illustrated in the next example I bring forward, the *Rhapsody of Judgment and Salvation*, which covers four chapters of *Isaiah*. The seven sections into which I have divided this composition do not make a succession in time. It is the fourth or middle section that stands out as a climax, presenting the Mountain of the Saved The Pendulum Movement in Rhapsodies Rhapsody of Judgment and Salvation. Isaiah xxv-vii towering above a prostrate world: on either side of this the other sections are varying pictures of the same judgment. The real movement of this rhapsody is the pendulum movement of alternation: — an alternation between successive pictures of Doom and Salvation. From the prominence of this alternation, and also because of the rapidity and obscurity of the transitions in this composition, I have thought it desirable to print it in full, with proper arrangement of parts. The sections of Judgment are distinguished by Roman, those of Salvation by Italic type. I quote the Revised Version (text or margin) exactly, except that for the formulæ commencing speeches (such as, "In that day shall be said," etc.) I substitute the names of the speakers at the head of the speeches. Paragraphs without such headings are scenic or prophetic descriptions.

ISAIAH'S
RHAPSODY OF JUDGMENT AND SALVATION

PRELUDE. — PROCLAMATION

Behold, the LORD maketh the earth empty, and maketh it waste, and turneth it upside down, and scattereth abroad the inhabitants thereof. And it shall be, as with the people, so with the priest; as with the servant, so with his master; as with the maid, so with her mistress; as with the buyer, so with the seller; as with the lender, so with the borrower; as with the taker of usury, so with the giver of usury to him. The earth shall be utterly emptied, and utterly spoiled: for the LORD hath spoken the word.

I

The earth mourneth and fadeth away, the world languisheth and fadeth away, the lofty people of the earth do languish. The earth also is polluted under the inhabitants thereof; because they have transgressed the laws, changed the ordinance, broken the everlasting covenant. Therefore hath the curse devoured the earth, and they that dwell therein are found guilty: therefore the inhabitants of the

earth are burned, and few men left. The new wine mourneth, the
vine languisheth, all the merryhearted do sigh. The mirth of tab-
rets ceaseth, the noise of them that rejoice endeth, the joy of the
harp ceaseth. They shall not drink wine with a song; strong drink
shall be bitter to them that drink it. The city of confusion is broken
down: every house is shut up, that no man may come in. There is
a crying in the streets because of the wine; all joy is darkened, the
mirth of the land is gone. In the city is left desolation, and the gate
is smitten with destruction.

2

*For thus shall it be in the midst of the earth among the peoples, as
the shaking of an olive tree, as the grape gleanings when the vintage
is done. These shall lift up their voice, they shall shout.*

VOICES FROM THE WEST
For the Majesty of the LORD!

VOICES FROM THE EAST
Wherefore glorify ye the LORD in the east!

VOICES FROM THE WEST
*Even the name of the LORD, the God of Israel, in the isles
of the sea!*

Voices of the Doomed

From the uttermost part of the earth have we heard songs, glory
to the righteous. But I said, I pine away, I pine away, woe is me!
the treacherous dealers have dealt treacherously; yea, the treacherous dealers have dealt very treacherously.

Voice of Prophecy

Fear, and the pit, and the snare are upon thee, O inhabitant of
earth. And, it shall come to pass, that he who fleeth from the noise
of the fear shall fall into the pit; and he that cometh up out of the
midst of the pit shall be taken in the snare.

3

For the windows on high are opened, and the foundations of the earth do shake. The earth is utterly broken, the earth is clean dissolved, the earth is moved exceedingly. The earth shall stagger like a drunken man, and shall be moved to and fro like a hut; and the transgression thereof shall be heavy upon it, and it shall fall, and not rise again. And it shall come to pass in that day, that the LORD shall punish the host of the high ones on high, and the kings of the earth upon the earth. And they shall be gathered together, as prisoners are gathered in the pit, and shall be shut up in the prison, and after many days shall they be visited. Then the moon shall be confounded, and the sun ashamed.

4

For the LORD of hosts shall reign in Mount Zion, and in Jerusalem, and before his elders shall be glory.

SONG OF THE ELDERS

O LORD, thou art my God; I will exalt thee;
   I will praise thy name;
For thou hast done wonderful things,
   Even counsels of old, in faithfulness and truth.

   For thou hast made of a city an heap;
   Of a defenced city a ruin:
   A palace of strangers to be no city;
   It shall never be built.
   Therefore shall the strong people glorify thee,
   The city of the terrible nations shall fear thee.

   For thou hast been a strong hold to the poor,
   A strong hold to the needy in his distress,
   A refuge from the storm,
   A shadow from the heat,
   When the blast of the terrible ones
   Is as a storm against the wall.

   As the heat in a dry place
Shalt thou bring down the noise of strangers;
   As the heat by the shadow of a cloud,
The song of the terrible ones shall be brought low.

And in this mountain shall the LORD of hosts make unto all peoples a feast of fat things, a feast of wines on the lees, of fat things full of marrow, of wines on the lees well refined. And he will destroy in this mountain the face of the covering that is cast over all peoples, and the veil that is spread over all nations. He hath swallowed up death for ever; and the Lord GOD will wipe away tears from off all faces; and the reproach of his people shall he take away from off all the earth: for the LORD hath spoken it.

SONG IN THAT DAY

Lo, this is our God;
   We have waited for him,
   And he will save us:
This is the LORD;
   We have waited for him, we will be glad
   And rejoice in his salvation.

For in this mountain shall the hand of the LORD rest, and Moab shall be trodden down in his place, even as straw is trodden down in the water of the dunghill. And he shall spread forth his hands in the midst thereof, as he that swimmeth spreadeth forth his hands to swim: and he shall lay low his pride together with the craft of his hands. And the fortress of the high fort of thy walls hath he brought down, laid low, and brought to the ground, even to the dust.

SONG IN THE LAND OF JUDAH

We have a strong city;
   Salvation will he appoint for walls and bulwarks.
Open ye the gates,
   That the righteous nation which keepeth truth may enter in.
Thou wilt keep him in perfect peace,
   Whose mind is stayed on thee, because he trusteth in thee.
Trust ye in the LORD for ever:
   For in the LORD JEHOVAH is an everlasting rock.

   For he hath brought down them that dwell on high, the lofty city:
   He layeth it low, he layeth it low, even to the ground;
   He bringeth it even to the dust.
   The foot shall tread it down;
   Even the feet of the poor,
   And the steps of the needy.

The way of the just is uprightness:
Thou that art upright dost direct the path of the just.
Yea, in the way of thy judgements, O LORD,
Have we waited for thee;
To thy name and to thy memorial
Is the desire of our soul.

With my soul have I desired thee in the night;
Yea, with my spirit within me will I seek thee early:
For when thy judgements are in the earth,
The inhabitants of the world learn righteousness.
Let favour be shewed to the wicked,
Yet will he not learn righteousness;
In the land of uprightness will he deal wrongfully,
And will not behold the majesty of the LORD.

5

PROPHETIC SPECTATOR

LORD, thy hand is lifted up, yet they see not; but they shall see thy zeal for the people, and be ashamed; yea, fire shall devour thine adversaries.

VOICES OF THE SAVED

LORD, thou wilt ordain peace for us: for thou hast also wrought all our works for us. O LORD our God, other lords beside thee have had dominion over us; but by thee only will we make mention of thy name.

PROPHETIC SPECTATOR

The dead live not, the deceased rise not: therefore hast thou visited and destroyed them, and made all their memory to perish.

VOICES OF THE SAVED

Thou hast increased the nation, O LORD, thou hast increased the nation; thou art glorified: thou hast enlarged all the borders of the land.

PROPHETIC SPECTATOR

LORD, in trouble have they visited thee, they poured out a prayer when thy chastening was upon them.

VOICES OF THE DOOMED

Like as a woman with child, that draweth near the time of her delivery, is in pain and crieth out in her pangs; so have we been before thee, O LORD. We have been with child, we have been in pain, we have as it were brought forth wind; we have not wrought any deliverance in the earth; neither have inhabitants of the world been born.

GOD (TO THE SAVED)

Thy dead shall live: my dead bodies shall arise. Awake and sing, ye that dwell in the dust: for thy dew is as the dew of herbs, and the earth shall cast forth the dead. Come, my people, enter thou into thy chambers, and shut thy doors about thee: hide thyself for a little moment, until the indignation be overpast. For, behold, the LORD cometh forth out of his place to punish the inhabitants of the earth for their iniquity: the earth also shall disclose her blood, and shall no more cover her slain.

6

VOICE OF PROPHECY

In that day the LORD with his sore and great and strong sword shall punish leviathan the swift serpent, and leviathan the crooked serpent; and he shall slay the dragon that is in the sea.

SONG IN THAT DAY

A Vineyard of wine, (sing ye of it,)
  I the LORD do keep it; I will water it every moment:
  Lest any hurt it, I will water it night and day.
Fury is not in me:
  Would that the briers and thorns were against me in battle,
  I would march upon them, I would burn them together.
Or else let him take hold of my strength,
  That he may make peace with me:
  Yea, let him make peace with me.
In days to come shall Jacob take root;
  Israel shall blossom and bud:
  And they shall fill the face of the world with fruit.

PROPHETIC SPECTATOR

Hath he smitten him as he smote them that smote him? or is he slain according to the slaughter of them that were slain by him? In measure, when thou sendest her away, thou dost contend with her; he hath removed her with his rough blast in the day of the east wind. Therefore by this shall the iniquity of Jacob be purged, and this is all the fruit to take away his sin; when he maketh all the stones of the altar as chalkstones that are beaten in sunder, so that the Asherim and the sun-images shall rise no more.

7

For the defenced city is solitary, an habitation deserted and forsaken, like the wilderness: there shall the calf feed, and there shall he lie down, and consume the branches thereof. When the boughs thereof are withered, they shall be broken off; the women shall come and set them on fire: for it is a people of no understanding; therefore he that made them will not have compassion upon them, and he that formed them will show them no favour.

VOICE OF PROPHECY

And it shall come to pass in that day, that the LORD shall beat out his corn, from the flood of the River unto the brook of Egypt, and ye shall be gathered, one by one, O ye children of Israel.

And it shall come to pass in that day, that a great trumpet shall be blown; and they shall come which were ready to perish in the land of Assyria, and they that were outcasts in the land of Egypt; and they shall worship the Lord in the Holy Mountain at Jerusalem.

Such is the Prophetic Rhapsody in its full development. Its effect is that of a World Drama; to attain this effect all literary forms concur in one, and even description has a subordinate place in representation. As the Rhapsody is a form of literature special to Hebrew Prophecy, it may be interesting to enquire into its origin as a distinct literary form.

Origin of the Prophetic Rhapsody

On the one side it may be regarded as an extension of Drama. In a previous chapter we have noted prophecies which were equivalent to brief dramatic dialogues, presenting the Divine yearning and the repentance of the rebellious people. Such dialogues were, however, abstract and general, with no note of particular time or place. The Hebrew people have strong dramatic feelings, but no theatre in which to give them vent; accordingly, when dialogue becomes determined by indications of time and place, such as in other literatures would be transferred to a theatric scene, these in Hebrew literature can be conveyed only by description. The addition of this scenic description to dialogue converts drama into rhapsody.

An illustration of a composition differing from dramatic dialogue by no more than this addition of description is afforded by one of the most beautiful of the compositions of Jeremiah, that on the Drought. Its speakers are God, the Prophet, and Repentant Israel.[1] Its dramatic action consists in the gradual moving of God from judgment to mercy; and dramatic effect is carried to the extent of representing Jehovah as a justly incensed God, who for a long time will not so much as look at the sinful nation, but addresses them only through the Prophet: at last he speaks his reproofs, and finally his mercy, to his people directly. To all this dialogue is prefixed a prelude picturing, in lyric description, the drought which is the scene and occasion of the whole.

[1] It is usually interpreted as a Dialogue of Intercession, with no speakers except God and the Prophet. No explanation of it is entirely free from difficulty, but the one given in the text seems to me the least difficult. (1) A great objection to other views is the conclusion: it seems impossible, without straining, to make the Prophet guilty of any fault (mistrust, etc., is suggested) for which he should be invited to repent. Nor is it easy to see why the Prophet should speak xv. 15-18 after the full assurance given him in xv. 11. On the other hand the Divine reply (xv. 19) seems a natural reference to the 'purged remnant' which in all prophecy appears as the only portion of the nation to be saved. No doubt verses 20, 21 refer to Jeremiah: but they are outside the rhapsody, being an epilogue added to this as to other important prophecies (compare i. 18 and vi. 27). (2) In two speeches which I assign to the Repentant People (xiv. 7-9, 19-22) the plural is uniformly used: and the lyric prologue has prepared us to hear Judah mourning. It is true that the third speech (xv. 15-18) uses the singular: but that immediately follows the speech of God (12-14) in which the singular is used, and which is undoubtedly addressed to the People and not to the Prophet. (3) The ordinary view ignores the marked distinction between "The Lord said *unto me*," in xiv. 11 (contrast 10), xiv. 14 (compare 17), xv. 1, as compared with the usual formula, "The Lord said," in xv. 11 (and 19), and the beautiful dramatic effect which this suggests.

Jeremiah xiv-xv   RHAPSODY OF THE DROUGHT

Prelude

Judah mourneth,
And the gates thereof languish;
They sit in black upon the ground;
And the cry of Jerusalem is gone up.
And their nobles send their little ones to the waters:
They come to the pits, and find no water;
They return with their vessels empty:
They are ashamed and confounded, and cover their heads.
Because of the ground which is chapt,
For that no rain hath been in the land,
The plowmen are ashamed, they cover their heads.
Yea, the hind also in the field calveth,
And forsaketh her young,
Because there is no grass.
And the wild asses stand on the bare heights,
They pant for air like jackals; their eyes fail,
Because there is no herbage.

Repentant Israel

Though our iniquities testify against us, work thou for thy name's sake, O Lord: for our backslidings are many; we have sinned against thee. O thou hope of Israel, the saviour thereof in the time of trouble, why shouldest thou be as a sojourner in the land, and as a wayfaring man that turneth aside to tarry for a night? Why shouldest thou be as a man astonied, as a mighty man that cannot save? yet thou, O Lord, art in the midst of us, and we are called by thy name; leave us not.

The Prophet

Thus saith the Lord unto this people, Even so have they loved to wander; they have not refrained their feet: therefore the Lord doth not accept them; now will he remember their iniquity, and visit their sins.

The Lord (*to the Prophet*)

Pray not for this people for their good. When they fast, I will not hear their cry; and when they offer burnt offering and oblation, I will not accept them: but I will consume them by the sword, and by the famine, and by the pestilence.

The Prophet

Ah, Lord God! behold, the prophets say unto them, Ye shall not see the sword, neither shall ye have famine; but I will give you assured peace in this place.

The Lord (*to the Prophet*)

The prophets prophesy lies in my name: I sent them not, neither have I commanded them, neither spake I unto them: they prophesy unto you a lying vision, and divination, and a thing of nought, and the deceit of their own heart. Therefore thus saith the Lord concerning the prophets that prophesy in my name, and I sent them not, yet they say, Sword and famine shall not be in this land: By sword and famine shall those prophets be consumed. And the people to whom they prophesy shall be cast out in the streets of Jerusalem because of the famine and the sword; and they shall have none to bury them, their wives, nor their sons, nor their daughters: for I will pour their wickedness upon them. And thou shalt say this word unto them, Let mine eyes run down with tears night and day, and let them not cease; for the virgin daughter of my people is broken with a great breach, with a very grievous wound. If I go forth into the field, then behold the slain with the sword! and if I enter into the city, then behold them that are sick with famine! for both the prophet and the priest go about in the land and have no knowledge.

Repentant Israel

Hast thou utterly rejected Judah? hath thy soul loathed Zion? Why hast thou smitten us, and there is no healing for us? We looked for peace, but no good came; and for a time of healing, and behold dismay! We acknowledge, O Lord, our wickedness, and the iniquity of our fathers: for we have sinned against thee. Do not abhor us, for thy name's sake; do not disgrace the throne of thy glory: remember, break not thy covenant with us. Are there any among the vanities of the heathen that can cause rain? or can the heavens give showers? art not thou he, O Lord our God? therefore we will wait upon thee; for thou hast done all these things.

The Lord (*to the Prophet*)

Though Moses and Samuel stood before me, yet my mind could not be toward this people: cast them out of my sight, and let them go forth. And it shall come to pass, when they say unto thee, Whither shall we go forth? then thou shalt tell them, Thus saith the LORD: Such as are for death, to death; and such as are for the sword, to the sword; and such as are for the famine, to the famine; and such as are for captivity, to captivity. And I will appoint over them four kinds, saith the LORD: the sword to slay, and the dogs to tear, and the fowls of the heaven, and the beasts of the earth, to devour and to destroy. And I will cause them to be tossed to and fro among all the kingdoms of the earth, because of Manasseh the son of Hezekiah king of Judah, for that which he did in Jerusalem. For who shall have pity upon thee, O Jerusalem? or who shall bemoan thee? or who shall turn aside to ask of thy welfare? Thou hast rejected me, saith the LORD, thou art gone backward: therefore have I stretched out my hand against thee, and destroyed thee; I am weary with repenting. And I have fanned them with a fan in the gates of the land; I have bereaved them of children, I have destroyed my people; they have not returned from their ways. Their widows are increased to me above the sand of the seas: I have brought upon them against the mother of the young men a spoiler at noonday: I have caused anguish and terrors to fall upon her suddenly. She that hath borne seven languisheth; she hath given up the ghost; her sun is gone down while it was yet day; she hath been ashamed and confounded: and the residue of them will I deliver to the sword before their enemies, saith the LORD.

THE PROPHET

Woe is me, my mother, that thou hast borne me a man of strife and a man of contention to the whole earth! I have not lent on usury, neither have men lent to me on usury; yet every one of them doth curse me.

THE LORD (*to the Prophet*)

Verily I will strengthen thee for good; verily I will intercede for thee with the enemy in the time of evil and in the time of affliction. — (*To Israel.*) — Can one break iron, even iron from the north and brass? Thy substance and thy treasures will I give for a spoil without price, and that for all thy sins, even in all thy borders. And I will make thee to serve thine enemies in a land which thou knowest not: for a fire is kindled in mine anger, which shall burn upon you.

REPENTANT ISRAEL

O LORD, thou knowest: remember me, and visit me, and avenge me of my persecutors; take me not away in thy longsuffering. Know that for thy sake I have suffered reproach. Thy words were found, and I did eat them; and thy words were unto me a joy and the rejoicing of mine heart: for I am called by thy name, O LORD God of hosts. I sat not in the assembly of them that make merry, nor rejoiced: I sat alone because of thy hand; for thou hast filled me with indignation. Why is my pain perpetual, and my wound incurable, which refuseth to be healed? wilt thou indeed be unto me as a deceitful brook, as waters that fail?

THE LORD

Therefore, if thou return, then will I bring thee again, that thou mayest stand before me; and if thou take forth the precious from the vile, thou shalt be as my mouth: they shall return unto thee, but thou shalt not return unto them.

EPILOGUE. — *To the Prophet*

And I will make thee unto this people a fenced brasen wall; and they shall fight against thee, but they shall not prevail against thee: for I am with thee to save thee, and to deliver thee, saith the LORD. And I will deliver thee out of the hand of the wicked, and I will redeem thee out of the hand of the terrible.

If, on the one hand, we thus see dramatic prophecy passing into rhapsody by the addition of an element of description, we can, looking to the other side, observe how discourse can sway in the direction of dramatic machinery, and so become rhapsodic. I have before drawn attention to such a prophecy as that of Zephaniah, in which the continuity of Divine speech is broken by outbursts of impersonal lyrics, exulting in delivered Zion, or triumphing over the threatened foe. Again, it is easy to understand how the fervour of prophetic oratory can suddenly change to realising the predicted future as if immediately present. The lengthy discourse in which Isaiah describes the Assyrian as the rod of God's anger, and pictures the reign of peace that would follow the Assyrian's overthrow, is throughout couched in the future tense: at just a single point the future tense gives place to the realistic present.

> He is come to Aiath, he is passed through Migron; at Michmash he layeth up his baggage: they are gone over the pass; "Geba is our lodging," they cry; Ramah trembleth; Gibeah of Saul is fled. Cry aloud with thy voice, O daughter of Gallim! hearken, O Laishah! O thou poor Anathoth! Madmenah is a fugitive; the inhabitants of Gebim gather themselves to flee. This very day shall he halt at Nob; he shaketh his hand at the mount of the daughter of Zion, the hill of Jerusalem.
>
> Behold the Lord, the LORD of hosts, shall lop the boughs with terror: and the high ones of stature shall be hewn down, and the lofty shall be brought low. And he shall cut down the thickets of the forest with iron, and Lebanon shall fall by a mighty one. And there shall come forth a shoot out of the stock of Jesse, and a branch out of his roots shall bear fruit.

In the same way most of the Doom Songs (except those of Ezekiel) are rhapsodic: the denunciations and predictions alternate with various modes of presenting the fulfilment of the same.

The Rhapsodic Discourse, as distinguished from the Rhapsody, is illustrated on the largest scale in a portion of *Jeremiah* which

Rhapsody from Jeremiah's Manifesto (ii-vi) I would describe as his Prophetic Manifesto. It is a long composition of five chapters, following the account of the prophetic call, and embodying the general spirit of Jeremiah's ministry. The greater part of it is discourse, marked by the mingling of imagery and pathetic appeal which distinguishes this prophet; I take it up at

iv. 5 the point where it abruptly passes into the dramatic form of rhapsody. While there is a slight suggestion of succession between its parts, in the fact that the threatened judgment seems to advance nearer and nearer, yet the main movement is the pendulum movement of alternation: — an alternation, not between judgment and salvation, but between the impending Doom and the Panic of those who are about to suffer it.

1

I reckon as first of the seven sections that which does not pass beyond the limits of discourse; though the discourse is approaching nearer and nearer to dramatic form in the direct appeals to Israel, and the imagined responses of the people. But at last the rhapsodic form becomes pronounced, and the alternation of Doom and Panic begins.

2

A Cry

Declare ye in Judah, and publish in Jerusalem, and say, Blow ye the trumpet in the land: cry aloud and say, Assemble yourselves, and let us go into the fenced cities. Set up a standard toward Zion: flee for safety, stay not: for I will bring evil from the north, and a great destruction. A lion is gone up from his thicket, and a destroyer of nations; he is on his way, he is gone forth from his place; to make thy land desolate, that thy cities be laid waste, without inhabitant.

THE PEOPLE

For this gird you with sackcloth, lament and howl: for the fierce anger of the LORD is not turned back from us.

THE LORD

And it shall come to pass at that day, that the heart of the king shall perish, and the heart of the princes; and the priests shall be astonished, and the prophets shall wonder.

THE PROPHET

Ah, Lord GOD! surely thou hast greatly deceived this people and Jerusalem, saying, Ye shall have peace; whereas the sword reacheth unto the soul.

3

A Cry to Jerusalem

A hot wind from the bare heights in the wilderness toward the daughter of my people, not to fan, nor to cleanse; — a full wind from these shall come for me: now will I also utter judgements against them. Behold, he shall come up as clouds, and his chariots shall be as the whirlwind: his horses are swifter than eagles.

THE PEOPLE

Woe unto us! for we are spoiled.

THE PROPHET

O Jerusalem, wash thine heart from wickedness, that thou mayest be saved. How long shall thine evil thoughts lodge within thee?

4

Voices from Dan and from the Hills of Ephraim

Make ye mention to the nations; behold, publish against Jerusalem, that watchers come from a far country, and give out their voice against the cities of Judah. As keepers of a field are they against her round about; "because she hath been rebellious against me," saith the Lord. Thy way and thy doings have procured these things unto thee; this is thy wickedness; surely it is bitter, surely it reacheth unto thine heart.

THE PEOPLE

My bowels, my bowels! I am pained at my very heart; my heart is disquieted in me; I cannot hold my peace; because thou hast heard, O my soul, the sound of the trumpet, the alarm of war. Destruction upon destruction is cried; for the whole land is spoiled: suddenly are my tents spoiled, and my curtains in a moment. How long shall I see the standard, and hear the sound of the trumpet?

GOD

For my people is foolish, they know me not; they are sottish children, and they have none understanding: they are wise to do evil, but to do good they have no knowledge.

5

Vision

I beheld the earth, and, lo, it was waste and void; and the heavens, and they had no light. I beheld the mountains, and, lo, they trembled, and all the hills moved to and fro. I beheld, and, lo, there was no man, and all the birds of the heaven were fled. I beheld, and, lo, the fruitful field was a wilderness, and all the cities thereof were broken down at the presence of the LORD, and before his fierce anger.

The Lord

The whole land shall be a desolation; yet will I not make a full end. For this shall the earth mourn, and the heavens above be black: because I have spoken it, I have purposed it, and I have not repented, neither will I turn back from it.

VISION continued

The whole city fleeth for the noise of the horsemen and bowmen; they go into the thickets, and climb up upon the rocks: every city is forsaken, and not a man dwelleth therein.

THE LORD

And thou, when thou art spoiled, what wilt thou do? Though thou clothest thyself with scarlet, though thou deckest thee with ornaments of gold, though thou enlargest thine eyes with paint, in vain dost thou make thyself fair; thy lovers despise thee, they seek thy life.

VISION continued

For I have heard a voice as of a woman in travail, the anguish as of her that bringeth forth her first child, the voice of the daughter of Zion, that gaspeth for breath, that spreadeth her hands, saying, Woe is me now! for my soul fainteth before the murderers.

6

Through these alternating passages of doom and panic the judgment has seemed to advance: at first it was only announced from a distance; in the last sections the desolation was fully seen, but only in vision. The next section is too lengthy to quote. As if with a reminiscence of Abraham's intercession for Sodom, God bids the prophet search Jerusalem through and through for a single just man, that he may pardon her. The prophet tries low and high in vain. Then the Lord reluctantly calls the enemy to go up and destroy, "but make not a full end." As if using the moments of waiting, God is represented as pouring out descriptions of the terrible foe — mighty men, whose quiver is an open sepulchre — and remonstrances against the hardness of heart that in the very presence of judgment will not turn to the judge. All seems in vain. The conclusion is "astonishment and horror": false prophets and subservient priests, and a people that loves to have it so! What will they do in the end? Now the panic appears; the destruction arrives, yet is still held under restraint.

THE PEOPLE

Flee for safety, ye children of Benjamin, out of the midst of Jerusalem, and blow the trumpet in Tekoa, and raise up a signal on Beth-haccherem: for evil looketh forth from the north, and a great destruction.

THE LORD

The comely and delicate one, the daughter of Zion, will I cut off. Shepherds with their flocks shall come unto her; they shall pitch their tents against her round about; they shall feed every one in his place.

THE ENEMY

Prepare ye war against her; arise, and let us go up at noon.

THE PEOPLE

Woe unto us! for the day declineth, for the shadows of the evening are stretched out.

THE ENEMY

Arise, and let us go up by night, and let us destroy her palaces. For thus hath the LORD of hosts said, Hew ye down trees, and cast up a mount against Jerusalem: this is the city to be visited.

THE LORD

She is wholly oppression in the midst of her. As a well casteth forth her waters, so she casteth forth her wickedness: violence and spoil is heard in her; before me continually is sickness and wounds.

7

Even in the presence of the destroying foe a final attempt is made by God at least to glean a remnant of Israel. But there is none to listen; the ear of the people is uncircumcised; they refuse to walk in the old paths, to hearken to the watchmen: the word of the Lord has become to them a reproach. "Therefore," cries Jehovah, "I am full of the fury of Jehovah; I am weary with holding in." The fury is to be poured out upon old and young, families and fields; the people from the north are stirred up against Zion, a people who are cruel, and have no mercy. There remains only the final panic.

THE PEOPLE

We have heard the fame thereof; our hands wax feeble: anguish hath taken hold of us, and pangs as of a woman in travail. Go not forth into the field, nor walk by the way; for there is the sword of the enemy, and terror on every side. O daughter of my people, gird thee with sackcloth, and wallow thyself in ashes: make thee mourning, as for an only son, most bitter lamentation; for the spoiler shall suddenly come upon us!

In the rhapsodies so far reviewed we have seen the movement that consists in a continuous advance, and the movement that advances only by alternations. There is a third type of movement in which the distinctness of the parts is more prominent than the progress from one part to another. *Movement by Phases*. Such divisions in the movement of a literary composition are felt to correspond to the 'Acts' of a drama, but, differing from these Acts by the absence of continuous succession, they should be indicated by some different name, such as 'Phases.' The prophecy of Amos is an illustration, and constitutes a single *Rhapsody of the Judgment to come*. *Amos's Rhapsody of the Judgment to come*. The first of the three divisions or 'Phases' into which it falls brings out Israel's part in a general judgment, and it is a piece of Lyric Prophecy. The second Phase is a series of appeals to Israel, and is in the form of Discourse. The third presents the coming of the judgment in the form of Dramatic Vision.

The portion constituting the first Phase has been cited at length in a previous chapter.[1] It is a chain of lyric woes denounced against various peoples: free recitative of prose detailing special features of each, while rhythmic refrains speak the common doom. It is clear that the various denunciations are so arranged as to lead up to that on Israel as a climax. A note of this prophet's treatment is his power of emphasising by holding back. What the judgment on Israel is to be is kept a mystery; the formula used for the other nations — devouring fire — does not appear in the last case, but the judgment is described only by its effects, — flight perishing from the swift, and the mighty unable to deliver himself.

<small>Phase I i, ii</small>

The second Phase is a series of appeals increasing in intensity. First, we have four general appeals, each ushered in by the cry, "Hear ye," or "Publish ye." Then follows a pleading in which discourse becomes lyrical. The successive warnings sent by God are enumerated — cleanness of teeth, the guilty city isolated by drought with abundance all around, blasting and mildew, pestilence after the manner of Egypt, and burning like that of Sodom and Gomorrah — and after each comes the refrain, "*Yet have ye not returned to me, saith the* LORD." The pleading turns to a threat:

<small>Phase II iii-vi</small>

> Therefore THUS will I do unto thee, O Israel: and because I will do THIS unto thee, prepare to meet thy God, O Israel.

The coming judgment still remains veiled under the mysterious *thus*. The last appeal takes the form of a lamentation, including a double woe: against those who desire the Day of the Lord, not seeing that it will be darkness and not light; and against those that are at ease in Zion, and put far away the evil day. The limit of appeal seems now to be reached: God

<small>v-vi. 7</small>

---

[1] Above, page 114.

swears by Himself that Jacob and his sins have become a thing of abhorrence. And the mystic judgment begins to take substance, as we hear of captivity in the east and the nation that is to afflict the whole land. vi. 8-14

With the third Phase the judgment appears sensibly to advance, as the series of visions pass before us. A visionary appearance of locusts at their work of destruction is seen: but when the destruction has proceeded a certain way the prophet interposes his intercession, and the Lord repents and says it shall not be. Another vision, and fire is seen devouring the great deep; but when it reaches the land the prophet again makes intercession, and the judgment is stayed. The next vision displays a plumbline: the exact limit has been reached, beyond which there can be no passing by of the iniquities of Israel. The emphasis of this as a turning-point is further seen by the way in which the prophet introduces here his digression, describing the efforts of those in authority to restrain him from prophesying evil to Israel. We are thus prepared for the next vision of summer fruit: Israel is ripe for her fall. With the final vision the judgment has begun. The Lord, standing on the altar of his house, bids smite the chapiters, that the thresholds may shake, and universal destruction of house and people may follow.

Phase III vii-ix. 6

vii. 10-17

ix. 1-6

> Though they dig into hell, thence shall mine hand take them; and though they climb up to heaven, thence will I bring them down. And though they hide themselves in the top of Carmel, I will search and take them out thence; and though they be hid from my sight in the bottom of the sea, thence will I command the serpent, and he shall bite them.

An Epilogue drops dramatic presentation for appeal; and further speaks of a remnant to be restored. Thus the last strain of this, as of other rhapsodies, can be the song of a golden age, when "the plowman shall overtake the reaper, and the treader of grapes him that soweth seed"; and the people shall be planted upon their land, to be plucked up no more.

Epilogue ix. 7-15

I have felt it less necessary to dwell in detail upon this beautiful prophecy of Amos, because the movement by phases which it illustrates will be found again in another composition, a colossal and wonderful example of the rhapsodic form, which needs a separate chapter for its consideration.

CHAPTER XVII

THE RHAPSODY OF 'ZION REDEEMED' [*Isaiah* XL–LXVI]

THE last twenty-seven chapters of our *Book of Isaiah* form a single composition: no less stupendous as a literary monument than supreme in importance as inspiration of Hebrew and Christian religion. To expound it would require a volume; all that I can attempt is to elucidate its outer literary form, well assured that here, as always, this must be an important factor in the interpretation. Isaiah's Rhapsody of 'Zion Redeemed'

Every reader feels a difficulty in catching the unity of the whole, however strongly he may feel the attraction of the parts. No narrative is carried on from beginning to end, though there is much to suggest progress of story; though reasoning abounds, there is no sign of a logical plan; if the reader seeks to take refuge in supposing a collection of many compositions, he is continually confronted with evidences of unity. The full force of this part of the Bible is brought out by considering it a Rhapsody, — the prophetic form made by the fusion of all literary forms in one; which can thus give the realistic emphasis of dramatic presentation to its ideas, while free at any point to abandon drama for discourse or lyric meditation. This *Rhapsody of Zion Redeemed* has a movement which, like that of other rhapsodies, is best compared to the succession of parts in an Oratorio. On the whole, this movement is so far an advance that, like many other prophecies, it works forward from an immediate judgment Its general movement and matter and deliverance, on to the final judgment of the nations and restoration of the remnant in a Messianic kingdom. But the seven divisions into which the whole falls are not seven stages in this advance, but (like those in the prophecy of Amos) seven different 'phases,' side by side in part and partly successive, each complete in itself and drawing matter from all parts of the national history, and all necessary to be exhibited before the action is consummated. The seven Phases may be described as follows: —

1

Judgment on Babylon

2

Jehovah's Servant and Desponding Zion

3

The Awakening of Zion

4

Jehovah's Servant Exalted

5

Zion Exalted

6

The Redeemer come to Zion

7

Judgment on Zion and the Nations

The mere reading of these titles suggests advance in the movement as a whole. Yet it is impossible to say that (for example) the sixth section either follows or precedes those standing before it: it embraces the whole action looked at from a particular point of view, and is placed where it is because of the relation of that point of view to the whole. Further, as the rhapsodic form can mingle dramatic realisation with the most spiritual meditation or imaginative idealising, so the matter of the whole prophecy extends from an immediate deliverance of Babylonian Captives, by the instrumentality of Cyrus, to a spiritual redemption of Zion, and final judgment of the nations by Jehovah. And similarly the hero of this rhapsody — the 'Servant of Jehovah' — appears at some points as Israel the nation, charged with a mission to itself and to the Gentiles; in other places it seems to individualise into a humanity that can suffer martyrdom, and, in the memorable central act of the rhapsody, has become a mystic personality, whose sufferings are at last recognised by the nations as vicarious.

Prelude

The Prelude embodies the spirit of the whole rhapsody in brief lyric and dramatic form. The Voice of God is heard commanding to speak comfort to Jerusalem, and cry to her that her warfare is accomplished, and her iniquity pardoned.   xl. 1-11
At once voices appear to take up the message and carry it on to its destination. A Voice cries to prepare in the wilderness a highway for God; every valley is to be exalted and every mountain and hill made low, the crooked is to be made straight and the rough places plain: the glory of the Lord is about to be revealed, and all flesh shall see it together. Another Voice in succession passes on the word; but here the   6
Voice of the Tidings is checked by the Voice of Despondency.

> What shall I cry?
> All flesh is grass,
> And all the goodliness thereof is as the flower of the field:
> > The grass withereth,
> > The flower fadeth;
> > Because the breath of the LORD bloweth upon it:
> Surely the people is grass.

But the Voice of the Tidings makes reply:

> The grass withereth,
> The flower fadeth:
> But the word of our God shall stand for ever.

Another Voice seems to sound from far on the road to Jerusalem: bidding to get up into the high mountain to tell the good tidings to Zion, to lift up the voice with strength, to say to the cities of Judah, Behold your God!

9

Phase I

The first Phase is the elaborate presentation of the Judgment on Babylon. The Voice of Prophecy strikes the key-note, celebrating the supremacy of Jehovah: who measureth the waters in the hollow of his hand, and meteth out heaven with a span, weighing the mountains in scales and the hills in a balance; before whom the nations are as a drop in a bucket; he taketh up the isles as a very little thing. To what, then, shall this God be likened? to a graven image, gilded by a goldsmith, with silver chains cast for it lest the god fall down? or wrought for the impoverished worshipper by a cunning workman out of a tree, chosen carefully lest the god might rot? Meanwhile He sitteth above the circle of the earth, and all the inhabitants thereof are but as grasshoppers; He calleth all the host of heaven by number and by name, and for that He is strong not one of them is lacking. The Voice of Prophecy then appeals to the desponding of Israel, who cry that their way is hid from God, and their judgment a thing passed away for ever. Have they not heard and known that the Creator of the ends of the earth fainteth not, neither is weary, but giveth power to the faint? Even the youths shall be weary and fail; but they that wait upon the LORD shall renew their strength; they shall mount up with wings as eagles; they shall run, and not be weary; they shall walk, and not faint.

xl. 12-xlviii

At this point the rhapsody becomes dramatic: a single scenic action is sustained for eight chapters, broken only by occasional outbursts of lyric song. The Nations are summoned to the bar of God to hear his will concerning the deliverance of his people; and the idea of the assembled Nations, once raised, is by little touches of allusion kept before us to the end.[1] There is no speaker in this scene except Jehovah: yet, by the pendulum-like alternation so common in prophecy,[2] and here seven times repeated, God is presented as addressing alternately the Nations and Israel, each in the presence of the other, pronouncing his foreordained counsel to the one, and proclaiming redemption to the other. Thus the assumed presence of the Nations on the one side and Israel on the other completes the dramatic reality of the scene.

   1. The Nations, away to the furthest islands of the west, are summoned to judgment: to hear of 'one from the east' raised up as an instrument of righteousness,[3] crushing the peoples in his path; and none but Jehovah hath wrought this from the beginning. — *A few verses present the panic of the assembling Nations: how the idolaters encourage one another: the carpenter cheering the goldsmith, and he that smootheth with the hammer him that smiteth the anvil; they look to the soldering of the idols, and strengthen them with chains for the coming shock.*

  xli

  xli. 1–20

  5–7

As if in contrast with such panic, Israel is summoned with words of comfort. He is the chosen Servant of Jehovah, who will be his Redeemer: causing mountains to be threshed and scattered out of his path, opening for him rivers on bare heights and fountains in the midst of valleys, while the wilderness

  8–20

---

[1] Such allusions are xli. 1, 21, 28–9; xliii. 9–10; xliv. 8–9; xlv. 20; xlviii. 6, 14. The fact that occasionally (xliii. 12; xliv. 8; xlv. 17) in addresses to the Nations the pronoun *You* or *Your* is casually used in reference to Israel adds to the general effect of the scene: each party is addressed in the presence of the other.

[2] Compare above, page 349.

[3] It is specially important in this prophecy to remember the twofold meaning in the Old Testament of the word 'righteousness': not only right doing, but also *setting right*, vindication, almost the equivalent of salvation. Compare xli. 2; xlii. 6; xlv. 8, 13; especially li. 5; and lvi. 1.

blooming with myrtle and acacia shall signify what the Holy One of Israel hath done for his people.

2. The idolatrous Nations are challenged to dispute, to produce their cause and their strong reasons; let their idols declare things to come that their godhead may be known;

xli. 21-xliii. 8

let them do good or do evil that the two parties may look one upon the other. — *A single verse conveys the silence of the Nations: the gods of their workmanship are things of nought.* — Then Jehovah produces his case: he has raised up 'one from the north,' 'from the rising of the sun,' to tread the Nations like clay, and make glad tidings for Zion. Who but Jehovah hath declared such counsel from the beginning? —

xli. 24

xli. 28 9

Again the verses present God as looking for an answer from the Nations and meeting only silence: he pronounces the molten images vanity and confusion.

The Divine Speaker now turns to Israel, and proclaims him to the Nations as his Servant:[1] and the service is to bring forth judgment to the Gentiles. Not by force, but by gentleness: he shall not cry nor shout; the bruised reed he shall not break, nor quench smoking flax; but he shall be sustained until he has become light and help to the peoples of the earth. — *A Lyric Outburst of Praise to Jehovah from the whole earth: let them that go down to the sea sing, let Sela and the villages of Kedar lift up the voice, let them shout from the top of the mountains. Jehovah hath long kept silence, but now will he cry like a travailing woman; he will waste mountains and make rivers islands, he will make darkness light and the crooked straight: and Israel shall never be forsaken.* — But as this song dies away, the proclamation is heard to describe this Servant of Jehovah as blind, as deaf, as hid in prison houses, and only now perceiving that it is He against whom the

xlii

10-17

18

---

[1] It seems to me impossible to understand the 'Servant' of these verses (xlii. 1-9) otherwise than as the nation of Israel. No one doubts that the 'Servant' of verses 18-25 is Israel: but these verses are a continuation of the beginning of the chapter, verses 10-17 being one of the lyric interruptions that occur at intervals and are outside the argument.

people has sinned that has given Israel for a spoil. Yet now his Maker has become his Redeemer. "When thou passest through the waters I will be with thee; and through the rivers, they shall not overflow thee." The Holy One of Israel is his saviour: he has given Egypt for ransom, and Ethiopia and Seba; he will say to the north, Give up, and to the south, Keep not back; and the imprisoning nations shall bring them forth, a blind people that hath eyes, a deaf people that hath ears.

3. The alternation of pleading continues. The assembled Nations are again challenged to bring witnesses, to show the foreseeing of counsel from of old. Their silence makes them witnesses for Jehovah, and Israel too is witness. There is no god but Jehovah, and he is the only saviour. xliii. 9–xliv. 5

Then to Israel their Creator and King tells how for their sake Babylon has been visited. The former deliverance from Egypt shall no more be remembered; a new thing shall be done, a way opened in the wilderness, and rivers in the desert. Yet Israel hath not called upon the Lord; hath wearied him with sins and not with sacrifices. Jehovah will blot out his transgressions for his own sake. Water shall be poured upon the thirsty, and streams upon the dry ground; the seed of Jacob shall spring up among the grass, as willows by the watercourses. "One shall say, I am the LORD'S; and another shall call himself by the name of Jacob; and another shall subscribe with his hand unto the LORD, and surname himself by the name of Israel." xliii. 14

4. Again Jehovah asserts his godhead, and pours scorn on the gods of the Nations. He is the first, and he is the last, and beside him there is no God, there is no Rock. The fashioners of graven images are plunged in confusion: the delectable things their work has created cannot witness for them to save them from shame. xliv. 6-28

> The smith maketh an axe, and worketh in the coals, and fashioneth it with hammers, and worketh it with his strong arm: yea, he is hungry, and his strength faileth; he drinketh no water, and is faint. The carpenter stretcheth out a line; he marketh it out with a pencil;

he shapeth it with planes, and he marketh it out with the compasses, and shapeth it after the figure of a man, according to the beauty of a man, to dwell in the house. He heweth him down cedars, and taketh the holm tree and the oak, and strengtheneth for himself one among the trees of the forest: he planteth a fir tree, and the rain doth nourish it. Then shall it be for a man to burn; and he taketh thereof, and warmeth himself; yea, he kindleth it, and baketh bread: yea, he maketh a god, and worshippeth it: he maketh it a graven image, and falleth down thereto. He burneth part thereof in the fire; with part thereof he eateth flesh; he roasteth roast, and is satisfied: yea, he warmeth himself, and saith, Aha, I am warm, I have seen the fire: and the residue thereof he maketh a god, even his graven image: he falleth down unto it and worshippeth, and prayeth unto it, and saith, Deliver me; for thou art my god.

So the worshipper of idols feeds upon ashes, with none to show him how his deceived heart has led him astray, till he cannot see the lie in his right hand.

But not so with Israel: theirs is not a made God, but the Maker of his people. And he has now redeemed them, blotting out as a thick cloud their transgressions, and as a cloud their sins.

xliv. 21

> *Sing, O ye heavens,*
> *For the LORD hath done it;*
> *Shout, ye lower parts of the earth;*
> *Break forth into singing, ye mountains,*
> *O forest, and every tree therein:*
> *For the Lord hath redeemed Jacob,*
> *And will glorify himself in Israel.*

Then thus saith to Israel his Redeemer, he who stretcheth out the heavens, he who frustrateth the tokens of liars, and maketh diviners mad: Cyrus is his Shepherd, and shall perform all his pleasure, even saying of Jerusalem, She shall be built.

5. To the Nations Jehovah proclaims Cyrus as his anointed, commissioned to do his work, for which the way shall be smoothed before him. Jehovah hath surnamed Cyrus, though Cyrus hath not known him. The authority

xlv. 1-xlvi. 4

of the proclamation is maintained: Jehovah is he who is the creator of light and of darkness, peace and evil are alike his instruments.

> *Drop down, ye heavens, from above,*
> *And let the skies pour down righteousness:*
> *Let the earth open, that they may be fruitful in salvation,*
> *And let her cause righteousness to spring up together.*

Shall not the work of the hands be used by him that has wrought it? Therefore the Creator of man has raised up Cyrus as an instrument of righteousness. For this shall the labour of Egypt, and the merchandise of Ethiopia, and the Sabeans, men of stature, come over unto him, accepting his bonds because of the God that is hidden in him: "Verily thou art a God that hidest thyself, O God of Israel, the Saviour." And let the assembled Nations know that there is no saviour but Jehovah: to Him must the ends of the earth look, and to Him every knee bow. His enemies shall be covered with confusion: and a few words of the Divine Speaker call up a picture of the idols of Babylon borne away into captivity, Bel bowing down over one beast, and another beast groaning under the weight of Nebo laid flat across him.

Then, with a sudden turn, the Speaker addresses Israel: their God is not a god to be borne in his people's arms, but in his arms has their God carried his people, from the womb he has borne them, and even to hoar hairs shall they be carried.   xlvi. 3

6. The proclamation before the Nations is resumed. The one God, whom no helpless idols can equal, whose is the counsel that is seen from the beginning to the end, will do his pleasure: he calls a ravenous bird from the east to execute his counsel, and his salvation shall no longer tarry. — *At once a lyric outburst calls tauntingly to the virgin daughter of Babylon to come down and sit in the dust, to sit on the ground without a throne; to cover herself with shame; to sit silent, to get her into darkness, for she*   xlvi. 5-xlviii. 13

xlvii. 1-5

shall no more be called the lady of kingdoms. — The Divine Speaker reminds Babylon of her cruelty to the captives of the Lord, and her careless confidence. Now all her losses shall come upon her at once, the day of evil breaking without any dawn to go before it; and all her astrologers, and stargazers, and monthly prognosticators shall be as stubble; there shall be none to save.

6-15

Upon Israel too the Divine rebuke falls: upon those who swear by the name of Jehovah, and make mention of the God of Israel, but not in truth nor in righteousness. Because of the iron sinew in their neck, and their brow of brass, has Jehovah told them the thing before it come to pass, lest they should say their idol had done it. From the womb they have been a transgressor, but for his name's sake God will defer his anger. He has refined Israel, but not as silver; He has tried him in the furnace of affliction, — He, the first and last, whose glory shall not be given to another.

xlviii. 1

7. For the seventh and last time in this High Court of Heaven and Earth God turns to the assembled Nations.[1] He whom Jehovah loveth shall perform his pleasure on Babylon, and his way shall be made prosperous. The Nations are bidden to listen, and already the voice of Jehovah's agent is heard: "From the time that it was, there am I: and now the Lord GOD hath sent me, and his spirit."

xlviii. 14-22

It remains to turn for the last time to Israel, that they may know their redeemer, who leads them by the way they should go. "Oh that thou hadst hearkened to my commandments! then had thy peace been as a river, and thy righteousness as the waves of the sea." The scene of judgment ends with a cry to go forth out of Babylon, that the whole earth may ring with a

xlviii. 17

---

[1] We have thus a sevenfold division of this, which is one of seven 'Phases' of the Rhapsody. Similarly the natural divisions of *Job*, *Joel* and *Solomon's Song* were found to be seven (see in the Literary Index). On the other hand, five seems to be the favourite number in Wisdom literature: five books in *Proverbs* and *Ecclesiasticus*, five Essays in *Ecclesiastes* and five Discourses in *Wisdom*.

cry of Jacob, the Lord's Servant, redeemed, and a second time led through the desert, while waters gush from the rock to quench his thirst.[1]

Phase II

The second Phase presents the Servant of Jehovah commencing the ministry proclaimed for him in the previous scenes. This Servant is distinctly called the nation Israel: but it is Israel reforming Israel, a nation with a mission to itself as well as to those outside.

xlix. 1-1

> Listen, O isles, unto me; and hearken, ye peoples, from far: the LORD hath called me from the womb; from the bowels of my mother hath he made mention of my name: and he hath made my mouth like a sharp sword, in the shadow of his hand hath he hid me; and he hath made me a polished shaft, in his quiver hath he kept me close: and he said unto me, Thou art my servant; Israel, in whom I will be glorified. But I said, I have laboured in vain, I have spent my strength for nought and vanity.

Then he speaks of the new commission which has roused him from such despondency.

> He saith, It is too light a thing that thou shouldest be my servant to raise up the tribes of Jacob, and to restore the preserved of Israel: I will also give thee for a light to the Gentiles, that thou mayest be my salvation unto the end of the earth.

As an opening of his commission he proclaims the salvation that is to bring Israel — the despised, the servant of rulers — and make him inherit desolate heritages. The captives shall feed in the ways, and on all bare heights shall be their pasture; they shall not hunger nor thirst, neither shall the heat nor sun smite them:

---

[1] The concluding words, "*There is no peace, saith the Lord, unto the wicked*," I understand as a prolonged *Amen*, or pious ejaculation of a scribe, at the conclusion of a section, without a place in the immediate context. Compare *Isaiah* ii. 22, and lvii. 21; and the doxologies ending the first four books of Psalms.

for he that hath mercy on them shall lead them, even by the springs of water shall he guide them.

> *Sing, O heavens;*
> *And be joyful, O earth;*
> *And break forth into singing, O mountains:*
> *For the LORD hath comforted his people,*
> *And will have compassion upon his afflicted.*

The voice of Desponding Zion is heard: this with the responses of the Servant of Jehovah makes a change to dialogue. She cries that Jehovah has forsaken her. — Can a woman forget her sucking child? Behold, she is graven on the palms of the Lord's hands: her waste places shall be built, and the children of her bereavement shall yet throng until the place is too strait for its inhabitants. — But how shall the barren and the exile bring forth new inhabitants? — Kings shall be her nursing-fathers, and queens her nursing-mothers: they shall bring her children in their bosoms. — Zion is still incredulous: shall the prey be taken from the mighty? — Mighty is He that contendeth for her: is Jehovah's hand shortened? have the children of God been disinherited?

xlix. 14

The discourse passes back into a soliloquy of Jehovah's Servant: and here the Servant appears to take more individual form. The Lord hath given him the tongue of the taught that he might know how to sustain with words him that is weary; morning by morning his ear is wakened to the Divine word. And he has not been rebellious: he has given his back to the smiters, and his cheeks to them that pulled off the hair; he hid not his face from shame and spitting: for He that justifieth him is near. And already he is become a judgment to those about him, to separate between those who obey his voice, even though they walk in darkness, and those who kindle a fire, and gird themselves about with firebrands: these he leaves to walk in the flame of their fire, and among the brands they have kindled; this only they have from him, that they shall lie down in sorrow.

l. 4

Phase III

The third Phase, in a mystical dramatic mode of realisation only possible in so spiritual a literary form as the rhapsody, presents the gradual Awakening of Zion under reiterated calls from God and the Celestial Hosts.

li.-lii. 12

Jehovah crieth to his people that seek him to look to their past and take comfort: to look unto the rock whence they were hewn, and to the hole of the pit whence they were digged. For the waste places of Zion shall again be as Eden: joy and gladness shall be found therein, thanksgiving, and the voice of melody. — *No response.*

Jehovah crieth comfort to his people from their glorious future: his righteousness is near, his salvation is gone forth. The heavens shall vanish away like smoke, and the earth wax old like a garment, but his salvation shall stand fast for ever. — *No response.*

Jehovah comforteth his people against the reproach of men. For there the moth shall eat like a garment, the worm shall eat them like wool: but his righteousness shall be for ever.

·The Celestial Chorus encourage Jehovah: calling to the Arm of the Lord to awake as in the days of old, when Egypt was cut in pieces, and the sea became a pathway for the redeemed. And the ransomed of the Lord shall again come with singing to Zion, everlasting joy upon their heads.

Jehovah yet again comforteth his people: will they fear man that shall die, and the son of man which shall be as grass, when the Maker of heaven and earth has said that the captive exiles shall speedily be loosed? For it is he who ruleth the sea that hath put his words in their mouth and covered them with the shadow of his hand. — *No response.*

The Celestial Chorus join in the cry to Jerusalem to awake, to stand up: she has drunk of the cup of staggering, and there has been none among all her sons to guide her. Therefore has Jehovah taken out of her hand the cup of staggering, and put it into the hands of them that afflict her. — *No response.*

The Celestial Chorus reiterate the cry to Zion to awake, to put on her strength, to put on her garments of beauty, shaking herself from the dust. For Jehovah hath said, she was sold for nought, and without money shall she be redeemed, and shall know that it is he, even Jehovah, who hath done it.

At last the awakening of Zion seems to begin. Beautiful upon the distant mountains are seen the feet of messengers bringing good tidings of good, publishers of salvation. — Now the watchmen of Zion have caught the word: they lift up the voice: no discordant notes, they see eye to eye how Jehovah is returning to Zion. — Now the waste places of Jerusalem break forth into joy, they sing together that the Lord hath redeemed Jerusalem. — Now the Lord's arm is made bare that all the nations of the earth can behold his salvation: and awakened Zion can see, as if present, the bearers of the sacred vessels departing out of Babylon, careful that no unclean thing mar their sacred office, and passing on with the God of Israel for their rearward.

lii. 7-12

Phase IV

We have reached the fourth and central Phase of the Rhapsody: the brief section which seems to stand out from the rest like the keystone of an arch, and presents the Servant of Jehovah prosperous and highly exalted, to the astonishment of the nations that had despised his marred visage, his form marred more than the sons of men. The Chorus of Nations, in a lyric song of gradually augmenting stanzas, express their astonishment at that which they can hardly believe; and bring out the mystery of a personality whose sufferings have been a bearing of the sufferings of others. Which of us (they ask) believed that which we heard, or recognised the Lord's hand, when we saw him grow up as a root out of a dry ground, without form or comeliness, despised and rejected of men? Surely he hath borne our griefs, and been wounded for our transgressions, when we esteemed him smitten of God and afflicted;

lii. 13-liii

liii

we were the sheep that had gone astray, and the Lord laid on him the iniquity of us all. In oppression he humbled himself; led as a lamb to slaughter he opened not his mouth; who of his generation considered that he was cut off from the land of the living, stricken for the people's transgression? Yet it pleased Jehovah to put him to grief: but he shall see of the travail of his soul and be satisfied, and by knowledge of him shall the righteous Servant make many righteous.

Phase V

From the Servant of Jehovah in his glory we pass to Zion exalted. The fifth Phase of the Rhapsody is a series of Songs for Zion in her Exaltation. The first Song celebrates Zion as Jehovah's Bride: "Thy maker is thy husband, the Lord of hosts is his name." _{liv-lv}

> For a small moment have I forsaken thee;
>   But with great mercies will I gather thee.
> In overflowing wrath
>   I hid my face from thee for a moment;
> But with everlasting kindness
>   Will I have mercy upon thee.

Like the rainbow pledge of old to Noah is this new covenant.

> For the mountains shall depart,
>   And the hills be removed;
> But my kindness shall not depart from thee,
>   Neither shall my covenant of peace be removed.

The second Song depicts Zion as a city of beauty: her foundations of sapphires and pinnacles of rubies, her gates of carbuncles, and all her border of pleasant stones. Zion is impregnable as she is beautiful: terror shall not come nigh her; no weapon formed against her shall prosper.

The third Song presents Zion calling to the nations with offers of a free covenant.

> Ho, every one that thirsteth, come ye to the waters,
> And he that hath no money;
> Come ye, buy, and eat;
> Yea, come, buy wine and milk
> Without money and without price.

Zion recites the sure mercies of David given to her as a covenant, and how she is to be a leader of the peoples, calling to her nations she knows not. The fourth Song makes the invitation more urgent: bidding seek the Lord while he may be found, the wicked forsaking his way and the unrighteous man his thoughts, and turning to the Lord who will abundantly pardon. For as the heavens are higher than the earth, so is Jehovah's abundance of mercy; and his word gone forth shall no more return empty than the rain shall descend to the earth without causing it to bud and bring forth.

lv. 6-13

> Ye shall go out with joy,
> And be led forth with peace:
> The mountains and hills shall break forth before you into singing,
> And all the trees of the field shall clap their hands.
> Instead of the thorn shall come up the fir tree,
> And instead of the brier shall come up the myrtle tree:
> And it shall be to the LORD for a name,
> For an everlasting sign that shall not be cut off.

Phase VI

The sixth section is long, and in parts obscure. As a whole it presents the work of redemption exercised upon Zion. It therefore stands appropriately before the final judgment that is to exalt a purified Zion amid the overthrow of the nations. But the redeeming work is an ideal picture that belongs to all periods of the nation's history, and it must not be limited to the restored exiles any more than it must be referred to the sin preceding exile: sin and redemption from sin have belonged to every period of Israel's history, and the return of sons and daughters to the City of Salvation is but a main incident used as a universal

lvi-lxii

image. The relation of this sixth Phase to the section that follows and the sections that precede is reflected in the opening words of the Servant of Jehovah. Playing upon the two meanings of the word he enjoins righteousness — that is, doing right — because of the near approach of God's righteousness — lvi. 1-8 that is, setting right, judgment and salvation. Then, with references back to the Babylonian exile which has inspired so much in the preceding sections, he speaks invitations to the stranger, and to the physically maimed, to join the Lord's people: the Lord's house shall be called an house of prayer for all peoples.

Then the Act seems to resolve itself into a series of pictures, in which the Servant of Jehovah is seen at his work for the redemption of the people. The first picture is one of unmeasured national corruption: all the beasts of lvi. 9-lviii the field coming to devour, and the watchmen blind — dumb dogs that cannot bark, dreaming, lying down, loving to slumber; meanwhile the righteous are perishing unheeded, with none to mark the lesson of their death. Suddenly the faithful Servant is among them: denouncing the sons of the sorceress, unmasking the abominations of the grove and murderous sacrifices lvii. 3 of the rock valleys, exposing the apostasy of the adulterous nation, and the depths of debasement to which they will descend in seeking any protector rather than their God. A second picture presents a different type of national character: a people that wearies with the length of the way, yet lvii. 10 says not, There is no hope: it finds a mysterious quickening of its strength, and, blind of heart, looks about to every source rather than the true one to explain the support it feels. But suddenly the Servant of Jehovah is seen smoothing the way before them, casting up the hollows and taking lvii. 14 stumbling-blocks away, while he proclaims that the high and lofty One that inhabiteth eternity dwells also with the contrite and humble spirit, not contending for ever, lest the spirit faint away, but restoring comforts after the iniquity has been chastised. A third picture is of those who love righteous ordinances and delight to draw near unto God; but they ask, Wherefore have we fasted, and God seeth not? To these the faithful Servant explains how they fast for contention and for their own pleasure. Is this the fast that the Lord has chosen, that a man should afflict his soul, and bow down his head like a rush, and spread sackcloth and ashes under his feet? Is not this the fast acceptable to the Lord, to loose the bonds of wickedness, and let the oppressed go free, to deal bread to the hungry, and cover the naked, and that thou hide not thyself from thine own flesh? Then shall thy light break forth as the morning; thy righteousness shall go before thee and the glory of Jehovah be thy rearward.

lviii

Then, all the several pictures growing together into one, we have the Servant of Jehovah identifying himself with the nation, and preaching that the Lord's hand is not shortened that it cannot save, but iniquities have come between the people and its God, until they grope like the blind, and stumble at noonday; until judgment is turned away backward, and truth fallen in the streets. And the Lord saw it, and it displeased him that there was no judgment, and none to interpose; wherefore his own arm wrought salvation. He put on righteousness as a breastplate, and a helmet of salvation on his head; he clothed himself with garments of vengeance, and was clad with zeal as a cloak: and he shall come like a rushing stream, which the breath of the Lord driveth. Thus A REDEEMER SHALL COME TO ZION.

lix

At once the lyric songs break out, bidding Zion arise, shine, for her light is come. Darkness shall cover the earth, and gross darkness the peoples: but Jehovah shall arise upon Zion, and nations shall be drawn to her light, and kings to the brightness of her sunrise. Her heart shall be enlarged and tremble as she beholds the multitudes of camels, the ships flying as doves to the windows, all bringing her sons and daughters from afar. Her gates shall be open day and night as the wealth of nations flows into her. Violence shall not be heard in her land; her officers shall be peace, and her exactors righteousness; her walls shall be

lx

called Salvation, and her gates, Praise: and her sun shall no more go down, for it shall be Jehovah, an everlasting light.

The lyric outburst subsides into a soliloquy of Jehovah's Servant upon his glorious task of preaching good tidings to the meek, binding up the broken-hearted, opening the prison to them that are bound, proclaiming the day of God's vengeance, and appointing to the mourners of Zion the garment of praise for the spirit of heaviness. He turns even then to speak words of promise to Zion, and Zion, no longer desponding, rejoices in the Lord who has covered her with the robe of righteousness as a bride is adorned with jewels. The Servant, in response, will for Zion's sake know no peace until her righteousness shine before all kings. She shall be named no longer Desolate, Forsaken: her land shall be Beulah, for her sons shall marry it, and her God shall rejoice over her as a bridegroom rejoices over his bride. Then the Servant of Jehovah cries to the Watchmen he has set upon the walls to give the Lord no rest until he fulfil his word to Zion. The section ends with a Chorus of Watchmen, who cry to go through the gates, to clear the way, to lift up the ensign that all nations can see: for the Lord's proclamation of salvation has been made to the end of the earth, and soon the name of Jerusalem will be the City Sought out.

lxi. 1

lxii. 1

lxii. 10

Phase VII

The seventh Phase is to bring the final Judgment, to which so much of what precedes has been pointing. Its keynote is struck by a Dramatic Vision of Judgment.

lxiii-lxvi

He who watcheth

Who is this that cometh from Edom,
    With crimsoned garments from Bozrah?
This that is glorious in his apparel,
    Marching in the greatness of his strength?

He who cometh

I that speak in righteousness,
Mighty to save.

He who watcheth

Wherefore art thou red
In thine apparel,
And thy garments
Like him that treadeth in the winefat?

He who cometh

I have trodden the winepress alone;
And of the peoples there was no man with me:
   Yea, I trod them in mine anger,
   And trampled them in my fury;
   And their lifeblood is sprinkled upon my garments,
   And I have stained all my raiment.
For the day of vengeance was in mine heart,
And the year of my redeemed is come.
And I looked, and there was none to help;
And I wondered that there was none to uphold:
Therefore mine own arm brought salvation unto me;
And my fury, it upheld me.
   And I trod down the peoples in mine anger,
   And made them drunk in my fury,
   And I poured out their lifeblood on the earth.

Then the Servant of Jehovah speaks, and gathers the whole national history into a liturgy of thanksgiving, confession, and supplication for judgment. He makes beginning with the lovingkindnesses of the Lord: he was the saviour of his people, in all their afflictions he was afflicted, and the angel of his presence saved them. But they were rebellious, and grieved his holy spirit; until he was turned to be their enemy and himself fought against them. Under his wrath have they become as the heathen; they have been delivered into the power of their iniquities; they have faded like a leaf which the

lxiii. 7-lxiv

wind of their iniquities driveth about. The holy cities have become a wilderness, Jerusalem a desolation; the holy and beautiful house where the fathers worshipped God is burned with fire. Yet is Jehovah their father, though Abraham know them not, and Israel refuse to acknowlege them. Oh that God would rend the heavens, and come down, that the mountains might flow down at his presence!

The response comes in the JUDGMENT, that finally separates between the holy and the evil: and the concluding phase of the rhapsody is the pendulum movement swinging to and fro between vengeance and glad salvation. lxv-lxvi

The rebellious, walking in their own way, and provoking God with their abominations — their works shall be recompensed into their own bosoms. *But there shall be a seed out of Jacob; the Lord's chosen shall inherit his mountains; Sharon shall be a fold of flocks, and the valley of Achor a place for herds to lie down in.* But those that prepare a table to Fortune and pour libations to Destiny, destined shall they be to the fortune of the sword: they shall perish, and leave only a name to curse by. *But he that blesseth himself shall bless himself by the God of Truth, for joy of the new heaven and the new earth, and the Holy Mountain in which the seed of the blessed shall forget their troubles. For the Lord's dwelling is not in a builded house, but in the poor and contrite spirit.* But they that choose their own ways, and delight in their own abominations, shall find Jehovah also choosing their delusions, and bringing their fears upon them. They persecute the fearers of the Lord, and challenge the Lord to glorify himself: — a shout from the city, a shout of Jehovah that maketh recompense. *But Zion cannot understand her deliverance, for before she has travailed she has brought forth. And Jerusalem and her lovers rejoice together, her peace flowing like a river.* While Jehovah shall come in fire and chariots of whirlwind to rebuke his enemies in the midst of their abominations: *and a standard shall be set up, that all nations and tongues can*

lxv. 1, 8

11, 16

lxvi. 3, 7

15

*see the Lord's glory, even to the isles afar off that have not heard
his fame. And out of all nations shall they bring the
brethren of Zion as an offering unto the Lord, and the
seed of Israel shall be before the Lord as long as the new heavens
and new earth shall remain. And all flesh shall come up
to worship at the holy feasts:* and they shall go forth and
look upon the carcasses of the transgressors, for their worm shall
not die, neither shall their fire be quenched.

CHAPTER XVIII

THE WORKS OF THE PROPHETS

WE have now passed in review all the various literary forms assumed by Prophecy. It remains to consider the contents of the prophetic books that have come down to us.

At the outset two important points call for notice. One is the recognition of what I will call Prophetic Sentences. In our examination of Wisdom literature we saw[1] that it partly consisted in isolated sayings,— the unit proverbs and the short maxims and epigrams enlarged from these; a considerable proportion of the books of wisdom was seen to be occupied with such independent literary brevities, and works that were specially consecutive in argument, such as *Ecclesiastes*, nevertheless exhibited portions of their whole contents given up to such miscellaneous matter. To a much smaller extent we saw in Lyric Poetry[2] a similar aggregation of brief poetic sayings or ejaculations to make longer poems. It is not surprising then that in Prophecy also we should find, besides formal discourses, isolated and independent Sentences, each a unit of prophetic thought on some single topic. Perhaps an ideal example of such Prophetic Sentences is given by a well-known passage of *Jeremiah*. This passage stands between an elegy of the mourning women describing a devastated land covered with carcasses, and another prophecy denouncing uncircumcised nations by name, and with them the uncircumcised in heart. Its distinctiveness from the context must be felt by every reader.

_{Prophetic Sentences}

---

[1] Above, pages 98, 292, 294.   [2] Above, page 164.

> Jeremiah
> ix. 23
>
> Thus saith the LORD, Let not the wise man glory in his wisdom, neither let the mighty man glory in his might, let not the rich man glory in his riches: but let him that glorieth glory in this, that he understandeth, and knoweth me, that I am the LORD which exercise lovingkindness, judgement, and righteousness, in the earth: for in these things I delight, saith the LORD.

Not only do such Prophetic Sentences exist, but from the way in which they appear in more than one place, they would seem to have somewhat of the floating character of proverbs. The cry of 'fear, and the pit, and the snare,' already seen in a work of Isaiah, occurs almost without a change in Jeremiah. "We have heard of the pride of Moab, that he is very proud," is a gnome-like sentence found both in Isaiah's and Jeremiah's Doom Songs on Moab; and the two have many other sentences in common. The three first sayings in Obadiah's Vision of Edom — those putting the ideas of an ambassador among the nations proclaiming the humiliation of Edom, of an eagle brought down from a mountain cleft, of grape-gatherers and robbers leaving gleanings — all occur in various parts of Jeremiah's Doom Song against the same nation. And a Prophetic Sentence made by negation of the proverb about fathers eating sour grapes and children's teeth being set on edge is found as an independent saying in *Jeremiah*, while it is expanded into an elaborate discourse by Ezekiel.

<small>Is. xxiv. 17, 18; Jer. xlviii. 43-4</small>

<small>Jer. xxxi. 29; Ez. xviii</small>

It is to be observed that such Prophetic Sentences are found in groups, chiefly at the close of a series of longer prophecies. One such group follows the words of encouragement given by Isaiah to Ahaz in the crisis made by the unnatural alliance of Israel with Syria against Judah.

> <small>Isaiah vii. 18-25</small>
>
> And it shall come to pass in that day, that the LORD shall hiss for the fly that is in the uttermost part of the rivers of Egypt, and for the bee that is in the land of Assyria. And they shall come, and shall rest all of them in the desolate valleys, and in the holes of the rocks, and upon all thorns, and upon all pastures.

⁎

> In that day shall the Lord shave with a razor that is hired, which is in the parts beyond the River, even with the king of Assyria, the head and the hair of the feet: and it shall also consume the beard.
>
> ***
>
> And it shall come to pass in that day, that a man shall nourish a young cow, and two sheep; and it shall come to pass, for the abundance of milk that they shall give he shall eat butter: for butter and honey shall every one eat that is left in the midst of the land.
>
> ***
>
> And it shall come to pass in that day, that every place, where there were a thousand vines at a thousand silverlings, shall even be for briers and thorns. With arrows and with bow shall one come thither; because all the land shall be briers and thorns. And all the hills that were digged with the mattock, thou shalt not come thither for fear of briers and thorns, but it shall be for the sending forth of oxen, and for the treading of sheep.

The isolation of the first passage is the clearer from the fact that in this portion of *Isaiah* there is no mention of Egypt: Assyria is the avenging force foreseen in that crisis. On the other hand, there is an individuality about each of the four passages, such as would readily give them currency as prophetic epigrams (so to speak): the prophecy of the fly and the bee, of the hired razor, of butter and honey, of briers and thorns. We have seen that repetition and reiteration play a great part in a prophet's ministry; such epigrammatic sayings would be repeated by the prophet on occasion after occasion of his preaching, until the text could pass into popular use, while the prophet's discourse on it would adapt itself to circumstances. Nor is it any objection against the separation of these four passages that they are all referred to a time expressed by the words "in that day:" on the contrary, we find a few phrases "in that day," "in those days," "the days come," that seem to be used as regular formulæ for introducing a prophecy.

Another series of such Sentences is found following Isaiah's Doom Song against Egypt. It differs from the last in the fact that all have a common thought,—the future conversion of Egypt; if the other Sentences were like proverbs, this series corresponds to the proverb cluster.

<small>Isaiah xix. 18-25</small>   In that day there shall be five cities in the land of Egypt that speak the language of Canaan, and swear to the LORD of hosts; one shall be called The City of Destruction.

※

In that day shall there be an altar to the LORD in the midst of the land of Egypt, and a pillar at the border thereof to the LORD. And it shall be for a sign and for a witness unto the LORD of hosts in the land of Egypt; for they shall cry unto the LORD because of the oppressors, and he shall send them a saviour, and a defender, and he shall deliver them.

※

And the LORD shall be known to Egypt, and the Egyptians shall know the LORD in that day; yea, they shall worship with sacrifice and oblation, and shall vow a vow unto the LORD, and shall perform it.

※

And the LORD shall smite Egypt, smiting and healing; and they shall return unto the LORD, and he shall be intreated of them, and shall heal them.

※

In that day shall there be a highway out of Egypt into Assyria, and the Assyrian shall come into Egypt, and the Egyptian into Assyria; and the Egyptians shall worship with the Assyrians.

※

In that day shall Israel be the third with Egypt and with Assyria, a blessing in the midst of the earth: for that the LORD of hosts hath blessed them, saying, Blessed be Egypt my people, and Assyria the work of my hands, and Israel mine inheritance.

It is clear that the recognition of such Sentences, not as an accident, but as a regular feature of prophetic literature, makes a <small>Recognition of Sentences in exegesis</small> great difference to the exegesis of particular passages. The documents which preserve the literatures of antiquity have not the clear separation of parts, or even of whole compositions, that modern printing has made for us a matter of course; and there is no element in exegesis more important, or more difficult, than the determination exactly where a literary section of Scripture begins and ends. Many discourses in the Bible seem to present perplexing and obscure lines of thought, simply because the discourse has been made to extend over passages which may better be considered as independent. I take a casual example. The portion of our *Book of Zechariah* which is numbered as chapters seven and eight is treated by most expositors as a single discourse. It opens with a formal enquiry as to the obligation of fasts, to which an answer is returned; near the end of this section there is another reference to fasts, and to their being days of gladness; the argument of the whole is supposed to be that the observance of moral duties, and the Messianic peace that this will bring — which are topics of intervening passages — would make fasts a gladness instead of a burden. But it must be confessed that the links in this chain of thought are very inconsequent; and the idea of the gladness of fasts is but little emphasised if it is to be the climax up to which a lengthy discourse has led. On the other hand, portions of the intervening matter have a strong appearance of independence.

_{Zechariah vii-viii}

_{viii. 18}

viii. 1-8   And the word of the LORD of hosts came to me, saying, Thus saith the LORD of hosts: I am jealous for Zion with great jealousy, and I am jealous for her with great fury.

∗

Thus saith the LORD: I am returned unto Zion, and will dwell in the midst of Jerusalem: and Jerusalem shall be called The City of truth; and the mountain of the LORD of hosts The holy mountain.

∗

Thus saith the LORD of hosts: There shall yet old men and old women dwell in the streets of Jerusalem, every man with his staff in his hand for very age. And the streets of the city shall be full of boys and girls playing in the streets thereof.

∗

Thus saith the LORD of hosts: If it be marvellous in the eyes of the remnant of this people in those days, should it also be marvellous in mine eyes? saith the LORD of hosts.

₊

Thus saith the LORD of hosts: Behold I will save my people from the east country, and from the west country: and I will bring them, and they shall dwell in the midst of Jerusalem; and they shall be my people, and I will be their God, in truth and in righteousness.

A full discourse stands next, on the same general subject, contrasting former turbulence with coming peace; then the succession of independent sayings is continued.

18-23 And the word of the LORD of hosts came unto me, saying, Thus saith the LORD of hosts: The fast of the fourth month, and the fast of the fifth, and the fast of the seventh, and the fast of the tenth, shall be to the house of Judah joy and gladness, and cheerful feasts; therefore love truth and peace.

₊

Thus saith the LORD of hosts: It shall yet come to pass, that there shall come peoples, and the inhabitants of many cities: and the inhabitants of one city shall go to another, saying, Let us go speedily to intreat the favour of the LORD, and to seek the LORD of hosts: I will go also. Yea, many peoples and strong nations shall come to seek the LORD of hosts in Jerusalem, and to intreat the favour of the LORD.

₊

Thus saith the LORD of hosts: In those days it shall come to pass, that ten men shall take hold, out of all the languages of the nations, shall even take hold of the skirt of him that is a Jew, saying, We will go with you, for we have heard that God is with you.

Of course, in the interpretation of this or any part of Scripture difference of opinion will come in. I am merely contending for the arrangement in isolated Sentences as a legitimate resource of exegesis. And with regard to any particular passage the question must be, not whether it is possible by ingenuity or by straining to weave it into a continuous whole, but whether, all things considered, any succession of words may be better regarded as a portion of a whole or as an independent aphorism.

There is one prophet to whom the present consideration applies with special force. From the time of St. Jerome there has been an agreement to recognise the prominence of *sententiæ* in Hosea; and the obscurity which all readers find in his writings seems largely due to the fact that this book of prophecy, like the *Book of Proverbs*, is made up of longer discourses mingled with abundance of Prophetic Sentences, each of these Sentences an isolated whole, yet all reflecting the general attitude of this prophet to the moral questions of his time. I venture upon a lengthy citation in order to give readers, accustomed to puzzle over Hosea's line of argument, an opportunity of appreciating the new interest that comes into the prophecy when large parts of it are presented as collections of prophetic epigrams.

> The days of visitation are come, the days of recompense are come; Israel shall know it: the prophet is a fool, the man that hath the spirit is mad, for the multitude of thine iniquity, and because the enmity is great.

Hosea ix. 7-x. 12

⁎

> Ephraim watcheth against my God: as for the prophet, a fowler's snare is in all his ways, and enmity in the house of his God.

⁎

> They have deeply corrupted themselves, as in the days of Gibeah: he will remember their iniquity, he will visit their sins.

⁎

> I found Israel like grapes in the wilderness; I saw your fathers as the firstripe in the fig tree at her first season: but they came to Baal-peor, and consecrated themselves unto the shameful thing, and became abominable like that which they loved.

⁎

> As for Ephraim, their glory shall fly away like a bird: there shall be no birth, and none with child, and no conception. Though they bring up their children, yet will I bereave them, that there be not a man left: yea, woe also to them when I depart from them!

⁎

Ephraim, like as I have seen Tyre, is planted in a pleasant place: but Ephraim shall bring out his children to the slayer.

※

Give them, O LORD: what wilt thou give? give them a miscarrying womb and dry breasts.

※

All their wickedness is in Gilgal; for there I hated them: because of the wickedness of their doings I will drive them out of mine house: I will love them no more; all their princes are revolters.

※

Ephraim is smitten, their root is dried up, they shall bear no fruit: yea, though they bring forth, yet will I slay the beloved fruit of their womb. My God will cast them away, because they did not hearken unto him: and they shall be wanderers among the nations.

※

Israel is a luxuriant vine, which putteth forth his fruit: according to the multitude of his fruit he hath multiplied his altars; according to the goodness of his land they have made goodly obelisks. Their heart is divided; now shall they be found guilty: he shall smite their altars, he shall spoil their obelisks.

※

Surely now shall they say, We have no king: for we fear not the LORD; and the king, what can he do for us?

※

They speak vain words, swearing falsely in making covenants: therefore judgement springeth up as hemlock in the furrows of the field.

※

The inhabitants of Samaria shall be in terror for the calves of Beth-aven: for the people thereof shall mourn over it, and the priests thereof that rejoiced over it, for the glory thereof, because it is departed from it. It also shall be carried unto Assyria for a present to king Jareb: Ephraim shall receive shame, and Israel shall be ashamed of his own counsel.

※

As for Samaria, her king is cut off, as foam upon the water. The high places also of Aven, the sin of Israel, shall be destroyed: the

thorn and the thistle shall come up on their altars; and they shall
say to the mountains, Cover us; and to the hills, Fall on us.

***

O Israel thou hast sinned from the days of Gibeah: there they
stood; that the battle against the children of iniquity should not overtake them in Gibeah. ***

When it is my desire, I will chastise them; and the peoples shall
be gathered against them, when they are yoked to their two transgressions. And Ephraim is an heifer that is taught, that loveth to
tread out the corn; but I have passed over upon her fair neck: I
will set a rider on Ephraim; Judah shall plow, Jacob shall break
his clods. ***

Sow to yourselves in righteousness, reap according to mercy;
break up your fallow ground: for it is time to seek the LORD till he
come and rain righteousness upon you.

The second of our preliminary considerations is the Prophetic
Cycle. Considerable part of our prophetic literature is found to
consist in series of discourses, or incidents, or rhapsodies, succeeding one another just as the contents *Cycles of Proph-ecy*
of a modern volume of sermons. But sometimes
separate prophecies are united together by some essential bond,
whether of structural connection or of related subject-matter. In
this second case the word Cycle seems appropriate. It has been
remarked in a former chapter that all the discourses of Malachi
have the same structural plan: the discourse near its commencement is interrupted by an imaginary objection, or more than one
objection, and these become the real starting-point of what follows. The recurrence of this scholastic device makes the whole
Book of Malachi a single Dialectic Cycle. Again, we have seen
how the denunciations against Israel and seven other nations at
the opening of *Amos* are in structure exactly parallel: they constitute a Cycle of Dooms. The last section of this prophecy is a
series of emblems (presented in vision), ascending one above
another in nearness to the crisis and issue: this is an Emblem

Cycle. Such illustrations of the term are easy; one or two usages need more discussion.

The portion of *Isaiah* that extends from chapter twenty-eight to chapter thirty-five is best considered as a Cycle and not merely a series of discourses. The bond of connection is very definite: all the discourses are animadversions on a certain political situation, but this is made a background for pictures of the restoration of Israel, or a remnant of Israel, in a golden age or Messianic kingdom. The political situation is the panic caused by the Assyrian invasion, and the efforts of the party of Israel's independence to restrain the nation from looking for support to the rival empire of Egypt.

<small>Isaiah xxviii-xxxv</small>

<small>xxviii</small> In the first discourse Isaiah denounces the dissoluteness of Judah's priestly and prophetic rulers as on a par with that of Israel's kingdom, and exposes the secret ground of their light-heartedness amid national apprehensions — the 'covenant with death and agreement with hell' they have made for themselves, so that the overflowing scourge will pass them by. This secret confidence in Egypt he calls a refuge of lies, and in contrast upholds Jehovah's foundation-stone laid in Zion, by the strength of which he will be a diadem of beauty to the residue that believe in him. In a later discourse, when an embassy has been openly sent to Egypt, the prophet pours contempt on the alliance with the "Boaster that sitteth still," which shall become to Israel like a breach ready to fall, swelling out in a high wall. But after foretelling ruin he springs to a glad future, gradually ascending from a state of external affliction relieved only by the blessing of spiritual guidance, to a golden tide in a plenteous land, when the light of the moon shall be as the light of the sun, and the light of the sun shall be sevenfold, and idols shall be utterly cast out. The same combination of elements marks all the discourses. The conclusion of the series is a companion picture of ideal destruction and ideal restoration. Edom is named as the foe, but the details show that this is used only as a type of hostile forces: for so universal is the destruction that all

<small>xxx</small>

the host of heaven are seen to moulder away, and the heavens roll together as a scroll; streams of earth become pitch and its dust brimstone, the smoke of it going up for ever;¹ palaces are overgrown with thorns and thistles, fit habitation for jackals, where the wild beasts meet with the wolves, and the satyr cries to his fellow. The contrasting picture¹ is of the wilderness and the solitary place being glad, and the desert blossoming as the rose; the glowing sand becomes a pool, the habitation of jackals green with reeds and rushes: and a way of holiness stretches across, over which the ransomed of the LORD return to Zion, with everlasting joy upon their heads. Discourses with such community of treatment, brought to such a common climax, make what may be called a Cycle of the Restoration.

xxxiv
xxxv

Again, there is a Vision Cycle of much literary interest in our *Book of Zechariah*. The hopes of the Temple-builders are strengthened by a series of visions; not only do these visions belong to the same dream and have a common reference, but further, by a beautiful touch of vision effect, they are enclosed in another 'Enveloping Vision,' which remains constant while the others come and go, dreams within a dream. The prophet relates how "in the night" he beheld horses, red, sorrel, and white, among the myrtle trees, and these are interpreted to him as spirits of ministration that go to and fro in the earth. This is the Enveloping Vision,—as it were the machinery for carrying out whatever by special vision may be made known: and it seems to remain in the background during all that follows. At present the report is that the earth sitteth still and is at rest; the angel of the Lord appeals for mercy on Jerusalem to tarry no longer, and is answered with comfortable words. The Lord will return to Jerusalem with mercies: and each of these mercies is symbolised in a vision, the

<small>Vision Cycle: Zechariah i. 7– vi. 8</small>

---

¹ It will be understood of course that the date of this prophecy, whether of its composition or of that to which it may refer, does not affect the argument: we are here concerned with the order of prophecies as they stand, whoever may be responsible for the arrangement.

prophet feeling himself, as it were, wakened from sleep to behold
each. The first vision is of Horns and Smiths: the former are interpreted of the nations that have lifted themselves up against Jerusalem, the latter of the forces that shall fray
these and cast them down. A second vision shows a man with a
measuring line, going to measure Jerusalem: for its inhabitants
shall increase till it must needs be inhabited as villages without
walls. The third vision presents the hierarchy of heaven, and
the High Priest Joshua (representative of the Temple-builders)
assailed by the Adversary: but the Adversary is rebuked, and
Joshua is clad in rich apparel, with a mitre set on his head. The
next appearance is of the Golden Candlestick: this final piece of
Temple furniture symbolises how Zerubbabel shall complete as well
as begin his good work. While the prophet watches this he is
aware of the two olive trees on either side of it: this is a separate
emblem, giving authority for associating the two 'sons of oil,'—
the prince Zerubbabel and the priesthood. Two more visions
foreshadow the moral purification of the land: the Flying Roll of
the Curse indicating crime purged out of the country, and Wickedness in the ephah pressed down by the weight of a talent showing
how the wickedness of the land shall be banished, as the visionary
figure is banished, into the wilderness. The succession of individual mercies concluded, the Enveloping Vision resumes: chariots
are now added to the horses, from between the two mountains of
brass: and they are to depart to the four winds of heaven to execute the will of the Lord. The unity that is implied in all Cycles
reaches a climax in such enveloping of symbolic details in the
symbol of that which is to provide for their execution.

These preliminary considerations disposed of, the remaining
task of this chapter becomes easy. In the Appendix to this work
I attempt to analyse the contents of each book of prophecy, separating discourses and sentences, indicating the nature of each,
and, where convenient, adding titles. Here it is only necessary
to sum up.

In several cases the contents of a prophetic work consist of a single composition. Obadiah, Nahum, and Zephaniah have left only a single Discourse. The *Book of Jonah* we have in a former chapter seen to be a single prophetic Epic. We have also seen that the books of *Joel* and *Amos* resolve themselves each into a single Rhapsody. A degree more varied are the prophetic works of Habakkuk, which consist of his *Rhapsody of the Chaldeans* and his *Ode of Judgment*. In *Haggai* we find four Occasional Discourses, regularly dated. And we have seen that the prophecy of *Malachi* may be regarded as a Dialectic Cycle.

Contents of Prophetic Books
Shorter books

The rest of prophetic literature shows more complexity. It may be pointed out that when we speak of 'The Book of the prophet Jeremiah,' we are using an ambiguous term. The whole works of this prophet, as of others, fall into several 'books'; just as what in ordinary parlance is called 'The Book of Psalms' appears in the Revised Version as five books, clearly separated by doxologies. So, with the exception of the nine mentioned in the preceding paragraph the works of the prophets divide themselves into more than one book for each author.

Our *Book of Isaiah* falls naturally into seven books.[1] The first is made up of general prophecies, ending with the Vision of the Call. Six chapters contain Occasional prophecies, one set relating to the Unholy Alliance of Israel with Syria, another inspired by an Assyrian Invasion. The fourth book contains the Doom Songs collected together: these may be considered to make a Cycle of Doom, as they are followed by the general *Rhapsody of Judgment* upon the whole earth. I have already in discussing the word 'cycle' described the next section of *Isaiah* as a Cycle of the Restoration. As a sixth book we have a brief historical excerpt, bringing out Isaiah's action in the great crisis of Sennacherib's invasion. The last book is the *Rhapsody of Zion Redeemed*.[2]

Isaiah

---

[1] Compare the Literary Index throughout.

[2] It will be understood that the question whether this section is from the same author as preceding parts of *Isaiah* is outside the scope of the present work.

The discourses of Jeremiah seem to be grouped in more numerous divisions, making ten books in all. After a section occupied by the prophet's Call, and general Manifesto of his ministry, we have a second containing miscellaneous discourses and sentences. Then follow several clear groups, founded on a Missionary journey, on the Drought, on Pottery, on Messages to Rulers. The seventh book is largely occupied with Controversies; the eighth contains the prophecies of the Restoration. A book follows of Incidental discourses and prophetic history; and the collection of Doom Songs concludes the series.

Jeremiah

The arrangement of Ezekiel's Works is very simple and clear. They fall into only three books: the first contains prophecies of Judgment, the third prophecies of the Restoration, each brought to a climax by the two parts of the connected Vision of Jerusalem judged and Jerusalem restored. The book separating these is occupied with the Dooms on the Nations.

Ezekiel

The *Prophecy of Daniel* makes two books: one of Prophetic Incidents and Interpretations of Visions, arranged in chronological order; the other a Cycle of Visions seen by the prophet himself. *Hosea* also falls into two divisions. The Emblem Prophecy of Gomer makes one. The other consists of discourses, brief rhapsodies, and especially long collections of prophetic sentences, but all uniting to convey the idea of the Lord's Controversy with Israel; perhaps, on the analogy of Wisdom literature, this might be called a Cluster of Prophecies. *Micah* has two very different sections; five chapters contain miscellaneous discourses, the last two the very dramatic prophecies fully discussed in a previous chapter. And our *Book of Zechariah* falls into three divisions, very diverse in character.[1] The first is miscellaneous, but mainly occupied with the elaborate Vision Cycle described above. The other two divisions contain discourses, the matter of which suggests their separation into two books.

Daniel

Hosea

Micah

Zechariah

[1] It will be understood that the question whether the three parts are by the same author is outside the scope of the present work.

This completes the list of Old Testament prophets. But the
New Testament furnishes a book which must be considered in this
connection. *The Revelation of St. John* is too
closely involved with modern theological questions [St. John's Revelation]
to admit of its being discussed in a work from
which distinctively religious matter is excluded. On the other
hand, in the literary study of Scripture it is impossible to ignore a
composition of such transcendent literary interest. If a reader
will apply to this book of Revelation a method which ought to be
applied to all parts of Scripture, and set himself to take in the
whole at a sitting, reading with his imagination on the stretch in
the way in which he would read Dante's *Hell, Purgatory*, and
Paradise, he will find, whatever his theological principles may be,
that this Vision Cycle is one of the literary wonders of the world.
I will be content with making two remarks on the subject, and
with these my treatment of Biblical Prophecy may be brought to
a conclusion.

The title contains the word 'revelation.' But in our discussion
of prophetic forms we saw that this word had two distinct meanings: revelation of the future, as in the visions of
Daniel, and revelation of the ideal, as in Ezekiel's [Meaning of the title]
Visions of Jerusalem, or the original revelation to
Moses in the mount. Which of these meanings applies, or do
they both apply, to the work of St. John? The popular mind has
seized upon the first of these, and looks upon St. John's *Revelation* as a prophetic riddle, the ingenious reading of which will give
a clue to events of past or future history, or will even enable the
present to be exactly located in some scheme of all time. But if
the words of the prologue, " the things which must shortly come
to pass," and the parallels with Daniel's visions, favour the view
that the revelation is a foreshowing, yet on the other hand the
equally close parallels with Ezekiel's visions, and the building up
of the whole structure upon symbolic symmetries, counterparts,
and antitheses, make it certain that the idealising of the world-
contest between good and evil is of the very essence of the

work.[1] Moreover, if both kinds of revelation belong to this book, they will mutually modify one another. Suppose that some specially distinctive detail of the symbolism suggests connection with some historic power or institution: then, by the influence of the other type of revelation, we must expect that historic reality to be idealised in the movement of the vision, so that it would still be hazardous exegesis to interrogate other details of the symbolism for further historic details. I have before remarked upon the way in which prophetic literature as a whole has suffered from the unfortunate narrowing of the word 'prophecy' in ordinary conversation to the single sense of prediction. No part of prophetic literature has suffered so much in this respect as St. John's *Revelation;* and the literary student, at all events, should address himself to those permanent spiritual interests of the book which are independent of times and seasons.

But the *Book of Revelation* presents another feature of the highest interest and significance. It may be expressed in a phrase of the vision itself: "The testimony of Jesus is the spirit of prophecy." Underlying the whole book is the idea that the "revelation of Jesus Christ" is a bringing together and enhancing of all previous revelations; and accordingly in the symbolic scenery of the visions, and the phrases by which they are described, the conceptions of Old Testament prophecy are continually appearing in new forms and combinations. At the outset, when the Apostle speaks of being 'in the Spirit,' we think of Ezekiel borne by the spirit to Jerusalem. The prefatory messages to the seven churches of Asia, with their individual details and rhythmic promises and threats, remind us of the chain of denunciations in similar form on seven nations with which Amos opens his prophecy, before he deals with his church of Israel. In the vision itself we begin at once to get details from Old Testament prophets. The personal

Association of its details with other prophecy

---

[1] I may be allowed to express my admiration of the way in which this element of interpretation has been worked out in the late Professor Milligan's *Revelation* (a volume of the Expositor's Bible, Hodder & Stoughton).

description of one coming with the clouds, of hair white as wool, a golden girdle, feet like burnished brass, eyes of fire, is entirely from Daniel; from Ezekiel come the rainbow round about the throne and the four living creatures. The naming of Him who is worthy to open the book as the 'Root of David' brings up the 'Branch' and 'Shoot' which have figured in the Messianic pictures of Isaiah; and the other appellative, 'the Lion' of the tribe of Judah,' takes us back to Primitive Prophecy and the Blessings of Jacob on the tribes. It is the same with the symbols that make up the succession of scenes. The book written within and without, the little book to be eaten and found sweet in the mouth and bitter in the belly, have both become familiar from the prophecy of Ezekiel; the golden candlestick of Zechariah's vision is multiplied sevenfold for this supreme revelation, and its appendage of the two olive trees now becomes the centre of a separate chapter of allegory; the incense symbolising the prayers of the saints realises the imagery of the psalms; if again the delivered psalmist has cried that God _{Psalm cxli. 2} has put a 'new song' in his mouth, the thought finds here a realisation in the mystic new song which none but the sealed of the Lord can learn. The prophetic conceptions undergo alteration and enlargement as they reappear. Zechariah's vision had presented spirits of ministration on the earth in the form of horses, white, red, black, grisled, — the colours being a picturesque detail: but the horses of *Revelation* — the white, the red, the black, the pale — have each a hue mystically connected with its office of judgment. Prophecy had frequently couched its mysteries under the image of a book sealed up: this consummation of all things presents the unsealing. Among the instruments of woe the trumpets represent the trumpet sound which in the rhapsodies had marked the commencement of panic, the bowls poured out repeat the regular image of the Doom Songs, — the cup of Jehovah's fury. The woes thus hurled upon the world are the 'plagues' of Egypt magnified: when locusts are mentioned, the mystic imagery of Joel is worked into the description; when hail is pictured, the expression "every stone about the weight of a talent" reads like a momentary finger-pointing to Zechariah's vision of Wickedness pressed down with the talent of lead. Where the form of woes goes outside the Egyptian plagues prophecy has other symbols to contribute, and the 'burning mountain' recalls Jeremiah's Doom of Babylon, as the star Wormwood the Doom of Babylon in *Isaiah*. Again, the recital of the number of the saved, tribe by tribe, recalls in its rhythm a similar recital of the portions of the tribes of *Ezekiel*. Of course a new chord has been struck in the vision that immediately follows: the "great multitude, which no man could number, out of every nation, and of all tribes and peoples and tongues, standing before the throne." But as the description is continued hallowed associations from old prophecy come in. That they have "washed their robes and made them white in the blood of the Lamb," combines Isaiah's promise that sins red as crimson should be as wool with Zechariah's vision of the filthy garments taken in the heavenly court from Joshua that he might be clothed in rich vestments; while the sweetly sounding promise —

> They shall hunger no more, neither thirst any more, neither shall the sun strike upon them, nor any heat, for the Lamb which is in the midst of the throne shall be their shepherd, and shall guide them unto fountains of waters of life —

has been spoken before by the Servant of Jehovah in the Isaiahan Rhapsody. Sometimes St. John's symbols or descriptive touches would fail to produce their effect if separated from the associations they recall. It would seem harsh in so mystic a scene to speak of exact numbers: but the phrase of the old processional psalm —

> The chariots of God are twenty thousand,
> Even thousands upon thousands —

renders it possible for *Revelation* to make the armies of the horsemen "twice ten thousand times ten thousand." Again we might see no point in the symbol of the balance held by the rider on the black horse, were it not that Ezekiel's mimic siege has accustomed us to associate famine with eating bread by weight and drinking water by measure. And when we reach the tumult of winds and sea and the beasts coming up out of the sea, the vision becomes pointless unless the prophecies of Daniel are assumed throughout.

It will be understood that the use in *Revelation* of the Old Testament prophecy is no borrowing or travelling backward; on the contrary, the conceptions of the prophets become intensified by being *massed* together, and ideas from diverse sources unite in a single new conception. The horror of nature that attends the opening of the sixth seal is given in a single description. Its first clause, as to the sun becoming black as sackcloth and the moon as blood, gives a phenomenon of change three times used by Joel. Then the stars falling from heaven, "as a shaken fig tree casts her unripe figs," unites Isaiah's expression of stars falling "as a fading leaf from the fig tree" with Nahum's application of the image of a shaken fig tree to the succession of fortresses yielded in a panic. Then the detail of the heavens being rolled up as a scroll recalls Isaiah's ideal ruin of Edom; that of the mountains and islands moving and fleeing has been a stock prophetic image; the idea of men's hiding in the caves and rocks has been used in Isaiah's opening manifesto, their crying to the rocks and mountains to fall on them and cover them has been pictured by Hosea. The final climax of the description — that the great day of wrath is come, and who is able to abide it? — borrows the refrain of Joel's rhapsody. Or again: when the angel casts his sickle to the earth, we at once recognise the consummation foreshadowed by Joel; but when the vintage so gathered is cast into the winepress of the wrath of God, the association is with the vision of judgment in the Isaiahan Rhapsody; when again blood comes out of the winepress and reaches even to the bridles of the horses, the image of that rhapsody has become united with an early picture of Isaiah, which represented the Assyrian flood deluging the land and reaching to the horses' necks. The song over Fallen Babylon recalls many such songs of old prophecy;

but before it has gone far the details have entirely changed, and identified the fallen power also with Tyre whose ruin is wept over by the merchant and the shipman: the suggestion is that all the bulwarks of evil are included in the Babylon of *Revelation*. To take a final example. The New Jerusalem seen with the measured symmetries of its walls and gates is the Jerusalem of Ezekiel. Its coming down as a bride adorned for her husband is the thought of one of the songs to Zion Exalted in the rhapsody of Isaiah; from another of these songs come the foundations of precious stones and pearly gates; yet another has foreshadowed the gates open day and night, the Divine Sun in the glory of which nations walk. And the additional picture of the river of water of life — with the trees of life, yielding their monthly fruits, and leaves for the healing of the nations — has brought us back to the visions of Ezekiel.

Even as a literary effect this building up of new conceptions out of details that come to us hallowed with the associations of past literature is eminently impressive. It is another form of that which in secular literature is the chain of 'classic' succession, by which Miltonic poetry will in its every detail echo some classic image or expression of Italian and Roman literature, as these in their turn had made their details suggest their origin in the classic poetry of Greece. The emblematic ideas of prophecy, however, go far beyond literary imagery; and, whether we consider matter or form, it is highly significant that the final outpouring of Scriptural Prophecy should be a Procession of symbolic visions in which the visionary symbols of all preceding prophecy have grown together into their consummation.

BOOK SIXTH

THE BIBLICAL LITERATURE OF RHETORIC

CHAPTER	PAGE
XIX. THE EPISTLES: OR WRITTEN RHETORIC	439
XX. SPOKEN RHETORIC: AND THE 'BOOK OF DEUTERONOMY'	444

CHAPTER XIX

THE EPISTLES: OR WRITTEN RHETORIC

THE word 'rhetoric' has several meanings. In the sense that belongs to its most common usage it has little connection with the purpose of the present work. Questions of style seem to me to belong to the study of language rather than to the study of literature; unless in such cases as the *Book of Wisdom*, where we saw a peculiarity of style of sufficient magnitude to make the composition a literary class by itself, the morphological distinctness of which must be kept in mind by one who would appreciate the argument. At present I am using the word 'rhetoric' in a different sense, — as the literature of address. The Biblical literature of address falls into two main divisions: the Epistle, or Written Address, and Oratory, the Spoken Address. *[Rhetoric: the Literature of Address]*

The Epistolary literature of the Bible constitutes a department of the highest importance as regards its subject-matter. But its treatment need occupy only a small space in a work of which the purpose is to note distinctions of literary form. All that is necessary is to point out that the generic term 'epistle' covers three classes of composition worth distinguishing, without reckoning the *Epistle of St. James*, which has already been treated as a part of Wisdom literature. *[Epistolary Literature: the Written Address]*

The first and largest class is made up of epistles in the strictest sense, — the Epistles of Pastoral Intercourse. These have the full form of epistolary correspondence: commencing with a salutation from the Apostle,[1] with whom other names are joined in some cases, to a distinct church or fellow-worker; ending with further salutations and sometimes an autograph message, and with greetings, general or by name. Sometimes messages to individuals, or about the treatment of individuals, appear in the body of the letter; information is given as to the writer's condition, or his prospective movements and the possibility of personal visits to his correspondents; reference is made to affairs of the church or person addressed, and even to financial questions or to the disposal of articles of luggage left behind. The matter of the epistle, moreover, is called forth by particular circumstances; though in treating the particular the writer can rise or digress to the deepest principles touched in the highest forms of expression. The *First Epistle to the Corinthians* is an ideal example of this type. Its earlier paragraphs are drawn from St. Paul by tidings he has heard of the Church at Corinth: tidings of factions, of moral laxity, of proceedings against brethren in secular courts. Then he turns to answer questions of principle, or of ecclesiastical policy, which have been conveyed to him on behalf of the Corinthian church; he thus treats of celibacy, of the idol feasts which constituted a burning question in the early days of Christianity, of the relation of the sexes in places of worship; the question of diverse spiritual gifts seems also to be among those put to him, and in treating it he is led to the famous outpouring on 'charity,' or 'love.' He concludes with a summary of the 'gospel' he has preached, but a summary really designed for a single purpose, to meet doubts that had arisen concerning the resurrection doctrine of the Apostles.

<small>Epistles of Pastoral Intercourse</small>

<small>I Corinthians</small>

The other pastoral epistles are, in their general character as a branch of literature, covered by this typical example. The *Second Epistle to the Corinthians* seems to have been called forth by the reception of the first. That to the *Galatians* is a personal remonstrance from St. Paul to churches with which he conceived himself to have a

<small>Other Pastoral Epistles</small>

---

[1] In the case of *II, III John* the writer appears only as 'The Elder.'

special bond of intimacy, and which had been disturbed by Judaising tendencies such as it was the mission of this Apostle to resist. The epistle to the *Philippians* was perhaps originated by a desire to heal local differences, if we may judge from an appeal to that effect addressed to individuals by name; but its matter as a whole is general. Those to the *Thessalonians* have an individual colour given to them by the prominence of discussions touching the expected near 'coming of Christ.' The epistles to *Timothy* are appeals to a 'child in the faith' and fellow-worker, touching his personal character as a teacher; but St. Paul also pronounces through him upon questions likely to be disputed by those amongst whom Timothy would labour. The epistle to *Titus* is a general summary of instruction to one left in charge of a district where much organising was to be done. The epistle to *Philemon* was a personal appeal sent by St. Paul with a runaway slave, now Christianised, and desiring to return to his master, a convert and friend of the Apostle. Of a similar personal character are the epistles (numbered second and third) of St. John, addressed to an unnamed lady and to Gaius.

_{iv. 2}

There is a clear distinction between such epistles of Pastoral Intercourse and two others, which may be designated Epistolary Treatises. The *Epistle to the Romans* is addressed, it is true, to a particular church: but it is the church of the world's metropolis, and one which the writer has never visited. The formalities of salutation quickly lead the writer to that which is his text: the new conception of a 'righteousness by faith,' which is salvation 'to the Jew first and also to the Greek.' What follows is a formal and ordered exposition of this conception, the writer throughout keeping before him the two parties of Jews and non-Jews, whose attitudes to the new doctrine would be so different. Commencing with first principles he gradually reaches a climax in the idea of a world redemption; if then he passes from argument to exhortation, yet his exhortations are only another form of his argument, and represent the gospel realised in practical life. The con-

<small>Epistolary Treatises</small>

<small>Romans</small>

clusion has the greetings, and references to the writer's movements, which belong to the pastoral epistles. The *Epistle to the Hebrews*
Hebrews lacks all epistolary form of opening, even the name of its author; at the close there is only a reference to the liberation of Timothy, and a salutation from 'them of Italy.' The whole is an elaborate and symmetrical argument, brilliant in style, addressed by a Hebrew to Hebrews, the purport of which is that the Law must give place to the Gospel as to a higher and fuller dispensation.

A third class of epistles is to be distinguished, which will include those to the *Colossians* and *Ephesians*, those of *Peter*, of *Jude*,
Epistolary Mani- and the *First Epistle of John*. Of these only the
festos epistle to the *Colossians* has the regular epistolary salutations and greetings. That named after the Ephesians is really a circular letter to churches, of which the church at Ephesus was only the chief, and in place of final greetings we here find a recommendation of the bearer of the epistle. The others have in our Bibles the title of 'general': St. Peter's are addressed "To the elect who are sojourners of the Dispersion in Pontus, &c.," and "To them that have obtained a like precious faith with us"; that of Jude, "To them that are called, beloved in God the Father, and kept for Jesus Christ"; the *First Epistle of St. John* has no address. I think this group would be correctly designated Epistolary Manifestos. The writer's whole conception of the truth and the life of which he is a minister is concentrated in a single deliverance, not for purposes of general argument or exposition (though both are found), but drawn out by some special situation of the church, and making appeal to the whole nature of those who read, intellectual and spiritual, whether in their private or corporate
Colossians and capacity. In the case of the Colossians and Ephe-
Ephesians sians the inspiring situation seems to be the rivalry of some other well-ordered systems of truth, and the purpose of the epistles is to put forward the Christian faith and life as satisfying every capacity of the fullest nature. St. Peter's ad-
I Peter dress to the Dispersion is clearly called out by an era of cruel persecution, which has naturally driven the Church to test

the foundations of the faith for which it is suffering. The *Epistle of Jude*, and the *Second Epistle of Peter* which has so much in common with it, are manifestos necessitated by evil attacking the Church from within: the perversion of the doctrine of 'liberty' into a bold antinomianism that set at defiance elementary morality as well as ecclesiastical order. St. John's Epistle seems in a general way to have originated in that which would be an accessory cause of the others, —the sense that the age was 'the last time' and the time of antichrists; in particular, the number of those who could bear personal witness to the life of Christ was fast disappearing, and the last pronouncements of those who still survived must be heard. *[margin: Jude and II Peter; I John]*

Reviewing all three classes I may add one remark. The Epistles occupy in the New Testament the place occupied by Prophecy in the Old Testament. The prophets ministered to a nation, and could move amongst their fellow-countrymen and bring to bear on them the power of vocal address. The Apostles addressed those who were scattered through distant cities, and could communicate with the Church as a whole only by letter. The Pastoral Epistles correspond to the Occasional Discourses and Prophetic Incidents which make up so large a proportion of prophetic literature. In our analysis of Prophecy we have also noticed the Prophetic Manifesto, embodying, like the Epistolary Manifestos, the preacher's general conception of his ministry. For the Epistolary Treatises there is no counterpart in prophetic literature; for the prophet speaks with authority, not by argument, as a representative of the God his hearers acknowledge. The analogous Old Testament form is rather to be sought in Wisdom literature. But if so, the conception of Wisdom is found to have altered; with a new world in which the Greek takes the intellectual lead Wisdom can no longer be mere reflection, but must arm itself with argument. In the passage from the Essays of Old Testament Wisdom to the Epistles named after Romans and Hebrews we have passed from Oriental to Western philosophy. *[margin: Old Testament counterparts of the Epistles]*

CHAPTER XX

SPOKEN RHETORIC: AND THE 'BOOK OF DEUTERONOMY'

THE department of Oratory, or Spoken Rhetoric, is represented in the Bible partly by the elaborate speeches already noted in the Drama of *Job*, attractive by their flowing elo-

Oratory or Spoken Rhetoric

quence and their pointed gnomic sayings. There are again numerous speeches scattered through the Old and New Testament, which, however, cannot well be appreciated from the literary standpoint, owing to the condensed form in which they are reported. Perhaps here also should be reckoned, in a class by themselves, the formal Prayers, or Addresses to God, of which Solomon's Dedicatory Prayer, and the apocryphal Prayer of Manasses are the chief examples. But the department includes one work of the highest literary importance in the fifth book of the Pentateuch, called by its Greek name of *Deuteronomy*.

This book of *Deuteronomy* might have for its second title '*The Orations and Songs of Moses before his ascent of Pisgah*.' The vast historic importance of the book, from its in-

Deuteronomy as a literary work

fluence on later Biblical writers, and the difficult questions surrounding its origin, have tended to divert attention from the literary interest attaching to its contents.[1] There is, perhaps, no other work in which so much is gained by attempting to read the whole at a sitting. For this exercise some preparation should be made, in the way of separating the substance from accessories. To begin with, there are some long parenthetic

---

[1] It may be well to remind the reader that questions of literary history are excluded from the present work. The analysis of *Deuteronomy* is analysis of the book as it stands, apart from any question how it has reached its present form.

explanations, which are obviously not to be understood as part of
the speeches in which they occur: in modern phraseology they
are foot-notes, and they should be marked off.[1] Other verses
should be separated as prefaces, titles, colophons, and the like.[2]
But in addition to these brief passages there is a lengthy section
of fifteen chapters which may be understood as the 'Book
of the Covenant' that is being mentioned continually in   xii-xxvi
the speeches; however important in itself, this section should, in
such an exercise as I am describing, be taken as read, and not
allowed to disturb the succession of orations. When, with these
preparations, the whole book is reviewed at a sitting, an intense
interest is thrown upon the orations from the pathetic situation in
which they are delivered: the leader of the Hebrews in their wan-
derings alone realising that promised land from which he alone
is excluded. This thought from time to time breaks out in the
cry — "The Lord was angry with me for your sakes"; and when
not spoken in words it is none the less present as inspiration of
the passionate appeals and denunciations with which Moses seeks
to make the Covenant, of which he has been the interpreter, a
power with the people when he is no longer present to uphold it.
There is also a crescendo of interest throughout the book: narrative review, appeal, ceremonial and terrible denunciation, farewell
and personal tenderness, a climax of song, simple story of the
solemn and pathetic end. Read in any way, *Deuteronomy* reveals
its rhetoric richness; read at a single sitting, it is seen to be oratory arranged to produce all the effect of Drama.

First Oration   i. 6-iv. 40
Moses' Announcement of his Deposition

The people are indicated as gathered together in the deep hollow that makes the bed of the Jordan, on its eastern side. Moses,
standing before them, commences in the calm tone of historic sur-

---
[1] They are: ii. 10-12; ii. 20-3; iii. 9 and 11 and again 14; x. 6-9.
[2] See throughout analysis in the Literary Index.

vey. He goes to the central incident of the people's history — the giving of the law on Horeb — and tells how the first movement forward revealed the growing numbers of the people, so that he could no longer support the cumbrance and burden and strife of so vast a nation.

> The LORD, the God of your fathers, make you a thousand times so many more as ye are, and bless you, as he hath promised you!

It thus became necessary to appoint captains of hundreds and fifties and tens; and in such organised form the people passed through the great and terrible wilderness, and reached Kadesh-Barnea. There the order came to advance on the foe. But though the spies sent on to explore brought back word of a good land, yet they made the heart to melt with their tale of cities great and fenced up to heaven, and children of the Anakim : until the people forgot the Lord their leader in the wilderness. Moses reviews how the Lord's wrath brake forth at the murmuring, and he sware that none save the faithful spies should enter the land : the children and little ones should alone inherit. Here for the first time comes the sad plaint that the Lord was angry with Moses for the people's sake, and he, too, must not pass over Jordan. The history continues to tell of the presumptuous courage that went up to the battle without the Lord, and was visited with defeat and rout. Then there is the turning back to the wilderness, and the eight and thirty years wandering while all the men of war of that generation were being gradually consumed : a wandering, nevertheless, that lacked not the Lord's watchfulness.

> The LORD thy God hath blessed thee in all the work of thy hand: he hath known thy walking through this great wilderness: these forty years the LORD thy God hath been with thee, thou hast lacked nothing.

With the crossing of the brook Zered the new era begins : the dread and the fear of Israel falls upon the peoples. In vain Sihon king of Heshbon and Og king of Bashan resist : their cities are taken, their people smitten and extirpated, their land divided among the tribes that had much cattle. It now appears how these signs of Jehovah's favour to his people stirred the personal hopes of Moses.

> And I besought the LORD at that time, saying, O Lord GOD, thou hast begun to show thy servant thy greatness, and thy strong hand: for what god is there in heaven or in earth that can do according to thy works, and according to thy mighty acts? Let me go over, I pray thee, and see the good land that is beyond Jordan, that goodly mountain, and Lebanon. But the LORD was wroth with me for your sakes, and hearkened not unto me: and the LORD said unto me, Let it suffice thee; speak no more unto me of this matter. Get thee up into the top of Pisgah, and lift up thine eyes westward, and northward, and southward, and eastward, and behold with thine eyes: for thou shalt not go over this Jordan. But charge Joshua, and encourage him, and strengthen him: for he shall go over before this people.

So, then, the office of Moses is to be ended : the words he has commanded are not to be added to, nor diminished from : it remains that the people shall keep them, and this shall be their wisdom and their understanding in the sight of the peoples, for no people can have a god so nigh or statutes so wise as theirs. But they must remember the occasion of the lawgiving, and how the mountain burned with fire unto the heart of heaven, and they heard the voice but saw no form ; they must take heed lest they make the form of anything in heaven or earth, to worship it ; and lest when they behold the sun and moon and all the host of heaven their hearts be lifted up and they worship these — these which the Lord has divided unto all the peoples under the whole heaven, whereas Israel he has chosen for his own inheritance. And he will be jealous over the people with whom he has made his covenant.

> For ask now of the days that are past, which were before thee, since the day that God created man upon the earth, and from the one end of heaven unto the other, whether there hath been any such thing as this great thing is, or hath been heard like it? Did ever people hear the voice of God speaking out of the midst of the fire, as thou hast heard, and live? Or hath God assayed to go and take

him a nation from the midst of another nation, by temptations, by signs, and by wonders, and by war, and by a mighty hand, and by a stretched out arm, and by great terrors, according to all that the LORD your God did for you in Egypt before your eyes? Unto thee it was shewed that thou mightest know that the LORD he is God; there is none else beside him. Out of heaven he made thee to hear his voice, that he might instruct thee: and upon earth he made thee to see his great fire; and thou heardest his words out of the midst of the fire. And because he loved thy fathers, therefore he chose their seed after them, and brought thee out with his presence, with his great power, out of Egypt; to drive out nations from before thee greater and mightier than thou, to bring thee in, to give thee their land for an inheritance, as at this day. Know therefore this day, and lay it to thine heart, that the LORD he is God in heaven above and upon the earth beneath: there is none else. And thou shalt keep his statutes, and his commandments which I command thee this day, that it may go well with thee, and with thy children after thee, and that thou mayest prolong thy days upon the land, which the LORD thy God giveth thee, for ever.

SECOND ORATION

v. 1-xi

THE DELIVERY OF THE COVENANT TO THE LEVITES AND ELDERS

The second oration of Moses is connected with a public ceremony: the handing over the Book of the Covenant into the custody of the Levites and Elders. The scene of the preceding oration is repeated, and Moses appears, with officials grouped round him representing the Levites and Elders, holding in his hands the Covenant of the Lord, now for the first time reduced to writing. As in the former speech, he goes for a starting-point to the scene at Horeb; he recites the commandments one by one as delivered by the great Voice amid fire and darkness; and he reminds the people how they came to him with words of panic:

> We have seen this day that God doth speak with man, and he liveth. Now therefore why should we die?

Their petition was that Moses might stand in their stead before the Lord, and all that the Lord commands by him they will do. Now therefore all the separate commandments and statutes and judgments of which Moses has thus been the interpreter have been gathered into one Covenant, the book Moses holds in his hands. His task is to commend it to their obedience before they hear it read. He commences with the great Name.

> Hear, O Israel: the LORD our God is one LORD: and thou shalt love the LORD thy God with all thine heart, and with all thy soul, and with all thy might. And these words, which I command thee this day, shall be upon thine heart: and thou shalt teach them diligently unto thy children, and shalt talk of them when thou sittest in thine house, and when thou walkest by the way, and when thou liest down, and when thou risest up. And thou shalt bind them for a sign upon thine hand, and they shall be for frontlets between thine eyes. And thou shalt write them upon the doorposts of thy house, and upon thy gates. And it shall be, that when the LORD thy God shall bring thee into the land which he sware unto thy fathers, to Abraham, to Isaac, and to Jacob, to give thee; great and goodly cities, which thou buildedst not, and houses full of all good things, which thou filledst not, and cisterns hewn out, which thou hewedst not, vineyards and olive trees, which thou plantedst not, and thou shalt eat and be full; then beware lest thou forget the LORD.

On the contrary, when their children ask them in the days to come, what mean these statutes and judgments, they shall tell how they were Pharaoh's bondmen in Egypt, and how Jehovah brought them out with wonders great and sore, and gave them these commandments to keep: and it shall be their righteousness if they observe the commandments of their God.

This Covenant shall be their distinction among the nations. The Lord will cast out the nations before them: — not suddenly, lest the beasts of the field increase upon them; but by little and by little will he cast them out. They shall make no covenant with them, nor give them sons and daughters in marriage.

> For thou art an holy people unto the LORD thy God: the LORD thy God hath chosen thee to be a peculiar people unto himself, above all peoples that are upon the face of the earth. The LORD did not set his love upon you, nor choose you, because ye were more in number

than any people; for ye were the fewest of all peoples: but because the LORD loveth you, and because he would keep the oath which he sware unto your fathers, hath the LORD brought you out with a mighty hand, and redeemed you out of the house of bondage.

The orator turns to the past to find ground for emphasising the keeping of the Covenant.

Thou shalt remember all the way which the LORD thy God hath led thee these forty years in the wilderness, that he might humble thee, to prove thee, to know what was in thine heart, whether thou wouldest keep his commandments, or no. And he humbled thee, and suffered thee to hunger, and fed thee with manna, which thou knewest not, neither did thy fathers know; that he might make thee know that man doth not live by bread only, but by everything that proceedeth out of the mouth of the LORD doth man live. Thy raiment waxed not old upon thee, neither did thy foot swell, these forty years. And thou shalt consider in thine heart, that, as a man chasteneth his son, so the LORD thy God chasteneth thee. And thou shalt keep the commandments of the LORD thy God, to walk in his ways, and to fear him. For the LORD thy God bringeth thee into a good land, a land of brooks of water, of fountains and depths, springing forth in valleys and hills; a land of wheat and barley, and vines and fig trees and pomegranates; a land of oil olives and honey; a land wherein thou shalt eat bread without scarceness, thou shalt not lack anything in it; a land whose stones are iron and out of whose hills thou mayest dig brass. And thou shalt eat and be full, and thou shalt bless the LORD thy God for the good land which he hath given thee. Beware lest thou forget the LORD thy God, in not keeping his commandments, and his judgements, and his statutes, which I command thee this day: lest when thou hast eaten and art full, and hast built goodly houses, and dwelt therein; and when thy herds and thy flocks multiply, and thy silver and thy gold is multiplied, and all that thou hast is multiplied; then thine heart be lifted up, and thou forget the LORD thy God, which brought thee forth out of the land of Egypt, out of the house of bondage; who led thee through the great and terrible wilderness, wherein were fiery serpents and scorpions, and thirsty ground where was no water; who brought thee forth water out of the rock of flint; who fed thee in the wilderness with manna, which thy fathers knew not; that he might humble thee and that he might prove thee, to do thee good at thy latter end:

and thou say in thine heart, My power and the might of mine hand hath gotten me this wealth. But thou shalt remember the LORD thy God, for it is he that giveth thee power to get wealth; that he may establish his covenant which he sware unto thy fathers, as at this day.

Moses turns to the future. They are this day to pass over Jordan, and soon they will see the nations, even the tall sons of Anak, going down before them. But let them beware lest they say in their heart: "For my righteousness hath the Lord brought me into the land." Not for their righteousness, but for the wickedness of them that dwell in the land. Not for their righteousness, for they have been ever a stiff-necked generation: and the orator gathers into one single view all the outbreaks of rebellion and sin which had marred the history of the people in the wilderness. Yet why this rebellious spirit?

What doth the LORD thy God require of thee, but to fear the LORD thy God, to walk in all his ways, and to love him, and to serve the LORD thy God with all thy heart and with all thy soul, to keep the commandments of the LORD, and his statutes, which I command thee this day for thy good? Behold, unto the LORD thy God belongeth the heaven, and the heaven of heavens, the earth, with all that therein is. Only the LORD had a delight in thy fathers to love them, and he chose their seed after them, even you above all peoples, as at this day.

Moses speaks, not to children which have not known, but to those who have seen all the works of the Lord done upon Egypt, and how the LORD their God is God of gods, and Lord of lords, the great God, the mighty, the terrible. Let them therefore circumcise their hearts, and so go over and possess the good land.

For the land, whither thou goest in to possess it, is not as the land of Egypt, from whence ye came out, where thou sowedst thy seed, and wateredst it with thy foot, as a garden of herbs; but the land, whither ye go over to possess it, is a land of hills and valleys, and drinketh water of the rain of heaven: a land which the LORD thy God careth for; the eyes of the LORD thy God are always upon it, from the beginning of the year even unto the end of the year.

If, then, the people keep faithfully the Covenant of the Lord, he will give them the rain in its season, the former rain and the latter rain, and the land shall yield her increase; but if they turn aside and serve other gods, the heavens shall be shut up, and the land shall not yield her fruit, and they shall perish quickly from off the good land their God has given them.

> Therefore shall ye lay up these my words in your heart and in your soul; and ye shall bind them for a sign upon your hand, and they shall be for frontlets between your eyes. And ye shall teach them your children, talking of them, when thou sittest in thine house, and when thou walkest by the way, and when thou liest down, and when thou risest up. And thou shalt write them upon the doorposts of thine house, and upon thy gates; that your days may be multiplied, and the days of your children, upon the land which the LORD sware unto your fathers to give them, as the days of the heavens above the earth.

Fresh promises follow of rewards for faithfulness: nations greater and mightier than themselves driven out before them, a border from the wilderness to Lebanon, from the hinder sea to the river Euphrates,—every place where the sole of their foot shall tread shall be theirs. In conclusion Moses refers to the blessing and the curse, which are to be the sanctions of the Covenant; and then must have come the time when he would hand over the Book of the Covenant in the eyes of the whole nation, to the Levites and Elders around him, to be read by them before the people on that day and many a day afterwards.

xxviii   THIRD ORATION
       AT THE REHEARSAL OF THE BLESSING AND THE CURSE

When the fifteen chapters containing the Book of the Covenant are concluded, a succession of paragraphs follow which need close attention. First we have an ordinance formally appointing the Ceremonial of the Blessing and Curse; and this is a provision for the future, since the places designated — Mounts

xxvii. 1-8

Ebal and Gerizim—are on the other side of Jordan. Next follow two verses in which it is said that Moses and the priests the Levites *spake* unto all Israel, to the effect that they had that day become the Lord's people, and must keep his commandments. Then verses describe how Moses "charged the people the same day," the point of the charge being the division of the tribes—six for the mountain of the Curse, and six for the mountain of the Blessing; the description brings out the antiphonal character of the ceremony, the Levites speaking, and the people responding with an Amen. Then follow the Curses in this full ritual form. But, instead of a similar series of Blessings, we find the matter of the Blessings put in oratorical language, which oratorical language continues into the matter of the Curses. The only way of satisfactorily interpreting such a succession of paragraphs is to suppose a *Rehearsal* of the Ceremony, the tribes being stationed upon opposite slopes in some spot resembling the mountains of Ebal and Gerizim; and, when the ceremony has proceeded as far as the conclusion of the Curses, Moses—since it is only a rehearsal—interrupts it, and takes the whole into his own hands. This gives us the third oration.

9-10

11-14

15-26

xxviii

Moses describes how, if the people observe the commandments of their God, they shall be blessed in city and in field, in the fruit of their body and the fruit of their ground and their cattle, in basket, in kneading-trough, when they come in and when they go out, and in all that they do.

> The LORD shall open unto thee his good treasury the heaven to give the rain of thy land in its season, and to bless all the work of thine hand: and thou shalt lend unto many nations, and thou shalt not borrow. And the LORD shall make thee the head, and not the tail; and thou shalt be above only, and thou shalt not be beneath; if thou shalt hearken unto the commandments of the LORD thy God.

But if the people shall not hearken unto the voice of the Lord their God, then curses shall come upon them and overtake them: curses in city and field, in basket and kneading-trough, in the fruit of body and of cattle and of field, curses when they come in and when they go out. Discomfiture and rebuke, consumption, fever, inflammation, fiery heat, the sword, blasting mildew, shall pursue them until they perish.

> And thy heaven that is over thy head shall be brass, and the earth that is under thee shall be iron. The LORD shall make the rain of thy land powder and dust: from heaven shall it come down upon thee, until thou be destroyed. The LORD shall cause thee to be smitten before thine enemies: thou shalt go out one way against them, and shalt flee seven ways before them: and thou shalt be tossed to and fro among the kingdoms of the earth.

There shall be madness, and blindness, and astonishment of heart; groping at noontide as the blind gropeth in darkness; sons and daughters shall be borne into captivity, and the eyes of parents shall look and fail with longing for them all the day; but there shall be nought in the power of their hand; for they shall be only oppressed, and crushed alway, and they shall be mad for the sight of their eyes which they shall see.

> Thou shalt carry much seed out into the field, and shalt gather little in; for the locust shall consume it. Thou shalt plant vineyards and dress them, but thou shalt neither drink of the wine nor gather the grapes; for the worm shall eat them. Thou shalt have olive trees throughout all thy borders, but thou shalt not anoint thyself with the oil; for thine olive shall cast its fruit. Thou shalt beget sons and daughters, but they shall not be thine; for they shall go into captivity.

The stranger in their midst shall mount higher and higher as they go down lower and lower: and all because they have not hearkened unto the voice of their God.

> Because thou servedst not the LORD thy God with joyfulness, and with gladness of heart, by reason of the abundance of all things: therefore shalt thou serve thine enemies which the LORD shall send against thee, in hunger, and in thirst, and in nakedness, and in want of all things: and he shall put a yoke of iron upon thy neck, until he have destroyed thee. The LORD shall bring a nation against thee from far, from the end of the earth, as the eagle flieth; a nation

whose tongue thou shalt not understand; a nation of fierce countenance, which shall not regard the person of the old, nor shew favour to the young: and he shall eat the fruit of thy cattle, and the fruit of thy ground, until thou be destroyed: which also shall not leave thee corn, wine, or oil, the increase of thy kine, or the young of thy flock, until he have caused thee to perish. And he shall besiege thee in all thy gates, until thy high and fenced walls come down, wherein thou trustedst, throughout all thy land: and he shall besiege thee in all thy gates throughout all thy land, which the LORD thy God hath given thee. And thou shalt eat the fruit of thine own body, the flesh of thy sons and of thy daughters which the LORD thy God hath given thee; in the siege and in the straitness, wherewith thine enemies shall straiten thee. The man that is tender among you, and very delicate, his eye shall be evil toward his brother, and toward the wife of his bosom, and toward the remnant of his children which he hath remaining: so that he will not give to any of them of the flesh of his children whom he shall eat, because he hath nothing left him; in the siege and in the straitness, wherewith thine enemy shall straiten thee in all thy gates. The tender and delicate woman among you, which would not adventure to set the sole of her foot upon the ground for delicateness and tenderness, her eye shall be evil toward the husband of her bosom, and toward her son, and toward her daughter; and toward her young one that cometh out from between her feet, and toward her children which she shall bear; for she shall eat them for want of all things secretly: in the siege and in the straitness, wherewith thine enemy shall straiten thee in thy gates.

If thou wilt not observe to do all the words of this law that are written in this book, that thou mayest fear this glorious and fearful name, THE LORD THY GOD; then the LORD will make thy plagues wonderful, and the plagues of thy seed, even great plagues, and of long continuance, and sore sicknesses, and of long continuance. And he will bring upon thee again all the diseases of Egypt, which thou wast afraid of; and they shall cleave unto thee. Also every sickness, and every plague, which is not written in the book of this law, them will the LORD bring upon thee, until thou be destroyed. And ye shall be left few in number, whereas ye were as the stars of heaven for multitude; because thou didst not hearken unto the voice of the LORD thy God. And it shall come to pass, that as the LORD rejoiced over you to do you good, and to multiply you; so the LORD will rejoice over you to cause you to perish, and to destroy you; and

> ye shall be plucked from off the land whither thou goest in to possess it. And the LORD shall scatter thee among all peoples, from the one end of the earth even unto the other end of the earth; and there thou shalt serve other gods, which thou hast not known, thou nor thy fathers, even wood and stone. And among these nations shalt thou find no ease, and there shall be no rest for the sole of thy foot: but the LORD shall give thee there a trembling heart, and failing of eyes, and pining of soul: and thy life shall hang in doubt before thee; and thou shalt fear night and day, and shalt have none assurance of thy life: in the morning thou shalt say, Would God it were even! and at even thou shalt say, Would God it were morning! for the fear of thine heart which thou shalt fear, and for the sight of thine eyes which thou shalt see. And the LORD shall bring thee into Egypt again with ships, by the way whereof I said unto thee, Thou shalt see it no more again: and there ye shall sell yourselves unto your enemies for bondmen and for bondwomen, and no man shall buy you.

xxix-xxxi. 8

FOURTH ORATION
THE COVENANT IN THE LAND OF MOAB

The fourth oration has this title in the text, although the scene appears to be the same. After a brief historic survey, Moses seems to review the different classes of people standing before him.

> Ye stand this day all of you before the LORD your God; your heads, your tribes, your elders, and your officers, even all the men of Israel, your little ones, your wives, and thy stranger that is in the midst of thy camps, from the hewer of thy wood unto the drawer of thy water: that thou shouldest enter into the covenant of the LORD thy God.

We are thus led to the special point of this day's speech. It is personal, as distinct from national religion. Moses fears lest there may be some man or woman, or some family or tribe, who may nourish idolatry in their hearts, and think to escape in the general righteousness;—

> lest there should be among you a root that beareth gall and wormwood; and it come to pass, when he heareth the words of this curse, that he bless himself in his heart, saying, I shall have peace, though I walk in the stubbornness of mine heart.

Moses declares that God will separate that man or that woman unto evil out of all the tribes of Israel, to bring upon him all the curses of the Covenant. As for such a tribe or family: the stranger from a far land, the children of the days to come, shall wonder to see the plagues of its land, and how it is brimstone, and salt, and a burning, like the ruin of Sodom, and they shall ask, Wherefore hath the Lord donĕ thus unto this land? And they shall say, Because they forsook the covenant of the Lord, the God of their fathers. The secret things of the sin belong unto the Lord our God; but the judgment when it is revealed will belong to us and to our children for ever.[1]

But Moses has additional words of mercy to speak, as well as of judgment. When all these things are come upon them, the blessing and the curse, and they call them to mind among all the nations whither they have been driven, then if they turn with all their heart unto the Lord he will turn their captivity, and gather their outcasts from the uttermost parts of heaven, and bring them again into the land of their fathers, and do them good, and put these curses upon their enemies: if only they turn unto the Lord with all their heart and with all their soul.

> For this commandment which I command thee this day, it is not too hard for thee, neither is it far off. It is not in heaven, that thou shouldest say, Who shall go up for us to heaven, and bring it unto us, and make us to hear it, that we may do it? Neither is it beyond the sea, that thou shouldest say, Who shall go over the sea for us, and bring it unto us, and make us to hear it, that we may do it? But the word is very nigh unto thee, in thy mouth, and in thy heart, that thou mayest do it.

The Leader of the people thus reaches the point of his final appeal. He calls heaven and earth to witness against them this day, that he has set before them life and death, the blessing and the curse. Therefore, he cries to them,

---

[1] This is the only point where the argument of the orations is at all difficult. The line of thought is given by verse 18 (of chapter xxix): the distinction of (*a*) man or woman, (*b*) family or tribe; then verses 20–21 follow the judgment on (*a*), verses 22–28 the judgment on (*b*).

Choose life, that thou mayest live, thou and thy seed: to love the
LORD thy God, to obey his voice, and to cleave unto him: for he is
thy life, and the length of thy days: that thou mayest dwell in the
land which the LORD sware unto thy fathers, to Abraham, to Isaac,
and to Jacob, to give them.

There remains the personal farewell. Moses tells how he is that day an hundred and twenty years old; and the mystic strength that had supported the people in the wilderness, so that their feet swelled not these forty years, is no longer vouchsafed to their leader: "I can no more go out and come in." And the Lord has said to him that he shall not go over Jordan. But while physical strength is failing, the words on the old man's lips are of strength and courage: a worn-out leader puts courage into the nation before him, and into Joshua, whom he installs as leader in his place. Thus with his cry of "Be strong, and of good courage," and "The Lord shall go before you," Moses retires from his office of leader, and leaves Joshua in his place.

The orations of Moses are concluded: but not yet his words. That very day, as he is presenting himself with Joshua his successor in the Tent of Meeting, the call comes to put his message to the people in the form of Song. His doctrine shall drop as the rain, his speech distil as the dew, while he sings of Jehovah the Rock, the God of faithfulness. When the nations were divided, Israel was retained by the Creator for himself.

Moses' Song xxxii. 1-43

> For the LORD's portion is his people:
> Jacob is the lot of his inheritance.
> He found him in a desert land,
> And in the waste howling wilderness.
> He compassed him about, he cared for him,
> He kept him as the apple of his eye:
> As an eagle that stirreth up her nest,
> That fluttereth over her young,
> He spread abroad his wings, he took them,
> He bare them on his pinions:

> The LORD alone did lead him,
> And there was no strange god with him.
> He made him ride on the high places of the earth,
> And he did eat the increase of the field;
> And he made him to suck honey out of the rock,
> And oil out of the flinty rock;
> Butter of kine, and milk of sheep,
> With fat of lambs,
> And rams of the breed of Bashan, and goats,
> With the fat of kidneys of wheat;
> And of the blood of the grape thou drankest wine.

The joyousness of the song clouds over, as it tells how Jeshurun waxed fat and kicked, and moved the Lord to jealousy with new gods, that came up but yesterday, whom their fathers did not know. The fire of Divine anger burns as from the lowest pit, devouring the increase of the earth. Visions of mischiefs heaped upon the faithless people pass before us, of arrows spent upon them, wasting hunger, burning heat, teeth of beasts, poison of crawling things, without the Sword bereaving and terrors within: only short of entire destruction does the judgment stop, lest the adversary should misdeem, and think that their hand, and not Jehovah's wrath, had done all. And how blind and void of wisdom must the nation be not to see the meaning of it all, and that their Rock has forsaken them!

> For their rock is not as our Rock,
> Even our enemies themselves being judges.

And the imagery flows forth to paint the loathly gods to which Israel has given preference — things of rottenness like grapes of Sodom, bitter as clusters of gall, poisonous as wine of dragons: — until, by a bold transition, the description is made to produce revulsion in the mind of God himself. He thinks with complacency of vengeance yet stored among his treasures, that he may use once more on his people's side: waiting till their strength is exhausted, and their last hope gone, and then raising himself in wrath to scorn their helpless idols, and recompense vengeance to their adversaries. And so with the joy of Jehovah returned to his fallen people, this Song of the Rock of Israel concludes.

Then the end comes. The whole people understand it, and all are waiting to see their Leader set out on the mystic journey on which none may accompany him. Heads of the tribes stand out from the masses of the people and line the route by which Moses must pass. The first sight of the whole nation, which he has ruled so long, seems to kindle in Moses a vision, which reaches us only dimly, in his words of Jehovah coming forth from amidst his holy ones, a fiery law at his right hand, the holy ones of the peoples sitting at his feet. Then, passing along the leaders of the tribes, he speaks last words to each: stirring words of past battle cries, or pregnant sayings destined to be watchwords in the future. Reuben, his men never few. Judah, sufficient of his hands. Levi—

The Passing of Moses. xxxii. 48-xxxiv

> Who said of his father, and of his mother,
>   I have not seen him;
> Neither did he acknowledge his brethren,
> Nor knew his own children,

when he took sides with Jehovah at the waters of strife. Benjamin, beloved of the Lord, who dwelleth between his shoulders. Blessings on the princely Joseph.

> Blessed of the LORD be his land:
> For the precious things of heaven, for the dew,
> And for the deep that coucheth beneath,
> And for the precious things of the fruits of the sun,
> And for the precious things of the growth of the moons,
> And for the chief things of the ancient mountains,
> And for the precious things of the everlasting hills,
> And for the precious things of the earth and the fulness thereof,
> And the good will of him that dwelt in the bush.

Zebulun, blessed in his going out over the seas, and Issachar in his tent life at home. Naphtali, with the blessings of the western sea and the sunny south; Asher, dipping his foot in the oil of his own vineyards, shod with the iron and brass of his mines. The whole line of the tribes past, Moses lifts hands and voice in the final blessing.

> There is none like unto God, O Jeshurun,
> Who rideth upon the heaven for thy help,
> And in his excellency on the skies.
> The eternal God is thy dwelling-place,
> And underneath are the everlasting arms.

From the height of lyric song we drop to simple, bare prose: fittest of forms to convey the solitary journey from which there is to be no return; the going up to the top of Pisgah, the long gaze over the land of promise; the lonely death; the burial in the sepulchre that no man knoweth. So the days of weeping in the mourning for Moses were ended.

APPENDICES

		PAGE
I. LITERARY INDEX TO THE BIBLE	.	. 465
II. TABLES OF LITERARY FORMS . . .		. 499
III. ON THE STRUCTURAL PRINTING OF SCRIPTURE	.	. 512
IV. USE OF THE DIGRESSION IN 'WISDOM' .	.	. 521
GENERAL INDEX	. . .	. 527

APPENDIX I

LITERARY INDEX TO THE BIBLE

In this first Appendix the whole Bible, and the more important parts of the Apocrypha, are divided up into the separate literary compositions of which they are composed. The form of each composition is indicated, and, in cases that admit of it, a suitable title is suggested. The arrangement follows the order in which the books of the Bible stand; the Appendix will therefore serve as a guide to Bible reading where it is desired to read from the literary point of view.

Reference figures (in brackets) are added to previous pages in which particular compositions have been discussed. The Appendix will therefore serve also as an Index to the present work.

It is suggested to the student to mark with pencil in his copy of the Revised Version the divisions and titles here suggested, or to make divisions and titles of his own. It is an immense help to literary appreciation to have the form of a piece of literature conveyed directly to the eye (as is done by the printer in all books except the Bible), instead of having to collect the form by inference while reading.

GENESIS

History Part I: Formation of the Chosen Nation.—Primitive History

Deals with the period preceding the appearance of the Chosen People as a Nation. An Historic Framework enclosing Epic Incidents (244).

i–xi	First Beginnings of the World
xii–l	The Patriarchal Succession

Merged in this History, yet separable for literary purposes, are various forms of Epic.[1]

EPIC STORIES

i–ii. 3	The Creation
ii. 4–iii	The Temptation in the Garden of Eden
iv. 1–15	Cain and Abel
vi. 9–ix. 17	The Flood

EPIC CYCLES

OF ABRAHAM.— *Call of Abraham (xii. 1–9)* — *Sarai and Pharaoh (xii. 10–20)* — *The Parting of Abraham and Lot, and the Raid on Sodom (xiii–xiv)* — *Sarai, Hagar, and the Promised Seed (xv–xvii)* — *The Judgment on Sodom (xviii–xix. 28)* — *Abimelech and Sarah (xx)* — *Birth of Isaac and casting off of Ishmael (xxi. 1–21)* — *Offering of Isaac (xxii. 1–19)* — *Burial of Sarah (xxiii)* — *Wooing of Rebekah (xxiv)*

OF ISAAC.— *Birth of Isaac and casting off of Ishmael (xxi. 1–21)* — *Offering of Isaac (xxii. 1–19)* — *Burial of Sarah (xxiii)* — *Wooing of Rebekah (xxiv)*

OF JACOB.— *Guileful obtaining of Isaac's blessing (xxvii. 1–40)* — *Flight of Jacob (xxvii. 41–xxviii)* — *How Jacob served under Laban (xxix–xxxii. 2)* — *Meeting of Jacob and Esau (xxxii. 3–xxxiii)* — *Blessing and Death of Jacob (xlvii. 28–l)*

EPIC HISTORY

xxxvii. 2–36 continued xxxix. i–xlvi. 7 and xlvi. 28–xlvii. 12	Joseph and his Brethren (232)

---

[1] The reader is warned against the common mistake of confusing Epic with Fiction. (Above, page 221.)

EXODUS, LEVITICUS, NUMBERS

History Part II: Migration of the Chosen Nation to the Land of Promise. — Constitutional History

Deals with the Chosen Nation up to their arrival at the Land of Promise. Successive Revelations of Law, and Incidents associated with these (245).

Exod. i–xviii	Slavery in Egypt, Deliverance, and Journey to Sinai
Exod. from xix and Leviticus	Constitution of the Nation at Sinai
Numbers	The March from Sinai and the Thirty-eight Years' Wandering

Merged in this History, but separable for literary purposes, are various forms of Epic.

EPIC HISTORY

Exodus i. 8–vi. 13 continued vi. 28–xi and xii. 21–39 and xiii. 17–xv. 21	*Moses and the Plagues of Egypt*

MIXED EPIC

Numb. xxii–xxiv	*The Story of Balaam (224 and 345 note)*

DEUTERONOMY

OR

The Orations and Songs of Moses

An Historic Framework enclosing the Farewell Orations and Songs of Moses. (Fully analysed above, Chapter XX.) *Portions described in italics may be omitted in the exercise of taking in Deuteronomy at a single sitting.*[1]

i. 1–2	*Title page to the whole book*
3–5	*Preface to the First Oration*
i. 6–iv. 40	First Oration: Moses' Announcement of his Deposition

[1] Several passages (i. 2; ii. 10–12; ii. 20–3; iii. 9, 11, 14; x. 6–9) should be marked off from the orations as 'explanatory footnotes.'

iv. 41-3	Editorial Note connecting the first and second Orations
44-9	Preface to the Second Oration
v. 1-xi. 32	Second Oration: The Delivery of the Covenant to the Levites and Elders
xii-xxvi	The Book of the Covenant
xxvii. 1-8	Ordinance appointing the Ceremony of the Blessing and the Curse
9-26	Rehearsal of the Ceremony (see page 452) interrupted by
xxviii	Third Oration: At the Rehearsal of the Blessing and the Curse
xxix. 1	Preface to the Fourth Oration
xxix. 2-xxxi. 8	Fourth Oration: The Covenant in the Land of Moab
xxxi. 9-13	Editorial Note: Arrangements for the regular reading of the Covenant
xxxi. 14-30	Preface to the Song of Moses
xxxii. 1-43	The Song of Moses: Jehovah our Rock
xxxii. 44-7	Colophon to the Song of Moses
xxxii. 48-xxxiii. 1	Preface to the Last Words of Moses
xxxiii. 2-29	The Last Words of Moses [2-3 and 26-9 General; 4-25 Blessings on particular tribes, a Document incorporated, of which 4-5 is the title]
xxxiv	Editorial Conclusion: The Passing of Moses

JOSHUA, JUDGES, RUTH, I SAMUEL

History Part III: The Chosen Nation in its Efforts towards Secular Government. — Incidental History

Deals with the Conquest of the Promised Land and Tentative Approach to Secular Government. Epic matter with connecting Historic Framework (246).

Joshua	Conquest of Canaan, including [xiii-xxii] Division of the Land
Judges	Sporadic attempts at secular government: including [viii. 22 and ix] first idea of secular kingship
I Samuel	Gradual establishment of secular kingship and rise of Prophets to represent the Theocracy

JOSHUA—I SAMUEL

The main interest in this group of books is the Epic element, to which the rest serves as connecting matter.

EPIC STORIES

Judges iii. 12–30	Ehud's Assassination of Eglon
iv–v	War of Deborah and Barak against Sisera
vi–viii. 28	Gideon and the Midianites
viii. 29–ix	Crowning of Abimelech by the Men of Shechem
x. 6–xii. 6	Jephthah and the Ammonites
xvii–xviii	Micah's Images and the Danish Migration
xix–xxi	The Benjamite War

EPIC CYCLES

OF JOSHUA.— *The Spies and the Woman of Jericho (ii) — The Passage of the Jordan (iii–iv) — The Siege of Jericho (v. 13–vi) — Siege of Ai and Sin of Achan (vii–viii. 29) — Embassy of the Gibeonites (ix) — League of the Five Kings (x. 1–27) — Joshua's Farewell (xxiii–xxiv)*

OF SAMSON.— *Birth of Samson (Judges xiii. 2–25) — Samson and the Woman of Timnah (xiv–xv. 8) — The Jawbone of an Ass (xv. 9–20) — The Gates of Gaza (xvi. 1–3) — Samson and Delilah (xvi. 4–22) — Death of Samson (xvi. 23–31)*

OF SAMUEL.— *Birth of Samuel (I Sam. i–ii. 11) — Call of Samuel and Dooming of Eli (ii. 12–iv) — The Ark and the Philistines (v–vii. 1) — The Anointing of Saul and the Retirement of Samuel (viii–xii) — The Anointing of David (xvi. 1–13) — The Witch of Endor (xxviii. 3–25)*

OF SAUL.— *The Anointing of Saul and the Retirement of Samuel (I Sam. viii–xii) — The Raid on Michmash (xiii. 15–xiv. 46) — War with the Amalekites and Breach between Samuel and Saul (xv) — The Witch of Endor (xxviii. 3–25)*

EPIC HISTORIES

Ruth	The Story of Ruth: An Idyl (235–8)
I Samuel xvi. 14 to xxviii. 2 continued xxix to II Samuel i	The Feud of Saul and David

II SAMUEL, I AND II KINGS

History Part IV: The Chosen Nation under a Secular Government and a Theocracy side by side. — Regular History

Deals with the period from the Settlement of the Monarchy to the Captivity. Systematic account of successive reigns (247).

II Samuel ii to I Kings xi	Reigns of David and Solomon
I Kings xii to II Kings xvii	Kingdoms of Judah and Israel side by side
II Kings from xviii	Kingdom of Judah and its Captivity

Merged in this History, yet separable for literary purposes, are various forms of Epic, especially Epic Prophecy.

EPIC HISTORY

II Sam. xiii–xx	*The Feud between David's Sons and the Revolt of Absalom*

PROPHETIC STORIES

II Samuel xi. 2 to xii. 25	*Nathan, David, and Bathsheba*
xxiv	*Gad and the Numbering of the People*
I Kings xiii. 1–32	*The Man of God and the Old Prophet of Bethel*
xiv. 1–18	*Ahijah and the Wife of Jeroboam*
xx. 35–43	*The Son of the Prophet and Ahab*
xxii. 1–40	*Micaiah and the Battle of Ramoth-gilead*

PROPHETIC CYCLE

OF ELISHA. — *Elisha's Parting from Elijah (II Kings ii. 1–18) — The Healing of the Waters (ii. 19–22) — The Mocking Children (ii. 23–5) — The Water Trenches (iii. 4–27) — The Vessels of Oil (iv. 1–7) — The Shunammite Woman (iv. 8–37) — Death in the Pot (iv. 38–41) — The Feeding of the Hundred Men (iv. 42–4) — The Healing of Naaman and Leprosy of Gehazi (v) — The Axe-head that swam (vi. 1–7) — The Expedition to arrest Elisha (vi. 8–23) — The Siege of Samaria (vi. 24–vii. 20) — The Shunammite Woman's Estate (viii. 1–6) — Hazael's Visit to Elisha (viii. 7–15) — Death of Elisha (xiii. 14–21)*

CHRONICLES—JOB 471

	PROPHETIC EPIC
I Kings xvii–xix continued xxi and II Kings i–ii. 18	The History of Elijah the Tishbite

CHRONICLES, EZRA, NEHEMIAH

History Part V : The Chosen Nation as a Church. — Ecclesiastical History

A compilation of Historical Excerpts, Memoirs, Documents, etc., all bearing upon the Ecclesiastical Organisation of the Nation as restored after the Exile (248).

I Chr.–II Chr. ix	Reigns of David and Solomon
II Chr. from x	Kingdom of Judah to its Captivity
Ezra i–vi	The Return under Zerubbabel, and Building of the Temple
vii–x	The Return of Ezra
Neh. i–vii	The Return of Nehemiah and Building of the Walls
viii–x	The Covenant under Ezra and Nehemiah
xi–xiii	Miscellaneous Memoirs of the Return

ESTHER

An Epic History (230).

JOB

A Dramatic Parable in a Frame of Epic Story

Fully analysed in the Introduction, above, pages 3–41.

i–ii	*The Story Opens*
	The Dramatic Parable
iii	Act I : Job's Curse
iv–xiv	Act II : First Cycle of Speeches
xv–xxi	Act III : Second Cycle of Speeches

xxii–xxx	Act IV: Third Cycle of Speeches[1]
xxxi	Act V: Job's Vindication
xxxii–xxxvii	Act VI: Interposition of Elihu
xxxviii–xlii. 6	Act VII: The Divine Intervention
xlii from 7	*The Story Closes*

[1] In the third cycle the speeches need re-arrangement, by the transference of three verses (2-4 of Chapter xxvi) to the commencement of the next chapter, and the consequent alterations of headings to speeches.

Then answered Eliphaz the Temanite, and said—
Chapter xxii

Then Job answered and said—
Chapters xxiii, xxiv

Then answered Bildad the Shuhite, and said—
Chapter xxv, continued in xxvi. 5-14

Then Job answered and said—
Chapter xxvi. 2-4, continued in xxvii. 2-6

Then answered Zophar the Naamathite, and said—
Chapter xxvii. 7 to end of Chapter xxviii

Then Job answered and said—
Chapters xxix, xxx

This conjectural re-arrangement of the speeches is based on the following consideration:

1. The utmost caution should be exercised in accepting conjectural emendations affecting the sense of a passage; but the same principle does not apply to changes in the arrangement of speeches, especially as the sacred books have passed through centuries in which the principles of parallelism were lost.

2. All critics recognise the difficulty of the text as it stands between Chapters xxvi and xxviii (inclusive), which has the effect of making Job take up a position antagonistic to his former contention and to his subsequent words: and some commentators resort to violent explanations, such as prolonged irony, etc.

3. The most marked feature of literary style in the book is its extreme parallelism; this makes it most improbable that the third colloquy should be imperfect, by the omission of a speech from Zophar, and a reply to him from Job. Moreover the change in the introductory formulæ when Chapters xxvii and xxix are reached — viz. *And Job again took up his parable and said* instead of the usual *Job answered and said* — is very suspicious.

4. The conjecture here adopted is substantially that of Grätz, which is to a large extent the same as Cheyne's. Some eminent critics (*e.g.* Davidson, Driver) are deterred from seeking a third speech for Zophar by the shortness of Bildad's third speech (xxv), which they take as an indication that the controversy is becoming exhausted. But the present conjecture lengthens Bildad's speech and removes this objection.

THE PSALMS

A Collection of Lyrics in Five Books

Compare above, Chapters V–VII generally

Book I

i	The Meditative and the Worldly Life (192)
ii	Ode: The Messiah (150)
iii	A Dramatic Lyric (179)
iv	A Liturgy of Devotion (168)
v	Of Consecration: A Meditation
vi	A Dramatic Lyric (177)
vii	A Liturgy of Judgment (168)
viii	Man the Viceroy of God (70, 185)
ix–x	A Dramatic Lyric, with double change (182 note).—Acrostic
xi	Trust: A Meditation
xii	A Dramatic Lyric
xiii	Judgment: A Meditation
xiv = liii	A Rhapsodic Meditation on Judgment (184)
xv = xxiv. 1–6	The Devout Life (101)
xvi	Trust: A Meditation
xvii	Judgment: A Meditation
xviii	Ode: David's Song of Deliverance (83)
xix	The Heavens above and the Law within (91–8)
xx	(Antiphonal) Benediction on the King
xxi	Benediction on the King
xxii	A Dramatic Lyric (178)
xxiii	Jehovah's Follower (187)
xxiv	Anthems for the Inauguration of Jerusalem (100, 154)
xxv	Liturgy of Devotion.— Acrostic
xxvi	Consecration: A Meditation
xxvii	A Dramatic Lyric, with double change (180, 186)
xxviii	A Dramatic Lyric
xxix	Ode: The Thunderstorm (147)
xxx	Anthem for the Inauguration of Jerusalem (154)
xxxi	A Dramatic Lyric (duplicated: page 182 note)
xxxii	A Monody of Experience

xxxiii	Festal Hymn
xxxiv	A Liturgy of Thanksgiving (167)
xxxv	An Elegy of Denunciation (159)
xxxvi	The Supreme Evil and the Supreme Good (97)
xxxvii	Judgment: A Meditation. — Acrostic
xxxviii	A Monody of Experience
xxxix	A Monody of Experience. — With refrain
xl (including lxx)	A Liturgy
xli	A Monody of Experience

Book II

xlii–xliii	Exile Song (63). — With refrain
xliv	An Elegy
xlv	Marriage Hymn
xlvi	Occasional: Deliverance from Sennacherib (154, 57). — With refrain
xlvii	Accession Hymn
xlviii	Occasional: Victory over Sennacherib (153)
xlix	Man that is in Honour: A Parable. — With refrain
l	Ode: On Judgment (150)
li	Penitence: A Meditation (94–5, 184 note)
lii	An Elegy of Denunciation
liii	See xiv
liv	A Dramatic Lyric
lv	An Elegy of Denunciation
lvi	A Dramatic Lyric. — With refrain
lvii	A Dramatic Lyric (179). — With refrain
lviii	An Elegy of Denunciation (189 note)
lix	A War Ballad. — With double refrain
lx (with cviii)	Occasional: Hymn of Defeat and Victory (181 note)
lxi	Exile Song
lxii	Liturgy of Devotion (167). — With refrain
lxiii	Exile Song
lxiv	Judgment: A Meditation
lxv	A Liturgy of Praise (164)
lxvi	Votive Hymn
lxvii	Festal Hymn — With refrain
lxviii	Processional Ode (144)
lxix	A Dramatic Lyric, with transition stage (183 note 2)

lxx (see xl)	Elegy of Denunciation
lxxi	A Dramatic Lyric
lxxii	Encomium: On the King

Book III

lxxiii	The Mystery of Prosperous Wickedness
lxxiv	An Elegy (158)
lxxv	A Song of Judgment
lxxvi	Occasional: Deliverance from Sennacherib (153)
lxxvii	A Monody of Experience (175)
lxxviii	National Anthem: Of the Kingdom of Judah (139, 143)
lxxix	An Elegy
lxxx	An Elegy (158). — With refrain
lxxxi	Festal Hymn
lxxxii	Elegy of Denunciation (188)
lxxxiii	Elegy of Denunciation
lxxxiv	A Song of God's House (185)
lxxxv	A Dramatic Lyric, with double change and transition stage (182)
lxxxvi	A Liturgy of Supplication (169)
lxxxvii	Salutation to Zion (159)
lxxxviii	An Elegy
lxxxix	Ode: On the Covenant (149)

Book IV

xc	Life as a Passing Day (189)
xci	The Shadow of the Almighty
xcii	Votive Hymn
xciii	Accession Hymn (161)
xciv	A Liturgy of Judgment (167)
xcv-c	Accession Hymns. — (For xcix see page 61)
ci	Anthem for the Inauguration of Jerusalem (155)
cii	An Elegy
{ ciii	The World Within and
{ civ	The World Without (150–3)
cv	National Anthem: Of the Undivided Nation in Canaan (142–3)
cvi	National Anthem: For the Captivity (142–3)

476 LITERARY INDEX TO THE BIBLE

Book V

cvii	Ode: Of the Redeemed (65, 148). — With double refrain
cviii (see lx)	A Dramatic Lyric, with double change
cix	An Elegy of Denunciation (159)
cx	Encomium: On the Ideal King
cxi–cxii	An Acrostic Hallelujah
cxiii–cxviii	The Hallel: a series of Hallelujah Psalms sung as one at the great feasts. — (For cxiv see page 59, and for cxvi and cxviii pages 161, 162)
cxix	The Law: An Acrostic Meditation (183)
cxx–cxxxiv	The Songs of Ascents (170–3)
⎰ cxx	Song of the Exile (171)
cxxi	The Lord thy Keeper (172, 54)
cxxii	Pilgrim Song: Salutation to Jerusalem (172)
cxxiii	Monody of the Exile (171)
cxxiv	Monody of the Exile (171)
cxxv	Pilgrim Song: Thoughts on Mount Zion (172)
cxxvi	Monody of the Exile (171)
cxxvii	Pilgrim Song: Work and Home (172, 97)
cxxviii	Pilgrim Song: Home Life (172)
cxxix	The Exile's Denunciation (171)
cxxx	The Exiled Nation's Liturgy of Penitence (172)
cxxxi	Pilgrim Meditation: On Simplicity (172)
cxxxii	Temple Hymn (172, 155)
cxxxiii	Pilgrim Song: Of Unity (172)
cxxxiv	Temple Song: Benediction of the Night Watch (172)
cxxxv	Hallelujah Psalm
cxxxvi	National Anthem: Of the Nation in the Wilderness (142–4)
cxxxvii	Elegy of the Exile (157–8)
cxxxviii	Judgment: A Meditation
cxxxix	A Dramatic Lyric (77, 90, 178)
cxl	An Elegy of Denunciation
cxli	Consecration: A Meditation
cxlii	A Monody of Experience
cxliii	A Monody of Experience (176)
cxliv	A Dramatic Lyric, with double change and refrain (182 note)
cxlv	Festal Hymn. — Acrostic
cxlvi–cl	Series of Hallelujah Psalms that can be sung as one

THE PROVERBS

A Miscellany of Wisdom in Five Books
Above, pages 284-8, 291, 323-4

i. 1-6	Title to the whole collection
7	Motto to the whole collection

Book I

Sonnets on Wisdom (284-6)

i-ix

i. 8-9	Epigram
10-19	Sonnet: The Company of Sinners (273)
20-33	Dramatic Monologue: Wisdom's Cry of Warning
ii	Sonnet: Wisdom the Preservative from Evil
iii. 1-10	Sonnet: The Commandment and its Reward (277)
11-20	Sonnet: Wisdom the Prize in View
21-6	Sonnet: Wisdom and Security
27-35	Sonnet: Wisdom and Perversity
iv. 1-9	Sonnet: The Tradition of Wisdom
10-19	Sonnet: The Two Paths
20-7	Sonnet: Wisdom and Health
v	Sonnet: The Strange Woman
vi. 1-5	Sonnet: Suretyship
6-11	Sonnet: The Sluggard (280-1)
12-19	A Pair of Sonnets: The Sower of Discord
20-35	Sonnet: The Folly of Adultery
vii-viii	Dramatic Monologue: Wisdom and the Strange Woman
ix	Sonnet of Sonnets: The House of Wisdom and the House of Folly [1-6 (Sonnet) is strophe to which 13-18 is antistrophe; 7-9 (Epigram) is strophe to which 10-12 is antistrophe]

Book II

The Proverbs of Solomon

x-xxii. 16

x-xxii. 16	Collection of isolated Unit Proverbs: no appearance of arrangement (286)

Book III

A Wisdom Epistle (286)

xxii. 17-xxiv

xxii. 17-21	Superscription to the Epistle
22-9	Disconnected Sayings [*Epigrams and Unit Proverbs*]
xxiii. 1-3	Epigram: Awe before Appetite
4-5	Epigram: Transitoriness of Riches
6-8	Epigram: Hospitality of the Evil Eye (262)
9-18	*Disconnected Sayings*
19-21	Epigram: Gluttony
22-5	*Disconnected Sayings*
26-8	Epigram: The Pit of Whoredom
29-35	Sonnet: Woes of Wine (277-8)
xxiv. 1-10	*Disconnected Sayings*
11-12	Epigram: The Duty of Rescue
13-14	Epigram: Wisdom and Honey (262)
15-22	*Disconnected Sayings*
Postscript	
xxiv. 23-5	Epigram: Respect of Persons
26-9	*Disconnected Sayings*
30-4	Sonnet: The Field of the Slothful (280-1)

Book IV

Solomonic Proverbs collected under Hezekiah (287)

xxv-xxix

xxv. 1	Title to Book IV
2-7	Proverb Cluster: On Kings
xxv. 8-xxvi. 2	*Disconnected Sayings*
xxvi. 3-12	Proverb Cluster: On Fools
13-16	Proverb Cluster: On Sluggards
17-26	Proverb Cluster: On Social Pests
xxvi. 27-xxvii. 22	*Disconnected Sayings*
xxvii. 23-7	Folk Song of Good Husbandry (287)
xxviii-xxix	*Disconnected Proverbs*

Book V

Shorter Collections (287)

xxx–xxxi

xxx — Proverbs of Agur. [xxx. 1-4 Sonnet: The Unsearchableness of God (278). 5-6 Epigram. 7-9 Number Sonnet: The Golden Mean. 10 Unit Proverb. 11-14 Sonnet: An Evil Generation. 15-16 Number Sonnet: Things never satisfied (275). 17 Epigram. 18-19 Number Sonnet: Things not to be known. 20 Epigram. 21-3 Number Sonnet: Things not to be borne. 24-8 Number Sonnet: Little and Wise. 29-31 Number Sonnet: Things stately in their going. 32-3 Epigram: The Restraining of Wrath]

xxxi. 1-9 — The Oracle of Lemuel's Mother (262)
10-31 — Anonymous Acrostic Sonnet: The Virtuous Woman

ECCLESIASTES, OR THE PREACHER

A Suite of Five Essays, broken by Miscellaneous Sayings

Fully analysed, pages 293-304. Compare also 309-10, 323-4

i. 1	Title to the whole [*founded upon the first essay*]
i. 2-11	Prologue: All is Vanity
i. 12-ii	Essay I: in the form of a Dramatic Monologue: Solomon's Search for Wisdom
iii. 1-iv. 8	Essay II: The Philosophy of Times and Seasons
iv. 9-v. 9	*Miscellaneous Maxims of Life*
v. 10-vi. 12	Essay III: The Vanity of Desire
vii. 1-22	*Miscellaneous Paradoxes of Life*
vii. 23-ix. 16	Essay IV: The Search for Wisdom, with Notes by the Way
ix. 17-xi. 6	*Miscellaneous Proverbs of Life*
xi. 7-xii. 7	Essay V: Life as a Joy shadowed by the Judgment [including Sonnet (xii. 1-7): The Coming of the Evil Days]
xii. 8-14	Epilogue: All is Vanity: Fear God

THE SONG OF SONGS

A Suite of Seven Dramatic Idyls

Fully analysed above, Chapter VIII

i. 2–ii. 7	Idyl I: The Wedding-Day
ii. 8–iii. 5	Idyl II: The Bride's Reminiscences of the Courtship
iii. 6–v. 1	Idyl III: The Day of Betrothal
v. 2–vi. 3	Idyl IV: The Bride's Troubled Dream
vi. 4–vii. 9	Idyl V: The King's Meditation on his Bride
vii. 10–viii. 4	Idyl VI: The Bride's Longing for her Home on Lebanon
viii. 5–14	Idyl VII: The Renewal of Love in the Vineyard of Lebanon

ISAIAH

A Prophetic Collection in Seven Books

Book I

General Prophecies

i. 2–vi

	Discourse: The Great Arraignment (329)
ii–iv	Discourse: The Latter Glory and the Present Judgment (330)
v. 1–7	Parable of the Vineyard
v. 8–30	Lyric Prophecy: A Sevenfold Denunciation
vi	The Prophet's Call

Book II

Prophecies on the Unholy Alliance

vii–x. 4

vii. 1–17	Prophecy of the sign 'Immanuel' (341 and note)
vii. 18–viii. 8	A Cluster of Prophetic Sentences: The Fly and the Bee (*vii. 18–19*) — *The Razor (20)* — *Butter and Honey (21–2)* — *Briers and Thorns (23–5)* — *Maher-shalal-hash-baz (viii. 1–4)* — *The River (5–8)*. — *Above, pages 418–9*
viii. 9–ix. 7	Rhapsodic Discourse: Light for the People that walk in Darkness
ix. 8–x. 4	Lyric Prophecy: Doom of the North (334)

Book III
Prophecy under an Assyrian Invasion
x. 5–xii

x. 5–xii	Rhapsodic Discourse: The Rod of the Lord and the Reign of Peace (386)

Book IV
A Cycle of Judgment
xiii–xxvii

xiii–xiv. 23	Doom Song on Babylon
xiv. 24–7	Doom Song on Assyria
28–32	Doom Song on Philistia
xv–xvi	Doom Song on Moab
xvii. 1–11	Doom Song on Damascus
12–14	A Doom Song
xviii	Doom Song on Ethiopia (with Refrain)
xix	Prophecy Cluster: Doom Song on Egypt (1–17) — followed by a series of Sentences on the Conversion of Egypt (18, 19–20, 21, 22, 23, 24–5). — Above, pages 419–20
xx	Emblem Prophecy against Ashdod
xxi	Visions of Doom: The Prophetic Watchman (355–8)
xxii. 1–14	Denunciation: The Panic of the Valley of Vision (358)
15–25	A Personal Denunciation
xxiii	Doom Song on Tyre
xxiv–xxvii	Climax of Book IV: A Rhapsody of Judgment (373–80)

Book V
A Cycle of the Restoration (426)
xxviii–xxxv

xxviii–xxxii	Discourses in the form of Animadversions upon the Political Situation [an Assyrian Invasion and question of the Egyptian Alliance] as a background for picturing the Redemption and the Golden Age (426)
xxviii	The Covenant with Death (426)
xxix	The Nightmare of Judgment upon Ariel
xxx	The Boaster that sitteth still (426)
xxxi–xxxii. 8	The Horses of Egypt and the Holy One of Israel
xxxii. 9–20	The Women that are at ease

xxxiii	Rhapsody of Salvation: [1 Prelude, 2 Israel, 3 Prophetic Spectator, 7 Scenic, 10 God, 14 Sinners in Zion, 15-24 Godly in Zion]
xxxiv-v	Finale to Book V: The Utter Destruction and the Great Redemption (426-7)

Book VI

The Invasion of Sennacherib
xxxvi-xxxix

xxxvi-ix	Historical Excerpt: Prophetic History of the Sennacherib Crisis

Book VII

Rhapsody of Zion Redeemed
xl-lxvi

Fully analysed above, Chapter XVII

xl. 1-11	Prelude
xl. 12-xlviii	Phase I: The Judgment on Babylon
xlix-l	Phase II: The Servant of Jehovah and Desponding Zion
li-lii. 12	Phase III: The Awakening of Zion
lii. 13-liii	Phase IV: The Servant of Jehovah Exalted
liv-lv	Phase V: Zion Exalted
lvi-lxii	Phase VI: A Redeemer come to Zion
lxiii-lxvi	Phase VII: Judgment on Zion and on the Nations

JEREMIAH

A Prophetic Collection in Ten Books

Book I

The Prophet's Call and Manifesto
i-vi

i	The Prophet's Call
ii-vi	Jeremiah's Manifesto: Discourse culminating in Rhapsody of Doom and Panic (386-91)

Book II

Miscellaneous Discourses and Sentences

vii-x

vii. 1-28	Discourse: The Temple of the Lord are we
vii. 29-viii. 3	Discourse: Tophet
viii. 4-ix. 9	Rhapsodic Discourse: The Hurt of the Daughter of my People [viii. 14 People, 16 Scenic, 17 God, 18 Prophet, 19 Captive People, 19(*b*) God, 20 Captive People, 21 (to end) Prophet who quotes God]
ix. 10-16	Discourse: A Lamentation for the Land
17-22	Discourse: The Mourning Women
23-6	*Prophetic (417) Sentences [23-4, 25-6]*
x. 1-16	Prophecy Cluster on Idolatry [1-10, 11, 12-16]
17-25	Scene of Panic

Book III

Prophecies of the Missionary Journey

xi-xiii

xi. 1-8	The Prophet's Commission: The Tour of Preaching the Covenant
9-17	Prophetic Intercourse: On Judah's Rejection of the Covenant
xi. 18-xii. 6	Prophetic Incident: The Conspiracy of Anathoth
xii. 7-17	Judah and his Evil Neighbours
xiii	Emblem Prophecy: The Girdle (336, 338)[1]

Book IV

The Drought and other Prophecies

xiv-xvii

xiv-xv	Rhapsody of the Drought (381-5)
xvi	Prophetic Intercourse: The Doom of the Land
xvii. 1-12	*Prophetic Sentences [1-2, 3-4, 5-8, 9-10, 11, 12]*
13-18	Prophetic Intercourse: A Prayer under Persecution
19-27	Discourse: On the Sabbath

[1] Found attached to the prophecies of the Missionary Journey, though with no necessary connection.

Book V

Discourses Founded on Pottery

xviii-xx

xviii. 1-17	Emblem Prophecy: Potter's Clay (336)
18-23	Prophetic Intercourse: The Conspiracy
xix-xx	Prophetic Incident: The Potter's Bottle (337), including (xx. 7-13) a Prophetic Meditation and (14-18) a Prophetic Curse

Book VI

Messages to Rulers

xxi-xxiii

xxi. 1-10	Prophetic Response: On the Approach of Nebuchadrezzar's Army
11-14	Message to the Royal House
xxii. 1-9	Message to the Royal House
10-12	Discourse: On Shallum
13-19	Discourse: On Jehoiakim
20-30	Discourse: On Coniah
xxiii. 1-8	Discourse: The Shepherds of Israel
9-40	Discourse: On False Prophets

Book VII

Occasional and Controversial Prophecies

xxiv-xxix

xxiv	Emblem Prophecy: The Figs (336)
xxv	The Cup of the Lord's Fury (354)
xxvi	Prophetic Controversy: Destruction of the Temple
xxvii-xxviii	Prophetic Controversy: The Yoke
xxix	Epistle: To the Elders of the Captivity

Book VIII

Prophecies of the Restoration

xxx–xxxi

xxx. 1–3	Preface to the Eighth Book
xxx. 4–22	Discourse (with Pendulum Structure): The Restoration of Judah (332)
xxx. 23–xxxi. 20	Rhapsodic Discourse: The Restoration of Israel
xxxi. 21–40	Prophetic Sentences [21-2, 23-6, 27-8, 29-30, 31-4 (*The New Covenant*), 35-7, 38-40]

Book IX

Incidental and Historical Prophecies

xxxii–xlv

xxxii–iii	Incident: The Anathoth Estate
xxxiv. 1–7	Incident: The Siege of the Fenced Cities
8–22	Incident: The Hebrew Servants
xxxv	Incident: The Rechabites
xxxvi	Incident: The Burning of the Roll
xxxvii–xliv	Prophecy merged in History: Crisis of the Siege and Abduction of Jeremiah to Egypt (341)
xlv	Prophetic Intercourse: Jeremiah and Baruch

Book X

Dooms of the Nations

xlvi–li

xlvi	Doom of Egypt (Twofold)
xlvii	Doom of the Philistines
xlviii	Doom of Moab
xlix. 1–6	Doom of the Children of Ammon
7–22	Doom of Edom
23–7	Doom of Damascus
28–33	Doom of Kedar and Hazor
34–9	Doom of Elam
l–li	Doom of Babylon (337)
lii–liii	*Historical Appendix to the Works of Jeremiah*

LAMENTATIONS

A Suite of Acrostic Elegies (157)

EZEKIEL

A Prophetic Collection in Three Books (430)

Book I

Prophecies of Judgment

i-xxiv

i-iii	Vision: The Prophet's Call
iv-v	Emblem Prophecy: The Mimic Siege (338-9)
vi-vii	Discourse: Against the Land of Judah (337-8)
viii-xi	VISION: JERUSALEM UNDER JUDGMENT (343-5)
xii. 1-16	Emblem Prophecy: Stuff for removing
17-20	Emblem Prophecy: Bread of Trembling
21-8	Discourse with Proverb Text
xiii	Discourse: Against False Prophets
xiv. 1-11	Prophetic Response: On False Enquirers
12-23	Discourse: On Vicarious Righteousness
xv	Parable: Of the Vine (345)
xvi	Parable: Of the Ungrateful Spouse (345)
xvii	Parable: Of the Eagle and the Cedar (345)
xviii	Discourse: The Proverb of Fathers and Children
xix	Discourse: A Lamentation for the Princes of Israel
xx. 1-44	Prophetic Response: A Vain Enquiry
45-9	Discourse: The Forest of the South
xxi	Emblem Prophecy: The Sword (337)
xxii	Discourse: The Bloody City
xxiii	Parable: Oholah and Oholibah (345)
xxiv. 1-14	Parable: Of the Caldron
15-27	Emblem Prophecy: Death of the Prophet's Wife (340)

Book II

Dooms of the Nations
xxv–xxxii

xxv	Cycle of Dooms [1–7, 8–11, 12–14, 15–17]
xxvi–xxviii	Threefold Doom on Tyre [xxvi; xxvii; xxviii. 1–19] and Doom on Zidon (359–61)
xxix–xxxii	Sevenfold Doom (361–3) on Egypt [xxix. 1–16; 17–21; xxx. 1–19; 20–26; xxxi; xxxii. 1–16; and 17–32]

Book III

Prophecies of the Restoration
xxxiii–xlviii

xxxiii. 1–9	Discourse: The Watchman
10–20	Dialectic Prophecy: Repentance
21–33	Discourse: News of the Fall of Jerusalem
xxxiv	Discourse: The Shepherds of Israel (330)
xxxv–xxxvi	Discourse: Mount Seir and the Mountains of Israel
xxxvii. 1–14	Vision: The Valley of Dry Bones (342)
15–28	Emblem Prophecy: The Joining of the Sticks
xxxviii–xxxix	Discourse: Gog of the Land of Magog
xl–xlviii	VISION: JERUSALEM RESTORED (343–5)

DANIEL

A Prophetic Collection in Two Books (430)

Book I

Prophetic Incidents and Interpretations of Visions
i–vi

i	Prophetic Incident: Daniel and the King's Meat
ii	Vision Interpretation: The Image and the Stone
iii	Prophetic Incident: The Burning Fiery Furnace
iv	Vision Interpretation: Nebuchadnezzar's Dream of the Tree cut down
v	Vision Interpretation: The Writing on the Wall (343)
vi	Prophetic Incident: The Den of Lions

Book II

A Cycle of Visions
vii–xii

vii	Vision of the Four Beasts (343)
viii	Vision of the Ram and the He-goat (343)
ix	Vision Prophecy: The Time of Restoration (343)
x–xii	Vision Prophecy: The Time of the End

HOSEA

A Prophetic Collection in Two Books

Book I

Gomer
i–iii

i–iii	Emblem Prophecy of Gomer (340)

Book II

The Lord's Controversy
iv–xiv

iv–vi	Discourse culminating in a Rhapsody [v. 8 Panic, 9 God, vi. 1 People, 4 God]
vii	Discourse of Denunciation
viii. 1–6	Discourse: The Idols and the Triumph of Judgment
7–14	*Prophetic Sentences* [7(a), 7(b), 8–9(a), 9(b)–10, 11, 12, 13, 14]
ix. 1–6	Discourse: Joy turned to Judgment
ix. 7–x	*Prophetic Sentences* [ix. 7, 8, 9, 10, 11–12, 13, 14, 15, 16–17; x. 1–2, 3, 4, 5–6, 7–8, 9, 10–11, 12, 13–15]
xi. 1–11	Dramatic Prophecy: The Divine Yearning (349–50)
xi. 12–xii	Discourse: Jacob's Doings and Recompense [1]
xiii–xiv. 8	A Drama of Repentance (350–1)
xiv. 9	*Epilogue Sentence to Book II*

[1] Marginal Reading of R. V. to xi. 12

JOEL

A Rhapsody of the Locust Plague (369-73)

AMOS

A Rhapsody of the Judgment to come (391-3)

OBADIAH

A Doom Prophecy upon Edom

JONAH

A Prophetic Epic (240, 337-8)

MICAH

A Prophetic Collection in Two Books

Book I

Miscellaneous Prophecies

i–v

	Rhapsody of Judgment Approaching [verse 8 The Prophet, 10-16 Scenic]
ii. 1-5	Discourse: Against Oppression
6-11	Discourse: Wickedness seeking to silence Prophecy
12-13	Discourse: A Vision of the Breaking Forth
iii	Discourse: Against Rulers and Prophets
iv-v	Discourse: The Mountain of the Lord's House

Book II

Dramatic Prophecies

vi–vii

vi. 1-8	The Lord's Controversy before the Mountains (347)
vi. 9-vii	The Lord's Cry and the Man of Wisdom (348-9)

NAHUM

A Rhapsodic Doom Prophecy upon Nineveh

HABAKKUK

A Prophetic Collection

i–ii	Rhapsody of the Chaldeans (365–7)
iii	An Ode of Judgment (147)

ZEPHANIAH

A Rhapsodic Discourse (120)

HAGGAI

Four Occasional Discourses, dated

ZECHARIAH

A Prophetic Collection in Three Books

Book I

Miscellaneous Discourses

i–viii

i. 1–6	The Prophet's Manifesto
i. 7–vi. 8	Vision Cycle (427)
vi. 9–15	Emblem Prophecy: The Crowning of Joshua
vii. 1–7	Response: On the Fasts (421–2)
8–14	Discourse of Denunciation (421–2)
viii. 1–8	Prophetic Sentences of Jerusalem Restored [viii. 1–2, 3, 4–5, 6, 7–8]
9–17	Discourse: The Seed of Peace for the Remnant of the People (421–2)
18–23	Prophetic Sentences of the Restoration [18–19, 20–22, 23]

Book II
Discourses
ix-xi

ix	Discourse: Thy King cometh
x-xi	Rhapsodic Discourse: The False Shepherds and the Flock of Slaughter

Book III
Discourses
xii-xiv

xii-xiii. 6	Discourse: The Fountain in the House of David
xiii. 7-9	Discourse: Against my Shepherd
xiv	Discourse: Vision of Judgment and the Golden Age (332)

MALACHI

A Dialectic Cycle of Six Discourses (346)

[i. 2-5; i. 6-ii. 9; ii. 10-16; ii. 17-iii. 6; iii. 7-12; iii. 13-iv. 6]

WISDOM OF SOLOMON

A Suite of Five Discourses in the Form of Text and Comment

Above, Chapter XIII: compare Appendix IV, and pages 323-4, 255 note

i. 1-11	Text [i. 1] and Discourse I: Singleness of Heart (310)
i. 12-vi. 11	Text [1. 12] and Discourse II: Immortality and the Covenant with Death (311-5)
vi. 12-ix	Text [vi. 12] and Discourse III: Solomon's Winning of Wisdom (315-6)
x-xi. 5	Text[1] [ix. 18, last clause] and Discourse IV: The World saved through Wisdom (317)
xi. 5-xix	Text[1] [xi. 5] and Discourse V: Judgments on the Wicked turning to Blessings on God's People (318-23: compare Appendix IV)

[1] In these two Discourses the text is made by the concluding words of the preceding Discourse.

ECCLESIASTICUS

OR

THE WISDOM OF JESUS THE SON OF SIRACH

A Miscellany of Wisdom in Five Books

Above, pages 289-92, 255 note, 323-4

Preface by the Author's Grandson

Book I

i-xxiii

i. 1-20	Sonnet: Wisdom and the Fear of the Lord
22-4	Epigram: Unjust Wrath
25-7	A Maxim
28-30	A Maxim
ii. 1-6	A Maxim
7-18	Sonnet: True and False Fear
iii. 1-16	Essay: Honour to Parents
17-28	Essay: Meekness
29-31	*Disconnected Sayings*
iv. 1-10	Essay: Consideration for High and Low
11-19	Essay: Wisdom's Way with her Children
20-8	Essay: True and False Shame
iv. 29-v. 3	*Disconnected Sayings*
v. 4-8	A Maxim
v. 9-vi. 1	Proverb Cluster: Government of the Tongue (265)
vi. 2-4	Epigram: Self-Will
5-17	Essay: On Friendship
18-37	Essay: On Pursuit of Wisdom
vii. 1-3	Epigram: Sowing Sin and Reaping
4-6	A Maxim
vii. 7-18	*Disconnected Sayings*
19-36	Essay: Household Precepts
viii. 1-ix. 16	Essay: Adaptation of Behaviour to Various Sorts of Men

ECCLESIASTICUS 493

ix. 17-x. 5	Essay: Wisdom and Government
x. 6-xi. 6	Essay: Pride and True Greatness
xi. 7-10	Proverb Cluster: Meddlesomeness
11-28	Essay: Prosperity and Adversity are from the Lord (268)
xi. 29-xiii. 24	Essay: Choice of Company
xiii. 25-xiv. 2	*Disconnected Sayings*
xiv. 3-19	Essay: On Niggardliness
xiv. 20-xv. 10	Essay: The Pursuer of Wisdom and his Reward
11-20	Essay: On Free Will
xvi. 1-23	Essay: No Safety for Sinners in Numbers
xvi. 24-xviii. 14	Essay: God's Work of Creation and Restoration
xviii. 15-18	Proverb Cluster: On Graciousness
19-27	Essay: On Taking Heed in Time
xviii. 28-9	*Disconnected Sayings*
xviii. 30-xix. 3	Three Temperance Maxims [30-31; 32-1 (*a*); 1 (*b*)-3]
xix. 4-17	Essay: Against Gossip (268)
xix. 20-xx. 13	Essay: Wisdom and its Counterfeits
xx. 14-31	*Disconnected Sayings*
xxi. 1-10	Proverb Cluster: Sin and its Judgment
11-26	Proverb Cluster: Wise Men and Fools
xxi. 27-xxii. 5	Proverb Cluster: The Hatefulness of Evil
xxii. 6-15	Proverb Cluster: Commerce with Fools Intolerable [including a Sonnet: 11-12]
xxii. 16-26	Essay: The Steadfast Friend and the Uncertain
xxii. 27-xxiii. 6	Sonnet: Watchfulness of Lips and Heart (279)
xxiii. 7-15	Essay: The Discipline of the Mouth
16-27	Essay: The Horror of Adultery

Book II

xxiv-xxxiii. 15

xxiv	Preface to Book II, into which is interwoven (3-22) a Dramatic Monologue: Wisdom's Praise of Herself (289-90)
xxv. 1-2	Number Sonnet: What Wisdom loves and hates (275)
3-6	A Maxim
7-11	Number Sonnet: The Love of the Lord (276)
13-15	Epigram: The Wrath of an Enemy

xxv. 16-xxvi. 18	Proverb Cluster: Women Bad and Good [xxv. 16-xxvi. 4 Essay; 5-6 Number Sonnet; 7-18 Sonnet]
xxvi. 28	Number Sonnet: The Backslider
xxvi. 29-xxvii. 2	A Maxim
xxvii. 3-10	*Disconnected Sayings*
11-15	Proverb Cluster: The Discourse of Wise and Fools
16-21	A Maxim
22-4	A Maxim
xxvii. 25-xxviii. 11	Essay: Retribution and Vengeance
xxviii. 12-26	Essay: On the Tongue (266)
xxix. 1-20	Essay: On Lending and Suretyship
21-8	Essay: The Blessing of a House of One's Own
xxx. 1-13	Essay: On the Chastisement of Children
14-25	Essay: On Health
xxxi. 1-11	Essay: On Riches
xxxi. 12-xxxii. 13	Essay: On Feasting
xxxii. 14-xxxiii. 6	*Disconnected Sayings*
xxxiii. 7-15	Essay: An Analogy

Book III

xxxiii. 16-xxxix. 11

xxxiii. 16-18	*Preface to Book III (290)*
19-23	Essay: On Giving and Bequeathing
24-31	Essay: On Servants
xxxiv. 1-8	Essay: On Dreams
9-12	A Maxim
xxxiv. 13-17	Sonnet: The Fearers of the Lord
xxxiv. 18-xxxv	Essay: On Sacrifices, Evil and Acceptable
xxxvi. 1-17	A Prayer for Mercy upon Israel
18-20	*Disconnected Sayings*
21-6	Essay: On Wives
xxxvii. 1-6	Essay: On False Friends
7-26	Essay: On Counsel and Counsellors (269-70)
xxxvii. 27-xxxviii. 15	Essay: On Disease and Physicians
xxxviii. 16-23	Essay: On Mourning for the Dead
xxxviii. 24-xxxix. 11	Essay: The Wisdom of Business and the Wisdom of Leisure

Book IV

xxxix. 12–xlii. 14

xxxix. 12–35	Preface into which is interwoven (16–31) a Rhetoric Encomium of God's Works
xl. 1–10	Essay: The Burden of Life
11–27	A Pair of Sonnets: A Garden of Blessing
28–30	A Maxim
xli. 1–4	Sonnet: On Death
5–13	Essay: The Posterity of Sinners
xli. 14–xlii. 8	Essay: On Things to be ashamed of
xlii. 9–14	Essay: Women as a Source of Trouble

Book V

Longer Works

xlii. 15–l. 24

xlii. 15–xliii	Rhetoric Encomium: The Works of the Lord
xliv–l. 24	Rhetoric Encomium: The Praise of Famous Men (29o)

Epilogue to the Whole: Number Sonnet of the Hated Nations (l. 25–6)—
 Colophon with Beatitude (27–9)
Author's Preface to the Whole (li)

ST. MATTHEW, ST. MARK, ST. LUKE, ST. JOHN

Each of these constitutes a single **Gospel**, which must be understood as a specific literary form (250)

THE ACTS OF THE APOSTLES

A continuation of one of the **Gospels**, and of the same literary form (251)

EPISTLE TO THE ROMANS

An Epistolary Treatise (441)

I, II CORINTHIANS

Epistles of Pastoral Intercourse (440)

GALATIANS

An Epistle of Pastoral Intercourse (440)

EPHESIANS

An Epistolary Manifesto (442)

PHILIPPIANS

An Epistle of Pastoral Intercourse (441)

COLOSSIANS

An Epistolary Manifesto (442)

I, II THESSALONIANS

Epistles of Pastoral Intercourse (441)

I, II TIMOTHY

Epistles of Pastoral Intercourse (441)

TITUS, PHILEMON

Epistles of Pastoral Intercourse (441)

HEBREWS

An Epistolary Treatise (442)

JAMES

A Wisdom Epistle (292)

i. *1*	*Superscription to the Epistle*
i. 2–4	A Maxim
5–8	A Maxim
9–11	A Maxim
12–27	Essay: On the Sources of the Evil and the Good in us (270–2)
ii. 1–13	Essay: On Respect of Persons
14–26	Essay: Faith and Works
iii. 1–12	Essay: On the Responsibility of Speech (267)
13–18	Essay: The Earthly Wisdom and the Wisdom from above
iv. 1–10	Discourse: On Worldly Pleasures
11–12	A Maxim (264)
iv. 13–v. 18	Discourse: The Judgment to come
19–20	A Maxim

I, II PETER

Epistolary Manifestos (442)

I JOHN

An Epistolary Manifesto (442)

II, III JOHN

Epistles of Pastoral Intercourse (441)

JUDE

An Epistolary Manifesto (443)

THE REVELATION

A Vision Cycle (431-6)

APPENDIX II

TABLES OF LITERARY FORMS

This second Appendix is intended for the technical student of Literary Morphology. It arranges in Tables all the literary forms found in Scripture, with the examples of them, so that each form can be studied by itself. In the case of very common forms, such as the simple Discourse, it has not been thought necessary to give the examples. The reference figures are to preceding pages of this book.

I.—FORMS OF LYRIC POETRY

LYRIC		
Folk Songs quoted.		Song of the Sword (*Genesis* iv. 23, 4).—Of the Well (*Numbers* xxi. 17, 18). Husbandry Song (*Proverbs* xxvii. 23-7).—War-Ballad (*Joshua* x. 12-13). Fragments of others in *Numbers* xxi.
Odes (127)	Triumphal Odes:	Deborah's Song (*Judges* v).—Song of Moses and Miriam (*Exodus* xv).
	National Anthems:	*Psalms* cv, lxxviii, cvi; cxxxvi.
	Processional Ode:	*Psalm* lxviii.
	Songs in Ode form:	Moses' Song (*Deuteronomy* xxxii).—Song of David (*Psalm* xviii).—Song of the Thunderstorm (*Psalm* xxix).—Prayer of Habakkuk (*Habakkuk* iii).
	Odes on Themes:	The World within and the World without (*Psalms* ciii, civ).—Ode of the Redeemed (cvii).—On the Covenant (lxxxix).—On Judgement (l).—On the Messiah (ii).
Occasional Psalms (153)	Anthems for the Inauguration of Jerusalem: *Psalms* xxx, xxiv, cxxxii, 1-9, ci.	
	Victory Hymns: *Psalms* xlvi, xlviii, lxxvi.	
	Hymn of Defeat and Victory: *Psalms* lx and cviii.	
	[Most of the Odes are Occasional Lyrics; and the next department of Elegies is closely akin.]	
Elegies (156)	Elegies Proper	On Saul and Jonathan (*II Samuel* i, 19-27). *Psalms* xliv, lxxiv, lxxix, lxx, lxxxviii, cii. Exile Songs: *Psalms* xlii-iii; lxi, lxiii; cxxxvii. Compare below: Songs of Ascents. Acrostic Elegies: *Lamentations of Jeremiah*.
	Elegies of Denunciation	National: lxxxiii. In Songs of Ascents: cxxix. Personal or Public: lii, lviii, lxxxii; lv; xxxv, lxx, cix, cxl. War Ballad: lxx.
	Encomia and Salutations	On the King: *Psalm* lxxii.—On the Ideal King: *Psalm* cx. To Zion: *Psalm* lxxxvii.—To Jerusalem (in the Songs of Ascents): cxxii.

LYRIC continued	Liturgical Psalms	Ritual Hymns (160)	Hallelujahs: *Psalms* cxiii–cxviii; cxxxv; cxlvi–cl; (acrostic) cxi–cxii. Accession Hymns: xlvii; xciii; xcv–c. Festal Hymns: xxxiii, lxvii; lxxxi; (acrostic) cxlv. Votive Hymns: lxvi; cxvi and (antiphonal) cxviii; xcii; *I Samuel* ii. 1–10; *Luke* i. 46–55, 68–79, and ii. 29–32. Benedictions: *Psalms* xx, xxi; xlv; *Numbers* vi. 24–6; *Psalm* cxxxiv. Doxologies: *Psalms* xli. 13, etc.; *Luke* ii. 14.
		Liturgies (164)	General xl. Of Praise: *Psalms* xxxiv, lxv. Of Supplication: lxxxvi. Of Penitence: cxxx. Of Devotion: iv, lxii; (acrostic) xxv. Of Judgment: vii, xciv.
	Dramatic Lyrics (174)		The 'Songs of Ascents' (170); *Psalms* cxx–cxxxiv. [Exile Songs: cxx, cxxiii, cxxiv, cxxvi, cxxix, cxxx. Pilgrim Songs: cxxi, cxxii, cxxv, cxxviii, cxxxviii, cxxxi, cxxxiii. Temple Hymns: cxxxii, cxxxiv.]
Simple: *Psalms* iii, vi, xii, xxii, xxviii, liv, lxxi, cxxxix. With Refrain: lvi, lvii. Duplicated: xxxi. With Transitional Stage: lxix (compare xiv).
With Double Dramatic change: *Psalms* xxvii, cviii. With Refrain: cxliv. With Transitional Stage: lxxxv. Antiphonal and Acrostic: ix–x.
	Monodies (183)		*Psalms* xxxii, xli; xxxix, lxxviii; xxxviii; cxlii, cxliii. In Songs of Ascents: cxxiii, cxxiv, cxxvi.
	Meditations (183)		Consecration: *Psalms* v. xxvi, cxli: (acrostic) cxix. Trust: xi, xvi. Penitence: li. Simplicity: cxxxi. Judgment: xiii, xiv (= liii), xvii, lxiv, cxxxviii; (acrostic) xxxvii.
	Psalms on Themes (185)		The Meditative and the Worldly Life (i)—The Devout Life (xv)—Life as a Passing Day (xc)—Work and Home (cxxvii)—Home Life (cxxviii).
Jehovah's Follower (xxiii)—The Shadow of the Almighty (xci)—The Lord thy Keeper (cxxi).
Man that is in Honour: A Parable (xlix)—The Mystery of Prosperous Wickedness (lxxiii).
The Heavens above and the Law within (xix)—The Supreme Evil and the Supreme Good (xxxvi).
Man the Viceroy of God (viii)—A Song of Judgment (lxxv)—A Song of God's House (lxxxiv)—A Song of Unity (cxxxiii).

II.—HISTORIC AND EPIC LITERATURE IN CONNECTION

HISTORY with EPIC (Page 244)

Primitive History: Formation of the Chosen Nation: *Book of Genesis.*
  Genesis i-xi: First Beginnings of the World. xii-l: Overlapping Succession of Patriarchs Abraham, Isaac, Jacob, Joseph.
  Historic Framework of Genealogies, Annals, and other connective matter (including Incidents explaining names of places or relations of world-families), enclosing the Epic Incidents.
  Epic Element: Epic Incidents: The Creation (in Sonnet form: i-ii. 3).—The Temptation in the Garden of Eden (ii. 4-iii).—Cain and Abel (iv. 1-15).—The Flood (vi. 9-ix. 17). **Epic Cycles** of Abraham (page 400)—of Isaac (page 466)—of Jacob (page 466). **Epic History:** Joseph and his Brethren (xxxvii. 2-36, xxxix. 1-xlvi. 7, and xlvii. 28-xlvii. 12).

Constitutional History: Migration of the Chosen Nation to the Land of Promise: *Books of Exodus, Leviticus, Numbers.*
  Exodus i-xviii: Slavery in Egypt, Deliverance, and Journey to Sinai. *Exodus* from xix and *Leviticus*: Constitution of the Nation at Sinai. *Numbers*: The March from Sinai and Thirty-eight Years' Wandering.
  Successive Revelations of the Law, and Incidents leading to or associated with these.
  Epic Element: Epic History: Moses and the Plagues of Egypt (*Exodus* i. 8-vi. 13; vi. 28-xi. 21-39; xiii. 17-xv. 21). **Mixed Epic:** Story of Balaam (*Numbers* xxii-xxiv).

Incidental History: The Chosen Nation in its Efforts towards Secular Government: *Books of Joshua* and *Judges*, and *First Book of Samuel* (including first chapter of *II Samuel*).
  Joshua: Conquest of Canaan and Division of the Land. *Judges*: Sporadic attempts at secular government and first conception of kingship (viii. 22 and ix). *I Samuel*: Gradual establishment of Secular kingship and rise of Prophets to represent Theocracy.
  Mainly Epic matter, but in a connective framework of summaries, fillings in between Incidents: and especially, a Doomsday Book of the conquered country.
  Epic Element: Epic Incidents: Ehud's Assassination of Eglon (*Judges* iii. 12-30)—War of Deborah and Barak against Sisera (iv-v)—Gideon and the Midianites (vi-viii. 28)—Crowning of Abimelech by the Men of Shechem (viii. 29-ix)—Jephthah and the Ammonites (x. 6-xii. 6)—Micah's Images and the Danish Migration (xvii-xviii)—The Benjamite War (xix-xxi). **Epic Cycles** of Joshua (page 469)—of Samson (page 469)—of Samuel (page 469)—of Saul (page 469). **Epic History:** Feud of Saul and David (*I Samuel* xvi. 14-xxviii. 2, and xxix to *II Samuel* i) and Story of Ruth (Idyl).

HISTORY with EPIC continued	Regular History: The Chosen Nation under a Secular Government and a Theocracy side by side: *Second Book of Samuel* and both *Books of Kings*. *I Kings* xii–*II Kings* xvii: *II Samuel* ii–*I Kings* xi: Reigns of David and Solomon. Kingdoms of Judah and Israel side by side. *II Kings* from xviii: Kingdom of Judah to its Captivity. Systematic account of successive reigns, with the Incidents narrated historically; documents, references to authorities. Epic Element: Epic History: The Feud between David's Sons and the Revolt of Absalom (*II Samuel* xiii–xx)—to which may be added (outside the period) the *Book of Esther*. Especially: Epic Prophecy. [See Table III.]	
	Ecclesiastical History	I, II *Chronicles* and sequel books of *Ezra* and *Nehemiah*: Documents, Genealogies, Statistics, Historical Excerpts: the matter abridged, amplified, arranged with reference to its bearing on the Ecclesiastical organisation of the Church as restored after the exile.
		The Four Gospels: the term **Gospel** must be understood as a specific literary form: they are not biographies, nor histories, but Authoritative Statements (cf. Protocols) of Acts and Words of the Founder of the Church. [The Fourth Gospel differs from the rest in its style, which is mainly based (522–3) on the form of Text and Comment.]
		Acts of the Apostles: a continuation of one of the Gospels: Authoritative Statement of the Proceedings of the Apostles in the early stages of founding the Church and opening it to the whole Gentile world.

III.—FORMS OF EPIC LITERATURE

EPIC

Verse Epic: Remarkably absent (page 223).			
Mixed Epic (page 224): Story of Balaam (*Numbers* xxii-xxiv) — The Story of the Blessing of Isaac (*Genesis* xxvii. 1-40) — The Story of the Blessing and Death of Jacob (*Genesis* xlvii. 28-l).			
Prose Epic (page 229)	**Epic Stories:** the Epic Incidents in Primitive History and Incidental History. [See Table II.]		
	Epic Cycles	Of Abraham (page 466) — of Isaac (page 466) — of Jacob (page 466) — of Joshua (page 469) — of Samson (page 469) — of Saul (page 469).	
	Epic Histories (organic wholes)	Joseph and his Brethren (*Genesis* xxxvii. 2-36; xxxix-xlvi. 7 and xlvi. 28-xlvii. 12). Moses and the Plagues of Egypt (*Exodus* i. 8-vi. 13; vi. 28-xi; xii. 21-39; xiii. 17-xv. 21). Feud of Saul and David (*I Samuel* xvi. 14-xxviii. 2 and xxix-*II Samuel* i). Feud between David's Sons and Revolt of Absalom (*II Samuel* xiii-xx). The Book of Esther. — The Book of Ruth (Epic Idyl).	
Epic Prophecy (page 238)	**Prophetic Stories:** Nathan, David, and Bathsheba (*II Samuel* xi. 2-xii. 25) — Gad and the Numbering of the People (*II Samuel* xxiv) — The Man of God and the Old Prophet of Bethel (*I Kings* xiii. 1-32) — Ahijah and the Wife of Jeroboam (*I Kings* xiv. 1-18) — The Son of the Prophet and Ahab (*I Kings* xx. 35-43) — Micaiah and the Battle of Ramoth-Gilead (*I Kings* xxii. 1-40).		
	Prophetic Cycles: Of Elisha (page 470) — of Daniel (compare page 487).		
	Prophetic Epics (organic wholes)	The History of Elijah the Tishbite (*I Kings* xvii-xix; xxi; *II Kings* i-ii. 18). The Book of Jonah.	

IV.—FORMS OF WISDOM LITERATURE

WISDOM The Biblical term corresponding to our Philosophy and Science	**Unit Proverb** (page 256)	Popular Proverbs: quoted in *I Samuel* x. 12, xxiv. 13; *Ezekiel* xvi. 44. Riddles (*Song of Songs* viii. 8-9; *Judges* xv. 16). [Cycle, or game of Riddles: *Judges* xiv.]
	Sayings or Sentences of the Wise: Unit of Thought in Unit of Form	Doctrine and Supplement: such as *Proverbs* x. 1; xvi. 32; xi. 31, etc. Doctrine distributed: such as *Proverbs* xx. 14; xv. 16; xxiv. 26.
		[Here may be mentioned the Fable (*Judges* ix. 8-15, *II Kings* xiv. 9) and the Parable (in the Gospels; or *II Samuel* xii. 1-6, xiv. 4-9). These, however, never attain distinctness as a separate literary form; the nearest approach to this is the **Dramatised Parable of the Book of Job**, in which Wisdom literature, Epic, Drama and Rhetoric are amalgamated.]
	Wisdom Literature tending Prosewards pages 263-272	Maxims (page 263): in the form of Texts with Comments. *Ecclesiasticus* i. 25-7, 28-30: ii. 1-6; v. 4-8; vii. 4-6; xi. 7-8, 10; xviii. 30-1; xviii. 32-xix. 1 (*a*); xix. 1 (*b*)-3; xx. 14-15, 24-6; xxi. 2, 22-4; xxii. 7-8, 13; xxv. 3-6; xxvi. 29-xxvii. 2; xxvii. 16-21, 22-4; xxxii. 18; xxxiv. 9-12; xl. 28-30. *St. James* i. 2-4, 5-8, 9-11; iv. 11-12; v. 19-20. *Ecclesiastes* iv. 9-12, 13-16; v. 1-7, 8-9; vii. 1-6, 8-10, 11-12, 13-14, 15-18, 20-2; x. 2-3, 5-7, 12-14; xi. 6. The Maxims enlarge into the Discourses: see *Wisdom of Solomon* (page 305)—*St. James* iv. 1-10; iv. 13-v. 18.
		Proverb Cluster: Aggregation of Unit Proverbs (with Epigrams and Maxims) on a common theme: *Proverbs* xxv. 2-7 The King—xxvi. 3-12 On Fools—xxvi. 13-16 On Sluggards—xxvi. 17-26 On Social Pests. *Ecclesiasticus* v. 9-vi. 1 Government of the Tongue—xi. 7-10 Meddlesomeness—xviii. 15-18 Graciousness—xxi. 1-10 Sin and its Judgment—11-26 Wise Men and Fools—xxi. 27-xxii. 5 Hatefulness of Evil—xxii. 6-15 Commerce with Fools Intolerable—xxv. 16-xxvi. 18 Women Bad and Good—xxvii. 11-15 Discourse of Fools.

WISDOM continued	Wisdom Literature (ending Proem own th continued) (page 264)	The Essay: *Ecclesiasticus* iii. 1-16 to Honour to Parents iii. 17-28 Meekness iv. 1-10 On Con siderateness for High and Low iv. 11-17 to Wisdom's Way with her Children iv. 20-31 True and False Shame vi. 5-17 Friendship vi. 18-37 Pursuit of Wisdom vii. 19-36 Household Precepts viii. 19, 19 Adaptation of Behaviour to Various Sorts of Men x. 17, x, 5 Wisdom and Government x. 6 to xi. 6 Pride and True Greatness xi. 11-28 Prosperity and Adversity from the Lord xi. 29, xiii. 24 Choice of Company xiv. 3-19 Niggardliness xiv. 20, xv. to The Pursuer of Wisdom and his Reward xv. 11-20 Free Will xvi. 1-23 No Safety for Sinners in Numbers xvi. 24, xviii. 14 God's Work of Crea tion and Restoration xviii. 15-27 On Taking Heed in Time xix. 4-17 Against Gossip xix. 20-xx. 31 Wisdom and its Counterfeits xxii. 16-26 The Steadfast Friend and the Uncertain xxiii. 7-15 The Discipline of the Mouth xxiii. 16-27 The Honored Adulteries xxv. 16-xxxvi. 4 Women Bad and Good xxvii. 25, xxviii. 1-11 Retribution and Vengeance xxviii. 12-26 On the Tongue - xxix. 1-20 On Lending and Suretyship xxix. 21 ff The Blessing of a House of One's Own xxxi. 1-11 Chastisement of Children xxx. 14-25 On Health—xxxi. 12 ff On Riches xxxi. 12-xxxii. 13 On Feasting xxxiii. 7-15 An Analogy xxxiii. 19-23 On Giving and Bequeathing xxxiii. 24-31 On Servants xxxiv. 1-8 On Dreams xxxiv. 18-xxxv Sacrifices, Evil and Acceptable xxxvi. 21-6 On Wives xxxvii. 1-6 False Friends xxxvii. 7-26 On Counsel and Counsellors xxxvi. 27-xxxviii. 15 Disease and Physicians xxxviii. 16-23 On Mourning for the Dead xxxviii. 24-xxxix. 11 There is one Wisdom for the Busy and one for the Man of Leisure xl. 1 to The Burden of Life xli. 5-13 The Posterity of Sinners xli. 14-xlii. 8 Things to be ashamed of xlii. 9-14 Women as a Source of Trouble. St. James l. 12-27 On the Sources of the Evil and the Good in us ii. 1-13 On the Respect of Persons ii. 14-26 On Faith and Works iii. 1-12 On the Responsibility of Speech iii. 13-18 The Earthly Wisdom and the Wisdom from above. *Ecclesiastes* 1. 12-ii Solomon's Search for Wisdom—iii iv. 8 The Philosophy of Times and Seasons (including a Sonnet) v. 10 vi. 12 The Vanity of Desire vii. 23 ix. 16 The Search for Wisdom, with Notes by the Way xi. 7-xii. 7 Life as a Joy shadowed by the Judgment (later part in Sonnet form).

The (Rhetoric) Encomium: *Ecclesiasticus* xxxix. 16-35 On God's Works (Inwoven into prelure to Book IV)—xliii. 15 xliii On the Works of the Lord—xliv-l. 24 On Famous Men (page 281). |

506

WISDOM continued	Wisdom Literature tending Versewards	**Epigram** (page 260): A Unit Proverb organically enlarged: *Proverbs* xxiii. 1-3 Awe before Appetite—xxiii. 4-5 The Transitoriness of Riches—xxiii. 6-8 Hospitality of the Evil Eye—xxiii. 19-21 Gluttony—xxiii. 26-8 The Pit of Whoredom—xxiv. 11-12 The Duty of Rescue—xxiv. 13-14 Wisdom and Honey—xxiv. 23-5 Respect of Persons—xxx. 32-3 The Restraining of Wrath—xxxi 4-9 Kings and Wine. *Ecclesiasticus* i. 22-4 Unjust Wrath—vi. 2-4 Self Will—vii. 1-3 Sowing Sin and Reaping—xxv. 13-15 The Wrath of an Enemy—xxvii. 5-7 Reasoning the Test of Men. Other Epigrams are: *Proverbs* i. 8-9; ix. 7-9, 10-12; xxii. 22-3, 24-5, 26-7; xxiii. 10-11, 13-14, 15-16, 17-18, 24-25; xxiv. 1-2, 3-4, 5-6, 15-16, 17-18, 19-20, 21-22, 28-29; xxv. 6-7, 9-10, 21-2; xxvi. 24-6; xxvii. 10, 15-16; xxx. 5-6, 17, 20. *Ecclesiasticus* v. 2-3, 14, 15; xiv. 1-2; xx. 16-17, 30-1; xxi. 11-12, 13-14, 15, 16-17, 19-21; xxii. 1-2; xxxii. 16-17, 20-2; xxxvi. 18-19; l. 28-9. *Ecclesiastes* x. 16-17, 20; xi. 3. **Fixed or Number Sonnet** (page 272): *Proverbs* vi. 16-19 The Sower of Discord—xxx. 7-9 The Golden Mean—xxx. 15-16 Things never satisfied—xxx. 18-19 Things not to be known—xxx. 21-3 Things not to be borne—xxx. 24-8 Little and Wise—xxx. 29-31 Things stately in their going. *Ecclesiasticus* xxiii. 16-18 (part of an Essay)—xxv. 1-2 What Wisdom hates and loves—xxv. 7-11 The Love of the Lord—xxvi. 5-6 Women Bad and Good—xxvi. 28 The Backslider—l. 25-6 The Hated Nations. **Free Sonnet** (pages 272-281): *Proverbs* i. 10-19 The Company of Sinners—ii. Wisdom the Preservative from Evil—iii. 1-10 The Commandment and its Reward—iii. 11-20 Wisdom the Prize in View—iii. 21-6 Wisdom and Security—iii. 27-35 Wisdom and Perversity —iv. 1-9 The Tradition of Wisdom—iv. 10-19 The Two Paths—iv. 20-7 Wisdom and Health—v. The Strange Woman—vi. 1-5, Suretyship—vi. 6-11 The Sluggard—vi. 12-19 (A Pair of Sonnets) The Sower of Discord—vi. 20-35 The Folly of Adultery— ix. (Sonnet of Sonnets) The House of Wisdom and the House of Folly—xxiii. 29-35 Woes of Wine—xxiv. 30-4 The Field of the Slothful—xxvii. 23-7 Folk Song of Good Husbandry—xxx. 1-4 The Unsearchableness of God—xxx. 11-14 An Evil Generation— xxxi. 10-31 (Acrostic) The Virtuous Woman. *Ecclesiasticus* i. 1-20 Wisdom and the Fear of the Lord—ii. 7-18 True and False Fear—xxii. 11-12 Fools and the Dead— xxii. 27-xxiii. 6 Watchfulness of Lips and Heart—xxvi. 7-18 Women Bad and Good— xxxiv. 13-17 The Fearers of the Lord—xl. 11-27 (A Pair of Sonnets) A Garden of Blessings—xli. 1-4 On Death. *Ecclesiastes* iii. 1-8 (part of an Essay) Times and Seasons—xii. 1-7 (part of an Essay) The Coming of the Evil Days. **Dramatic Monologue** (page 282): *Proverbs* i. 20-33 Wisdom's Cry of Warning—vii-viii. Wisdom and the Strange Woman. *Ecclesiasticus* xxiv. 3-22 Wisdom's Praise of Herself. Compare *Ecclesiastes* i. 12-ii. Solomon's Search for Wisdom—*Wisdom of Solomon* ii. 1-20 and v. 3-13 The Wicked before and after Death—vi-ix Solomon on Wisdom.

V.—FORMS OF PROPHETIC LITERATURE

PROPHECY

A specially Biblical department of literature — in form akin to all departments, but in matter presenting a direct Divine message

The Prophecy or Prophetic Discourse (328): generic term as distinguished from more specialised forms below. Its essence is a Divine Message [**Burden** (A.V.) or **Oracle** (R.V.)]: compare *Jeremiah* xxiii. 26-40]. The Burden and the recommendatory matter are fused together.—**Prototype**: The Ten Commandments (compare *Exodus* xx and *Deuteronomy* v).
Notable Prophetic Discourses are: The Grand Arraignment (*Isaiah* i)—Ezekiel on the Shepherds of Israel (xxxiv)—Discourse with pendulum structure (*Jeremiah* xxx. 4-22).
Among the Discourses are found groups of **Prophetic Sentences** (like the series of isolated proverbs). Compare *Isaiah* vii. 18-viii. 8; xix. 18-25; *Jeremiah* ix. 23-6, xvii. 1-12, xxxi. 21-40: *Hosea* viii. 7-14; ix. 7-x. 15; *Zechariah* viii. 1-8; viii. 18-23. (Page 417.)
A **Book of Prophecy** is made up of Discourses or other Oracles grouped according to subject, date, etc.: thus, Literary Index above shows seven books in Isaiah, etc. What our Biblical titles call 'The Book of the Prophet', etc., is really made up of several 'books', just as the 'Book of Psalms' in A.V. is shown to contain five 'books' in R.V. (Page 429.)
A **Prophetic Cycle** (425) is made up of Discourses structurally connected: A Cycle of Dooms (*Isaiah* xiii-xxvii)—Cycle of the Restoration (*Isaiah* xxviii-xxxv).

Doom Songs: Utterances against particular Nations or Cities: partly corresponding to Satires and Philippics of other literatures (353).—**Prototype**: The Curse (*Genesis* ix. 25)

Nineveh: *Nahum*. Assyria: *Isaiah* xiv. 24-7.
Babylon: *Isaiah* xiii-xiv. 23; *Isaiah* xxi. 1-10; *Jeremiah* l-li.
Egypt: *Isaiah* xix; *Jeremiah* xlvi. 3-12 and 14-28; *Ezekiel* xxix-xxxii (Sevenfold).
Tyre and Zidon: *Isaiah* xxiii. *Ezekiel* xxvi-xxviii (Threefold).
Philistia: *Isaiah* xiv. 28-32; *Jeremiah* xlvii; *Ezekiel* xxv. 15-17.
Damascus: *Isaiah* xvii. 1-11; *Jeremiah* xlix. 23-7.
Moab: *Isaiah* xv-xvi; *Jeremiah* xlviii; *Ezekiel* xxv. 8-11.
Edom: *Jeremiah* xlix. 7-22; *Ezekiel* xxv. 12-14; *Obadiah*.
Ammon: *Jeremiah* xlix. 1-6; *Ezekiel* xxv. 1-7.
Others: *Isaiah* xvii. 12-14; xviii; xx; xxi. 11-17; *Jeremiah* xlix. 28-39.

Books of Dooms: *Jeremiah* xlvi-li; *Ezekiel* xxv-xxxii.
Cycle of Dooms: *Isaiah* xiii-xxvii; *Ezekiel* xxv; *Amos* i-ii.

Prophetic Lyrics (333): Triumph Song over Babylon (*Isaiah* xlvii. 1-5)—Ezekiel's Doom on Egypt (xxxii. 17-32)—Isaiah's Sevenfold Denunciation (v. 8-30)—his Doom of the North (ix. 8-x. 4). **Prototype**: Blessings and Last Words (Of Jacob, *Genesis* xlix. 2-27; Of Moses, *Deuteronomy* xxxiii. 2-29; Of David, *II Samuel* xxiii. 1-7).

| PROPHECY continued | Symbolic Prophecy (336-45) | **Emblem Prophecy** (336): [compare modern Emblem Poetry]: Discourse with Objective or Symbolic Text. **Prototype**: Ceremonial Worship, especially the Scapegoat, the Ark of the Covenant. Examples: The Girdle (*Jeremiah* xiii)—Potter's Clay (*Jeremiah* xviii. 1-17)—Figs (*Jeremiah* xxiv)—Map (*Ezekiel* xxi. 18-23)—various: *Ezekiel* xxxvii. 15-28; *Zechariah* vi. 9-15; xi. 4-17. The Emblem may come at the close (*Jeremiah* xix. 10; li. 61-4). Emblem action may be gesture (*Ezekiel* vi. 1,11)—probably with reiteration (compare *Jeremiah* xiii. 12-13; *Ezekiel* vii. 2-6)—or sustained dumb show: the Mimic Siege (*Ezekiel* iv-v); the Removal of the Stuff (*Ezekiel* xii. 1-16)—it extends to symbolic demeanour and manner of life (*Ezekiel* xxiv. 15-27; *Hosea* i-iii). Through the permanence of some emblems [compare *Jeremiah* xliii. 8-10; *Isaiah* viii. 1-4] the Emblem tends to coalesce with the **Sign of the Prophet**, that is, miraculous symbol guaranteeing the prophecy. **Prototype**: Moses' Signs to Pharaoh. Compare *Isaiah* vii. 10-16; *Jeremiah* xliv. 29; *Ezekiel* iv. 3; *Isaiah* lv. 13; *Matthew* xii. 38-40.

Vision Prophecy (342): in elementary form hardly distinguishable from Emblem Prophecy: the emblem presented in vision. **Prototype**: Jacob's Dream (*Genesis* xxviii. 12-14). Examples: *Amos* vii-ix; *Zechariah* i. 7-vi. 8; *Isaiah* lxiii. 1-6; especially Ezekiel's Valley of Dry Bones (xxxvii. 1-14). As the Emblem tends to coalesce with the Sign so the Vision Emblem passes into Revelation. This has two different senses: (A) **Revelation of the Future**: **Prototype**: Pharoah's Dreams (*Genesis* xli).
    Of this three stages traceable. (1) Vision supernatural and symbolic, Interpretation natural. [*Daniel* ii Dream of Stone cut without hands—iv Of the tree cut down—v Of the Writing on the Wall.] (2) A supernatural and symbolic Interpreter, Vision itself in direct speech. [*Daniel* ix The Time of Restoration—x-xii Time of the End.] With this connect the **Prophetic Call** [*Isaiah* vi; *Jeremiah* i; *Ezekiel* i-iii]. (3) Both Vision and Interpretation symbolic and supernatural. [*Daniel* ix Of the Four Beasts—viii Of the Ram and He-Goat.] (B) **Revelation of Law and Pattern**: the Symbolic passing over into the Ideal. **Prototype**: the Revelation to Moses in the Mount (*Hebrews* viii. 5). Examples: Ezekiel's Companion Visions of Jerusalem under Judgment (viii-xi) and Jerusalem Restored (xl-xlviii) combine A and B (pages 343-5).

Vision Cycles: *Amos* vii-ix; *Zechariah* i. 7-vi. 8—*Revelation* of St. John.

The Prophetic Parable (345): Emblem text narrated instead of being presented. **Prototype**: the Fable (*Judges* ix. 8-15). Examples: Ezekiel's Parable of the Vine (xv)—of the Spouse (xvi)—of the Eagle and Cedar (xvii)—of Oholah and Oholibah (xxiii)—of the Caldron (xxiv. 1-14)—Isaiah's Parable of the Vineyard (v. 1-7). Compare the Parables of Christ. |

PROPHECY continued		
	Prophetic Intercourse (345)	With God: Prototype: Abraham's Intercession (*Genesis* xviii. 22-33).—Examples: *Jeremiah* xi-xii. 6; xvi; xvii. 13-18; xviii. 18-23; xxxi. 23-6; *Ezekiel* iv. 14; *Habakkuk* i-ii.—Compare above: the Prophetic Calls.
		With Inquirers: the Response: compare as Prototype the primitive Inquiry of the Lord (*Genesis* xxv. 23; *1 Samuel* xxviii. 6).—In the Prophetic Books: *Jeremiah* xxi. 1-10; xlii. 1-22; *Ezekiel* xiv. 1-11; xx. 1-44; *Zechariah* vii. 1-7.
		With this connect Dialectic Prophecy: Discourse founded on an interruption from an imaginary disputant.—Examples: *Isaiah* xxviii; *Jeremiah* xiii. 12-14; *Ezekiel* xxxiii. 10-20; *Micah* ii. 6-11.—The whole of *Malachi* is a Dialectic Cycle.
		With the World: Prophetic Incidents and Controversies.—Conspiracy of Anathoth (*Jeremiah* xi. 18-xii. 6)—The Potter's Bottle (*Jeremiah* xix-xx)—Controversy of the Temple (*Jeremiah* xxvi)—Of the Yoke (*Jeremiah* xxvii-viii)—The Anathoth Estate (*Jeremiah* xxxii-iii)—The Siege (*Jeremiah* xxxiv)—The Rechabites (*Jeremiah* xxxv)—The Burnt Roll (*Jeremiah* xxxvi)—Jeremiah and Baruch (xlv)—Daniel and the King's Meat (*Daniel* i)—The Burning Fiery Furnace (iii)—The Den of Lions (vi).
		Prophecy and History interwoven: *Isaiah* xxxvi-ix; *Jeremiah* xxxvii-xliv; *Jeremiah* lii-iii; *Haggai*.—Compare Epic Prophecy (Table III) and the *Book of Jonah*.
	Dramatic Prophecy (347): *Micah* vi. 1-8 The Lord's Controversy before the Mountains—*Micah* vi. 9-vii The Lord's Cry and the Man of Wisdom—*Hosea* xi. 1-11 The Divine Yearning—*Hosea* xiii-xiv A Drama of Repentance.—A Dramatic scene of Panic (*Jeremiah* x. 17-25) is a link between this type and the Rhapsody.—Compare generally: *The Book of Job*.	
	The Prophetic Rhapsody (364-94)	The RHAPSODY OF ZION REDEEMED (*ISAIAH* XL-LXVI)—Above, Chapter XVII.
		Rhapsodies of Judgment (*Isaiah* xxiv-xxvii)—Of Salvation (*Isaiah* xxxii)—Of the Drought (*Jeremiah* xiv-xv)—Of the Locust Plague (*Joel*)—Of the Judgment to Come (*Amos*)—Of Judgment Approaching (*Micah* i)—Of the Chaldeans (*Habakkuk* i-ii).
		Rhapsodic Discourses: Discourses merging in Rhapsodies, or becoming rhapsodic at particular points.—*Isaiah* xxx. 9-ix. 7; *Isaiah* x. 5-xii; *Jeremiah* ii-vi; *Hosea* viii. 4-ix. 9; *Jeremiah* xxx. 23-xxxi. 20; *Hosea* iv-vi. The *Book of Zephaniah* is a Discourse interrupted by (impersonal) lyric outbursts—*Zechariah* x-xi mingles other types with Emblem Prophecy. Most of the Doom Songs (except those of Ezekiel) are rhapsodic at points.
	An exalted form of poetic presentation in which all literary forms are amalgamated	

VI.—LITERATURE OF ADDRESS

ADDRESS or Rhetoric	Oratory or Spoken Address (444-61)	The Orations of Moses in *Deuteronomy*. Miscellaneous Speeches (apparently only in condensation): *Joshua* xxiii, xxiv. *Acts* ii. 14-36; iii. 12-26; v. 35-9; vii. 2-53; x. 34-43; xv. 7-21; xvii. 22-31; xx. 18-35; xxii. 1-21; xxiv. 2-8 and 10-21; xxvi. 1-23.
	Formal Prayers: Address to God: *II Samuel* vii. 18-29; *I Kings* viii. 22-53; *Acts* iv. 24-30; (apocryphal) Prayer of Manasses; *Wisdom* ix; *Ecclesiasticus* xxxvi. 1-17; li. 1-12.	
	Epistle or Written Address (439-13)	Pure Epistles (Pastoral Intercourse): *I, II Corinthians, Galatians, Philippians, I, II Thessalonians, I, II Timothy, Titus, Philemon, II, III John.* Epistolary Treatises: *Romans, Hebrews.* Wisdom Epistle: *James.* Epistolary Manifestos: *Ephesians, Colossians, I, II Peter, I John, Jude.*

VII.—LITERATURE OF IDYL

IDYL	Epic Idyl: *Book of Ruth* (235-8)
	Lyric Idyl: *The Song of Songs* (194-217)

APPENDIX III

ON THE STRUCTURAL PRINTING OF SCRIPTURE

In Biblical, as in other versification, the structure which appeals to the ear and the mind can also be conveyed to the eye by proper modes of printing. The devices of spacing stanzas and indenting lines, which in English verse are used to mark out correspondences of rhyme or metre, can be employed to indicate analogous relations of parallel clauses.

The subject is best treated by examples. The system of structural printing followed for the most part in the present work I will illustrate by an arrangement of a famous passage from *Ecclesiastes*.

    Remember also thy Creator in the days of thy youth:
        Or ever the evil days come,
        And the years draw nigh
            When thou shalt say, I have no pleasure in them;

    Or ever the sun,
        And the light,
        And the moon,
        And the stars,
    Be darkened,
    And the clouds return after the rain:

    In the day when the keepers of the house shall tremble,
    And the strong men shall bow themselves,
    And the grinders cease because they are few,
    And those that look out of the windows be darkened,
    And the doors shall be shut in the street;
    When the sound of the grinding is low,
    And one shall rise up at the voice of a bird,
    And all the daughters of music shall be brought low;
    Yea, they shall be afraid of that which is high,

> And terrors shall be in the way;
> And the almond-tree shall blossom,
> And the grasshopper shall be a burden,
> And the caper-berry shall fail:
>
> Because man goeth to his long home,
> And the mourners go about the streets:
>
>> Or ever the silver cord be loosed,
>> Or the golden bowl be broken,
>> Or the pitcher be broken at the fountain,
>> Or the wheel broken at the cistern;
>
> And the dust return to the earth
>> As it was,
> And the spirit return unto God
>> Who gave it.

The system is illustrated in all its essential features by this passage. Two of the principles underlying it are obvious: that similar clauses are similarly indented, and that stanzas are separated by spaces. It involves, however, two other points that need more explanation.

The first of these points is raised by the opening stanza. When this stanza, or rather, the portion of it which follows the introductory first line, is examined, it is seen to be essentially a couplet, of which one member is

> Or ever the evil days come,

and the other member is

> And the years draw nigh when thou shalt say, I have no pleasure in them.

Considered from every point of view except one, these clauses are exactly parallel with one another. But when viewed in reference to the *mass* of the two they are found strangely unequal: the epithet of a single word 'evil' in the one clause has to balance it in the other the long collocation of words, 'when thou shalt say, I have no pleasure in them.' Yet this collocation of words does not present itself to our ears as a clumsy enlargement of the second clause, but, on the contrary, as a valuable addition to the rhetoric richness of the whole passage. I would meet such a case by separating the collocation of words so as to make it an element in the general structure, and at the same time indenting it so as to indicate its subordination to the previous line, in the sense of which it is a single detail.

> Or ever the evil days come
> And the years draw nigh
> When thou shalt say, I have no pleasure in them.

It will be seen that the device of indenting is thus used not only to bring together lines which are co-ordinate with one another, but also (occasionally) to distinguish a portion of the whole rhetoric mass which is subordinate to another portion. I believe that no system of parallel printing will be found practicable which does not provide for subordinate as well as co-ordinate indenting.

Another point illustrated by the extract from *Ecclesiastes* is the way in which parallel printing, besides affecting lines closely contiguous, can also convey to the eye correspondences between clauses widely sundered from one another. The passage cited is a poetic *tour-de-force* of extreme boldness; the infirmities of old age, which usually good taste would veil, are here enumerated in all their minuteness. Yet the effect is one of beauty, because the symptoms of decay are not expressed directly, but suggested under shadows of oriental symbolism, — by symbols sometimes unintelligible to the Western reader, whereas others of them have from this passage been imported into familiar speech. At just three points in the whole poem the symbolism is dropped, and direct speech has a moment's prominence: in the opening line, bidding remember God in youth; once further on, where a string of symbols gives place to the simple words —

> Because man goeth to his long home
> And the mourners go about the streets;

and again at the conclusion which speaks of the dust returning to the earth and the spirit to God. As the passage is printed above it will be seen that these three passages stand out from all the rest by their common indenting on the extreme left.

The system of structural printing thus illustrated aims at reflecting the Higher Parallelism. I have drawn attention in the body of this work (page 73) to the distinction between the Lower and the Higher Parallelism: between the disposition of a passage in simple figures, like couplets and quatrains, and, on the other hand, the suppression of these figures in order to let higher correspondences appear, such as belong to the thought of the passage as a whole. By way of illustration I gave two arrangements of a passage from the *Book of Job* (see pages 74-6). The arrangement illustrating the Higher

Parallelism was able to keep distinct to the eye the two strains of thought which in that passage are continually crossing one another. The same effect may be secured in the close of the sixty-fifth psalm: as here arranged it will be seen that the left-hand lines express the general visitation of the God of nature, and the resulting bountiful harvest, while the right-hand lines put the special gift of rain with the richness of pasturage the rain produces.

> Thou visitest the earth, and waterest it:
>> Thou greatly enrichest it,
>> The river of God is full of water:
> Thou providest them corn, when thou hast so prepared the earth;
> Thou waterest her furrows abundantly,
> Thou settlest the ridges thereof,
> Thou makest it soft with showers,
> Thou blessest the springing thereof,
> Thou crownest the year with thy goodness:
>> And thy paths drop fatness,
>> They drop upon the pastures of the wilderness,
>> And the hills are girded with joy:
>> The pastures are clothed with flocks,
> The valleys also are covered over with corn:
> They shout for joy, they also sing.

Many similar effects of Higher Parallelism can be conveyed by structural printing. In the arrangement of *Psalm* lxxvii on page 175 it will be clear how a block of similar lines makes an enumeration of troubled emotions, then an indentation to the right voices the prayer of trouble; again left-hand lines express the struggle out of trouble to the confidence born of memories, and a change to right-hand lines introduces the comforting memories: the whole struggle, in the proportion of its parts, is reflected to the eye. The similar psalm cited on pages 176-7 separates the alternating trouble and confidence notwithstanding the irregularity of the alternations. In the psalms of double dramatic change (see pages 180-3) the retrogression to the time of affliction is marked off by indentation, and this arrangement conveys at once to the eye how the close of the psalm is a return to the mood of the opening. On page 206 is given the happy dream of the bride (in *Canticles*): a glance shows how the lines indented to the right make an approach to a refrain. In the passage of the Reciting Chorus on the following page the left-hand lines exclaim at a sight, the right-hand lines describe it: the whole has the further effect of introversion. For the poems called in this work Sonnets, some structural printing is essential to bring out the correspondence of their parts: this has been fully explained and illustrated on pages 273-7. I will add one more example, on a larger scale, of the kind of printing I advocate: it is the section of *Job* which gives the hero's long-delayed vindication of his innocence.

> I made a covenant with mine eyes;
> How then should I look upon a maid?
>> For what portion should I have of God from above?
>> And what heritage of the Almighty from on high?
>> Is it not calamity to the unrighteous,
>> And disaster to the workers of iniquity?
>> Doth not he see my ways,
>> And number all my steps?
>
> If I have walked with vanity
> And my foot hath hasted to deceit;
>> (Let me be weighed in an even balance,
>> That God may know mine integrity;)
> If my step hath turned out of the way,
> And mine heart walked after mine eyes,
> And if any spot hath cleaved to mine hands:
> Then let me sow, and let another eat;
> Yea, let the produce of my field be rooted out.
>
> If mine heart have been enticed unto a woman,
> And I have laid wait at my neighbour's door:
> Then let my wife grind unto another,
> And let others bow down upon her.
>> For that were an heinous crime;
>> Yea, it were an iniquity to be punished by the judges:
>> For it is a fire that consumeth unto Destruction,
>> And would root out all mine increase.
>
> If I did despise the cause of my manservant or of my maidservant,
> When they contended with me,
>> What then shall I do when God riseth up?
>> And when he visiteth, what shall I answer him?
>> Did not he that made me in the womb make him?
>> And did not one fashion us in the womb?
> If I have withheld the poor from their desire
> Or have caused the eyes of the widow to fail;

Or have eaten my morsel alone,
And the fatherless hath not eaten thereof;
  (Nay, from my youth he grew up with me as with a father,
  And I have been her guide from my mother's womb;)
If I have seen any perish for want of clothing,
Or that the needy had no covering;
If his loins have not blessed me,
And if he were not warmed with the fleece of my sheep;
If I have lifted up my hand against the fatherless,
Because I saw my help in the gate:
Then let my shoulder fall from the shoulder blade,
And mine arm be broken from the bone.
  For calamity from God was a terror to me,
  And by reason of his excellency I could do nothing.

If I have made gold my hope,
And have said to the fine gold, Thou art my confidence;
If I rejoiced because my wealth was great,
And because mine hand had gotten much;
If I beheld the sun when it shined,
Or the moon walking in brightness;
And my heart hath been secretly enticed,
And my mouth hath kissed my hand:
  This also were an iniquity to be punished by the judges:
  For I should have lied to God that is above.

If I rejoiced at the destruction of him that hated me,
Or lifted up myself when evil found him;
  (Yea, I suffered not my mouth to sin
  By asking his life with a curse;)

If the men of my tent said not,
Who can find one that hath not been satisfied with his flesh?
The stranger did not lodge in the street;
But I opened my doors to the traveller;

If after the manner of men I covered my transgressions,
By hiding mine iniquity in my bosom;
Because I feared the great multitude,
And the contempt of families terrified me,
So that I kept silence, and went not out of the door —

Oh that I had one to hear me!
(Lo, here is my signature, let the Almighty answer me;)
And that I had the indictment which mine adversary hath written!
Surely I would carry it upon my shoulder;
I would bind it unto me as a crown.
I would declare unto him the number of my steps;
As a prince would I present it to him.

If my land cry out against me,
And the furrows thereof weep together;
If I have eaten the fruits thereof without money,
Or have caused the owners thereof to lose their life:
Let thistles grow instead of wheat,
And cockle instead of barley!

It is abundantly clear that the whole of this elaborate deliverance is constructed on three notes, and the resultant three strains stand distinct to the eye. It is as if Job were adapting rhetorically a prescribed formulary of vindication to a great variety of particulars. In *Psalm* vii. 3 a similarly constructed passage is also a formulary of self-vindication.

O LORD my God, if I have done this;
If there be iniquity in my hands;
If I have rewarded evil unto him that was at peace with me;
(Yea, I have delivered him that without cause was mine adversary:)
Let the enemy pursue my soul, and overtake it;
Yea, let him tread my life down to the earth,
And lay my glory in the dust!

It is, however, the *Lower Parallelism* of figures that has obtained the widest acceptance at the present day. Besides the use of it in the commentaries of scholars, it has been followed in a few popular works, an example of which is the Golden Treasury Psalter. This follows a condensed notation, resting upon the use of the 'hanging indent.' The opening of *Psalm* lvii, in full rhythmic structure, would stand as follows:

Be merciful unto me, O God, be merciful unto me,
    For my soul fleeth unto thee for refuge,
        Yea, under the shadow of thy wings shall be my refuge,
Until this peril be overpast!

I will call unto the most high God,
Even to God who doeth good unto me.

>   That he send from heaven and save me,
>   And put to shame him that would eat me up,
>   Yea, that God send forth his mercy and truth.
>
>   My soul is among lions, I lie even among ravening men,
>   With the children of men, whose teeth are spears and arrows,
>   And their tongue a sharp sword.

To make, in this way, separate stanzas of these triplets, couplet and quatrain loses space, and spreads the whole out further than may be desirable. The more compact structural scheme, instead of spacing, retains the 'hanging indent' (to the extreme left) for the first line of each figure: and the other lines of the figure are made subordinate.

>   Be merciful unto me, O God, be merciful unto me,
>   For my soul fleeth unto thee for refuge,
>   Yea, under the shadow of thy wings shall be my refuge,
>   until this peril be overpast!
>   I will call unto the most high God,
>   even to God who doeth good unto me,
>   That he send from heaven and save me,
>   and put to shame him that would eat me up,
>   Yea, that God send forth his mercy and truth!
>   My soul is among lions. I lie even among ravening men,
>   With the children of men, whose teeth are spears and arrows,
>   and their tongue a sharp sword.

I doubt the advantages of this condensed structure, except where the figures are very simple and uniform. I have used it on pages 47 and 54.

There is, however, a mode of printing Scriptural verse that reflects no parallelism at all, whether higher or lower, but simply distinguishes the lines of verse, all lines being uniformly indented. This is the mode followed in the Revised Version of the Bible. Standing by itself, this *Verse Structure* seems a very insufficient representation of the rhythmic poetry of the Bible. But it may be a useful adjunct to the Higher Parallelism; where there are no special correspondences to be indicated, it is better to fall back upon this neutral verse structure than upon the lower parallelism that rests upon figures and not sense.

Yet another structural notation, which may be called *Centric Printing*, is followed (for example) by Dr. Samuel Cox in his admirable translation of *Job*. This device is attributed to the poet Southey, and he has used it in the elaborate verse system of his *Kehama* and *Thalaba*. Its law is simple, — that the centre of each line corresponds with the centre of the page.

> Thy sons and thy daughters
> were eating and drinking wine in their eldest brother's house;
> and, behold,
> there came a great wind from the wilderness,
> and smote the four corners of the house,
> and it fell upon the young men,
> and they are dead;
> and I only am escaped alone to tell thee.

Though not without beauty to the eye, this mode of printing seems inadequate to the requirements of Biblical versification, as merely separating clauses, and not co-ordinating them. But it may have a real place in the expression of speech which is on the borderland between prose and verse, and I have used it in such passages (*e.g.* page 4).

As to the choice between these systems of structural printing, I would lay it down as a principle of rhythmic analysis that there is in these questions no right and wrong, but only better and worse. A given passage may be expressed in many different arrangements, and that will be the best which draws out of it the greatest symmetry. And even the sense of symmetry will vary according to the conception of a particular passage or the purpose of a particular citation.

APPENDIX IV

ON THE USE OF THE DIGRESSION IN THE 'BOOK OF WISDOM'

I have remarked in Chapter XIII upon a peculiar feature of literary style that characterises the *Wisdom of Solomon*. This is the use in that book of the Digression, not as an accident or a makeshift, but as an end in itself. The exact usage may be described by the term Digressive Subordination: a succession of digressions, and digressions from those digressions, each receding further from the original line of thought. It is difficult to find an illustrative parallel without going to literature of a very different order; but perhaps one is to be found in a feature of oriental fiction which French criticism has entitled *histoires à tiroir*. I refer to such fiction as is known to the West by the *Arabian Nights* or the *Fables of Bidpai*: the original story introduces a personage who tells a number of stories, in one of which a company entertain one another with stories; and the process is continued, story enclosed within story, like a set of Chinese boxes. Not dissimilar to such story subordination is the digressive subordination of the work we are considering; as perhaps the following scheme will help to make clear.

> *For evil thoughts and works separate from God*
> *For Wisdom takes fright at even a wicked word*
> *For that which fills all things must hear every murmur*

Each line represents a whole paragraph of the original. It will be seen that the third line is a comment upon the second, and the second upon the first; or, if we read the other way, the second line is a digression from the first, and the third, being a digression from the second, is doubly a digression from the first.

The argument represented by the above scheme I will quote in full (i. 2–11). Seek the Lord (urges the author) with singleness of heart:

Because he is found of them that tempt him not, and is manifested to them that do not distrust him. For crooked thoughts separate from God, and the Supreme Power, when it is brought to the proof, putteth to confusion the foolish;

Because wisdom will not enter into a soul that deviseth evil, nor dwell in a body that is held in pledge by sin. For a holy spirit of discipline will flee deceit, and will start away from thoughts that are without understanding, and will be put to confusion when unrighteousness hath come in. For wisdom is a spirit that loveth man, and she will not hold a blasphemer guiltless for his lips; because God beareth witness of his reins, and is a true overseer of his heart, and a hearer of his tongue:

Because the spirit of the Lord hath filled the world, and that which holdeth all things together hath knowledge of every voice: therefore no man that uttereth unrighteous things shall be unseen, neither shall Justice, when it convicteth, pass him by. For in the midst of his counsels the ungodly shall be searched out; and the sound of his words shall come unto the Lord to bring to conviction his lawless deeds: because there is an ear of jealousy that listeneth to all things, and the noise of murmurings is not hid. Beware then of unprofitable murmuring, and refrain your tongue from backbiting: because no secret utterance shall go on its way void, and a mouth that belieth destroyeth a soul.

In seeking an explanation of this marked feature of literary style, one remark may be ventured. The *Wisdom of Solomon*, however Greek it may be in origin and modes of thought, is nevertheless a contribution to Hebrew literature, and to the long literary period that intervenes between the Old and New Testament. But the main religious literature of this period was the oral literature of commentary, which, from the time of Ezra, maintained itself and gathered strength, until, in the Christian era, it took written shape in the Talmud. It would be strange if that which made so large a part of Jewish religious life had left no trace in the written literature of the times; and we have seen that the whole of the *Wisdom of Solomon* falls into the shape of texts and comments. But there is a close connection between the comment and the digression: a digression may be looked upon as a comment upon that point of the discourse from which it digresses. Hence the prominence of the digression in the Book of *Wisdom* may be connected with the influence of the oral literature of commentary upon written literature.

This influence is found to extend to the literature of the New Testament. In the style of St. Paul the digression is almost as prominent as in the book which is the subject of this Appendix. It is also specially observable in the

Gospel of St. John: the apparent repetitions and involutions of its style lose their difficulty when text and comment are separated.

In the beginning was the Word, and the Word was with God, and the Word was God.
[*The same was in the beginning with God. All things were made by him; and without him was not anything made. That which hath been made was life in him; and the life was the light of men. And the light shineth in the darkness; and the darkness overcame it not. There came a man sent from God, whose name was John. The same came for witness, that he might bear witness of the light, that all might believe through him. He was not the light, but came that he might bear witness of the light. The true light, which lighteth every man, was coming into the world. He was in the world, and the world was made by him, and the world knew him not. He came unto his own, and they that were his own received him not. But as many as received him, to them gave he the right to become children of God, even to them that believe on his name: which were born, not of blood, nor of the will of the flesh, nor of the will of man, but of God.*]

And the word became flesh, and dwelt among us, full of grace and truth.
[*And we beheld his glory, glory as of the only begotten from the Father. John beareth witness of him, and crieth, etc.*]

In the same way care is often needed in this Gospel to distinguish exactly where a discourse of Jesus ends, and the Evangelist's comment begins. Thus the Discourse to Nicodemus should probably end with verse 15, and verses 16-21 are the words of St. John.

To return to the *Book of Wisdom*. That such digressive subordination is not the result of confused or lax thought, but is an end in itself, is strongly suggested by the fact that, in the most elaborate examples, the process is carried on to the point of reversing itself, and the dropped threads are picked up one by one, till the argument has returned to the original line of thought by stages as regular as those by which it had departed from it. Another scheme may illustrate this.

With the loathsome plague of vermin compare —
   But note nemesis: vermin on foolish vermin-worshippers —
      Not but what all idolatry is folly, as corrupting God's gifts —
         For idolatry in its origin is a corruption —
      All idolatry is folly, but there are degrees of folly —
   Vermin-worship was the vilest and deserved such doom —
With that loathsomeness compare the tasty quails of the Israelites.

The reader must understand that each of these lines has to do duty for what in the original is a train of argument running sometimes to several pages. It will be seen that each of the successive digressions is further removed from the original thought, until the discussion on the origin of idolatry represented by the fourth line stands three degrees distant from the argument of the opening line; then the argument returns on its steps, each of the previous digressions is resumed and concluded, and the first line of thought is recovered. It may be added that, once the key to the arrangement is caught, the points of junction in the text will be seen to be clearly marked; and the whole complex of thought gives the impression of symmetry and finish.

The portion of the text represented by this second scheme (from xi. 15 to xvi. 4) is too long to quote in full, but I give a condensation, indented so as to bring out the digressive subordination. References are inserted indicating the exact point at which each digression leads off.

Appetite (it is argued, though the argument is not apparent until after the close of the digressions in xvi. 4) *is one of the things in reference to which the enemy was punished, and the righteous nation benefited. The Egyptians suffered a plague of VERMIN.*

> *Note: Vermin on vermin-worshippers* (xi. 16): *by what things a man sinneth, by these he is punished. The choice of that punishment in kind over all other modes of punishment evidences the mercy of the omnipotent lover of lives (such a reminder to the sinner being part of his way of convicting little by little, as when hornets were sent upon the Canaanites before the final destroyers came). God's sovereignty over all makes him forbearing to all; teaching his people to be lovers of men, and giving them hope in the time of their own chastisement.— The Egyptians were justly chastised with their own abominations, because they were so far gone in the FOLLY OF IDOLATRY.*
>
>> *For all idolatry is folly* (xiii. 1): *to see God's works, and not recognise the Creator. Least blameable are those who mistake the heavenly bodies or beautiful works of nature for God (though, knowing so much, these might have known more). But miserable indeed are those who rest their hopes in dead things: gold, silver, useless stone, or even refuse of a tree carved in an idle hour into a god; the workman prayeth all help from this which is in all things helpless: accursed idolater that turns what God has created into CORRUPTION.*
>>
>>> *For idolatry is a corruption of life* (xiv. 12), *and not one of the things which have been from the beginning. Origin of idola-*

try: perhaps an image of a lost child, honoured with rites, that afterwards grow into a law. Or, an image of a king, made for flattery in his absence, forced by the art of the artificer into a beauty that in time draws worship: thus stocks and stones become invested with the incommunicable Name. *Moral corruption follows*: the conflict within the idolaters' hearts caused by their loss of the knowledge of God they consider peace, and organise for it rites and ceremonies, which admit foul sin; besides that the empty idols are no restraint upon perjury.

But we have knowledge of the true God (xv. 1), and are not led into folly by the devices of men's art to worship dead images. Such a fool is the potter, who out of clay makes vessels for clean uses and the contrary (he decides which), and out of this same clay mouldeth a god—though he was himself earth but lately, and into earth will shortly return: he is full of anxiety, not about the shortness of his term, but in matching himself against the goldsmith's work, as if life were a plaything; or a fair for making gain: he beyond other idolaters must know that he sinneth.

The vermin-worshippers of Egypt were further gone than all in the folly of idolatry (xv. 14): they made their gods, not only the senseless idols of the nations, but also creatures that in themselves are hateful and void of beauty. Hence they were worthily punished through these same abominations which they worshipped.

But (xvi. 2) *instead of this plague of vermin*, through which the Egyptians came to loathe their necessary food, the people of God received benefits in the matter of food,—quails of rare flavour to satisfy dainty appetite: having suffered want just enough to know what the torment of the enemy would be.

In conclusion, the remark often made in reference to the literary style of St. Paul, may be applied also to the *Book of Wisdom*,—that what is in form a digression will be found, as regards the matter, to be an advance in the course of the argument.

www.ingramcontent.com/pod-product-compliance
Lightning Source LLC
Chambersburg PA
CBHW031946290426
44108CB00011B/694